The Legal Case for TREASON Against DONALD J. TRUMP

People's Constitutional Case

THE DOCWRITEREVIEW COLLECTIVE

The Legal Case for TREASON against Donald J. Trump

The People's Constitutional Case

Published by DocWriteReview Library of Congress Preassigned Control Number:

ISBN: 978-1-965060-37-7 — Paperback

ISBN: 978-1-965060-39-1 — eBook

AI Disclosure: This work was researched, drafted, and developed with the assistance of artificial intelligence tools, including Claude (Anthropic), ChatGPT (OpenAI), and NotebookLM (Google). All research, analysis, legal arguments, editorial judgment, and final content decisions were made by the human authors. The authors retain full responsibility for the accuracy, conclusions, and legal arguments presented in this work.

Credit Line:

Cover Design by Arlene A. Smith-Scott

Cover Image of Donald J. Trump is a Pixabay image.

Stay Connected!

UNLOCK A WEALTH OF knowledge and exclusive deals! Sign up now to receive free updates and special discounts on services and products related to grant writing, commercial lending, and much more. Don't miss out, join our community today!

Website: www.DocWriteReview.com

Email: Info@DocWriteReview.com

This book is dedicated to Jerald Johns, Adam D. Smith, Matthew S. Morris, John Luke E. Morris, Solomon Alleyne, and the future generations who will inherit the republic they never asked to defend.

Without the Constitution of the United States, where would we be.

Contents

Prologue

You were not supposed to write this book.

A prosecutor was. Or a special counsel. Or a congressional committee with subpoena power and the institutional authority to compel testimony, review classified documents, and present findings to a waiting nation.

None of them did.

So the citizens did.

□ □ □

This book is what happens when the institutions designed to hold power accountable decide that accountability is too expensive. It is a legal argument, built from the public record, applied to the constitutional standard the Framers wrote into Article III, Section 3. It does not claim what it cannot prove. It claims what the documented record establishes.

Twenty-eight chapters. Seven parts. One question.

Did Donald J. Trump commit treason against the United States of America?

□ □ □

The Constitution defines only one crime. Not murder. Not fraud. Not bribery. One crime so fundamental to the survival of a republic that the Framers named it first, defined it precisely, and surrounded it with strict evidentiary requirements to ensure it could never be used as a political weapon.

They named it treason because they feared it most. They feared it most because they knew what history had shown, across every republic that had risen and fallen before theirs: the greatest threat to a free people is not the enemy at the gates. It is the person inside the gates who opens them.

This book argues that person has been identified. The argument is legal, not rhetorical. The evidence is documented, not assumed. And the standard applied is the one the Framers wrote, not the one that political convenience would prefer.

□ □ □

Betrayal by a President should have consequences.

The institutions that were supposed to impose those consequences failed. The Congress that was supposed to check the President chose party over Constitution. The judiciary that was supposed to adjudicate the accountability claim was compromised before the claim could be made. The Department of Justice that was supposed to prosecute the misconduct was dismantled from within. And the men who held the power to stop it calculated, correctly in the narrow sense, that their survival was worth more than their oath.

So the citizens picked up the brief.

You do not have to be a lawyer to understand this case.

You have to be a citizen.

This book was written for you.

Introduction

The Law of Treason in America

The Constitutional Standard, Its Elements, Its History, and Why It Applies Here

A Note on Structure

In federal court, a legal brief has a precise structure: a Statement of the Case (what this is about), a Statement of Law (what the law requires), and an Argument (how the facts satisfy the law). This book follows that structure deliberately.

The narrative Introduction, The Highest Crime, is the Statement of the Case. This Legal Introduction is the Statement of Law. Parts I through VII are the Argument. The reader who understands the law before encountering the evidence is a reader who can evaluate the argument on its merits rather than on the strength of the rhetoric.

That is the purpose of this Legal Introduction. It establishes the constitutional standard with full rigor, including its narrowness, its high evidentiary bar, and the documented reasons courts have historically found it difficult to satisfy. By doing so, it demonstrates that this book is not stretching the law to fit the facts. It is applying the law as written. That distinction is the difference between a legal argument and a political screed.

* * *

Section I: The Only Crime the Constitution Defines

Open any federal criminal statute and you will find crimes defined by Congress, murder, fraud, espionage, sedition. Treason is different. It is the only crime whose definition is written directly into the Constitution itself, in Article III, Section 3. The Framers did not leave its definition to Congress because they understood, from direct historical experience, that governments weaponize accusations of betrayal against political enemies.

In England, treason had been used as a political weapon for centuries. Henry VIII had wives and ministers executed for treason. The Stuart kings used treason charges against parliamentary opponents. The Framers had witnessed the British Crown attempt to define colonial resistance as treason. They were not interested in giving any future American government the same tool.

So they wrote the definition themselves, into the document that no ordinary Congress could amend without supermajority ratification, and they wrote it narrowly.

> *"Treason against the United States, shall consist only in levying War against them, or in adhering to their Enemies, giving them Aid and Comfort. No Person shall be convicted of Treason unless on the Testimony of two Witnesses to the same overt Act, or on Confession in open Court." — Article III, Section 3, Constitution of the United States*

Note the word only. The Framers did not say treason consists of levying war or adhering to enemies. They said it consists only in those two things. The word only is a deliberate restriction. It means that whatever else a person might do, however corrupt, however dishonest, however damaging to the nation , it is not treason unless it falls within one of those two categories.

This narrowness is not a weakness of the treason clause. It is its strength. It means that when the evidence does satisfy the constitutional standard, the conclusion carries the full weight of the Republic's most solemn legal judgment. This book argues that the evidence satisfies that standard. Before making that argument, it is essential to understand precisely what the standard requires.

* * *

Section II: The Two Prongs: Levying War and Adhering to Enemies

Prong One: Levying War Against the United States

The first prong of the treason clause, levying war, has been interpreted by the Supreme Court to require more than individual violence or even organized criminal activity. It requires an assemblage of persons organized for the purpose of using force to overturn or resist the authority of the government.

The controlling precedent is Ex parte Bollman, decided by the Supreme Court in 1807 under Chief Justice John Marshall. Aaron Burr's conspirators were alleged to have assembled forces in the Ohio Valley with the intention of seizing New Orleans and potentially separating the western territories from the United States. Marshall held that levying war requires an actual assemblage of men for the purpose of executing a treasonable design. Mere conspiracy, without assembly, is not sufficient.

This requirement, actual assembly, directed force, treasonable purpose, shapes the analysis of Part I of this book. The assemblage at the Ellipse on January 6, 2021, the march to the Capitol, and the breach of the building during the active certification of the presidential election represent exactly the kind of organized, directed force against a constitutional act that Ex parte Bollman's framework addresses. The question is not whether an assemblage occurred. It is whether the assemblage was directed toward a treasonable purpose, and whether the person who directed it understood and intended that purpose.

Prong Two: Adhering to Enemies — Giving Aid and Comfort

The second prong, adhering to enemies by giving them aid and comfort, is the more complex and more central prong for the analysis developed in Parts II through VII of this book.

Adhering means alignment of purpose. It does not require formal agreement, written contract, or explicit communication of intent. Courts have held that adherence is established by the pattern of conduct, by a consistent record of acting in ways that serve the enemy's objectives, conceal that service, and continue it despite the government's own documented findings of hostile intent.

Aid and comfort means actual assistance that strengthens the enemy's position or weakens the United States. The Supreme Court in Cramer v. United States (1945) held that aid and comfort must be an overt, physical deed, action, not mere intention. But the deed need not be military. Diplomatic concessions that benefit the enemy. Financial arrangements that enrich the enemy or deprive the United States of strategic resources. The systematic destruction of alliance structures that contain the enemy. The concealment of the enemy's hostile operations through official denial. These are the categories of aid and comfort that Parts II through VII document.

* * *

Section III: The Required Elements — Every One Must Be Proven

A treason conviction requires proof of every element beyond a reasonable doubt. This book does not argue for conviction, that authority belongs to a jury in a properly constituted proceeding. It argues that the evidence, evaluated against these elements, is sufficient to submit the question to a jury. The distinction is legally significant. Here are the elements.

Element One: Allegiance

The accused must owe allegiance to the United States. This element is rarely contested in modern cases. A natural-born or naturalized citizen owes permanent allegiance. A person who takes the presidential oath and assumes the office of Commander in Chief owes the highest form of allegiance the Constitution recognizes, not merely as a citizen, but as the officer constitutionally charged with preserving, protecting, and defending the Constitution itself.

The presidential oath is not merely a ceremony. It is a legal commitment. Its breach is not merely a policy failure. In the context of the other elements, its breach is the foundation of the treason analysis.

Element Two: An Enemy

The accused must have adhered to an enemy of the United States. This is the most legally contested element in the modern context, and Chapter 4 of this book addresses it in full. The short version of the argument is this: the Supreme Court in Cramer v. United States defined enemy as any party united in hostile purpose against the United States. It did not require a formal declaration of war. It required hostile purpose and hostile action. The Intelligence Community Assessment of January 2017, confirmed by bipartisan Senate investigation across five published volumes, established that a foreign power engaged in a systematic campaign of hostile action against the United States, against its election infrastructure, its democratic institutions, and its alliance structures. That finding, made by the agencies of the federal government itself, is the evidentiary foundation for the enemy element.

Element Three: An Overt Act

The accused must have committed an overt act of aid and comfort , a real, physical deed, not merely a thought, a statement, or an intention. Cramer v. United States established this requirement firmly and the Supreme Court has never retreated from it. The overt act requirement is the constitutional bulwark against treason prosecutions based on political speech or association.

This book identifies multiple categories of overt acts across Parts I through VII. They include the withholding of congressionally authorized military assistance to a nation under active Russian military attack, documented by the Government Accountability Office as a violation of federal impoundment law. They include the systematic deconstruction of NATO's collective defense commitments across both presidential terms. They include the financial arrangements between the President's family enterprises and the sovereign wealth funds of foreign governments simultaneously benefiting from presidential policy decisions. They include the direction of an armed assemblage against the constitutional certification of a presidential election. Each is an overt, physical deed with documented consequences.

Element Four: Two Witnesses to the Same Overt Act

The two-witness rule is the most demanding evidentiary requirement in American law. The Constitution requires not merely two witnesses to the act, but two witnesses to the same overt act. This requirement, which the Supreme Court has interpreted strictly, means that circumstantial evidence alone cannot establish treason, however compelling. Two witnesses must testify to the same specific physical deed.

This book does not claim to fully satisfy this requirement for every overt act it documents. What it demonstrates, chapter by chapter, is that the public record, including congressional testimony, diplomatic communications, intelligence findings, and contemporaneous documentation by government officials, provides the witness categories from which the two-witness requirement could be satisfied in a properly constituted proceeding. Part VI, covering a 43-day period in early 2026, contains the richest and most contemporaneously documented witness record in the entire analysis.

Element Five: Specific Intent

Treason requires specific intent, the accused must have known they were giving aid and comfort to an enemy of the United States, and must have intended to do so. Negligence is not treason. Even recklessness is not treason. The intent requirement means that the pattern of conduct documented in this book must be evaluated not merely for its consequences, though those consequences are severe and documented, but for what it reveals about the actor's knowledge and purpose.

The architecture of denial documented in Part V, the sustained pattern of false statements specifically designed to conceal the conduct documented in Parts II through IV, is the primary evidence of specific intent. A person who had no treasonous intent would have no motive to deny, obstruct, and misrepresent the conduct at the center of this case. The denials are not separate from the treason argument. They are evidence of it.

* * *

Section IV: How Courts Have Interpreted the Treason Clause — The Case Studies

Cramer v. United States (1945) — The Overt Act Requirement

Anthony Cramer was a German-born American citizen who met with two German saboteurs, Thiel and Kerling, who had been landed in the United States by submarine in 1942 as part of Operation Pastorius, a German military mission to sabotage American war industries. Cramer knew Thiel and Kerling were German agents operating against the United States. He met with them publicly. He drank with them. He held money for them. He did not report them to the government.

The Supreme Court reversed his treason conviction. The reason is legally crucial for understanding this book's argument. The Court held that the overt acts the government proved, the meetings in public restaurants, did not, on their face, constitute aid and comfort to the enemy. A meeting, even a knowing meeting, is not itself aid and comfort unless it provides concrete assistance to the enemy's hostile mission. The Court found that the government's two witnesses could testify to Cramer meeting with the saboteurs, but could not testify to what was discussed or what assistance was provided. The overt act, as witnessed, did not satisfy the constitutional standard.

The lesson for this book's analysis: the overt acts it documents are not meetings. They are policy decisions with measurable consequences, the withholding of military assistance, the deconstruction of alliance commitments, the financial arrangements, the armed assemblage. These are not ambiguous social encounters. They are documented governmental acts whose consequences for the enemy and the United States are themselves part of the evidentiary record.

Chandler v. United States (1948) — The Objective Standard for Intent

Robert Henry Best and Douglas Chandler were American citizens who made propaganda broadcasts for Nazi Germany during World War II. Both were convicted of treason. Their convictions established what is now known as the Chandler standard for intent: whether a reasonable person in the defendant's position would have known that the acts would give aid and comfort to the enemy.

This objective standard matters for the analysis in Parts V and VI. The denials and misrepresentations documented in Part V demonstrate not merely consciousness of guilt, they demonstrate that the actor knew the conduct would be understood as giving aid and comfort if disclosed. The concealment is itself evidence of the subjective intent, and the Chandler objective standard supplements it: a reasonable person in the position of the Commander in Chief, with access to the full intelligence record of Russian hostility, cannot claim ignorance of what the documented pattern of conduct meant.

The Rosenberg Case (1953) — Espionage Act as Treason Substitute

Julius and Ethel Rosenberg passed atomic bomb secrets to the Soviet Union during the late 1940s. They were not charged with treason. They were charged under the Espionage Act, convicted, and executed. The government's decision not to charge treason was deliberate and strategic: the Soviet Union was not formally at war with the United States, making the enemy element legally contested. The two-witness rule made the specific intent element difficult to satisfy with the available evidence. The Espionage Act offered a lower bar and a surer conviction.

The Rosenberg case established a pattern that has governed every subsequent case involving conduct that might constitute treason but is prosecuted under substitute statutes. The government's routine use of the Espionage Act and the Trading with the Enemy Act as treason substitutes is itself part of the story this book tells.

United States v. Abu Ali (2005) and United States v. Hammoud (2004) — The Functional Enemy Doctrine

The post-9/11 cases that addressed treason and material support to terrorist organizations developed what scholars now call the functional enemy doctrine — the principle that enemy status attaches to any entity that is engaged in sustained hostile action against the United States, regardless of whether that entity has been formally designated as an enemy through a declaration of war.

This doctrine, developed in the circuit courts and never repudiated by the Supreme Court, is the legal foundation for Chapter 4's argument that a foreign power can constitute an enemy under Article III without a declaration of war, if the Intelligence Community has formally and unanimously established its sustained hostile purpose and hostile action against the United States.

* * *

Section V: The Espionage Act and the Trading with the Enemy Act — The Government's Substitute Tools

The Espionage Act

The Espionage Act of 1917, codified at 18 U.S.C. § 793 et seq., prohibits the unauthorized gathering, transmission, or retention of national defense information with intent or reason to believe it will be used to the injury of the United States or the advantage of a foreign nation. It does not require proof of an enemy. It does not require two witnesses to the same overt act. It does not require specific intent to commit treason, only reasonable cause to believe the information would damage national security.

The Espionage Act has served as the government's primary tool for prosecuting conduct that functionally resembles treason but cannot satisfy the constitutional standard. The Rosenbergs, Aldrich Ames, Robert Hanssen, Jonathan Pollard, and dozens of others were prosecuted under the Espionage Act rather than the treason clause. In June 2023, the Espionage Act was used to indict a former president for the first time in American history. That indictment was subsequently dismissed and later dropped on procedural grounds unrelated to the merits. But the indictment established that the conduct, measured against the Espionage Act's elements, presented a federal criminal case.

The Trading with the Enemy Act

The Trading with the Enemy Act, codified at 50 U.S.C. § 4301 et seq., prohibits commercial, financial, or material transactions with a designated enemy of the United States. It is simpler than treason in one critical way: you do not have to prove that the transaction advanced any particular hostile mission. Conducting business with an enemy state is itself the violation.

In the Cramer case, Justice Department attorneys debated between treason and Trading with the Enemy Act charges. The Act was considered because it was significantly easier to prove. After the Supreme Court reversed Cramer's treason conviction, he pleaded guilty to violating the Trading with the Enemy Act and served six years.

Why This Book Addresses Treason Rather Than Its Substitutes

The government's routine use of the Espionage Act and the Trading with the Enemy Act as treason substitutes is itself part of the story this book tells. When prosecutors consistently choose the easier statutory path, avoiding the two-witness rule, the enemy definition, the specific intent requirement, they avoid the constitutional question that the treason clause was designed to answer: did this person betray their country?

The Rosenbergs were convicted of espionage. But constitutional scholars have debated for seven decades whether their conduct constituted treason under Article III. This book makes that constitutional argument about conduct in the 21st century, because the argument belongs in the civic and historical record regardless of whether any prosecutor ever makes it in a court of law.

* * *

Section VI: Why This Case — The Specific Application

Having established what treason is, what its elements are, and how courts have interpreted it across two centuries, the Legal Introduction concludes by stating plainly why this book applies that framework to the documented conduct of Donald Trump.

The argument is not that Trump is obviously guilty of treason in a manner that would guarantee conviction in a properly constituted court. Given the immunity ruling in Trump v. United States (2024), the complexity of the enemy definition, the difficulty of the intent element, and the institutional reluctance to charge the highest crime against a former or current president, conviction is a distant prospect. This book does not pretend otherwise.

The argument is more precise and more constitutionally significant than a conviction claim: the factual record documented in Parts I through VII, when measured against the constitutional standard established in Sections I through V of this Legal Introduction, satisfies the legal definition of treason at the level required to submit the question to a jury.

That is all a treason brief needs to establish. The jury decides. The constitutional framework provides the standard. The evidence provides the facts. The argument provides the connection between them.

A republic that cannot make that argument, that lacks the constitutional vocabulary and civic courage to apply its own foundational law to the conduct of its own leaders , is a republic that has already surrendered the protection the treason clause was designed to provide.

The following Parts make the argument. The reader now has the law.

* * *

PART I

THE DOMESTIC FRONT

Levying War Against the Constitutional Order

Chapter One

Why Treason? A Betrayal of the American People

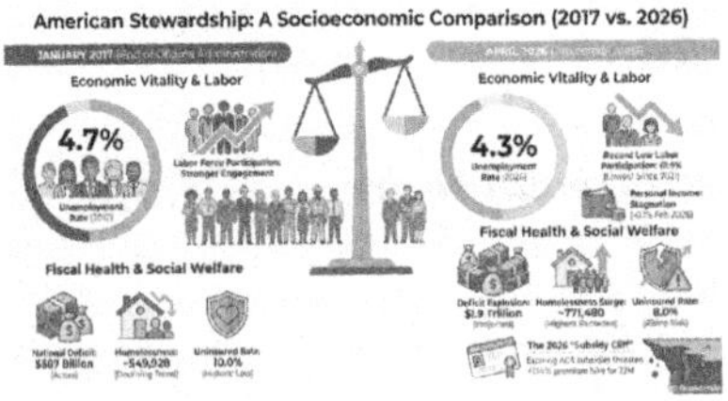

The Oath, the Pattern, and the Standard

The word "treason" appears in the Constitution only once.

That is not an accident.

Think of the Constitution as the operating manual for the most ambitious democratic experiment in human history. Most of the offenses a government official can commit, Congress defines and Congress can redefine. Fraud. Bribery. Obstruction. These are serious crimes, but they live in the federal code, subject to revision. The Framers left those definitions to the legislature on purpose.

Treason they wrote themselves, directly into the document. Not because they were angry, but because they were afraid, afraid of the exact thing they had just escaped: a government that turns the accusation of betrayal into a weapon against its own citizens. They had watched the British Crown charge colonists with treason for the crime of disagreeing. They were not going to hand that weapon to any future American government.

So they built a fence around the word. A high one. They said treason could only mean two things: levying war against the United States, or adhering to its enemies and giving them aid and comfort. Two things. That is all. And then they added the hardest evidentiary requirement in American law, the two-witness rule, to make sure no one could ever be convicted on the word of a single accuser.

That fence is this book's foundation, not its obstacle.

When the evidence clears a fence that high, the conclusion on the other side carries the full weight of the Republic's most solemn legal judgment. This chapter explains why the evidence documented in the pages that follow clears it. Not by cataloguing political grievances. Not by appealing to anger or fear. But by identifying, in plain terms, the four categories of documented conduct that correspond to specific constitutional elements and that Parts II through VII develop in exhaustive detail.

A political brief lists harms and assigns blame. A legal brief identifies elements and documents evidence. This book is the second kind of document. This chapter sets the terms on which that legal argument rests.

□ □ □

I. The Contract and the Oath

Here is a useful way to think about the presidential oath. Imagine you hire a property manager to run a building you own. The building belongs to you and your neighbors collectively. You give this manager extraordinary authority: the keys to every door, the power to sign contracts on your behalf, the ability to call in security, to negotiate with other buildings, to set the rules of the house. In exchange, the manager signs a contract committing to act in your interests and your neighbors' interests, not his own.

The presidential oath is that contract. The Constitution expresses it in thirty-five words:

> *"I do solemnly swear that I will faithfully execute the Office of President of the United States, and will to the best of my Ability, preserve, protect*

> *and defend the Constitution of the United States." — Presidential Oath of Office, Article II, Section 1*

The oath is not ceremonial, any more than a closing document at settlement is ceremonial. It is the legal instrument through which the President's authority is established. Every official act that follows, every order issued, every treaty negotiated, every pardon granted, derives its legitimacy from the allegiance the oath creates.

The Preamble identifies who the allegiance is owed to. Not a party. Not a donor class. Not a foreign government.

> *"We the People of the United States, in Order to form a more perfect Union, establish Justice, insure domestic Tranquility, provide for the common defence, promote the general Welfare, and secure the Blessings of Liberty to ourselves and our Posterity, do ordain and establish this Constitution for the United States of America." — Preamble, U.S. Constitution*

Those six purposes, a more perfect union, justice, domestic tranquility, the common defense, the general welfare, and the blessings of liberty, are the terms of the stewardship. They are what the property manager promised to protect.

Going back to our analogy: a property manager who secretly signs contracts benefiting a rival building, who lets the security systems deteriorate while telling residents everything is fine, who pockets payments from outside parties while making decisions that harm the people he was hired to serve, has not merely done a bad job. He has betrayed the trust that gave him the keys.

The chapters that follow document that betrayal in constitutional terms. This chapter identifies the four categories of conduct that make the legal argument necessary.

□ □ □

II. The Four Categories of Documented Conduct

The treason clause requires specific elements: allegiance, an enemy, an overt act witnessed by two persons, and specific intent. Parts II through VII document each element in detail. This chapter provides the framework: the four categories of conduct that, taken together, form the pattern the legal argument analyzes.

Think of these four categories the way a structural engineer thinks about the load-bearing walls of a building. You can argue about the paint color, the flooring, the layout of the rooms. But the load-bearing walls are not decorative. They are what holds the structure up. These four categories are the load-bearing walls of the legal case. Everything else in the book connects to one of them.

Each category is documented in the public record. Each connects directly to a specific constitutional element. And each is addressed in full in the chapters that follow.

First Category: The Russia Alignment

The Intelligence Community Assessment of January 2017, issued by the agencies of the federal government itself and confirmed across five bipartisan volumes of the Senate Intelligence Committee, established that a foreign power engaged in a sustained campaign of hostile action against the United States, targeting its election infrastructure, its democratic institutions, and its alliance structures.

What followed over the next eight years presents a pattern that is, at minimum, difficult to explain by accident. Think of it this way: if you hired a contractor to waterproof your basement and every decision that contractor made, without exception, made the flooding worse rather than better, at some point you stop calling it incompetence. Incompetence produces random failures. A pattern this directionally consistent, where every choice benefits the same party and every justification was contradicted by the government's own classified record, requires a different explanation.

Part II documents that pattern: American policy aligning systematically with Russian strategic objectives, American intelligence findings publicly contradicted and undermined, congressionally authorized military assistance to a nation under active Russian military attack withheld, and NATO's collective defense commitments weakened at the precise moments of maximum Russian strategic advantage.

Chapter 4 examines the legal question of whether Russia meets the constitutional definition of "enemy." Chapter 5 documents the Mueller-to-Helsinki pattern of alignment. Chapter 6 documents the systematic deconstruction of NATO's collective defense commitments. The reader will evaluate the legal argument on its merits.

Second Category: The Financial Entanglements

The Framers were practical people. They had watched European monarchies corrupted not by dramatic acts of sabotage but by something far more mundane: money. A foreign king sends gifts to a minister. The minister makes decisions that benefit the foreign king. Nobody calls it treason. Everybody understands what it is.

That is precisely why the Constitution contains not one but two Emoluments Clauses, one barring foreign payments, one barring domestic ones. The Framers were not going to let the new Republic be purchased the way the old monarchies had been. The clauses are the constitutional version of a conflict of interest policy, the kind every serious organization requires of its officers and agents.

The financial conduct documented in Chapter 9 establishes a pattern of payments from foreign governments and their representatives to Trump Organization properties during both presidential terms, and cryptocurrency token purchases by entities connected to foreign sovereign wealth funds during periods when those governments' relationships with the United States were active matters of presidential policy. The conflict of interest is documented in financial records, diplomatic correspondence, and congressional investigative findings.

For the treason analysis, the financial entanglements are not merely a separate constitutional violation. They are evidence of the corruption motive that connects the Russia alignment to the intent element. A President who makes foreign policy decisions that enrich himself through his family businesses is not performing an official act in the constitutional sense. He is, as Chapter 11 argues, performing a private transaction using the mechanisms of office.

Chapter 9 documents the financial conduct in full. Chapter 11 addresses the immunity question and the private act distinction that the financial entanglements directly implicate.

Third Category: The January 6 Assemblage

On January 6, 2021, an armed assemblage of persons marched from the Ellipse to the Capitol building during the active constitutional certification of a presidential election and breached the building by force, interrupting the certification for several hours.

The Supreme Court established the controlling legal standard for this kind of event in 1807, in Ex parte Bollman. Chief Justice John Marshall held that levying war against the United States requires an actual assemblage of persons organized for the purpose of executing a treasonable design. Not a speech. Not a conspiracy. An actual gathering of people, directed toward a treasonable purpose.

Here is the legal question Part I of this book addresses: Was the assemblage at the Capitol on January 6 a spontaneous riot that got out of hand, or was it a directed force operation against a constitutional act in progress? The answer matters because the treason clause answers it differently in each case. The January 6 Select Committee spent two years and interviewed hundreds of witnesses to answer exactly that question. Their findings, and the seven-part scheme they documented, are the factual predicate for Part I's legal analysis.

This chapter does not prejudge that analysis. It identifies the event for what it is in the legal framework: the factual predicate for the levying war prong of the treason clause.

Chapter 2 documents the breach of allegiance and the seven-part scheme. Chapter 3 examines the Commander in Chief's role and the constitutional significance of the Ellipse speech and the events that followed it.

Fourth Category: The Architecture of Denial

There is a principle that experienced investigators apply to complex cases: innocent people make mistakes, but they do not build systems. A single false statement might be a mistake. A false statement on the same subject, made to multiple audiences, over multiple years, using multiple different justifications, each one contradicted by the government's own records, is not a mistake. It is a structure.

The pattern documented in Part V spans both presidential terms and touches every subject addressed in the first three categories. Lies about the Russia investigation. Lies about the 2020 election. Lies about the content of ceasefire agreements. Lies about whether tariffs are paid by foreign countries or by American consumers. Lies about the fiscal impact of legislation that tripled the national deficit. Pardons issued to persons convicted of crimes committed in connection with protecting the President from investigation. Officials fired for fulfilling their legal obligations. Witnesses intimidated into silence.

The Chandler standard for intent, established in the 1948 treason conviction of an American who broadcast Nazi propaganda, holds that intent is established when a reasonable person in the defendant's position would have known that the acts gave aid and comfort to the enemy. Think of it this way: a person who parks in a no-parking zone might claim they did not see the sign. A person who covers the sign, argues the sign is fake, fires the parking officer, and pays a lawyer to have the sign declared unconstitutional has told you everything you need to know about their state of mind.

The architecture of denial is not separate from the treason argument. It is evidence of the intent behind the conduct the other three categories document.

Part V, Chapters 12 through 17, documents the architecture of denial in full, across every subject the pattern touches. Chapter 17 synthesizes the pattern and its legal significance for the specific intent element.

□ □ □

III. What This Chapter Is and Is Not

The Legal Introduction to this book established the constitutional standard with full rigor. It acknowledged the narrowness of the treason clause, the difficulty of the enemy element in the modern context, the demanding requirements of the two-witness rule, and the significant procedural obstacle created by the Supreme Court's immunity ruling in Trump v. United States (2024). It stated plainly that conviction is a distant prospect and that this book does not claim otherwise.

That honesty is this book's primary source of credibility. Think of it the way you would think about an expert witness. An expert who concedes the limits of the evidence is more persuasive than one who claims the evidence proves everything. The concession demonstrates that the expert has evaluated the evidence honestly, not selectively. A legal argument that overstates its case is not a legal argument. It is advocacy. The distinction between a legal brief and a political screed is the willingness to acknowledge what the evidence does not establish, as well as what it does.

This chapter does not establish that Donald Trump is guilty of treason. That determination belongs to a jury in a properly constituted proceeding. What this chapter establishes is the framework for the argument that the evidence, evaluated against the constitutional standard, is sufficient to submit the question to a jury.

That is all a treason brief needs to show. And it is the argument this book makes.

The reader will notice that this chapter does not contain an extended inventory of domestic policy harms, sections on immigration enforcement, reproductive rights, LGBTQ protections, tariff economics, homelessness statistics, housing policy, and the psychic costs of the administration's rhetoric. Those harms are real. Many are documented. Some are addressed in Parts III and VII where they bear on specific elements of the legal argument.

But an opening chapter of a legal brief is not the appropriate place for them. A reader who disagrees with the characterization of any one of those policy areas, and reasonable people do disagree about immigration enforcement, tariff policy, and housing strategy, has been given a reason to distrust the entire argument before the legal evidence has been presented. This book asks readers to evaluate the argument on its merits. That invitation requires the book to lead with its merits.

The four categories identified in Section II are not policy grievances. They are documented factual predicates for specific constitutional elements. That is the foundation on which this book rests. Everything that follows is built on it.

□ □ □

IV. The Standard the Reader Should Apply

Before proceeding to Part I's detailed examination of the January 6 assemblage and the seven-part scheme, the reader deserves a plain statement of what this book asks of them.

It does not ask for agreement. It does not ask for prior political alignment with its conclusions. It asks for the same standard a juror would be instructed to apply: evaluate the evidence against the legal elements, assess whether each element has been established by the documented record, and reach whatever conclusion that evaluation honestly supports.

Think of yourself, for the purposes of this book, as a juror in the most consequential case ever brought in American constitutional history. You are not being asked to convict. You are not being asked to acquit. You are being asked to read, evaluate, and decide. A juror who evaluates the evidence honestly and concludes the government has not established guilt is not failing the Republic. A citizen who reads this book honestly and concludes the argument has not been made is not wrong.

The book does not ask for a predetermined verdict. It asks for a fair reading of the case.

That reading begins with the law, which the Legal Introduction has provided. It continues with the domestic front. Part I begins on the next page.

□ □ □

Chapter Two

The Breach of Allegiance: When the Oath Became a Lie

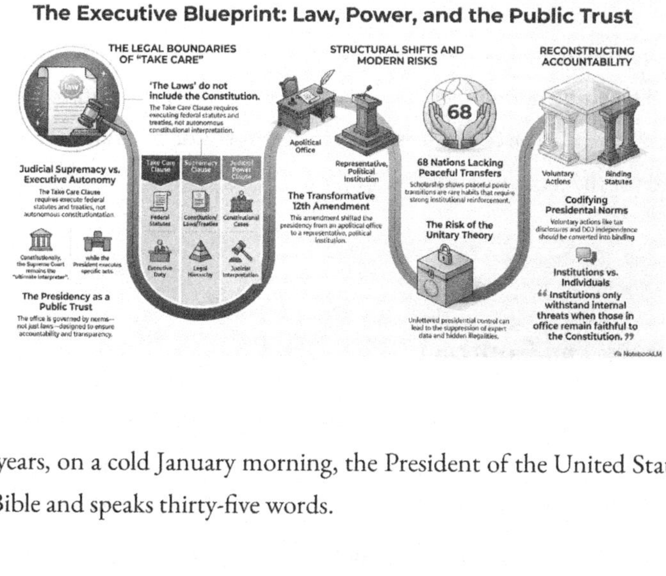

Every four years, on a cold January morning, the President of the United States places a hand on a Bible and speaks thirty-five words.

> *"I do solemnly swear that I will faithfully execute the Office of President of the United States, and will to the best of my Ability, preserve, protect and defend the Constitution of the United States."* — **Presidential Oath of Office, Article II, Section 1**

Most citizens view this as a ceremony. A formality. A ritual moment of pageantry before the real work begins.

The law views it differently. The law views it as a contract.

And not just any contract. The most consequential contract in American democracy, made in public, before the world, by the one person in the entire Republic who will be given the authority of the entire executive branch of the federal government. Every dollar the government spends, every agency that enforces every law, every military asset on every base around the world, all of it flows from the authority that oath creates.

That is what is at stake when the oath is spoken. And that is what is at stake when the oath is broken.

This chapter is about how that oath was broken. Not once, not accidentally, not through policy disagreement or political miscalculation. Systematically. Deliberately. Over years. In ways whose full legal significance the country is only now beginning to understand.

To understand the treason of January 6, 2021, you must first understand the years that preceded it. They were not politics as usual. They were the dismantling of the concept of allegiance itself, piece by piece, institution by institution, norm by norm, until the ground was prepared for the ultimate act.

□ □ □

Section One: The Contract

The oath is not merely ceremonial because the Constitution does not do merely ceremonial things. Every word in the founding document was chosen deliberately, argued over in the heat of a Philadelphia summer, and refined through drafts and debates that consumed months of the most brilliant political minds of their generation.

The treason statute, 18 U.S.C. section 2381, reflects this precision. It does not apply to everyone in the world. It applies specifically to whoever, owing allegiance to the United States, levies war against them or adheres to their enemies. A foreign enemy can kill Americans, destroy property, and attack military installations without committing treason. Treason is a betrayal of relationship. It is the crime of a citizen, and especially an officer, who turns against the state they swore to protect.

The Presidential Oath is the specific, documented, public establishment of that allegiance. And its language was chosen with a care that the Framers would want us to remember.

The Framers Chose Every Word on Purpose

At the Constitutional Convention of 1787, the delegates debated the Presidential Oath at length. An early draft required the President to protect the Constitution to the best of his judgment and power. Those two words, judgment and power, would have meant something specific and significant in constitutional law. They would have granted the President discretionary authority to interpret the Constitution independently, to decide for himself what the law meant, and to act on that interpretation even when the courts disagreed.

The delegates rejected those words. Deliberately. On the record.

They replaced judgment and power with a single word: ability. The shift was not cosmetic. In constitutional logic, judgment denotes discretion, the right to decide what the law is. Ability denotes diligence and personal effort. By choosing ability, the Framers were saying something precise: the President is a servant of the law's existing interpretation, not a creator of a new one. He executes the laws. He does not define them.

This is not a minor technical distinction. It is the foundational principle that separates a constitutional executive from a king.

The Take Care Clause: What the President Is Actually Required to Do

Article II, Section 3 of the Constitution contains a provision that sounds simple but carries enormous weight. It says the President shall take care that the laws be faithfully executed.

Legal scholars have spent decades analyzing exactly what the laws means in that sentence. The answer, established through careful analysis of the constitutional text and the drafting history of the Convention, is precise and important. The laws in the Take Care Clause refers to federal statutes and treaties, the output of the legislative process, the bills that Congress passes. It does not include the Constitution itself.

This is not a loophole or an oversight. It is the design. The Constitution is fundamental law, interpreted by the Judiciary. Ordinary laws are executive law, executed by the President. Article III and Article VI use the exact same three-part list, the Constitution, laws, and treaties, to define both the law of the land and the scope of judicial power. Article II conspicuously omits the Constitution from the President's execution duty. The Judiciary interprets the Constitution. The President executes what Congress enacts.

Think of it this way. If you hire a construction manager to build a house according to blueprints, the manager's job is to follow the blueprints as the architect has interpreted them. The manager does not get to decide the blueprints mean something different than what the architect says and then build accordingly. That is the architect's job. The President is the construction manager. The Supreme Court is the architect. The Framers designed it that way on purpose.

When a President claims the authority to interpret the Constitution independently, to override certified election results based on his personal reading of the law, to pressure the Vice President to act on a legal theory that every court and every legal authority had rejected, he has not exercised a constitutional power. He has claimed a power the Framers specifically and deliberately withheld from him. That is not a policy dispute. That is a breach of allegiance.

The presidency is not a monarchy. It is a temporary assignment of power, bound by the oath and bounded by the law. The outrageousness of the conduct documented in this chapter was not found in tweets, insults, or boorish behavior. It was found in the systematic repudiation of that oath. The President did not act as a steward of the public trust. He acted as a man who believed the United States government existed to serve him.

□ □ □

Section Two: The Profiteer

Article I, Section 9 of the Constitution contains a provision known as the Foreign Emoluments Clause. It prohibits any person holding federal office from accepting any present, emolument, office, or title of any kind whatever from any king, prince, or foreign state without the consent of Congress.

The Framers placed this in the very first article of the Constitution. They feared, above almost everything else, a President who could be bought.

They had good reason. They had watched the monarchies of Europe corrupt their governments through a steady flow of gifts, payments, and arrangements between foreign sovereigns and the officials who were supposed to be acting in the public interest. They were not going to let that happen in the new Republic. So they wrote it into the foundational law of the land, right at the beginning, before they even got to the structure of the executive branch in Article II.

Donald Trump took office in January 2017 refusing to divest from his businesses. He did not place his assets in a blind trust, the standard practice through which modern presidents have historically separated their private financial interests from their public duties. He placed them in a revocable trust managed by his sons, to whom he remained financially connected. The trust was revocable at any time. He could access the assets whenever he chose. The separation was in name only.

What Happened Next

The results were immediate and unprecedented in the history of the modern presidency.

Foreign governments seeking favor with the new administration began booking rooms at the Trump International Hotel in Washington, D.C. The Saudi government paid for rooms at a time when it was actively seeking American support for the blockade of Qatar, a diplomatic position that directly served Saudi strategic interests. The governments of Malaysia, the Philippines, and Turkey held events at Trump properties. Diplomatic missions from countries with active business before the American government chose Trump venues with a consistency that no reasonable observer could attribute to coincidence.

The line between the public treasury and private pockets had been erased.

But the outrageousness was not merely the money itself. It was the signal the money sent. To every foreign government watching, to every diplomat calculating how to get favorable treatment from the American executive branch, the message was clear. The United States government was no longer purely an instrument of foreign policy or the public good. It had become, at least in part, a franchise. Access and influence could be purchased. And the purchase price ran through the President's family businesses.

This is what the Emoluments Clause was written to prevent. The Framers understood that when a President's personal financial interests are served by the decisions of foreign governments, those governments have acquired something no foreign government is supposed to have: leverage over the President of the United States.

The Second Term: The Crypto Dimension

The second term introduced financial conflicts the Framers could not have imagined but would certainly have recognized. World Liberty Financial, a cryptocurrency venture connected to the Trump family, sold tokens to investors including entities linked to foreign sovereign wealth funds. These purchases created documented financial relationships between the President's family and foreign governments during the same period that those governments' relationships with the United States were active matters of presidential policy.

The conflict of interest is not hypothetical or theoretical. It is documented in financial records and congressional investigative findings. When the decisions a President makes about foreign policy can enrich his family, and when the families of foreign governments buy into that enrichment, the allegiance question answers itself.

> *"Loyalty was not owed to the Constitution. It was owed to the brand."*
> **The pattern established by the Trump Organization's operations during both terms**

That is not the allegiance the oath requires. That is its opposite.

□ □ □

Section Three: The Shakedown

In the summer of 2019, the President of the United States picked up the phone and called the newly elected leader of Ukraine.

Ukraine was not a casual diplomatic contact. It was a strategic ally on the front lines of Russian military aggression, a nation fighting a war against the same foreign power that the United States intelligence community had unanimously identified as the primary adversary to American democracy. Congress had authorized $391 million in military assistance for Ukraine. That money had been appropriated by the legislature, signed into law, and was sitting in the pipeline waiting to be delivered to a nation that needed it to survive.

The President held that money. He froze the transfer. And then he got on the phone with the Ukrainian President and asked for a favor.

The favor was not related to American national security. It was not about Ukrainian corruption in any general sense. It was specific. He wanted Ukraine to announce a public investigation into Hunter Biden, the son of the man who was at that moment the leading challenger for the Democratic presidential nomination.

He wanted opposition research. And he was willing to trade $391 million in congressionally authorized military aid for it.

What the Law Says About What Happened

The Government Accountability Office, a nonpartisan congressional watchdog, investigated the aid freeze and issued its finding in January 2020. The conclusion was unambiguous. The Office of Management and Budget had violated the Impoundment Control Act of 1974, the federal law that prohibits the executive branch from refusing to spend congressionally appropriated funds.

But the legal violation goes deeper than the Impoundment Control Act. Return to the Take Care Clause and what it actually requires. The President shall take care that the laws be faithfully executed. Congress had passed a law authorizing $391 million in military assistance to Ukraine. That law existed. It was on the books. The faithful execution of that law required delivering the aid.

Instead, the President froze the aid and conditioned its delivery on a foreign government taking a specific action that would benefit his personal political campaign.

This is not a policy dispute about the appropriate level of military assistance to a foreign ally. A policy dispute looks like this: I believe $391 million is too much, and I am sending Congress a revised budget proposal asking for $200 million instead. That is a legitimate exercise of executive policy judgment, subject to congressional review.

What actually happened looks like this: I am withholding the money Congress has already appropriated and authorized, and I will release it when you do something that helps my campaign. That is not policy. That is extortion. It is the use of official government power, the power of the purse and the authority of the Commander in Chief, as a personal political weapon.

He traded national security for opposition research. He used the American taxpayer's money as leverage for his own electoral benefit. When a President uses the power of his office not to advance the interests of the United States but to advance his own political survival, he has demonstrated where his allegiance lies. It lies with himself. Not the state he was sworn to defend.

The Testimony That Made It Plain

When the House of Representatives investigated the Ukraine aid freeze, the witnesses who came forward under oath told a consistent story.

Ambassador William Taylor testified that no corruption concerns had been raised through normal diplomatic channels, the process through which genuine policy concerns about foreign aid are normally communicated. Dr. Fiona Hill, the National Security Council's top Russia expert, testified that the corruption pretext offered to the public was not the real reason for the hold. Ambassador Gordon Sondland provided the clearest account.

> *"Was there a quid pro quo? As I testified previously, with regard to the requested White House call and White House meeting, the answer is yes."*

— Ambassador Gordon Sondland, House Intelligence Committee testimony, November 2019

Four witnesses. One consistent account. The stated justification was false. The real motivation was personal political benefit. And the mechanism was the weaponization of congressionally appropriated national security funds against a nation that was fighting the country the American intelligence community had identified as our primary foreign adversary.

If there is a more direct example of a President placing his own interests above the security of the United States, it does not readily come to mind.

□ □ □

Section Four: The Assault on the Rule of Law

The Presidential Oath requires the President to preserve, protect and defend the Constitution. The Constitution establishes three co-equal branches of government. It establishes a system of checks and balances specifically designed to prevent any single branch, including the executive, from accumulating unchecked power.

From the moment he took office, the conduct documented in the public record treated these checks not as constitutional requirements to be respected but as annoyances to be crushed.

The pattern was consistent and documented across both terms. Federal judges who ruled against the administration were publicly attacked by name, including characterizations of their rulings as the work of Obama judges or Clinton judges, a systematic effort to teach the public to evaluate judicial decisions not by their legal reasoning but by the political affiliation of the president who appointed the judge. The free press was branded the enemy of the people, a phrase with a specific and chilling historical resonance, used to prepare the public to disbelieve the institutional watchdog that the First Amendment was specifically designed to protect.

FBI Director James Comey was fired after refusing to pledge personal loyalty and declining to drop an investigation into the conduct of the National Security Advisor.

The President subsequently acknowledged to Russian officials, in the Oval Office, that the firing had relieved great pressure on the Russia investigation. He said this to the representatives of the foreign government whose relationship with his administration was the subject of the investigation he had just ended.

The Departmentalism Danger: Why This Matters Constitutionally

There is a legal theory called Departmentalism that some scholars have used to justify expanded executive authority. It argues that because the Constitution created three equal branches, each branch has the independent authority to interpret the Constitution within its own sphere. Under the strong version of this theory, the President can decline to execute statutes he personally concludes are unconstitutional, even if the courts have ruled otherwise.

The Framers considered and rejected this theory in the specific and documented way described in Section One of this chapter. They removed judgment and power from the Presidential Oath and replaced it with ability. They designed the Take Care Clause to require execution of statutes, not independent constitutional interpretation. And they gave Article III courts the structural jurisdiction over all cases arising under the Constitution, the exact scope of authority they withheld from the executive.

But the danger of Departmentalism is not merely theoretical. It is practical and it is documented. When a President adopts the view that he is empowered to independently interpret the Constitution, the results are predictable. Election results certified by state officials, confirmed by sixty federal courts, and affirmed by every legal authority consulted, including the President's own Attorney General, become subject to override based on the President's personal conclusion that the results were fraudulent. A Vice President is pressured to act on a legal theory every qualified authority has rejected because the President has decided his interpretation supersedes the judiciary's. A mob is directed to the Capitol to enforce by physical force a constitutional interpretation that failed in every legal forum where it was tested.

When the head of the executive branch treats the law as a tool for personal protection rather than a framework for governance, he breaks the allegiance that holds the republic together. Justice Sotomayor's dissent in Trump v. United States captured what this means in practice: 'In every use of official power, the President

is now a king above the law.' The Framers wrote the Take Care Clause and the Presidential Oath specifically to prevent exactly this result.

The Inspector General Purge: Removing the Watchdogs

The inspectors general of the federal government are the internal oversight mechanism of the executive branch. They are the officials responsible for detecting fraud, waste, and abuse within the agencies they oversee. They report not only to the executive but to Congress, providing the legislative branch with the independent information it needs to exercise its constitutional oversight function.

Between April and May of 2020, multiple inspectors general were fired or had their removal attempted across the national security apparatus. Intelligence Community Inspector General Michael Atkinson was fired specifically for performing his legal obligation, forwarding a whistleblower complaint about the Ukraine aid freeze to Congress as the law required. State Department Inspector General Steve Linick was fired while conducting an investigation into conduct involving the Secretary of State.

The firing of officials for performing their legal duties is not a policy decision. It is the removal of accountability. And accountability, in the constitutional design, is not optional. It is the mechanism through which the oath is enforced.

When the President removes the people whose job it is to catch him breaking the law, he is not cleaning house. He is clearing the field. He is creating the conditions in which the breach of allegiance documented in this chapter can continue and deepen without institutional resistance.

□ □ □

Section Five: The Pardon as Promise

Article II, Section 2 gives the President the power to grant reprieves and pardons for offenses against the United States.

This power was placed in the Constitution for good reasons. History records instances where it served justice beautifully, where innocent people were freed, where mercy was appropriately extended to those who deserved a second chance, where the rigidity of the criminal law was softened by the human judgment of a compassionate executive.

The pardon power, properly used, is a check on the harshness of the justice system. It is one of the most genuinely humane provisions in the entire Constitution.

Donald Trump used it as a payment system.

The Pattern: What the Pardons Have in Common

To understand what happened, you need to look not at any individual pardon in isolation but at the pattern across all of them. Patterns tell the truth that individual cases can obscure.

Roger Stone was convicted of seven felony counts: obstruction of justice, witness tampering, and five counts of lying to Congress. His crimes were committed in connection with protecting the President from federal investigation. His conviction followed proceedings in which evidence established his coordination with the Trump campaign about WikiLeaks, which the Mueller Report identified as the conduit for Russian-stolen Democratic Party emails. Stone refused to cooperate with federal investigators. He was commuted in July 2020 and fully pardoned in December 2020.

Paul Manafort was convicted of eight counts of financial fraud and tax evasion and pleaded guilty to two counts of conspiracy. The Senate Intelligence Committee's bipartisan finding that Manafort shared internal campaign polling data with Konstantin Kilimnik, a person the Committee assessed was a Russian intelligence officer, is one of the most damaging single findings in the entire Russia investigation record. Manafort declined to provide significant cooperation against the President. He was fully pardoned in December 2020.

Michael Flynn pleaded guilty to lying to FBI agents about his contacts with Russian Ambassador Sergei Kislyak, specifically his discussions about sanctions during the presidential transition, a period when a new administration is legally prohibited from conducting foreign policy. Flynn cooperated with the Mueller investigation for a period and then withdrew his cooperation. He was fully pardoned in November 2020.

The common thread running through every one of these pardons is not mercy. It is not rehabilitation. It is not justice. The common thread is that every person pardoned either declined to cooperate with investigations into the President's own conduct or withdrew their cooperation after providing limited information.

A presidential pardon issued to a person who was convicted of crimes committed in connection with protecting the President from investigation is not mercy. It is payment. It is the use of a constitutional power, designed for justice and compassion, as a tool for purchasing the silence of witnesses. That is bribery executed through the mechanism the Constitution provides but never designed for this purpose.

The January 6 Pardons: Ratifying the Attack

In January 2021, as he was preparing to leave office, the President told the mob that had attacked the Capitol that he loved them and that they were very special. The statement was not merely emotional. It was a signal.

When he returned to office in January 2025, he kept the promise that signal implied.

Within his first days back in office, the President pardoned the January 6 defendants. Not selectively. Not after individual review of the specific facts of each case. Broadly and sweepingly, including individuals who had been convicted of seditious conspiracy, individuals who had assaulted police officers with flagpoles, fire extinguishers, and other weapons, individuals whose jury-proven conduct represented the most direct attack on the constitutional process of certifying a presidential election in American history.

When a President pardons those who attacked the Capitol to keep him in power, he is not exercising mercy toward the remorseful. He is ratifying the attack itself. He is telling every militia group, every violent organization, every person in the country willing to use force on his behalf: if you fight for me and the legal system catches you, I will use the constitutional power of the pardon to ensure you do not suffer the consequences.

That is a standing offer to a private army.

And a President who maintains a standing offer to a private army, promising them immunity from the legal consequences of violence committed in his political interest, has not merely abused the pardon power. He has established the conditions for continued and escalating political violence. He has signaled that allegiance to the President supersedes allegiance to the law. And he has told future assemblages exactly what they need to hear before they march.

> *"When a President pardons his private army, he is not the head of state. He is a faction leader. And faction leaders do not serve the Republic. They consume it."* **The constitutional logic of the January 6 pardons**

□ □ □

Section Six: The 220 Years He Tried to End

Here is a fact about democracy that most Americans have never had occasion to consider, because they grew up in the only country where it has been true long enough to feel like the natural order of things.

Most nations on earth have never successfully transferred political power from one rival party to another through a peaceful election.

A 2014 study by political scientist Adam Przeworski analyzed 3,000 elections conducted between 1788 and 2008, across every nation that held them. His finding was striking. Sixty-eight countries in that sample had never, in their entire history, experienced a peaceful transfer of power between rival political parties. Not once. In sixty-eight nations, every time power changed hands, it changed through force, through coup, through assassination, through collapse, or through a system so rigged that the opposition never had a genuine chance.

The peaceful transfer of power is not the natural state of human political organization. It is the exception. It is the miracle. And it is extraordinarily difficult to achieve and extraordinarily easy to destroy.

How America Built the Habit: 1793 and 1801

The American version of this miracle was built in two stages, each of which required extraordinary acts of voluntary restraint by powerful men who could have chosen otherwise.

The first stage was 1793. George Washington, who had commanded the Continental Army, won the Revolutionary War, and been elected unanimously as the first President of the United States, resigned his military commission. He gave the power back. He walked away from it. He returned to private life. The artist John Trumbull called this one of the highest moral lessons ever given the world, because it established something that no founding document alone could establish: the precedent that military power is subordinate to civilian authority, and that the person who holds power does not own it.

The second stage was 1801. John Adams, the sitting President of the United States, lost the presidential election to Thomas Jefferson. The two men hated each other. Their political philosophies were diametrically opposed. Adams had every institutional mechanism available to him, he controlled the federal government, to make it very difficult for Jefferson to take over.

He left anyway.

Jefferson called what happened the Revolution of 1801. He noted that the revolution occurred by the suffrage of the people rather than the sword. What he meant was that for the first time in the history of the world, a head of state had surrendered the reins of government to a bitter political rival without force, without bloodshed, and without the victorious party having to fight its way into power.

That moment, January 4, 1801, is the foundation on which everything that followed was built. Every peaceful election, every gracious concession speech, every transition of power in the 220 years between Adams handing power to Jefferson and January 6, 2021 rests on that single precedent.

What the Norm Requires: Loser's Consent

Political scientists have a name for the principle that makes peaceful transfer of power possible. They call it loser's consent.

Loser's consent is the willingness of the defeated party to accept the legitimacy of the electoral outcome and the authority of the victor, even when accepting that outcome means losing power, losing policy influence, and potentially facing political retribution from the new administration. It is not a law. It cannot be enforced by courts. It is a norm, a shared understanding that both sides will abide by the result of the process even when the result is painful.

Democracy depends on loser's consent in a way that it depends on nothing else. Without it, every election becomes a potential conflict between the side that wins and the side that refuses to accept that it lost. Without it, the peaceful transfer of power that Adams demonstrated in 1801, the miracle that 68 nations have never managed to achieve, becomes impossible.

John Adams wrote in 1761, more than a decade before the Revolution: The very ground of our liberties is the freedom of elections.

He was right. And the freedom of elections depends entirely on the willingness of the loser to accept the result.

January 6: The Attack on 220 Years

On November 3, 2020, the American people voted. The result was certified by every state, reviewed by sixty federal courts, confirmed by the Department of Justice, and affirmed by the President's own Attorney General, who stated publicly that there was no evidence of fraud sufficient to change the outcome.

The President refused loser's consent.

He did not merely dispute the results in court, which is a legitimate legal remedy available to any candidate. He disputed them in court, lost, and then continued. He pressured state officials to change certified results. He organized a scheme to submit fraudulent electoral certificates from states his opponent had won. He pressured the Vice President to act on a legal theory that every court and every legal authority had rejected. And when all of those mechanisms failed, he directed an armed mob to the Capitol to stop by force the constitutional process that would confirm his defeat.

The attack on January 6 was not merely an attack on a building. It was not merely an attack on the members of Congress who were inside. It was an attack on the 220 years of accumulated precedent that stretches from John Adams walking out of the President's House in 1801 to the moment the first rioter broke a Capitol window in 2021.

It was an attempt to end the miracle.

What the Scholars Said

Legal scholars studying the January 6 attack have noted something important about the relationship between the constitutional text and what happened that day. The January 6 Report identified the attempt to override court-certified election results not merely as a moral failure but as a textual failure, a clear dereliction of the duty the Take Care Clause imposes.

When a President claims the authority to override the legal system based on a personal interpretation of the Constitution, when he substitutes his own judgment for that of sixty federal courts, for that of his own Attorney General, for that of the state officials whose legal responsibility it was to certify the results, he has violated the specific and deliberate design of the Framers who removed judgment and power from the Presidential Oath and replaced it with ability.

He has claimed to be the architect when the Framers built him to be the construction manager. And when the construction manager decides to tear down the building rather than accept the architect's blueprint, the building does not survive.

The Perpetual Task

The constitutional scholar Charles Krauthammer wrote that the task of merely maintaining strong and sturdy the structures of a constitutional order is unending, the continuing and ceaseless work of every generation.

He was describing what makes democracy different from every other system of government. Democracy is not a destination you arrive at and then inhabit forever. It is a practice. It requires active, ongoing commitment from the people who live inside it and especially from the officials who are temporarily entrusted with its power.

The oath that opens this chapter is not the starting point of that commitment. It is its public expression. The commitment itself must be carried in the conduct of every day in office, in every decision about where allegiance lies, in every choice between the interests of the public trust and the interests of the person who holds it.

What the documented record of the conduct examined in this chapter shows is a sustained, systematic choice to place personal interest, financial gain, political survival, and loyalty to a private faction above the constitutional allegiance the oath established.

That choice has a name.

It is called a breach of allegiance.

And a breach of allegiance by the person who holds the highest office in the Republic, sustained across years and across institutions, directed against the constitutional order itself, is the definition of the crime the Framers placed in Article III, Section 3.

The next chapter documents what that breach looked like when it was finally, physically, violently acted upon. On January 6, 2021, the groundwork laid by years of emoluments violations, extortion of allies, assault on the rule of law, and weaponization of the pardon power came to its logical conclusion.

The preparation was complete. The ground had been laid. And the levying of war began.

□ □ □

Chapter Three

The Commander in Chief's Role: The Oath, the Ellipse, and the Seven-Part Scheme

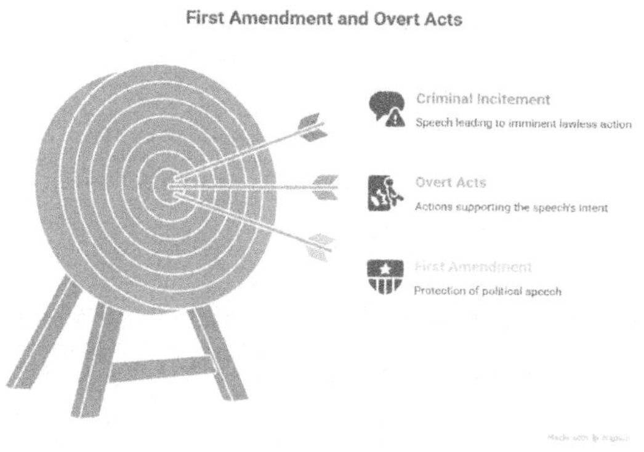

Every story has a villain. But the best stories, the ones that actually tell the truth, do not present their villain as simply evil. They show you how a person chose, step by step, to become what they became.

This chapter is about choices.

Specifically, it is about the choices made by the President of the United States in the weeks and months before January 6, 2021, the choices made on January 6 itself, and the legal significance of each choice measured against the oath of office that made Donald Trump the most powerful person in the world.

Those choices did not happen in a vacuum. They were made against a background of documented fact: that sixty federal and state courts had reviewed the claims of fraud and rejected them, that the President's own Attorney General had told him the claims were nonsense and bullshit, that the President's own campaign data team had told him in early November his chances of victory were very bleak, and that every state official whose legal responsibility it was to certify the results had done so without finding evidence of fraud sufficient to change the outcome.

The President knew all of this. The record proves he knew it. And he made his choices anyway.

What follows is a military prosecution brief disguised as a chapter. It documents how the President recruited the force, armed and disarmed the security environment, commanded the movement, and sustained the attack through 187 minutes of deliberate inaction. At the end of each overt act, the witnesses who can constitutionally establish that act are identified, because this book is not theorizing. It is building a case.

□ □ □

The Oath as a Legal Document

When you are sworn in as President of the United States, you do not simply promise to do your best. You take a specific oath, written into the Constitution itself, that has two parts.

The first part is active. You swear to faithfully execute the office of President. That means doing your job, the actual duties the Constitution assigns to the executive branch.

The second part is defensive. You swear to preserve, protect, and defend the Constitution of the United States. That means the document itself, the system of government it establishes, and the constitutional processes it protects.

The certification of Electoral College votes under 3 U.S.C. section 15 is one of those protected constitutional processes. It is not merely a formality. It is the legal mechanism by which the peaceful transfer of power occurs. When a President directs force against that process, he is not merely breaking a law. He is violating the oath that is the legal foundation of his own authority. He is using the power the oath gave him to destroy what the oath required him to protect.

> *"I do solemnly swear that I will faithfully execute the Office of President of the United States, and will to the best of my Ability, preserve, protect and defend the Constitution of the United States."* **Presidential Oath of Office, Article II, Section 1**

That oath is not a formality. Under the treason framework established in Chapter 2, it is the specific, constitutional, documented statement of allegiance. When a President violates it through directed force against a constitutional process, the allegiance element of the treason analysis is not merely satisfied. It is violated at the highest possible level.

With that established, let us look at the overt acts. One by one. With their witnesses named.

□ □ □

Overt Act One: The December 19 Tweet and the Recruitment of the Force

Before we can understand the speech at the Ellipse on January 6, we need to understand what happened seventeen days earlier. Because the Ellipse speech did not create the assemblage. It activated it. The assemblage had been recruited weeks in advance, and the recruitment was documented in a single tweet.

The Invitation

On December 19, 2020, the President of the United States sent a message to his tens of millions of social media followers.

> *"Big protest in D.C. on January 6th. Be there, will be wild!"* **President Donald Trump, Twitter, December 19, 2020**

Three words carried the legal weight: be there and wild. To an ordinary citizen scrolling through a news feed, this might have seemed like a campaign rally announcement. To the Proud Boys, the Oath Keepers, the Three Percenters, and the other militia organizations that had been monitoring the President's communications for instructions, it was received as something different. They understood it as a direct order from their Commander in Chief.

The January 6 Committee documented what happened in the hours following that tweet. The head of the Florida chapter of the Oath Keepers sent a message to members declaring an alliance with the Proud Boys and instructing them to shut this ship down. Militia organizations that had historically operated separately began coordinating in encrypted communication channels. Intelligence officials tracking domestic extremist networks noted what they described as red flags, the emergence of what analysts called a blended ideology, historically nonaligned violent groups uniting around a single specific objective.

The Proud Boys established an encrypted operational channel they called the Ministry of Self Defense. Inside that channel, they conducted tactical planning for January 6 that included maps of Washington, D.C. identifying police positions, tactical formation discussions, and designated entry points. This was not the preparation of people who were coming to Washington to hear a speech and wave flags.

The Roger Stone and Michael Flynn Connection

The connection between the White House and these militia groups was not abstract or theoretical.

Roger Stone, one of the President's longest-serving political associates, maintained documented communication with militia leaders in the weeks before January 6. On the day itself, Stone's personal security detail was provided by members of the Oath Keepers, several of whom have since been convicted of seditious conspiracy. Michael Flynn, the former National Security Advisor who had been pardoned just weeks earlier, maintained similar documented lines of contact with militia organizers.

Stone and Flynn served as the connective tissue between the White House's political operation and the violent organizations assembling in Washington. The Stop the Steal infrastructure, which organized both the rally and the logistical coordination of militia groups, ran from these organizers directly into the White House communications network. Text messages between rally organizers and White House staff documented that coordination in writing.

Why This Satisfies the Bollman Standard

Chapter 1 established that the Supreme Court's controlling definition of levying war, from Ex parte Bollman in 1807, requires an actual assemblage of persons for the purpose of executing a treasonable design. The assemblage cannot be merely a spontaneous crowd. It must be organized, directed, and aimed at a constitutional target.

The December 19 tweet is the legal proof that the assemblage was not spontaneous. It was recruited. The militia organizations that received the tweet as a call to arms and responded by establishing operational planning channels, coordinating across previously separate groups, and traveling to Washington armed and tactically prepared, constitute precisely the assemblage Bollman requires. The President recruited them with a tweet. His associates coordinated them through encrypted channels and personal relationships. And three weeks later, he activated them with a speech.

A general does not stumble accidentally upon an army at the gates of a city. He summons it. The December 19 tweet was the summons. The Ellipse speech was the battle order. And the Capitol was the target.

> **THE WITNESSES:** *The December 19 tweet is a public document. Its reception and interpretation by militia groups is documented in the January 6 Committee's Final Report, through intelligence analysis, and through the trial testimony of convicted Proud Boys and Oath Keepers leaders who confirmed they understood it as a directive. Roger Stone's communications with militia leaders are documented in the Committee's investigation. Michael Flynn's coordination is documented in Committee witness testimony.*

□ □ □

Overt Act Two: The Armed Assembly and the Magnetometer Order

On the morning of January 6, 2021, before the President walked to the podium at the Ellipse, his staff brought him information that should have stopped everything.

Thousands of his supporters were refusing to enter the secured rally area through the magnetometer checkpoints. The reason was not that the lines were too long or the morning was too cold. The reason was that they were carrying weapons: knives, handguns, AR-15 rifles, bear spray, brass knuckles, and spears fastened to flagpoles. They could not pass through metal detection screening without triggering the equipment and facing detention.

The President was told this directly. He was informed that the crowd pressing against the perimeter of his rally was an armed crowd. He understood what that meant.

His response was not alarm. It was not a call to security officials to manage the situation. It was not a request that armed individuals be turned away from the event.

> *"Take the fucking mags away. They're not here to hurt me. Let my people in. They can march to the Capitol from here."* **President Donald Trump, to White House staff, morning of January 6, 2021, documented in House Select Committee testimony**

Read that sequence carefully, because each element carries specific legal weight.

Take the fucking mags away: a direct order to remove the security screening that was preventing armed individuals from entering the rally.

They're not here to hurt me: an explicit acknowledgment that the crowd was armed, combined with an assessment that the weapons were not a threat to him personally. He was not concerned that his supporters were carrying deadly weapons. He was concerned they were being kept at a distance.

They can march to the Capitol from here: a statement of intent. Not a hope. Not a prediction. A plan. He knew the crowd was armed. He removed the security screening. And he identified the destination.

Why Armed Assembly Elevates the Legal Standard

The distinction between an unarmed crowd and an armed one is not merely a matter of danger. It is a matter of legal categorization. An unarmed crowd that gets out of control is a riot, a serious crime, but a crime that falls under ordinary criminal law. An armed crowd, organized in advance, directed by a commander who knows they are armed, deployed toward a specific constitutional target, falls under a different legal category entirely.

Under Ex parte Bollman, levying war requires an assemblage of persons in force. Force, in this context, is not merely the energy of a crowd. It is the capacity for organized coercion backed by the credible threat or use of weapons. When the President of the United States orders the removal of security screening for an armed crowd and then directs that armed crowd toward the seat of the constitutional government, he has not merely incited a riot. He has deployed an armed force.

This distinction is what elevates the January 6 charge from ordinary criminal incitement to the specific constitutional standard of levying war. Bollman's requirement of an assemblage in force is satisfied not merely by the numbers of people present, but by the weaponry they carried and the President's documented knowledge of that weaponry when he ordered the security screening removed.

The National Guard Void: Withholding the Defense

There is a second dimension to the armed assembly analysis that is equally important and often underemphasized.

In the days before January 6, the Capitol Police, the District of Columbia government, and federal officials made repeated requests and offers related to National Guard deployment. The Department of Defense has documented that requests for Guard support in connection with January 6 were significantly delayed and in some cases rebuffed at the White House level. The Guard was not positioned in advance despite documented intelligence assessments that the day could turn violent and despite the specific tactical planning by militia groups that intelligence officials had flagged.

On the day itself, as the Capitol was being overrun, frantic requests for National Guard deployment were made by Capitol Police, by members of Congress, and by Vice President Pence, who was not in the formal chain of command but who issued unambiguous orders to military officials to get the Guard to the Capitol and put down the situation. The National Guard did not arrive in force until hours into the assault.

The Commander in Chief, the only person in the United States government with the constitutional authority to deploy military force, made no calls to the Secretary of Defense, the Attorney General, or the Secretary of Homeland Security during those hours.

A commander who deploys an armed force against a target and simultaneously withholds the defense of that target is not a bystander. He is an active participant in the outcome. By deploying the armed assemblage and denying the defense, the President did not merely allow the assault on the Capitol to proceed. He ensured its success for as long as he chose not to intervene. That is the Aid and Comfort prong of the treason clause, executed through the mechanism of command authority.

> **THE WITNESSES:** *The magnetometer order is documented in Cassidy Hutchinson's sworn testimony before the House Select Committee and corroborated by the testimony of Secret Service agents present at the Ellipse. The President's knowledge that the crowd was armed is established by multiple witnesses who were present at the morning briefing. The National Guard delay and the void in the President's command authority during the assault are documented in the Committee's Final Report, in Pentagon records, and in the testimony of Vice President Pence's staff regarding his unilateral orders to the military.*

□ □ □

Overt Act Three: The Ellipse Speech and the Battle Order

At 12:00 p.m. on January 6, 2021, the President of the United States walked to the podium at the Ellipse and began speaking to the armed crowd his December 19 tweet had recruited and whose metal detector screening he had ordered removed ninety minutes earlier.

The speech lasted over an hour. It repeated false claims about the election that sixty courts had rejected, that the President's own Attorney General had called nonsense, and that the President's own campaign data team had told him were not supported by evidence. The President knew these claims were false when he made them. The documentary record, including the audio recordings of Steve Bannon from October 31, 2020 revealing the strategy of declaring victory regardless of the actual vote count, and the early November assessments from campaign staff that his chances of success were very bleak, establishes that the fraud narrative was a premeditated construction, not a sincere belief.

The President told his supporters that if they did not fight like hell they would not have a country anymore. He told them that he would be marching with them to the Capitol. He directed them toward the building where the constitutional certification process was underway.

The word peacefully appeared once in the speech. The phrase fight like hell appeared multiple times. The crowd heard what it was designed to hear.

The First Amendment Question and Why the Overt Acts Answer It

The First Amendment protects political speech, even extreme political speech, even speech that makes reasonable people furious. The Supreme Court established in Brandenburg v. Ohio in 1969 that speech can only be punished as criminal incitement if it is directed to producing imminent lawless action and is likely to actually produce that action.

The Ellipse speech, read in isolation, presents a genuine First Amendment question. Skilled defense lawyers argued that fight like hell is political rhetoric, that the crowd's subsequent actions were their own responsibility, and that the President cannot be held legally accountable for what his listeners chose to do.

But the Ellipse speech does not stand in isolation. It stands at the end of a sequence of overt acts, each of which supplies the element the speech alone cannot carry.

The December 19 tweet established that the assemblage was recruited, not spontaneous. The magnetometer order established that the President knew the assemblage was armed. The motorcade demand, which is addressed below, established that the President intended to personally lead the armed assemblage to the Capitol. And the 187 minutes of deliberate inaction, which follows, established that the President sustained the assault by choosing not to stop it.

Together, these overt acts satisfy the Brandenburg standard that the speech alone might not. The speech was not merely advocacy of change. It was a battle order delivered to a recruited, armed, tactically prepared force, by a commander who had already tried to personally lead them to the constitutional target and who would spend the next three hours ensuring they were not stopped.

The Motorcade: The Intent to Be Present

At 1:17 p.m., seven minutes after the President left the Ellipse stage, the presidential motorcade was waiting. He got in and demanded to be taken to the Capitol.

Multiple witnesses documented what followed. Metropolitan Police Department Officer Mark Robinson, who had participated in over a hundred presidential motorcades, testified that he had never witnessed a discussion in which the President so adamantly contradicted the Secret Service's professional security assessment. The President was described by witnesses as irate, furious, and physically animated. He told his Secret Service lead agent and the vehicle's driver: I'm the President and I'll decide where I get to go.

The motorcade returned to the White House. But the agents did not stand down. They remained on standby, because as of 1:25 p.m. the President was still planning to hold at the White House and then move to the Capitol. That plan was not officially canceled until 1:55 p.m., when security conditions at the Capitol had deteriorated beyond any possibility of a presidential arrival.

The President did not abandon the plan because he changed his mind. He abandoned it because the Secret Service would not take him.

This is the overt act that Marshall's Burr refinement requires. It is the open deed that proves the President's intent to be legally or actually present at the levying of war. He tried to go. He was stopped. That is the difference between a person who incites and a commander who leads.

THE WITNESSES: *The Ellipse speech is a public record with thousands of witnesses present. The motorcade confrontation is documented in testimony from Officer Mark Robinson of the Metropolitan Police Department, Secret Service lead agent Robert Engel, the vehicle's driver, and multiple White House staff members who were briefed on the incident. Cassidy Hutchinson's testimony before the House Select Committee included her account of what she was told about the confrontation by those present. Multiple witnesses corroborate the core facts.*

□ □ □

Overt Act Four: The Pence Pressure Campaign

What happened to Vice President Mike Pence in the weeks before January 6 is one of the most extraordinary legal stories in the history of American democracy. Not because the theory advanced against him was sophisticated. But because it was deployed despite being universally recognized as legally defective by everyone involved, including the lawyer who wrote it.

The Eastman Theory and Its Acknowledged Bankruptcy

The President, through his attorney John Eastman, advanced a legal theory that the Vice President of the United States possessed the unilateral authority to reject certified electoral votes during the Joint Session of Congress and to send the election to the House of Representatives, where the outcome would favor the incumbent.

The Vice President's constitutional role during the Joint Session is established by Article II and the Twelfth Amendment and clarified by the Electoral Count Act of 1887. That role is ministerial. The Vice President presides. He opens the envelopes containing the certified electoral votes of the states. He ensures the votes are handed to the tellers. He has no substantive authority to determine which votes are valid or to reject slates certified by state officials.

White House Counsel Pat Cipollone told the President this directly and described the Eastman plan as a murder-suicide pact. Greg Jacob, the Vice President's own counsel, rejected the theory in writing, in real time, as Eastman presented it. The entire senior leadership of the Department of Justice told the President it was illegal. The bipartisan Lost, Not Stolen report, co-authored by prominent Republican legal minds including Benjamin Ginsberg, exhaustively reviewed the 2020 election and found no legal or factual pretext for the Vice President to deviate from his ministerial role.

And John Eastman himself, in a private conversation with Greg Jacob, acknowledged that the Supreme Court would likely reject his theory by a vote of nine to zero.

A legal theory its own author concedes would lose nine to zero in the Supreme Court is not a legal argument. It is a pretext.

The Pressure Campaign

Despite universal legal rejection, the President maintained and escalated his pressure campaign against the Vice President for weeks.

In private confrontations, the President called Pence a wimp and used profane language to express his contempt for Pence's refusal to comply. On the morning of January 6, in a phone call documented by multiple witnesses, the President reportedly berated the Vice President and told him he would go down in history as a coward.

In public, the President used the Ellipse speech itself as a pressure mechanism, telling tens of thousands of assembled supporters, including the armed militia members whose metal detector screening he had already ordered removed, that he hoped Mike is going to do the right thing. He said this knowing that his armed supporters were about to march to the building where Pence was presiding over the certification process.

And then, at 2:24 p.m., while the Capitol was being overrun by those supporters and while Pence was being evacuated from the Senate chamber by Secret Service agents who were navigating a hallway that rioters had entered, the President sent a tweet telling the world that Pence did not have the courage to do what was necessary.

Secret Service protective intelligence agents monitoring social media in real time assessed the tweet immediately. Their documented conclusion: the tweet would further enrage the mob and enlarge the target on the Vice President's back.

The President of the United States, knowing his armed supporters were inside the Capitol hunting for the Vice President, publicly identified the Vice President as a coward who deserved the mob's anger. That is not political commentary. Under the broadcaster precedents established in the World War II treason cases, speech delivered in service of an ongoing violent assault against a constitutional officer, by the commander of the force conducting that assault, is an overt act of direction and command.

The Constitutional Significance

The Pence pressure campaign matters to the treason analysis for a reason that goes beyond the specific targeting of an individual. The Vice President was the constitutional officer presiding over the specific function that the assemblage was organized to disrupt. The pressure campaign was the legal mechanism. The armed mob was the physical mechanism. They were both aimed at the same target: the completion of the certification process that would confirm the President's electoral defeat.

Under the Bollman standard, the treasonous design requires an assemblage aimed at preventing a constitutional function of the United States government. The Pence pressure campaign and the armed mob were components of a unified design with a single objective. The President deployed both simultaneously.

> **THE WITNESSES:** *The Pence pressure campaign is documented in extraordinary detail. Mike Pence's own contemporaneous notes record his constitutional analysis and his refusal. Greg Jacob, Pence's counsel, testified before the House Select Committee about every step of the pressure campaign and about Eastman's private acknowledgment that the theory would fail nine to zero. Marc Short, the Vice President's Chief of Staff, documented the campaign and Pence's resistance. Pat Cipollone, the White House Counsel, testified about the murder-suicide pact characterization. The 2:24 p.m.*

tweet is a public document. The Secret Service protective intelligence assessment of its likely effect on the mob is documented in Committee findings.

□ □ □

Overt Act Five: The 187 Minutes and the Deliberate Void

From 1:10 p.m., when the President left the Ellipse stage, to 4:17 p.m., when he finally released a video asking the mob to go home, 187 minutes elapsed. What the President did, and what he chose not to do, during those 187 minutes is documented in testimony from dozens of witnesses who were present.

The most important legal fact about those 187 minutes is not merely what the President failed to do. It is the contrast between what he failed to do and what he actively chose to do instead. Because during those 187 minutes, the President was not passive. He was making choices. He just was not making the choices that his oath required.

What the President Did Not Do

During 187 minutes of armed assault on the United States Capitol, the Commander in Chief of the United States Armed Forces made zero calls to the Secretary of Defense. Zero calls to the Attorney General. Zero calls to the Secretary of Homeland Security. Not a single call to any of the officials who had the legal authority and the available resources to deploy force to defend the Capitol and protect the constitutional process being disrupted inside it.

The Vice President, who had no formal military authority, issued unambiguous orders to military officials from a secure location within the Capitol complex. The Capitol Police, the Metropolitan Police Department, and members of Congress were calling frantically for help. The National Guard was not deployed in force until hours into the assault.

The Commander in Chief was watching television.

What the President Did Do

What the President was doing during those 187 minutes was documented by the witnesses who were present with him in the dining room adjacent to the Oval Office.

He was watching Fox News coverage of the assault. He was making phone calls, but not to law enforcement or defense officials. He was calling his personal attorney Rudy Giuliani and contacting members of Congress to continue coordinating delays to the certification process, the same process the mob at the Capitol was physically attempting to prevent.

At 2:13 p.m., White House Counsel Pat Cipollone told Chief of Staff Mark Meadows they needed to go see the President immediately. Meadows replied: He doesn't want to do anything, Pat.

At 2:26 p.m., House Minority Leader Kevin McCarthy called the President and pleaded for help. The President's response, as documented in testimony: Well, Kevin, I guess they're just more upset about the election theft than you are.

At 2:38 p.m., under pressure from his daughter Ivanka and other aides, the President sent a tweet asking supporters to remain peaceful. He did not tell them to leave. He did not mention the Capitol. He did not ask anyone to stop. The assault continued.

At 4:17 p.m., nearly three hours after the violence began, and only after it was clear that the certification process could not be stopped, the President released a video. He told the mob to go home. He added: We love you. You're very special.

The Legal Significance: Command Authority as Overt Act

The 187 minutes are legally significant not merely as evidence of dereliction of duty but as affirmative evidence of command authority exercised in service of the assault.

A Commander in Chief who deploys an armed force toward a constitutional target, monitors the progress of the assault on television, declines every request and every mechanism available to stop it, and releases the armed force only after it becomes clear the objective cannot be achieved, has not been passive. He has been directing.

Rioter Stephen Ayres, who was inside the Capitol during the assault, testified before the House Select Committee about what happened when the President's 4:17 p.m. video was finally released. The mob literally left right after, Ayres testified. That single observation establishes two things. First, that the President had the power to end the assault at any point during those 187 minutes and chose not to use it. Second, that the mob understood its presence at the Capitol as contingent on the President's continued implicit authorization. When he withdrew that authorization, they left.

A force that leaves when its commander says leave was there because its commander told it to stay.

The 187 minutes are not evidence of a President who lost control of events. They are evidence of a President who maintained control of events and exercised that control to sustain the assault on the constitutional process he had spent weeks trying to stop through legal means. The command authority was real. The evidence that it was exercised, both in the deployment and in the deliberate withholding of the recall, is documented by the witnesses who were in the room.

> **THE WITNESSES:** *The 187 minutes are documented by an extraordinary array of witnesses. Cassidy Hutchinson, the White House Chief of Staff's senior aide, was present and testified in detail about the President's conduct, the television watching, the refusal to act, and the specific conversations with Cipollone and Meadows. Keith Kellogg, the National Security Advisor to the Vice President, was also present and testified. Pat Cipollone, White House Counsel, testified about his repeated attempts to get the President to intervene. Ivanka Trump's efforts to get her father to act are documented in Committee testimony. Kevin McCarthy's phone call with the President, and the President's chilling response, is established in Committee testimony and in McCarthy's own contemporaneous accounts. Stephen Ayres testified about leaving the Capitol immediately after the 4:17 p.m. video was released, establishing the command relationship between the President and the mob. All of these are witnesses to the same set of overt acts. The constitutional two-witness requirement is satisfied many times over.*

□ □ □

The Seven-Part Scheme: Force Was Never the First Plan

The Capitol was not the first plan. It was the last plan.

The House Select Committee documented a coordinated seven-part scheme to prevent the certification of the 2020 election results, a scheme that used every available mechanism of governmental power before turning to force when the other mechanisms failed. Understanding the scheme in its entirety is essential to understanding why January 6 is not merely a riot that got out of hand, but the culmination of a premeditated conspiracy.

The Seven Mechanisms, in Order

The first mechanism was the Department of Justice. The President attempted to use the DOJ to provide a veneer of governmental authority to his fraud claims. He sought to replace Acting Attorney General Jeffrey Rosen with Jeffrey Clark, a subordinate official who was willing to send letters to state legislatures falsely claiming the DOJ had identified significant concerns about election integrity. The entire senior leadership of the Department of Justice threatened mass resignation if Clark was appointed, warning the President that Clark would be leading a graveyard. The plan was abandoned only because the institutional resistance was total.

The second mechanism was pressure on state officials. In Georgia, the President called Secretary of State Brad Raffensperger and asked him to find 11,780 votes, one more than Biden's margin. The call was recorded. In Arizona, the President and Rudy Giuliani pressured House Speaker Rusty Bowers to hold a hearing to decertify Biden electors, despite Bowers stating he would not break his oath. In Michigan, state legislative leaders were invited to the White House to be pressured into overturning their state's results. Every state official who was pressured refused.

The third mechanism was the fake elector scheme. The Trump campaign organized supporters in seven swing states to meet on December 14, 2020 and sign fraudulent certificates claiming to be the legitimate presidential electors for their states, despite Biden having won those states. These fraudulent documents were transmitted to Congress and the National Archives to provide a pretext for Pence to reject the actual, certified electoral slates on January 6.

The fourth mechanism was the pressure campaign on Vice President Pence, documented in detail in Overt Act Four above.

The fifth mechanism was the ongoing dissemination of false claims through public communications, fundraising operations that raised approximately $250 million from supporters who were told the money was for an Election Defense Fund that did not exist, and coordinated messaging designed to maintain the pressure necessary to keep the political operation moving.

The sixth mechanism was the Ellipse rally and the march to the Capitol, documented above as Overt Acts One through Three.

The seventh mechanism was the 187 minutes of deliberate inaction during the assault, documented above as Overt Act Five.

What the Scheme Proves

The seven-part scheme is the most important structural element of the treason analysis in this chapter, because it answers the most powerful defense argument available.

That defense argument goes like this: the President genuinely believed the election was stolen, he pursued legal remedies through the courts and the political process, and when those remedies failed, his supporters spontaneously reacted in a way he did not intend and could not control.

The seven-part scheme destroys that argument. A person who genuinely believes he has been wronged pursues the legal remedy, and when the legal remedy fails, he accepts the result. A person who pursues seven sequential mechanisms over two months, each designed to overturn a specific legal finding, and then turns to physical force when the seventh mechanism is the last one standing, is not pursuing justice. He is pursuing power through whatever means are available. And when physical force is the last available means and he deploys it, the deployment is premeditated, not spontaneous.

> *"There were two groups of family. We called them kind of my team and Rudy's team. I didn't mind being characterized as being part of team normal."* **Bill Stepien, Trump Campaign Manager, House Select Committee testimony**

> *"I repeatedly told the President in no uncertain terms that I did not see evidence of fraud that would have affected the outcome of the election."*
> **William Barr, Attorney General, House Select Committee testimony**

The President was told by his own campaign manager and his own Attorney General that the evidence did not support his claims. He continued anyway. He continued through sixty court losses, through the resignation threats of his entire Justice Department leadership, through the refusals of Republican state officials in Georgia, Arizona, Michigan, Wisconsin, and Pennsylvania. And when every legal and political mechanism was exhausted, he deployed the armed force he had recruited in December and activated in January.

Each component of the scheme, viewed alone, might be characterized as aggressive politics. Viewed together, as a coordinated campaign with a single purpose, preventing the constitutional transfer of power through whatever means were available, they form the treasonous design that the assemblage of January 6 was organized to execute. The Capitol was where the design ran out of legal options and turned to force. That transition from legal manipulation to physical force is the moment that Bollman's standard of levying war is met.

□ □ □

The Seditious Conspiracy Bridge: From Federal Verdicts to Treason

Before this chapter closes, there is one more legal element to establish, because it answers the most technical objection to the treason argument.

That objection goes like this. Even granting everything documented above, the accused was not physically present at the Capitol. He did not break a window or push through a door. Chief Justice Marshall's refinement of the Bollman standard in the Burr trial required that a defendant be legally or actually present at the overt act of war. The accused was in the dining room watching television.

The seditious conspiracy verdicts answer this objection directly.

Twelve federal jury verdicts were returned against leaders of the Proud Boys and Oath Keepers for seditious conspiracy. These were not guilty pleas or negotiated outcomes. These were trial verdicts, reached by twelve citizens in each case who heard the evidence, applied the law, and concluded beyond a reasonable doubt that the defendants had conspired to use force to prevent, hinder, or delay the execution of a law of the United States.

That law was the Electoral Count Act. That force was the mob that the President recruited with the December 19 tweet, armed by removing the magnetometer screening, directed with the Ellipse speech, and sustained through 187 minutes of deliberate inaction.

Under federal law, a person who organizes, directs, and sustains a criminal conspiracy is legally present at every overt act committed by the members of that conspiracy in furtherance of its objectives. The Proud Boys leaders convicted of seditious conspiracy were legally present at every act of violence committed by their members inside the Capitol, even those they did not personally witness. The same legal principle applies to the person who recruited those leaders with a tweet, connected them to the White House through political associates, provided them with an armed crowd by removing the metal detector screening, directed them to the Capitol with a speech, and then sustained their assault through three hours of deliberate silence.

Legal presence at the levying of war is established by the direction of the force, the organization of the assemblage, and the overt acts taken to advance the treasonable design. All of those elements are present in the documented record.

The twelve seditious conspiracy verdicts do not merely support the treason argument. They establish as a matter of proven legal fact every element of the assemblage that the Bollman standard requires. The factual predicate for the levying of war has been established in federal court, by twelve juries, beyond a reasonable doubt. What the treason analysis adds is the question of who directed it. This chapter has answered that question with specific, dated, witnessed, documented overt acts.

The Capitol was not the first plan. It was the last plan. When every legal and political mechanism was exhausted, force remained. And when force was deployed, the person who deployed it watched from a dining room, declining for 187 minutes to exercise the command authority he had spent weeks using to build the assemblage that was now breaking through the windows of the People's House.

That is levying war. Not metaphorically. Constitutionally.

The next chapter asks what it means when the person who commits these acts simultaneously dismantles every institution capable of holding him accountable for committing them.

□ □ □

PART II

THE FOREIGN FRONT

Adhering to Enemies, Giving Aid and Comfort to Russia

Chapter Four

Who Is the Enemy? Russia and the Modern Definition of Hostility

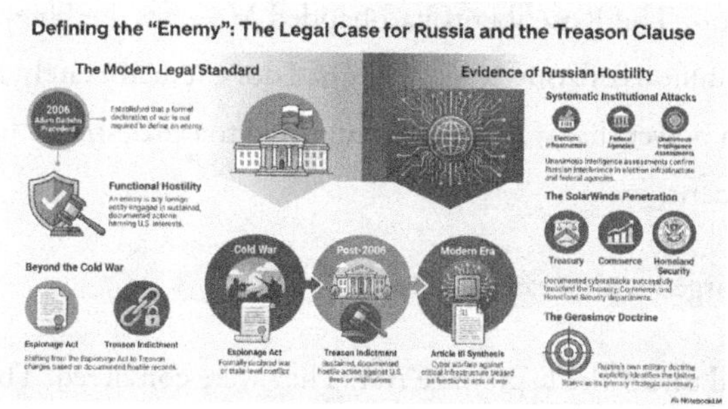

Before we can prove that someone aided an enemy, we have to prove there was an enemy.

That sounds simple. In practice, it is the most legally contested element in the entire treason argument, and this chapter addresses it head on. Not with rhetorical confidence, but with the precision the law requires.

The word enemy appears in the Constitution only once, in Article III, Section 3, in the definition of treason. The Framers did not define it further. They left that work to the courts and to the evidence. For most of American history, courts interpreted enemy narrowly, requiring a formal declaration of war, a recognized adversary state, a condition of open armed conflict that left no legal ambiguity about who was fighting whom.

That narrow interpretation served the Republic tolerably well for a century and a half. Then the nature of warfare changed. And the law had to decide whether it would change with it, or whether it would allow the Constitution to become, in a phrase Justice Jackson used in a different context, a suicide pact.

The law changed. This chapter tells the story of how it changed, what the current standard requires, and why the documented record of Russian hostile action against the United States satisfies that standard today.

□ □ □

Section One: The Cold War Dilemma and the Enemy the Law Would Not Name

In 1951, Julius and Ethel Rosenberg were put on trial for passing atomic bomb secrets to the Soviet Union. The Rosenbergs had handed Moscow the blueprint for weapons capable of killing millions of Americans. They had done it deliberately, knowingly, and in service of a foreign power that was openly committed to the destruction of the American system of government.

They were not charged with treason.

They were charged under the Espionage Act. They were convicted. They were executed. And the word treason never appeared in the indictment, because the Department of Justice made a calculated strategic decision that the constitutional bar was too high and the risk of failure was too great.

The reason is important and it is the legal foundation for everything that follows in this chapter.

The Soviet Union, in 1951, was not at war with the United States in the formal sense that Article III had historically required. There was no declaration of war. There were ambassadors in Washington and in Moscow. There were treaties. There were diplomatic communications. The two nations were locked in a global struggle for dominance that consumed the entire second half of the twentieth century, that killed Americans in Korea and Vietnam and in intelligence operations around the world, that threatened nuclear annihilation on a daily basis. But it was called a Cold War precisely because the formal legal threshold of declared armed conflict had not been crossed.

And so, for fifty years, whenever the government needed to prosecute someone for betraying the United States to the Soviet Union, it reached for the Espionage Act instead of the treason clause. Because the Espionage Act did not require the accused to have aided an enemy. It only required the unauthorized transmission of national defense information. The enemy question never had to be answered.

That era of legal caution served as the standard for half a century. Then came the 21st century and a new kind of threat. And the Department of Justice made a decision that changed the law forever.

□ □ □

Section Two: The Supreme Court's Definition, From Cramer to the Modern Era

Before the Gadahn precedent, which this chapter will reach shortly, there is a constitutional foundation that deserves its own treatment because it is the oldest and highest legal authority on what enemy means in the treason clause.

In 1945, the Supreme Court decided Cramer v. United States, the landmark case that established the overt act requirement for treason and that this book has cited repeatedly in the preceding chapters. Justice Robert Jackson, writing for the majority, did not merely address the overt act question. He also addressed the enemy question. And what he wrote has been sitting in the constitutional record for eighty years, waiting for a set of facts that made it necessary to read it carefully.

Justice Jackson's Definition

Justice Jackson wrote that an enemy, for purposes of the treason clause, is the party or parties opposed to the United States in hostile action. He elaborated that enemy status attaches to any entity united in hostile purpose against the United States.

Read those phrases again. Opposed to the United States in hostile action. United in hostile purpose against the United States.

Notice what those phrases do not require. They do not require a formally declared war. They do not require a recognized nation-state with a seat at the United Nations. They do not require an exchange of ambassadors' expulsion orders or a breaking of diplomatic relations. They require hostile action and hostile purpose.

Jackson was writing in the context of World War II, where the enemy was obvious and the hostile action was kinetic and the hostile purpose was declared in the formal sense. But the principle he articulated is not limited to that context. The principle is functional: if a foreign entity is acting against the United States with hostile purpose, the law may recognize it as an enemy regardless of the diplomatic formalities surrounding the relationship.

The Supreme Court defined enemy as any party united in hostile purpose against the United States. It did not say declared enemy. It did not say enemy at war. It said hostile purpose. That definition was written in 1945 and it has never been overruled. It is still the constitutional standard today.

The Gap Between Cramer and the Modern Threat

The gap between Cramer's 1945 definition and the modern threat landscape is not a gap in the law. It is a gap in the facts. The law, as Justice Jackson wrote it, was always broad enough to encompass functional hostility regardless of formal diplomatic status. What changed in the twenty-first century was not the law but the technology through which hostile purpose is expressed.

In 1945, hostile action looked like armies crossing borders and navies shelling coastlines. In 2016, hostile action looked like intelligence officers operating behind keyboards in St. Petersburg, deploying digital weapons against election infrastructure, generating and distributing disinformation at industrial scale, and penetrating the secure networks of federal agencies. The weapon changed. The hostility did not.

And the law, as Justice Jackson wrote it, addresses hostility, not the particular weapon through which hostility is expressed.

□ □ □

Section Three: The Gadahn Precedent and the Functional Definition of Enemy

In 2006, the Department of Justice indicted Adam Gadahn, a California-born American, for treason. Gadahn had joined al-Qaeda, appeared in propaganda videos praising the September 11 attacks, and called for further violence against the United States.

The indictment answered a question that had been legally open since 1787. You do not need a formally declared war to have an enemy under the treason clause. You do not need a nation-state with a flag and a capital and a military in uniform. You need a foreign entity engaged in sustained, documented, hostile action against the United States, with the purpose of harming American interests, American institutions, or American lives.

Al-Qaeda had no flag. It had no capital. It had no diplomatic relations with the United States. It was not a recognized state under any principle of international law. And yet the Department of Justice indicted an American citizen for treason in service of al-Qaeda, because the functional reality of what al-Qaeda was doing to the United States satisfied every element of the constitutional definition that Justice Jackson had articulated in Cramer sixty years earlier.

Opposed to the United States in hostile action? Yes. The September 11 attacks killed nearly three thousand Americans. United in hostile purpose against the United States? Yes. Al-Qaeda had published statements of war against the United States, recruited fighters specifically to attack American targets, and organized and funded the most devastating attack on American soil since Pearl Harbor.

If al-Qaeda qualifies as an enemy under the treason clause, then the Russian Federation, a sovereign nation-state with a military command structure, a published doctrine of warfare against the United States, and a documented record of executing that doctrine against American election systems, federal agencies, and democratic institutions, presents an even stronger legal case.

This is not a radical legal argument. It is the logical extension of a precedent the Department of Justice itself established.

The Three Criteria the Gadahn Precedent Established

The functional enemy definition that emerged from the Gadahn indictment has three specific criteria. An entity satisfies the constitutional definition of enemy if it is a foreign entity, if it is engaged in sustained and documented hostile action against the United States, and if its actions are specifically intended to harm American institutions, interests, or lives.

Each of these criteria is examined against the Russian Federation's documented record in the sections that follow. But first, there is a conceptual bridge that must be built, because the most predictable objection to the Russia-as-enemy argument is that cyber warfare is not real warfare.

That objection is wrong. And it is important to explain precisely why it is wrong.

□ □ □

Section Four: The Digital Border and Why Cyber Warfare Is Warfare

There is an argument that opponents of the Russia-as-enemy position will make, and it deserves to be addressed directly rather than avoided.

The argument goes like this. Al-Qaeda killed people. Russia hacked computers. These are not the same thing. The treason clause was written for real wars with real soldiers and real weapons. Cyber operations, however damaging, are intelligence activities, not acts of war. A country that conducts espionage is not an enemy in the constitutional sense. The United States conducts intelligence operations against other nations too. If intelligence operations make a country an enemy, everyone is everyone's enemy.

This argument sounds plausible until you examine what actually happened and what the law and military doctrine actually say about it.

What the Pentagon and NATO Say

The United States military and NATO, the alliance that has been the primary collective defense architecture against Russian military aggression for seventy years, have both formally and officially recognized that cyber attacks on critical infrastructure constitute acts of war that can trigger the same collective defense response as a physical military attack.

NATO's determination that a sufficiently severe cyber attack on a member nation can trigger Article 5, the collective defense clause that says an attack on one is an attack on all, is not a theoretical policy position. It is an operational military doctrine, adopted by the alliance specifically in response to the demonstrated reality of Russian cyber capabilities.

The Pentagon's own Cyber Strategy documents treat hostile cyber operations against American critical infrastructure as acts of war subject to military response. The United States Cyber Command, a full combatant command of the United States military with the same operational standing as the commands responsible for Europe, the Pacific, and the Middle East, exists specifically because the United States military has determined that cyberspace is a domain of warfare equivalent to land, sea, air, and space.

This is not opinion. This is the official, published, operational doctrine of the United States military. When the military says cyber attacks are acts of war, the law can hear it.

The Border Analogy

There is an analogy that makes this concrete for any reader who has never worked in national security.

Imagine that a foreign nation sent a team of soldiers across the physical border of the United States into a federal building in Washington, D.C. The soldiers did not shoot anyone. They broke into the secure filing rooms of the Treasury Department, the Commerce Department, and the Department of Homeland Security. They photographed every classified document they could find. They installed listening devices in every secure conference room. And they left, carrying with them the most sensitive intelligence the federal government possessed.

Would anyone argue that this was not an act of war? That because no bullets were fired and no one died, the sovereign border of the United States had not been violated and the hostile intent of the foreign nation had not been demonstrated?

Of course not. The physical penetration of federal buildings by foreign military operatives would be recognized immediately and universally as an act of war.

Now describe the SolarWinds attack of 2020, in which Russian intelligence services penetrated the networks of the Treasury Department, the Commerce Department, and the Department of Homeland Security, accessed classified information, and installed surveillance capabilities in secure communications systems.

The only difference between those two scenarios is the medium through which the border was crossed. In the first, the soldiers walked through a door. In the second, they walked through a network connection. The sovereign border of the United States is not defined only by its physical perimeter. It is defined by the integrity of its governmental systems, its elections, and its institutions.

When a foreign power hacks into federal agencies, penetrates election infrastructure, and manipulates the information environment through which American citizens make democratic decisions, they are not merely spying. They are penetrating the sovereign borders of the United States through a digital door. In the 21st century, a cyber soldier is not fundamentally different from a soldier crossing a physical border. The weapon has changed. The hostility has not.

18 U.S.C. Section 2331 and the Laws of Armed Conflict

The legal framework for this conclusion is not constructed from analogy alone. It is grounded in statutory law and in the evolving laws of armed conflict that govern international military operations.

18 U.S.C. section 2331, the federal statute defining international terrorism, has been interpreted and applied in ways that increasingly recognize digital operations as qualifying hostile acts when they target critical infrastructure. The laws of armed conflict, which the United States military is required to follow and which govern when and how force may be used, have been formally updated to address cyber operations. The International Committee of the Red Cross, the authoritative interpreter of international humanitarian law, has recognized that sufficiently destructive cyber operations can constitute attacks in the legal sense, triggering the same protections and the same response rights as physical attacks.

The legal evolution is real, documented, and consistent with the Cramer definition of hostile purpose and the Gadahn definition of functional enemy. A foreign entity that conducts sustained cyber operations against American critical infrastructure is engaged in hostile action against the United States regardless of whether the operations involve bullets or bytes.

□ □ □

Section Five: The Gerasimov Doctrine and the Declaration That Is Not Called One

In traditional warfare, a declaration precedes the attack. A nation formally announces a state of war, and the legal and military machinery of conflict begins.

Russia did not declare war on the United States in 2013 or 2016 or 2020. But Russia did something in some ways more legally significant. It published a manual.

In February 2013, General Valery Gerasimov, the Chief of the General Staff of the Russian Federation, published an article in the Military-Industrial Courier, a Russian military journal. The article, which became known in Western military and intelligence circles as the Gerasimov Doctrine, described Russia's strategic approach to modern warfare with a candor that is almost unprecedented in the public military literature of a major power.

What the Doctrine Says

Gerasimov described a model of conflict in which the distinction between war and peace is deliberately blurred, in which non-military means of achieving political and strategic goals have surpassed the power of conventional weapons in their effectiveness, and in which the primary theater of operation is not the battlefield but the information environment, the political system, and the social fabric of the adversary nation.

He described a model in which the internal instability of a target nation, the erosion of public trust in its institutions, the amplification of social divisions, and the manipulation of its democratic processes are not side effects of warfare but its primary objectives.

He explicitly identified the United States as Russia's primary strategic adversary.

And then Russia executed the doctrine against the United States with a precision and a scale that its own published manual described.

The Doctrine as Legal Evidence of Hostile Intent

In a treason prosecution, one of the most difficult elements to establish is intent. The accused must have acted with knowledge that they were aiding an enemy and with the intent to benefit that enemy at the expense of the United States. Intent is usually inferred from circumstantial evidence, from the pattern of conduct, from the consciousness of guilt demonstrated by lies and concealment.

The Gerasimov Doctrine eliminates the ambiguity about Russia's intent. Russia told us what it intended to do. It wrote it down. It published it under the name of the Chief of the General Staff. And then it did exactly what it said it would do.

In traditional warfare, a declaration of war is the legal instrument that establishes that a state of hostility exists. It tells the other nation and the world that the declaring nation is committed to using force to achieve its objectives. The Gerasimov Doctrine functions as precisely this kind of declaration, not addressed to the United States government through diplomatic channels, but published in a military journal and executed through the GRU, Russia's military intelligence service.

The law does not require an enemy to be polite enough to declare war through proper diplomatic channels. It only requires the enemy to act with hostile intent against the United States. Russia published its hostile intent in a military doctrine in 2013. Then it executed that intent in 2016, 2017, 2018, 2019, and 2020. The publication is the declaration. The execution is the hostile action. Together, they satisfy the Cramer standard of hostile purpose and the Gadahn standard of sustained documented hostility.

□ □ □

Section Six: The Documented Record of Russian Hostile Action

With the legal framework established, the Cramer definition of hostile purpose, the Gadahn standard of functional enemy, the cyber-equals-kinetic argument, and the

Gerasimov Doctrine as the declaration of hostile intent, we can now turn to the specific documented record of Russian hostile action against the United States.

This record is not opinion. It is not partisan. It is the sworn and documented assessment of the United States Intelligence Community, a bipartisan Senate Intelligence Committee that was controlled by Republicans for most of its investigation, and the federal agencies whose networks were penetrated.

The 2016 Election Interference: Attacking the Foundation of Democracy

In January 2017, the Intelligence Community Assessment, compiled by the CIA, NSA, and FBI under the direction of the Director of National Intelligence, reached a unanimous conclusion.

> *"We assess with high confidence that Russian President Vladimir Putin ordered an influence campaign in 2016 aimed at the US presidential election, Russian intelligence obtained and maintained access to elements of multiple US state or local electoral boards, and Russian military intelligence used the Guccifer 2.0 persona and DCLeaks.com to release US victim data obtained in cyber operations publicly and through WikiLeaks."*
> **Intelligence Community Assessment, January 6, 2017**

High confidence, in the terminology of the intelligence community, is the highest possible assessment level. It means the conclusion is supported by high-quality intelligence that leaves little room for doubt. The IC does not use high confidence casually. It uses high confidence when the evidence is overwhelming and the analytical conclusions are robust.

The finding that Vladimir Putin personally ordered the influence campaign against the 2016 election is supported by high-confidence intelligence from multiple independent sources across three separate agencies, each of which reached the same conclusion independently.

The Senate Intelligence Committee published five volumes of findings between 2018 and 2020, expanding on the IC assessment with specific details about Russian operational methods, specific targets, specific outcomes, and specific connections between Russian intelligence operations and the Trump campaign. The Committee was chaired and controlled by Republicans throughout most of the investigation. Its findings are bipartisan. They are not the conclusions of one party. They are the institutional consensus of the United States government.

The SolarWinds Attack: Penetrating the Sovereign Digital Border

In December 2020, the cybersecurity firm FireEye announced the discovery of a massive intrusion into American government and private sector networks that had been ongoing, undetected, for approximately nine months. The intrusion used a compromised software update from a company called SolarWinds to gain access to the networks of more than eighteen thousand organizations, including the Treasury Department, the Commerce Department, the Department of Homeland Security, parts of the Pentagon, and numerous other federal agencies.

The attack was attributed by the United States intelligence community to Russia's SVR, the Foreign Intelligence Service. The scope of what Russian intelligence accessed during those nine months of undetected presence in American government networks has never been fully disclosed publicly, because the full disclosure would itself constitute a security risk. What is publicly known is that the attackers had access to email communications, classified documents, and operational systems across the most sensitive areas of the American government.

Using the border analogy from Section Four: Russian intelligence spent nine months inside the buildings of the federal government, with full access to classified materials, listening to secure communications, and reading the most sensitive documents the American government possessed. They were never seen. And when they finally left, the full extent of what they had taken was not known and may never be fully known.

That is not espionage in the colloquial sense of a spy stealing a document. That is a sustained military intelligence operation penetrating the sovereign governmental infrastructure of the United States. Under the Cramer standard of hostile purpose, and under the Gadahn standard of sustained documented hostile action, this is enemy conduct.

The 50-State Probing: Targeting the Machinery of Democracy

Beyond the specific intrusions documented above, the Senate Intelligence Committee confirmed that Russian intelligence probed the election systems of all fifty states in the period surrounding the 2016 election. Not the states where the election was close. Not the states that mattered strategically. All fifty states.

The purpose of probing all fifty states is not to gather intelligence about election outcomes. A nation interested in intelligence about election outcomes does not need to probe Wyoming or Hawaii. The purpose of probing all fifty states is to map the vulnerabilities of the entire election infrastructure, to understand how it works, where its weak points are, and how it could be manipulated or disrupted at scale.

That is not the behavior of a nation conducting routine intelligence gathering. That is the behavior of a nation preparing the battlefield.

> **THE WITNESSES:** *The witnesses who can establish Russia's hostile status are among the most senior intelligence officials in the history of the United States. James Clapper, the Director of National Intelligence who oversaw the compilation of the January 2017 Intelligence Community Assessment, testified publicly about the findings and their implications. James Comey, the Director of the FBI, whose agency contributed to the ICA and conducted the Crossfire Hurricane investigation of Russian election interference, testified extensively before Congress. John Brennan, the Director of the CIA, testified about Russian hostile intent and publicly characterized the Helsinki Summit, addressed in the next chapter, as treasonous. Mike Pompeo, who served as CIA Director before becoming Secretary of State, confirmed the intelligence community's assessment of Russian interference. These are not partisan witnesses. They are the sworn testimony of the men who held the most sensitive intelligence positions in the United States government during the period in question.*

□ □ □

Section Seven: The Counterarguments and Why They Do Not Close the Case

This book made a commitment in its Legal Introduction, and it will keep that commitment here. The strongest counterarguments to the Russia-as-enemy position must be acknowledged honestly, because a legal argument that cannot withstand scrutiny of its weakest points is not a legal argument. It is advocacy.

There are three serious counterarguments. Each is addressed below. None of them closes the case against the argument this chapter makes, but each of them identifies a genuine legal uncertainty that a jury would have to resolve.

Counterargument One: The United States and Russia Maintain Diplomatic Relations

The United States has an embassy in Moscow and Russia has an embassy in Washington. The two nations have ambassadors, treaties, and diplomatic communications. A formally recognized diplomatic relationship is not consistent with a state of war, and the traditional legal understanding of enemy under Article III was developed in the context of declared armed conflict between nations that had severed their diplomatic ties.

The rebuttal: diplomatic relations and enemy status are not mutually exclusive under the modern functional standard. The United States designates certain nations as state sponsors of terrorism, imposes comprehensive sanctions, and treats those nations as adversaries across every dimension of foreign policy, while simultaneously maintaining formal diplomatic contact precisely because the relationship is adversarial and the channel of communication serves strategic purposes. The existence of an ambassador does not preclude hostile purpose. It often exists because hostile purpose must be managed through some channel. The Gadahn precedent establishes that functional hostile action, not formal diplomatic status, is the legal standard. Under that standard, diplomatic relations are one factor a jury would consider, not a threshold that forecloses the argument.

Counterargument Two: No Court Has Definitively Ruled Russia Is a Legal Enemy

The second counterargument is procedural rather than substantive. There is no judicial precedent declaring Russia a legal enemy under Article III. The Gadahn indictment addressed a non-state actor. The extension of that precedent to a sovereign nation-state during a period of nominal peace is a legal step that no court has yet taken. Courts are conservative institutions. They do not take novel legal steps lightly, particularly on a question as consequential as the definition of enemy under the highest-stakes provision of the Constitution.

The rebuttal: the absence of prior precedent is not a bar to indictment. It is precisely the function of federal courts to apply established legal principles to novel fact patterns. The Cramer definition of hostile purpose and the Gadahn standard of functional enemy are established principles. The documented record of Russian hostile action against the United States is a novel fact pattern. Applying established principles to novel facts is what courts do. The question of whether Russia qualifies as an enemy, at the indictment stage, is not a question that must be answered before the indictment is brought. It is a question that is presented to a jury along with the full evidentiary record.

Counterargument Three: This Is the Most Legally Contested Element in the Book

The final counterargument is an acknowledgment that the preceding two counterarguments reflect a genuine legal reality. The enemy definition is the most legally contested element in the treason argument presented in this book. The levying of war argument in Chapters 2 and 3 rests on documented overt acts with named witnesses and established jury verdicts. The adherence and aid and comfort arguments in the chapters that follow rest on documented conduct with named witnesses and bipartisan governmental findings.

The enemy definition argument rests on the application of a functional legal standard to a contested factual question in a novel legal context. That does not make it wrong. It makes it a jury question.

In a treason prosecution, the determination of enemy status is not made by legal scholars or by the authors of books. It is made by twelve citizens, presented with the full evidentiary record, instructed on the applicable legal standard, and

asked to apply one to the other. The Cramer standard, the Gadahn precedent, the Gerasimov Doctrine, the Intelligence Community Assessment, the Senate Intelligence Committee findings, the SolarWinds penetration, and the fifty-state probing together constitute the evidentiary record that would be presented to that jury. Whether that record satisfies the constitutional standard is the jury's question to answer. This book argues that it does. The reader is entitled to evaluate that argument with the full benefit of the strongest objections to it.

□ □ □

Section Eight: The Adversary in the Embassy and the Nature of Modern Hostility

There is a broader observation about the relationship between diplomatic ties and enemy status that deserves its own section, because it addresses a confusion that pervades public discussion of this issue.

The United States maintains diplomatic relations with many nations it simultaneously treats as adversaries across every substantive dimension of foreign policy. Iran has had no formal diplomatic relations with the United States since 1980, and yet the United States conducts covert operations against Iranian nuclear facilities, imposes comprehensive sanctions on the Iranian economy, and has launched military strikes against Iranian-aligned forces across the Middle East.

China maintains formal diplomatic relations with the United States, has an enormous embassy in Washington, and conducts hundreds of billions of dollars in annual trade with American companies. The United States military and intelligence community also formally classify China as the most significant long-term strategic competitor and threat to American national security. Both things are simultaneously true.

North Korea presents the most extreme case. The United States and North Korea do not have formal diplomatic relations. North Korea regularly threatens to destroy the United States with nuclear weapons. And yet no American court has ever ruled that North Korea is a legal enemy under Article III, because the question has never been litigated.

The point is this: the formal diplomatic relationship between two nations tells us relatively little about the functional nature of that relationship. The United States has learned, over decades of managing complex relationships with adversarial powers, that maintaining a diplomatic channel to a hostile nation is often strategically useful precisely because the relationship is hostile. You negotiate with adversaries. You communicate with enemies. The presence of an ambassador is not evidence of peace. It is often evidence of managed conflict.

Russia's ambassador in Washington and America's ambassador in Moscow are evidence that the United States government has made a strategic decision to maintain a communication channel with a nation it has publicly, unanimously, and repeatedly identified as a hostile power engaged in active operations against American democratic institutions. That strategic decision is legitimate and defensible. It does not, however, transform Russia's documented hostile actions into something other than hostile actions.

□ □ □

Section Nine: The Synthesis and What the Next Chapter Asks

The enemy question, for purposes of the treason argument in this book, resolves to this.

The Supreme Court defined enemy in 1945 as any party united in hostile purpose against the United States. The Department of Justice established in 2006 that enemy status does not require a formally declared war or a recognized nation-state, only sustained, documented, hostile action with the intent to harm American institutions, interests, or lives. The Pentagon and NATO have formally recognized that cyber warfare against critical infrastructure constitutes hostile action equivalent to physical military attack. Russia published its hostile intent in a military doctrine in 2013 and then executed that doctrine against American election systems, federal agencies, and democratic institutions across multiple election cycles. The unanimous Intelligence Community Assessment confirmed these findings in January 2017. The bipartisan Senate Intelligence Committee confirmed and expanded those findings between 2018 and 2020. The most senior intelligence officials in the United States government testified to the same conclusions under oath.

Russia is not an enemy in the declaration-of-war sense that would have been required in 1945. Russia is an enemy in the functional, documented, hostile-purpose sense that the modern legal standard requires.

Whether a jury would find Russia's documented conduct sufficient to satisfy the constitutional standard is not a question this chapter can answer with certainty. It is a jury question, and it would be argued on both sides with competent counsel and the full weight of the evidentiary record.

What this chapter has established is that the enemy argument is legally viable. It survives the motion to dismiss. It reaches the jury. And the jury would hear the Cramer definition, the Gadahn precedent, the Gerasimov Doctrine, the Intelligence Community Assessment, and the testimony of the Directors of National Intelligence, the FBI, and the CIA.

That is what the enemy question looks like when it is answered by the law rather than by politics.

The next chapter asks a different question. Now that the enemy is identified, what did the accused do to help it? What does the documented record of the Russia alignment look like when it is measured against the Cramer standard of actual aid and the Haupt standard of intent transforming ambiguous acts into treasonous ones?

The answer begins with a press conference in Helsinki, Finland, on July 16, 2018.

□ □ □

Chapter Five

Bad Faith and the Russia Alignment: From Mueller to Helsinki

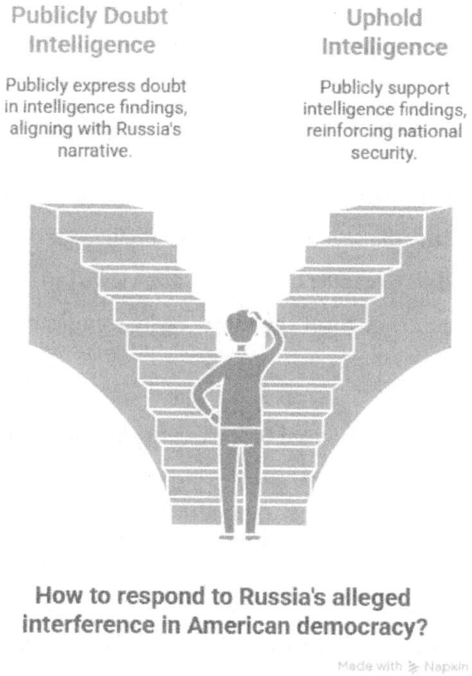

Here is a simple exercise.

Suppose you run a company. Your biggest competitor has been caught breaking into your offices, stealing your files, and spreading damaging lies about you to your customers.

Your entire security team, unanimously and without a single dissenting voice, tells you exactly who did it, exactly what they took, and exactly how they did it. The evidence is overwhelming. The conclusion is beyond any reasonable doubt.

And then you hold a press conference and say you believe your competitor when he says he did not do it.

What would your board of directors think?

What would a jury think?

That is the Helsinki Summit of July 2018, translated into language that does not require a law degree. And the legal analysis is not complicated. When the President of the United States stands beside the leader of a nation that his own intelligence community has unanimously documented as attacking American democracy, and publicly says he has no reason to doubt that leader's denial, he is not making a diplomatic statement. He is making a choice. He is choosing the enemy's narrative over his own country's unanimous professional judgment. He is giving Russia exactly what Russia needed and could not give itself: the voice of the American President endorsing its lie.

This chapter documents the pattern of conduct that surrounds that choice. The contacts, the clearance overrides, the shadow diplomacy, the intelligence dismissals, the sanctions failures, and the second-term acceleration. Each act, viewed individually, might be explained. Viewed together, they form the most legally significant pattern in the entire treason argument.

But before we look at the acts, we need to look at the law that tells us what to do with them.

□ □ □

Section One: The Legal Framework for Adherence Treason

The treason clause has two prongs. The first, levying war, was addressed in Chapters 2 and 3. The second is adherence treason: adhering to enemies, giving them aid and comfort.

This prong is where the Russia alignment argument lives. And it operates under a set of legal principles that this chapter will apply explicitly to the specific overt acts documented in what follows.

What Haupt Teaches About Ordinary Acts

In Chapter 1, this book introduced Haupt v. United States to explain how an innocent-seeming act, a father helping his son find a job and buy a car, became treason. The principle Haupt established is essential for the Russia alignment analysis.

The Court held in Haupt that seemingly commonplace acts meet the constitutional threshold for treason if they are performed with the specific intent to assist an enemy's hostile mission. The actor does not have to know every detail of the enemy's plan. He does not have to participate in the mission directly. He only has to know enough about the enemy's objectives that his act advances them, and he must perform the act with that knowledge and that purpose.

Applied here: when a President dismisses intelligence assessments documenting Russian election interference, fails to implement congressionally mandated sanctions against Russia, and shares classified intelligence with Russian officials in the Oval Office, each act might be individually defended as a policy choice or an exercise of executive discretion. But when each act is performed against a background of documented Russian hostile action, with documented knowledge of that hostile action, and with documented benefits flowing to Russia as a result, the Haupt standard transforms the individually ambiguous into the collectively treasonous.

What Kawakita Teaches About Intent

Kawakita v. United States established that treasonous intent may be inferred from conduct, statements, and professions of alignment with an enemy. The Court held that even insubstantial acts constitute aid and comfort if they embolden the enemy. And it held that intent is established not by a single confession but by the cumulative pattern of what a person does and says over time.

The Kawakita standard is the legal foundation for the cumulative pattern argument that runs through this entire chapter. No single act documented below is, by itself, a slam-dunk treason case. The Helsinki Summit, standing alone, might be defended as a diplomatic misstep. The CAATSA sanctions failure, standing alone, might be defended as an executive policy judgment about the proper pace of implementation. The Oval Office intelligence disclosure, standing alone, might be defended as the President's broad authority over classified information.

But Kawakita does not evaluate acts in isolation. It evaluates them as a pattern from which intent is inferred. And the pattern documented in this chapter, spanning two terms, covering every major dimension of the Russia relationship, consistently benefiting Russia and consistently harming American national security interests, is the pattern from which the Kawakita inference of treasonous intent is drawn.

The Specific Intent Requirement and the Mixed Motive Doctrine

Adherence treason is a specific intent crime. The defendant must not only intend the act but must intend to betray the country by means of the act. This is the hardest element in the entire treason analysis, and it is important to address it honestly.

The defense will argue that every act documented in this chapter had an innocent alternative explanation. The Helsinki statement was a diplomatic preference for engagement over confrontation. The CAATSA delay was a judgment about the proper sequence of sanctions implementation. The Oval Office disclosure was an exercise of the President's absolute authority over classified information. The Ukraine aid freeze was a legitimate policy concern about corruption. None of these acts, the defense will say, was motivated by a desire to betray the United States.

The law's response to this argument comes from the broadcaster treason cases of World War II. In those cases, courts established what is called the mixed motive doctrine. Under this doctrine, a patriotic motive does not negate a treasonous intent. If an actor has the conscious objective of helping the enemy succeed, the requisite mental state for treason is present, even if the actor also believes, sincerely or insincerely, that their actions will ultimately benefit the United States.

The question is not what the actor told himself about why he was doing it. The question is whether the conscious objective of the act was to advance the enemy's mission. Intent is a jury question, inferred from the totality of conduct. And the totality of conduct documented in this chapter points consistently in one direction.

□ □ □

Section Two: Helsinki, July 16, 2018 — The Lie as the Overt Act

On July 16, 2018, the President of the United States stood beside Vladimir Putin at a joint press conference in Helsinki, Finland, and delivered one of the most extraordinary statements ever made by an American president on foreign soil.

The Intelligence Community Assessment of January 2017 had concluded with high confidence that Putin personally ordered the influence campaign against the 2016 election. The FBI, CIA, and NSA had all independently reached the same conclusion. The Senate Intelligence Committee, controlled by Republicans, had confirmed those findings with five volumes of detailed evidence. The President had been briefed on all of it.

At the Helsinki press conference, a reporter asked whether the President believed his intelligence community's conclusion or President Putin's denial.

> *"President Putin says it's not Russia. I don't see any reason why it would be."* — **President Donald Trump, Helsinki press conference, July 16, 2018**

The reaction was immediate and it came from officials of both parties, from intelligence community leaders who had served under Republican and Democratic administrations, and from congressional leaders who had seen the classified evidence.

Former CIA Director John Brennan, who had overseen the January 2017 Intelligence Community Assessment, used a word that legal scholars noted carefully. He called the Helsinki statement treasonous. He was not using the word loosely or rhetorically. He was making a specific legal characterization of a specific act. A President who publicly endorses an adversary's denial of its own documented hostile operations against the United States has, in Brennan's assessment, provided aid and comfort to that adversary in the specific constitutional sense.

Former Director of National Intelligence James Clapper described the statement as very disturbing. Former Director of the NSA Admiral Mike Rogers expressed alarm. These are not political operatives or partisan commentators. They are the men who ran the agencies whose unanimous conclusions the President had just publicly rejected in favor of Vladimir Putin's denial.

The Kawakita Analysis of Helsinki

Under the Kawakita standard, the legal test for an overt act of aid and comfort is whether the act gave the enemy heart and courage to continue its hostile mission. The Helsinki statement did precisely that.

Russia's primary objective, in conducting the 2016 election interference campaign, was not merely to influence a single election. It was to undermine American confidence in its own democratic institutions and to establish a narrative of American electoral chaos that would delegitimize the results of American elections globally. The Gerasimov Doctrine describes this objective explicitly: weaken the adversary by undermining public trust in its institutions.

The American President publicly validating Russia's denial of its own interference campaign, at a press conference with Putin standing at his side, delivered to Russia exactly what the Gerasimov Doctrine described as the strategic objective. It told the world that the adversary's narrative had presidential endorsement. It told American allies that the American President did not stand with the unanimous conclusion of his own intelligence community. It told Russia that its operations had not only succeeded in their immediate objective but had produced the additional benefit of American presidential cover.

Under Kawakita, that is heart and courage to continue. Under Cramer, that is actual aid that actually advanced the enemy's mission. Under the Haupt analysis, it was performed against a background of documented Russian hostile action and with full knowledge of that action.

THE WITNESSES: *The Helsinki statement is a public document, delivered on international television before hundreds of witnesses. Former CIA Director John Brennan, former DNI James Clapper, and former NSA Director Admiral Mike Rogers each made documented public statements characterizing the Helsinki press conference as alarming or treasonous. Senate Intelligence Committee members of both parties expressed documented alarm. The President's own National Security Advisor at the time, John Bolton, documented his concerns in his memoir. The constitutional two-witness requirement is satisfied many times over for this overt act.*

□ □ □

Section Three: The Mueller Report as a Treason Document

The Mueller Report has been read primarily as an obstruction of justice document. Volume II documented eleven episodes of potential obstruction by the President. That reading is correct as far as it goes.

But Volume I of the Mueller Report, read through the lens of the treason framework, tells a different story. It documents the foundation on which the Helsinki betrayal was built: more than 140 contacts between Trump campaign officials and Russian nationals during the 2016 presidential campaign.

Those 140 contacts are legally significant not merely as evidence of relationship but as evidence of receptivity. A campaign that receives an offer of Russian government assistance and responds by agreeing to a meeting has demonstrated, at minimum, a willingness to benefit from the hostile operations of a foreign power against a domestic political opponent. Under the adherence treason standard, receptivity to enemy assistance is the beginning of the alignment that culminates in the overt acts documented later in this chapter.

The Trump Tower Meeting

In June 2016, campaign principals including the candidate's son Donald Trump Jr., his son-in-law Jared Kushner, and campaign chairman Paul Manafort met with Russian government-linked operatives at Trump Tower in New York. The meeting had been arranged by email, and the purpose was stated explicitly: receiving damaging information on Hillary Clinton as part of Russia's support for Donald Trump.

> *"If it's what you say I love it especially later in the summer."* — **Donald Trump Jr., email response to offer of Russian government assistance, June 3, 2016**

The Trump Tower meeting did not produce usable opposition research. But it established something more important for the treason analysis. It established that the campaign's senior leadership, when offered assistance from a foreign government as part of that government's support for the candidate, did not report the offer to the FBI, did not decline the meeting, and did not publicly disclose the contact. They accepted the meeting and said they loved the offer.

Under the complicity framework that legal scholar J. Richard Broughton has applied to adherence treason, the actor must associate himself with the venture, participate in it as something he wished to bring about, and seek by his actions to make it succeed. Accepting a meeting with Russian government-linked operatives offering campaign assistance as part of Russia's support for the candidate is association with the venture. Saying I love it is participation in something the actor wished to bring about.

Manafort and the Grave Counterintelligence Threat

The Senate Intelligence Committee's most damaging single finding in its five-volume report was about Paul Manafort, the Trump campaign chairman. Manafort shared internal campaign polling data with Konstantin Kilimnik, a Ukrainian political operative whom the Committee assessed was a Russian intelligence officer.

The Committee characterized this finding with specific language that deserves to be read carefully: a grave counterintelligence threat.

Not a concerning finding. Not a troubling discovery. A grave counterintelligence threat.

The Committee was controlled by Republicans throughout the majority of the investigation. The characterization of Manafort's data sharing as a grave counterintelligence threat is a bipartisan institutional conclusion, not a partisan political attack. It reflects the Committee's assessment that internal campaign polling data in the hands of a Russian intelligence officer could have been used to target specific voter populations, to focus disinformation campaigns, and to tailor influence operations for maximum effectiveness.

Manafort was pardoned in December 2020. The pardon pattern is addressed in Chapter 2. But for the purposes of the treason analysis, the pardon carries a specific legal significance here. The campaign chairman who shared data with a Russian intelligence officer, which the bipartisan Senate Intelligence Committee called a grave counterintelligence threat, was pardoned by the President whose campaign he had managed. Under the Haupt standard, the pardon of the person who committed the most damaging act of potential Russian assistance in the campaign record is itself evidence of the intent underlying the pattern.

□ □ □

Section Four: The Shadow State — Clearance Overrides, Backchannels, and Amateur Diplomats

The Mueller Report documented the contacts. But the structure that enabled those contacts to continue into the administration, and into the second term, relied on a specific mechanism that has received less legal attention than it deserves: the privatization of American foreign policy into the hands of individuals who could not pass a basic background check.

Treason is not always committed by armies crossing borders or spies passing documents. It is often committed by individuals who, for reasons of personal gain, political loyalty, or financial entanglement, create the conditions through which an adversary's interests are advanced. The individuals documented in this section were those conditions.

The Kushner Problem: Access Without Clearance

Jared Kushner, the President's son-in-law, was appointed Senior Advisor to the President. He was assigned a portfolio that, by any reasonable assessment, represents the most sensitive areas of American foreign policy: brokering peace in the Middle East, managing relations with China, and maintaining the administration's Russia posture.

In early 2017, career security professionals in the White House Personnel Security Office completed their review of Kushner's application for a top-secret security clearance. Their recommendation was that the clearance be denied. The documented reasons for that recommendation included Kushner's initial failure to disclose foreign contacts on his security forms, his financial entanglements with foreign entities, and counterintelligence risks flagged by the FBI.

In a normal administration, a security clearance denial ends an employee's access to classified information. It is the government's formal institutional judgment that the individual presents an unacceptable risk.

The President ordered the clearance granted over the objections of career intelligence officials.

> *"Senior White House officials were told by the President to grant his son-in-law a security clearance over the objections of career intelligence officials."* — **House Oversight Committee Report, April 2019**

The legal significance of this override for the treason analysis is specific and important. A security clearance denial is not a bureaucratic technicality. It is the government's way of saying: this person is a counterintelligence risk. By overriding that denial, the President knowingly preserved a channel of access for an individual whom the government's own security apparatus had flagged as compromised.

Under the Haupt standard, an act that seems administrative becomes treasonous when performed with knowledge of the enemy's potential interest in the access being granted. The President knew the clearance had been denied. He knew the stated reasons. He granted it anyway. And Kushner then engaged in diplomacy with foreign powers, including entities with direct connections to Russian financial interests, using the classified access his father-in-law had ordered provided.

The Backchannel That Failed

Before the inauguration, Kushner met with Russian Ambassador Sergei Kislyak. What emerged from intelligence reports about that meeting was one of the most extraordinary revelations of the early administration period.

Kushner had proposed using Russian diplomatic communications facilities to set up a secret communications channel with the Russian military. The purpose, as described in intelligence reports, was specifically to bypass American intelligence monitoring.

Read that again slowly. A senior official of the incoming United States government asked a foreign adversary's ambassador to use the foreign adversary's own secure communications infrastructure to establish a channel of communication that American intelligence services could not monitor.

A United States official who asks a foreign adversary to use their secure lines to bypass American monitoring is not conducting diplomacy. He is not engaging in creative back-channel communications of the kind that have occasionally served legitimate purposes in American foreign policy history. He is treating the American intelligence community as the threat to be circumvented, and the foreign adversary as the partner to be protected from American oversight.

This is the behavior of a cutout. It is the structure through which intelligence tradecraft operates when an asset needs to communicate with a handler without detection by the asset's own government.

The backchannel was not successfully established. But the attempt was documented. And Kushner remained in the White House for four years, with the top-secret clearance that career intelligence professionals had recommended denying.

The Second Term: The Witkoff Pattern

The second term did not continue the pattern of the first term. It removed the remaining guardrails.

In 2025, as the administration reshaped American policy toward Russia and the Middle East, the State Department was systematically sidelined. Career foreign service officers whose institutional knowledge and professional expertise represented the accumulated diplomatic capacity of the United States government were removed, retired, or marginalized. The National Security Council was purged of officials who had expressed dissenting views. The formal mechanisms of American diplomacy were hollowed out.

In their place, the President relied on Steve Witkoff, a New York real estate developer with no diplomatic experience, no background in the substantive policy areas he was negotiating, and a financial history intertwined with the very markets where American policy was shifting.

The choice of Witkoff over professional diplomats is not merely a management preference. It is a legal structure. Diplomacy conducted by private real estate developers rather than sworn federal officers operates outside the records retention laws that bind the State Department. It occurs without the oversight of career foreign service officers whose institutional knowledge includes the ability to recognize when negotiating positions serve American interests versus when they serve other interests. And it allows negotiations to be conducted in a manner that is functionally indistinguishable from business deal-making.

When the President's personal envoy negotiates American policy with foreign sovereign wealth funds, entities that are often direct extensions of foreign intelligence services, without the oversight structures that professional diplomacy provides, the line between the Republic's interests and the individuals' financial interests becomes impossible to draw from the outside.

A President who replaces professional diplomats with unqualified, financially entangled personal loyalists is not exercising executive discretion about personnel. He is creating the structural conditions through which aid can flow to foreign interests without the institutional safeguards designed to prevent exactly that. Under Haupt, the structure itself becomes the overt act when it is established with knowledge of the interests it serves.

THE WITNESSES: *The Kushner clearance override is documented in the House Oversight Committee's April 2019 report, in testimony from* *career White House security officials, and in reporting confirmed by multiple former White House staff. The backchannel attempt is documented in intelligence reports cited by the Washington Post and confirmed by former intelligence officials. John Kelly, the former White House Chief of Staff, and the former White House Counsel both had documented knowledge of the clearance override. The Witkoff appointments and the State Department marginalization are documented in congressional testimony, reporting from foreign service officers, and diplomatic correspondence.*

□ □ □

Section Five: The Pattern of Intelligence Dismissal

The Helsinki Summit did not happen in isolation. It was the most visible moment in a pattern that began before the 2016 election and continued through both terms. The pattern has a consistent structure. American intelligence agencies document Russian hostile action. The President dismisses, contradicts, or ignores the finding. Russia benefits from the dismissal.

Under the Kawakita standard, intent is inferred from the totality of conduct over time. A single instance of dismissing an intelligence finding might be a policy disagreement. A consistent pattern of dismissing intelligence findings specifically about the nation that Chapter 4 has established as a functional enemy, across years, across agencies, across administrations, is the pattern from which the Kawakita inference of treasonous intent is drawn.

CAATSA: The Law the President Would Not Enforce

In 2017, Congress passed the Countering America's Adversaries Through Sanctions Act, known as CAATSA, with overwhelming bipartisan support. The legislative record of CAATSA's passage reflects a congressional determination that the President's executive discretion over Russia policy could not be trusted to produce the sanctions response that the documented Russian hostile action required. Congress took the unusual step of mandating specific sanctions against Russia and limiting the President's authority to waive them.

The President did not implement the sanctions as required. The State Department, which was responsible for reporting on compliance, issued determinations that effectively created an implementation gap. Congress had to threaten additional legislation to compel partial compliance. The full sanctions regime mandated by CAATSA was never implemented with the speed or completeness that the law required.

Under the Cramer standard, the act must actually advance the enemy's mission. Sanctions are one of the primary tools through which the United States imposes costs on adversaries for hostile conduct. Failing to implement sanctions mandated by Congress specifically in response to documented Russian hostile action against American elections reduces the cost Russia pays for that hostile conduct. Under Cramer, reduced cost to an adversary that is conducting hostile operations against the United States constitutes actual aid.

The Oval Office Disclosure: Giving Russia What Russia Needed

In May 2017, the President met with Russian Foreign Minister Sergei Lavrov and Russian Ambassador Sergei Kislyak in the Oval Office. The meeting itself was unusual: it was arranged at Russian request, it excluded the American press while allowing Russian state media photographers, and it occurred the day after the President fired the FBI Director who was overseeing the Russia investigation.

During the meeting, the President shared classified intelligence. The intelligence was later reported by allied services to have been so sensitive that its disclosure jeopardized a critical intelligence source operating in or near a Russian-aligned territory. The source, whose identity and operational details were protected by the classification, was potentially a human asset whose life and continued operation depended on the information remaining secret.

When the New York Times reported the disclosure, the administration initially denied it. The President then confirmed it publicly.

> *"I get great intel. I have people brief me on great intel every day. And in order to share with Russia which I have the absolute right to do, facts pertaining to terrorism and airline flight safety."* — **President Donald Trump, Twitter, May 16, 2017**

He shared the intelligence. He confirmed it publicly. He expressed no regret. He characterized it as an exercise of his absolute right.

Under Cramer, the question is whether the act actually advanced the enemy's mission. Compromising an intelligence source operating against a Russian-aligned target advances Russia's mission directly. It removes an American capability. It potentially eliminates a human asset. It signals to the Russian intelligence service, which was present in the Oval Office when the disclosure occurred, that American intelligence operations against their interests could be compromised through the President's casual exercise of his classification authority.

The disclosure was made to the foreign minister and ambassador of the nation that the Intelligence Community Assessment had, four months earlier, unanimously concluded had conducted hostile operations against the United States. Under Haupt, an act performed with knowledge of an adversary's hostile mission, that advances that mission, is an overt act of aid and comfort regardless of the stated justification.

> **THE WITNESSES:** *The Oval Office meeting is documented by Russian state media photographs, by contemporaneous reporting from multiple news organizations, and by former officials who were briefed on its contents. The disclosure of classified intelligence and its impact on allied intelligence sources is documented in reporting from the Washington Post confirmed by current and former intelligence officials. The President's own public confirmation of the disclosure, quoted above, is the most direct witness testimony available: his own words.*

□ □ □

Section Six: The Second Term — Acceleration Without Guardrails

The first term established the pattern. The second term removed the people who had been preventing the pattern from becoming policy.

John Kelly had refused to implement the most extreme Russia-related directives. H.R. McMaster had pushed back on intelligence dismissals. James Mattis had resigned over alliance management concerns that directly implicated the Russia posture. Pat Cipollone had documented his objections in writing. The inspectors general who would have flagged violations of appropriations law and foreign policy protocols had been fired.

When the second term began in January 2025, those guardrails were gone. What replaced them was the accelerated version of every pattern documented in this chapter.

Ukraine Aid Suspension: Repeating the 2019 Violation at Scale

Military assistance to Ukraine, a nation actively resisting Russian military aggression in a war that Russia initiated in 2022, was rapidly suspended in the early weeks of the second term. The suspension was implemented through executive action rather than legislation. Congress had authorized the assistance. The President declined to deliver it.

The legal analysis is identical to the 2019 Ukraine aid freeze documented in Chapter 2. Congress had authorized funds for the specific purpose of supporting a nation resisting Russian military aggression. The executive branch impounded those funds. The Government Accountability Office had found the 2019 freeze violated the Impoundment Control Act. The second-term suspension repeated the same legal violation at a larger scale and with the same strategic beneficiary.

Under Cramer, withholding military assistance from a nation actively resisting the identified enemy advances the enemy's military mission directly. Every weapon that does not reach Ukraine is a weapon Russia does not have to defeat. Every dollar withheld from Ukraine's defense is a dollar Russia does not have to spend matching. The aid suspension is not a policy preference about the appropriate level of American involvement in a foreign conflict. It is an act that materially advances the military mission of the nation this book has established as a functional enemy of the United States.

March 5, 2026: The Most Precisely Timed Act in the Record

On March 5, 2026, one week into the unauthorized Iran war that Chapter 17 addresses in full, the President announced that Russia would be temporarily allowed to export its oil to India without sanctions.

The timing is the legal argument, and it deserves the specific analysis that the Haupt standard provides.

The Iran war had caused global oil prices to spike sharply. Russia, as one of the world's largest oil exporters, was receiving a substantial financial windfall from those price spikes. American sanctions on Russian oil, imposed following Russia's 2022 invasion of Ukraine, had been one of the primary tools constraining Russian revenue and reducing the funds available to the Russian military.

At the precise moment that Russia was profiting most from a conflict that American military action had created, American sanctions that constrained Russian oil revenues were lifted.

Under Haupt, the context and timing of an act are the evidence of the intent behind it. An act performed at the precise moment that it provides maximum benefit to the identified enemy, in the context of a sustained pattern of conduct that consistently benefits that enemy, is not coincidence. It is the Kawakita inference made concrete: the pattern of conduct demonstrates the conscious objective of aiding the enemy's mission.

The sanctions relief provided Russia with additional revenue at the precise moment Russia was profiting from American military action. The revenue funds the Russian military. The Russian military is engaged in active warfare against a U.S. partner nation in Europe. Under Cramer, that is actual aid. Under Haupt, the timing transforms a facially neutral executive action into an overt act of adherence.

> **THE WITNESSES:** *The Ukraine aid suspension is documented in congressional appropriations records, executive branch communications, and testimony from State Department and NSC officials. The March 5, 2026 Russia sanctions relief announcement is a public presidential statement, reported contemporaneously by multiple major news organizations and con-*

firmed in Treasury Department communications. The correlation between the announcement and the Iran war's energy market effects is documented in Federal Reserve, IMF, and commodity market records.

□ □ □

Section Seven: The Cumulative Pattern and the Kawakita Inference

The adherence treason argument in this chapter does not rest on any single overt act. It rests on a cumulative pattern. And it is important to state clearly why a cumulative pattern argument is legally appropriate and legally sound.

In criminal law, intent is almost never proven by direct evidence. Defendants do not confess their purposes. Intent is proven by the pattern of conduct, by the consistency of choices, and by the relationship between the actor's choices and the outcomes that result from them. The Kawakita standard, which permits the inference of treasonous intent from conduct and statements over time, exists precisely because the Framers understood that the most dangerous betrayals are the ones conducted through a thousand individually defensible choices rather than through a single dramatic act.

The pattern documented in this chapter covers every major dimension of the Russia relationship across two terms. The campaign accepted a meeting from Russian government-linked operatives offering assistance as part of Russia's support for the candidate. The administration shared classified intelligence with Russian officials in the Oval Office. The administration failed to implement congressionally mandated sanctions against Russia. The administration's most senior foreign policy official publicly validated Russia's denial of its own hostile operations against American democracy. The administration overrode career security professionals to grant a top-secret clearance to an individual they had flagged as a counterintelligence risk. The administration replaced professional diplomats with personal loyalists operating outside the oversight structures of American foreign policy. The administration suspended military assistance to the nation actively resisting Russian military aggression. And the administration lifted sanctions on Russian oil at the precise moment Russia was profiting most from American military action.

Every choice in that pattern benefits Russia. Every choice in that pattern harms American national security interests. Every choice is made against a background of documented knowledge of Russian hostile action against the United States. And every choice is made despite the specific, documented, sworn objections of the professional national security officials whose institutional responsibility was to prevent exactly the harm that resulted.

The standard for treason is not a single smoking gun. It is a pattern from which intent can be inferred. The Kawakita standard permits that inference. The Haupt standard transforms individually ambiguous acts into treasonous overt acts when performed with knowledge of the enemy's mission. The Cramer standard measures actual harm to American interests. Applied to the cumulative pattern documented in this chapter, all three standards point in the same direction. Whether a jury would find that conclusion beyond a reasonable doubt is the jury's question to answer. This chapter has built the record on which that question can be fairly put.

The next chapter asks a different question. Now that the enemy has been identified and the pattern of adherence has been established, how did the institutions designed to stop this conduct, the free press, the independent judiciary, the congressional oversight mechanisms, come to be systematically dismantled? And what does the law say about the dismantling of accountability as part of the treasonous design?

□ □ □

Chapter Six

The Dismantling of NATO: Aid and Comfort Through Strategic Destruction

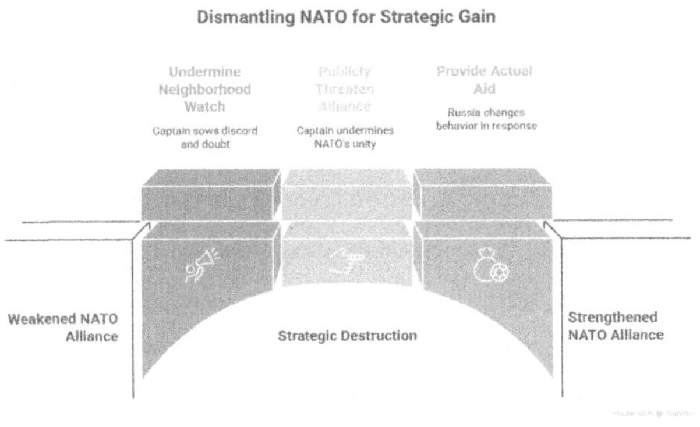

Imagine you live in a neighborhood where one family has been making threats against everyone else for years. They have broken into houses. They have cut phone lines. They have intimidated anyone who tried to speak out.

Your neighborhood has a watch program. Every family participates. The agreement is simple: if anyone comes for one of us, the rest of us respond together. That agreement is the only thing keeping the threatening family in check, because they know that attacking any one of us means fighting all of us.

Now imagine that the neighborhood captain starts telling everyone the watch program is unfair, that your neighborhood pays too much and the other families do not pay enough, that maybe the program is not worth it after all. He says this loudly, repeatedly, in front of the threatening family.

What does the threatening family think? They think the watch program is falling apart. They think they can start making moves.

That is NATO. And that is what happened to it.

This chapter documents how the most consequential military alliance in the history of the modern world was systematically weakened, publicly threatened, and functionally undermined over nine years, in ways that directly served the documented strategic objective of the nation this book has established as a functional enemy of the United States.

It also documents something the editorial analysis of this book's previous chapters identified as legally essential: that the aid was not merely potential. Under the Cramer standard, the aid must be actual. Russia must have actually changed its behavior in response. The evidence shows that it did.

□ □ □

Section One: Why NATO Is a National Security Asset, Not Just a Treaty

The North Atlantic Treaty Organization was founded in 1949 in the immediate aftermath of World War II. The Framers of NATO understood something that the architects of the post-World War I international order had failed to grasp: peace in Europe is not a natural condition. It is an engineered one. It requires architecture. It requires commitment. And most importantly, it requires credibility.

NATO's power comes not primarily from the weapons it deploys. It comes from the credibility of the commitment it represents. When any NATO member is attacked, all NATO members respond. That guarantee is the reason Russia has not militarily invaded a NATO member in the seventy-five years since the alliance was founded. The cost is too high.

The moment that guarantee becomes uncertain, the arithmetic of Russian aggression changes. Russia does not need NATO to dissolve completely before it begins to recalculate its options. It only needs to believe that the guarantee is sufficiently in doubt that the cost of testing it has come down.

The United States intelligence community has formally identified Russian dismantlement of NATO as a primary Russian strategic objective. The Gerasimov Doctrine, addressed in Chapter 4, describes NATO cohesion as the primary obstacle to Russian regional dominance and outlines the degradation of allied confidence as a primary tool of hybrid warfare. Every public act of NATO deconstruction, every statement of doubt about Article 5, every threat of withdrawal, is a strategic gift to the nation this book has established as a functional enemy of the United States.

> **In military strategy, the destruction of an adversary's deterrent capability is the highest form of aid that can be provided to that adversary's enemy. NATO is America's primary deterrent against Russian aggression in Europe. Undermining NATO is not a policy disagreement about alliance management. Under the Aid and Comfort framework, it is the delivery of America's most strategically valuable asset to the adversary whose primary objective is to acquire it.**

□ □ □

Section Two: The Congressional Prohibition and the Youngstown Analysis

Before documenting the specific overt acts of NATO deconstruction, this chapter must address a legal dimension that the editorial analysis identified as essential: the President's authority to withdraw from or functionally undermine NATO is not unconstrained. Congress has spoken. And when Congress has spoken, the constitutional analysis of what the President may do changes dramatically.

The Statutory Barrier

Congress passed legislation prohibiting the use of federal funds to facilitate any withdrawal from NATO that lacks either a two-thirds Senate majority or an explicit Act of Congress. The statute was passed with broad bipartisan support by legislators who had reviewed the intelligence assessments identifying Russian dismantlement of NATO as a primary strategic objective of the Russian Federation.

The existence of this statutory prohibition is legally significant for the treason analysis in a specific way. It establishes, as a matter of legislative record, that Congress determined that NATO membership is a national security interest whose protection required an explicit statutory limit on executive discretion. When Congress passes a law prohibiting a specific action because that action serves a foreign adversary's documented strategic objective, and the President takes that action anyway, the constitutional framework provides a specific analytical tool.

The Youngstown Analysis

In Youngstown Sheet and Tube Company v. Sawyer, decided by the Supreme Court in 1952, Justice Robert Jackson, the same Justice whose Cramer opinion defines the overt act standard for the treason clause, wrote the most influential framework in American constitutional law for analyzing executive power.

Jackson established three categories. In Category One, the President acts with explicit or implied congressional authorization, and his power is at its maximum. In Category Two, Congress has been silent, and the President acts in a constitutional gray zone. In Category Three, the President acts in direct contradiction of congressional will, and his power is at its lowest ebb.

When the President threatens to withdraw from NATO in defiance of a statute specifically prohibiting that withdrawal, he is operating in Youngstown Category Three. His power is at its lowest ebb. He is not exercising executive discretion. He is acting in direct contravention of the expressed will of Congress.

A President whose actions benefit a foreign adversary, and whose legal authority to take those actions has been specifically limited by Congress because of that adversarial benefit, is operating at the precise intersection of constitutional usurpation and aid and comfort to the enemy. The statutory prohibition does not create the treason. But it removes the defense that the action was a legitimate exercise of executive foreign policy authority.

□ □ □

Section Three: The First Term — Systematic Deconstruction

The pattern of NATO undermining began almost immediately after the January 2017 inauguration and proceeded through a series of documented, witnessed, and publicly recorded acts that, individually, might be characterized as management disputes and, collectively, form a sustained campaign of alliance deconstruction.

The June 2017 Summit: The Missing Words

At the NATO summit in Brussels in June 2017, every NATO leader delivered or reaffirmed a public commitment to Article 5, the collective defense guarantee that is the foundational principle of the entire alliance. Every leader except one.

The President of the United States delivered a speech at the summit that did not mention Article 5. The omission was not accidental. Senior White House staff had been given a draft version of the speech that included an explicit Article 5 affirmation. The affirmation was removed from the speech before it was delivered. Allied governments noticed immediately. Diplomatic cables from European capitals documented their alarm in terms that have rarely been used to describe the conduct of a sitting American president toward the alliance.

The strategic significance of the omission was understood by every government present. Article 5 derives its deterrent power from the credibility of the commitment it represents. The credibility of that commitment depends on the American President publicly and unequivocally reaffirming it at every opportunity. A summit speech that conspicuously avoids the affirmation that every other leader made is not a neutral act. It is a signal. And the signal was received.

The Private Withdrawal Discussions

John Bolton, who served as National Security Advisor, documented in his memoir that the President privately discussed withdrawing the United States from NATO during his first term. James Mattis, who served as Secretary of Defense, resigned specifically over concerns about the administration's posture toward the alliance and toward the broader framework of American relationships with allied nations. John Kelly, who served as White House Chief of Staff, made documented public statements about the threat the President's conduct posed to allied confidence in American commitments.

These are not anonymous sources or partisan critics. They are the three most senior national security officials who served in the Trump administration during the period in question. They witnessed the private discussions. They saw the directives. They documented their concerns. And they put their names to their accounts.

The NATO Funding Lie and Its Strategic Function

Throughout the first term, the President characterized NATO as a protection racket in which the United States was being exploited by European allies who refused to pay their fair share. The characterization was factually wrong in a way that was documentable, specific, and legally significant beyond mere inaccuracy.

> *"The United States cannot protect you if you do not pay."* **President Donald Trump, characterizing NATO obligations at multiple summits and press conferences, 2017 to 2020**

NATO members do not pay the United States for protection. Each member nation funds its own military, with a benchmark goal of spending two percent of gross domestic product on defense. The United States military budget is large because United States global strategic interests extend far beyond Europe and require a global force. The size of the American defense budget reflects American global commitments, not European freeloading.

This misrepresentation served a specific strategic function. It recast the alliance from a mutual defense arrangement, in which American participation serves American strategic interests, into a protection racket in which America was being exploited by ungrateful allies. That reframing is precisely Russia's preferred characterization of NATO. It is the narrative Russia needs its own population and the international community to accept in order to justify Russian aggression and undermine allied solidarity.

When the President of the United States delivers Russia's preferred NATO narrative to the American public through the credibility of his office, the broadcaster precedents established in the World War II treason cases, which this book addressed in Chapter 5, apply directly. Speech delivered in service of an enemy's strategic narrative, by the most powerful voice in the democratic world, is more strategically valuable to that enemy than any kinetic military operation.

□ □ □

Section Four: The French Blueprint — How to Destroy an Alliance Without Leaving It

The threat of formal withdrawal from NATO is not the most dangerous form of NATO deconstruction. Formal withdrawal requires congressional action under the statute described in Section Two of this chapter. It is slow, visible, and legally contestable.

The more dangerous approach is functional dismantlement: remaining a formal member of the alliance while systematically withdrawing the capabilities, commitments, and credibility that make the membership meaningful. This approach has a historical precedent. And the current administration appears to be following it.

The 1966 de Gaulle Model

In 1966, French President Charles de Gaulle withdrew France from NATO's integrated military command structure while remaining a signatory to the North Atlantic Treaty. He ordered American and NATO military installations off French soil. He retained French nuclear forces under purely national command, withdrawing them from the collective NATO nuclear umbrella. France remained, on paper, a NATO member. In practice, it had removed its most strategically valuable contributions from the alliance's operational capacity.

De Gaulle's half-exit demonstrated something that strategic analysts have studied for sixty years: you can functionally neuter an alliance from within without triggering the legal and diplomatic consequences of formal withdrawal. The alliance continues to exist. The member continues to attend summits. But the deterrent credibility that the alliance's power rests on is quietly hollowed out.

The 2026 Application

Constitutional law analysts examining the administration's April 2026 posture have identified a pattern consistent with the de Gaulle model, adapted for the current legal environment. The administration cannot easily achieve formal NATO withdrawal without triggering the statutory prohibition described in Section Two. But it can achieve the functional equivalent through a series of individually defensible executive actions.

Command decoupling: reducing American participation in NATO's integrated military command structure while remaining a formal member. Logistical denial: closing or reducing American military installations in Europe, which house approximately 100,000 American personnel and constitute the forward presence that makes the Article 5 commitment credible to adversaries. Nuclear umbrella retraction: redefining the American nuclear deterrent as a purely national asset rather than a collective guarantee, reducing the alliance's nuclear deterrence to the combined arsenals of the United Kingdom and France, approximately 515 warheads, against Russia's 6,257.

That arithmetic deserves its own sentence. A functional American withdrawal from NATO's nuclear umbrella would leave the remaining European alliance members facing a 12 to 1 nuclear disadvantage against Russia. This is not a policy adjustment. It is the strategic transformation of the European security environment in a direction that directly serves Russia's documented primary objective.

□ □ □

Section Five: April 2026 — From Deconstruction to Announced Destruction

On April 1, 2026, the President of the United States said publicly that he was beyond reconsideration on the question of pulling the United States out of NATO. He called the alliance a paper tiger.

Secretary of State Marco Rubio said on Fox News the same week that the administration would have to reexamine whether or not this alliance that has served this country well for a while is still serving that purpose, or whether it has become a one-way street where America is simply in a position to defend Europe but when we need the help of our allies they are going to deny us basing rights and deny us overflight.

White House Press Secretary Karoline Leavitt characterized the Iran war as a test that the alliance had failed, saying that member states had turned their backs on the American people.

On April 9, 2026, after a two-hour meeting at the White House between the President and NATO Secretary General Mark Rutte, the President posted on TruthSocial in capital letters:

"NATO WASN'T THERE WHEN WE NEEDED THEM, AND THEY WON'T BE THERE IF WE NEED THEM AGAIN."

At the subsequent press conference, Rutte was asked directly, multiple times, whether the President had threatened to withdraw from NATO during their meeting. He declined to answer. He would not deny the threat had been made.

Alliance leaders do not decline to deny existential threats unless the threat was made.

The Zakharova Synchronization: When the Enemy Echoes the President

What happened in the hours following the President's April 9 TruthSocial post provided one of the most legally significant moments in the entire NATO chapter of this book.

Russian Foreign Ministry spokeswoman Maria Zakharova, the official public voice of the Russian government's diplomatic position, echoed the President's paper tiger language within hours of his post. Russian state media, which operates as a direct extension of the

Russian government's information operations, amplified the President's characterization of NATO as unreliable and the alliance as functionally broken.

This synchronization is not merely rhetorically significant. It is legally significant for the adherence treason analysis.

The Gerasimov Doctrine, which this book addressed in Chapter 4 as Russia's published declaration of hostile intent, specifically identifies the degradation of Western public confidence in collective defense institutions as a primary tool of hybrid warfare. When Russia's official spokeswoman echoes the American President's language describing NATO as a paper tiger within hours of its publication, two things have been established. First, Russia understood the President's statement as an advancement of its own strategic objective. Second, Russia was coordinating its information operations with the American President's public messaging, whether through explicit coordination or through the opportunistic amplification of a message that served Russia's interest.

> **When the enemy's official spokesperson echoes the President's words within hours and amplifies them through state media, the enemy is not merely observing the deconstruction of the alliance that protects America. They are synchronizing their information warfare with it. That synchronization is adherence. It is the visible evidence of what aid and comfort looks like when it is delivered through a press conference rather than a military operation.**

□ □ □

Section Six: The Cramer Test — Did Russia Actually Receive Aid and Comfort?

The Supreme Court's Cramer standard requires that the overt act actually advance the enemy's mission. It is not enough to provide something that could theoretically help the enemy. The aid must be real. The comfort must be actual. The enemy's mission must have been advanced by what the accused did.

This is the legally essential question for the NATO chapter. Did Russia actually change its behavior in response to the NATO deconstruction documented above? Is there evidence that the enemy received actual aid, not merely potential aid?

The answer from the intelligence record and the military posture record is yes.

The Russian Military Response

Intelligence assessments available to Congress and documented in allied diplomatic cables confirmed that the Kremlin interpreted the President's April 2026 statements as a signal that the Article 5 commitment was genuinely in doubt. Russian military forces increased their operational activity along the borders of the Baltic states, Estonia, Latvia, and Lithuania, NATO members whose geographic position makes them the most exposed to Russian conventional military pressure and whose defense depends most directly on the credibility of Article 5.

Russian hybrid warfare operations in the Suwalki Gap, the narrow land corridor between Poland and Lithuania that is the only overland connection between the Baltic states and the rest of NATO Europe, increased in tempo and sophistication during the spring of 2026. Intelligence analysts assessed that Russian planners were testing the corridor's vulnerability in a manner consistent with preparation for potential interdiction.

These developments were not coincidental with the President's April 2026 statements. They were responses to them. Intelligence community assessments documented that Russian military planning had updated its assumptions about NATO cohesion based specifically on the President's public statements and on the evidence of alliance fracturing produced by the Iran war.

Under the Cramer standard, this is actual aid. Russia did not merely receive comfort in the psychological sense of feeling encouraged. Russia received strategic intelligence, derived from the President's own public statements, that altered its military calculus about what it could do in Eastern Europe without triggering the collective defense response that had deterred it for seventy-five years.

The Deterrence Destruction

There is a dimension of the Cramer actual aid analysis that is unique to the NATO context and that deserves specific attention.

In most treason cases, the aid can be measured concretely: documents transferred, intelligence disclosed, money provided. NATO's deterrence value is different. It is not a tangible asset that can be transferred. It is a psychological and strategic reality that exists only as long as it is believed.

When the President of the United States publicly characterizes the alliance as a paper tiger, as beyond reconsideration for dissolution, and as an organization that will not be there when needed, he is not transferring NATO's assets to Russia. He is destroying NATO's deterrence value. And deterrence destroyed is not recoverable in the way that a document can be returned or a payment reversed.

Every Russian military planner who updated their threat assessment of NATO cohesion after April 2026 was responding to an irreversible change in NATO's strategic posture. The ally whose commitment made Russian aggression too costly had publicly questioned that commitment. The calculus of deterrence had shifted. And deterrence, once diminished in the enemy's calculation, does not return to its prior level simply because the President later issues a clarifying statement.

This is the Aid and Comfort of strategic destruction. Not a weapon delivered. Not a secret disclosed. But the deliberate erosion of the one thing that stood between Russian military ambition and European security. Under Cramer, that erosion is actual aid because it actually advanced Russia's primary documented strategic objective.

□ □ □

Section Seven: The Legal Synthesis — Aid and Comfort Through Deterrence Destruction

The treason clause does not require the transfer of weapons or money. It requires adherence to an enemy, giving them aid and comfort. The law of adherence treason, as the preceding chapters have established, is satisfied by any overt act that actually advances the enemy's mission, performed with knowledge of the enemy's objectives and with the intent, inferred from the cumulative pattern of conduct, to make the enemy's mission succeed.

Applied to the NATO conduct documented in this chapter, the synthesis is this.

The United States Congress, on a bipartisan basis, identified Russia as a threat requiring sanctions and containment, and passed legislation specifically prohibiting executive withdrawal from NATO because NATO was identified as the primary mechanism of that containment. The President privately discussed withdrawal, publicly questioned Article 5, removed the Article 5 affirmation from the 2017 summit speech, characterized the alliance using the specific narrative that Russian state media and Russian diplomatic messaging had been using to undermine it, threatened dissolution in April 2026 in statements that Russian official spokeswoman Maria Zakharova echoed within hours, and took actions during the Iran war that produced the specific alliance fracturing that Gerasimov's hybrid warfare doctrine described as a primary strategic objective.

Under the Kawakita standard, the public statements gave the enemy heart and courage. The Zakharova synchronization confirmed that the enemy received and acted on that encouragement.

Under the Cramer standard, the subsequent Russian military posturing in Eastern Europe and the Suwalki Gap demonstrates that the aid was actual, not theoretical. Russia updated its military calculus. Russia increased its operational pressure in the areas most sensitive to NATO credibility. The enemy did not merely receive comfort. They acted on it.

Under the Youngstown analysis, the President's actions in the face of an explicit congressional prohibition place his authority at its lowest ebb, stripping the legal cover of executive foreign policy discretion from the conduct and exposing it to the full weight of the constitutional standard.

A President who undermines the alliance that is the primary mechanism of containment against the nation's primary documented adversary, in defiance of a congressional prohibition, in a manner that echoes the adversary's own information warfare messaging, and that produces documented changes in the adversary's military posture, has satisfied the constitutional definition of ad-

hering to enemies, giving them aid and comfort. The destruction of deterrence is the delivery of aid. The Cramer standard is met.

> **THE WITNESSES:** *The first-term conduct is witnessed by John Bolton (National Security Advisor, documented in published memoir), James Mattis (Secretary of Defense, documented in resignation letter and subsequent statements), and John Kelly (White House Chief of Staff, documented in public statements and confirmed by multiple former administration officials). The June 2017 summit speech omission of Article 5 is documented in the draft speech records and in diplomatic cables from allied governments. The April 2026 statements by the President, Secretary Rubio, and Press Secretary Leavitt are public records. The reaction of NATO Secretary General Mark Rutte is documented in press conference transcripts in which he declined, multiple times, to deny that a withdrawal threat had been made. The Zakharova synchronization is documented in Russian Foreign Ministry press conference records and Russian state media archives. The Russian military posture changes in the Baltic states and Suwalki Gap are documented in intelligence assessments cited in congressional testimony and allied diplomatic communications.*

□ □ □

The NATO chapter closes with a number that deserves to stand alone on the page, because it captures more than any legal argument can.

If the United States functionally withdraws from NATO's nuclear umbrella, the remaining European members of the alliance would face Russia with a combined arsenal of approximately 515 nuclear warheads, the weapons held by the United Kingdom and France. Russia possesses 6,257 nuclear warheads.

That is a 12 to 1 Russian advantage.

The Framers wrote the treason clause because they understood that the greatest danger to a republic is not the enemy at the gates. It is the person inside the gates who opens them.

The next chapter documents what it looks like when that person also controls the economic instruments through which the nation finances its own survival, and what happens when those instruments are turned against the people they were built to protect.

□ □ □

Chapter Seven

The Iran War Nexus: Using Israel as a Geopolitical Instrument

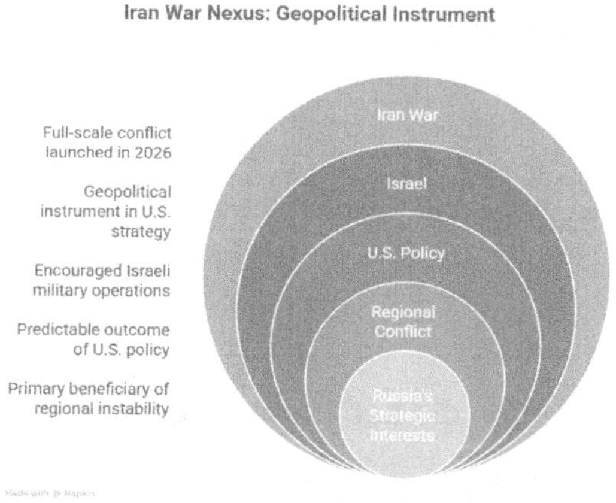

This chapter requires a careful statement at the outset.

Supporting Israel is not treason. American support for Israeli security is a longstanding bipartisan policy with deep roots in American foreign policy, strategic interests, and moral commitments. Nothing in this chapter argues otherwise.

What this chapter argues is more specific and more legally precise.

The manner in which U.S., Israeli, and Iranian relations were structured across two terms, from the Iran Deal withdrawal in 2018 through the full-scale war launched on February

28, 2026, created conditions for regional conflict that predictably and foreseeably served Russian strategic interests. More specifically, the administration did not merely support Israel. It encouraged Israel to conduct military operations that the United States would historically have restrained, knowing that such operations would trigger the escalation that Russia's own published doctrine had identified as a strategic objective.

The legal argument is not about Israel. It is about who benefits when a President consistently chooses the path that produces maximum regional instability over the path that produces containment and stability. Under the Cramer standard, the aid must be actual. Under the Kawakita standard, intent is inferred from the pattern of choices. Under the Haupt standard, what appears to be support for an ally becomes treasonous when the primary beneficiary of the resulting chaos is an identified enemy.

Russia did not fire a single shot in the Iran war. Russia condemned it publicly and loudly. And Russia was, by the unanimous assessment of European analysts and the documented movement of global energy markets, the primary strategic winner of every day that war continued.

That is the chapter's legal argument. Now here is the evidence.

□ □ □

Section One: The Thread That Unraveled Everything — The 2018 Iran Deal Withdrawal

In May 2018, the United States withdrew from the Joint Comprehensive Plan of Action, the multilateral nuclear agreement negotiated by the United States, the United Kingdom, France, Germany, Russia, China, and the European Union. The deal had constrained Iran's uranium enrichment, capped its centrifuge operations, reduced its stockpile of enriched uranium, and provided for regular IAEA inspections.

At the time of withdrawal, the International Atomic Energy Agency had certified that Iran was in compliance with its obligations. Not partially compliant. Not conditionally compliant. In compliance.

The withdrawal was justified publicly by claims of Iranian non-compliance. The documented reality was the opposite.

The Mattis Testimony

In October 2017, seven months before the withdrawal, Secretary of Defense James Mattis testified before the Senate Armed Services Committee. He was asked directly: is the JCPOA in the national security interest of the United States?

> *"I believe the agreement to be imperfect but has value."* — **Secretary of Defense James Mattis, Senate Armed Services Committee, October 2017**

Mattis recommended staying in the agreement. The U.S. intelligence community did not support the assessment that diplomacy had failed. European allies, whose own intelligence services monitored Iranian nuclear activity, opposed withdrawal unanimously. The IAEA, whose verification mission existed specifically to determine whether Iran was complying, said Iran was complying.

The public justification and the documented reality were different. That discrepancy is a fact. What it means for the legal analysis is addressed in Section Five of this chapter, where the intent inference is drawn from the pattern of choices.

The Predictable and Predicted Consequences

The officials who opposed withdrawal did not merely argue that it was unwise. They specifically predicted what would follow, and their predictions were documented in writing before the withdrawal occurred.

Iran would accelerate its nuclear program. It did, eventually reaching enrichment levels far beyond those permitted under the deal. Iran would deepen its economic and strategic relationship with Russia and China, the two nations that had the most to gain from Iran's isolation from the West. It did, and that deepening alignment with Russia became one of the primary geopolitical consequences of the withdrawal. Iranian proxy attacks on

American forces and regional allies would accelerate. They did, producing the escalation cycles that led directly to the 2026 war.

These were not unintended consequences. They were foreseen by the officials who opposed the withdrawal and documented in the record before the withdrawal occurred. Under the Haupt standard, an act performed with knowledge of the consequences it will produce is not an act whose consequences can be described as unintended.

□ □ □

Section Two: The Green Light Strategy — How Israel Was Used

The administration did not merely support Israel. American support for Israeli security has always included both enablement and restraint, providing weapons and intelligence while simultaneously exercising diplomatic pressure to prevent escalations that would serve adversarial interests or destabilize regions in ways that harmed American strategic objectives.

What changed under this administration was the restraint. The restraint disappeared.

The Escalation Sequence

The road from the 2018 Iran Deal withdrawal to the February 28, 2026 war followed a specific documented sequence. The Soleimani assassination of January 2020 was conducted without congressional notification, in a manner that military advisors warned would trigger escalation cycles. The Twelve-Day War of June 2025 saw American and Israeli forces conduct the first direct strikes on Iranian nuclear sites, destroying approximately 50 percent of Iran's missile stockpile. And the full-scale war designated Operation Epic Fury began on February 28, 2026, launched during active negotiations that the Omani mediating team had described as showing significant progress.

At each step, diplomatic off-ramps were available and were not taken. Military options were chosen. Regional conflict was sustained and deepened rather than contained and resolved. And at each step, a signal was sent to Israel and to the region that American restraint had been replaced by American enablement.

The Twelve-Day War of June 2025 is the clearest illustration of this dynamic. Israeli military operations that previous administrations would have discouraged, because they predictably produced the escalation cycles that the United States would then be drawn into, were instead supported and enabled. The U.S. posture had shifted from Israel's partner in managed deterrence to Israel's partner in regional transformation. And the chaos produced by regional transformation is precisely what Russia's published doctrine had identified as the strategic objective.

The Outsourced Escalation

There is a legal concept relevant to this analysis that comes from the law of complicity: the principle that a person who directs an act through a third party is legally responsible for the act, even if they did not personally perform it.

When an administration signals, through posture and policy and the absence of historical restraint, that Israeli military operations against Iran will be supported rather than discouraged, it is not neutral. It is direction through a proxy. The administration does not have to order the strikes. It only has to make clear that the strikes will be welcomed, that the escalation they produce will be managed with American support, and that the restraint that historically existed has been removed.

Under the Haupt standard, the administration is legally present at the overt acts produced by that signal, even when it is not physically present at the location where the strikes occur. The direction of the force through the proxy is the overt act. The resulting chaos, and the specific beneficiary of that chaos, are the aid and comfort.

The administration did not merely support Israel. It removed the restraint that had historically prevented Israeli military operations from producing the specific kind of regional chaos that Russia's own published doctrine identified as a strategic objective. When a President outsources military escalation to a proxy ally, knowing the primary beneficiary of the resulting chaos is the adversary, the Aid and Comfort is delivered through a third party. The legal responsibility does not disappear because the strikes were conducted by another nation's air force.

□ □ □

Section Three: Operation Epic Fury — The War That Served Russia

At approximately 1:00 in the morning on February 28, 2026, the United States and Israel launched coordinated military strikes against Iran. The operation was designated Operation Epic Fury by the United States and Operation Roaring Lion by Israel. It involved approximately 2,000 strikes targeting military installations, nuclear infrastructure, and Iranian leadership.

Among those killed on the first day of strikes was Supreme Leader Ayatollah Ali Khamenei.

The operational scale of Operation Epic Fury was significant by any historical measure. But the strategic consequences, particularly for Russia, are what matter for the legal analysis in this chapter.

The Economic Windfall Russia Did Not Have to Earn

The Iran war triggered an immediate and severe shock to global energy markets. The Strait of Hormuz, the narrow waterway through which approximately 20 percent of the world's oil supply transits daily, was effectively closed. Tanker traffic through the strait fell by 94 percent within 24 hours of the February 28 strikes. Brent crude oil prices surged toward $100 per barrel, with analysts projecting a rise to $150 to $200 per barrel if the closure persisted for three months.

Russia is one of the world's largest oil exporters. Under the sanctions imposed following Russia's 2022 invasion of Ukraine, Russian oil revenues had been significantly constrained. Those constraints depended on global oil prices remaining at levels where Russia's discounted oil, sold to circumvent sanctions, still generated enough revenue to fund its military operations in Ukraine.

The Iran war changed those economics overnight. At $100 per barrel, Russia's oil revenues increased substantially even after applying the sanctions discount. At $120 per barrel, where prices moved during the most intense phase of the Strait of Hormuz closure, Russia was receiving a financial windfall of tens of billions of dollars that it had not expected, had not planned for, and had not had to spend a single ruble in military operations to generate.

European Union President Antonio Costa, in documented public statements, described Russia as the only winner of the Iran war crisis. This was not a partisan characterization. It was the assessment of a European institutional leader examining the documented movements of global energy markets and their documented benefit to the Russian economy.

The Military Resource Drain

The Iran war consumed American military resources in a specific and measurable way that produced direct strategic benefit to Russia.

Operation Epic Fury utilized precision-guided munitions, Patriot air defense interceptors, and naval assets at a scale that drew down stockpiles that the United States had been building specifically for the potential requirement of defending NATO's eastern flank against Russian military aggression in Europe. The U.S. defense industrial base, which had already been strained by the provision of munitions to Ukraine, faced additional pressure from the Iran war's demands.

The EU defense commissioner, in documented statements cited in allied diplomatic communications, warned that American military costs were overstretched, making Washington incapable of providing sufficient military aid to Ukraine while simultaneously consuming precision-guided munitions in the Middle East. This was not a hypothetical risk. It was a documented assessment by the officials responsible for European defense coordination.

Under the Cramer standard, the aid must be actual. The documented drawdown of American military resources that would otherwise be available for the European theater, where Russia is engaged in active warfare against a U.S. partner nation, is actual aid to Russia measured in depleted stockpiles and diverted production capacity.

Russia's Strategic Passivity as Legal Evidence

There is an element of the Russian response to Operation Epic Fury that is counterintuitive and legally significant.

Russia condemned the strikes loudly. Russian Foreign Ministry spokeswoman Maria Zakharova described them as Satanism in all its glory. Foreign Minister Sergei Lavrov claimed Russia had been misled by Israeli assurances. Former President Dmitry Medvedev made statements about nuclear weapons that were designed to influence international opinion. Russian state media amplified Iranian casualty figures and framed the conflict in civilizational terms for domestic and Global South audiences.

And Russia provided no material military support to Iran. Not a single weapons system. Not a single combat unit. Not a single operational asset. Russia watched Iran absorb American and Israeli strikes while delivering rhetorical support from a safe distance.

This behavior is not the behavior of an ally caught off guard by a crisis affecting a partner. It is the behavior of a principal that has achieved its strategic objective without military cost and has no reason to risk that objective by entering a conflict that is already going exactly as its published doctrine described.

Russia did not need to fire a shot in the Iran war to win it. It only needed America to start it. The Gerasimov Doctrine described exactly this outcome as the objective of hybrid warfare: force the adversary to consume resources in a theater that serves your interests, collect the economic windfall from the resulting energy market disruption, and watch the alliances fracture without spending a single ruble on military action. Russia's strategic passivity in the face of the Iran war is not evidence that Russia was uninvolved in its strategic consequences. It is evidence that the strategy worked exactly as designed.

□ □ □

Section Four: The Constitutional Breach — War Without Congress

Chapter 3 of this book established the Youngstown framework for analyzing executive power. When the President acts in direct contravention of congressional will, his authority is at its lowest ebb. When he acts during a period of congressional prohibition, the constitutional cover of executive foreign policy discretion is stripped away.

The Iran war, like the first-term CAATSA sanctions failures and the NATO threats analyzed in Chapter 6, was conducted in the face of specific congressional limitation. Article I, Section 8 of the Constitution grants Congress, and Congress alone, the power to declare war. The War Powers Resolution of 1973 requires the President to notify

Congress within 48 hours of committing forces to hostilities and to obtain congressional authorization within 60 days.

Operation Epic Fury was launched without prior congressional authorization. It was launched without prior congressional notification. It was launched during active negotiations that diplomats described as productive. And it was launched based on a stated justification, imminent threat from Iranian nuclear development, that the administration's own military briefers contradicted in closed congressional sessions, telling legislators that there was no intelligence suggesting Iran was planning to attack American forces first.

The Timing as the Evidence of Intent

A President genuinely seeking to eliminate Iran's nuclear threat would not launch a bombing campaign while his diplomats were at the negotiating table with Iranian counterparts who had, according to the Omani mediating team, shown significant willingness to make concessions.

The timing of the February 28 strikes, during active negotiations, is not merely a diplomatic blunder. It is evidence of intent. It establishes that the objective of the war was not the elimination of a nuclear threat through the most available mechanism, which at that moment was a diplomatic negotiation showing progress. The objective was war. And the question the Kawakita standard puts to a jury is: why would a President choose war over diplomacy when diplomacy was working, if not because war served a purpose that diplomacy could not?

The Gerasimov Doctrine provides the answer. War in the Middle East served Russia's strategic objectives in ways that a negotiated nuclear agreement with Iran did not. A negotiated agreement would have stabilized the Middle East, reduced energy market volatility, freed American military and diplomatic resources for the European theater, and halted the process of driving Iran into Russia's strategic orbit. War did the opposite of all of these things.

The Youngstown Analysis

Chapter 6 introduced the Youngstown framework for the NATO conduct. It applies with equal force to the Iran war.

Congress had passed the War Powers Resolution specifically to prevent presidents from unilaterally committing the nation to sustained armed conflict. The Iran war was not a brief emergency use of force in response to an imminent threat. It was a sustained military campaign of 40 days involving 2,000 strikes, the assassination of a foreign head of state, and the closure of a global maritime chokepoint. Every day after the initial 48-hour notification window, and every day after the 60-day authorization deadline, the war continued without congressional authorization.

The Senate War Powers resolution to end the unauthorized war failed 47 to 53. The House version failed 212 to 219. These narrow margins are documented on the record by named senators and representatives. They establish, as a matter of congressional testimony, that the war lacked constitutional authorization. The President's authority was at its lowest ebb. And the beneficiary of the war conducted at the lowest ebb of constitutional authority was Russia.

> **THE WITNESSES:** *The War Powers violation is documented in the congressional voting record, in the testimony of Senators Kaine and Paul and Representatives Khanna and Massie, in the Pentagon's closed-session briefings to Congress in which military officials stated there was no intelligence suggesting Iran was planning to attack American forces first, and in the public statements of the Brennan Center for Justice and the ACLU characterizing the war as unconstitutional. The Omani mediating team's assessment that negotiations were showing significant progress at the time of the strikes is documented in diplomatic communications cited in international press reporting.*

□ □ □

Section Five: The Oil Strategy — When Foreign Policy Becomes Resource Seizure

The stated justification for Operation Epic Fury was the elimination of Iran's nuclear threat and the protection of American security interests. As the war progressed through March and April 2026, a different set of objectives became visible in the public statements of the President himself.

Taking the Strait

On March 9, 2026, ten days into the war, the President stated publicly that he was considering taking over the Strait of Hormuz. Not controlling it temporarily to restore commercial transit. Not securing it as a military objective during active hostilities. Taking it over. The language was possessive and permanent.

As negotiations in Islamabad broke down in April, the President declared a full naval blockade of Iran. He announced that the United States Navy would intercept any vessel that had paid transit tolls to the Iranian government, which had been charging shipping companies as much as $1 million per ship to transit the Strait. United States Navy destroyers entered the Strait for the first time since the war began to conduct clearing operations. CENTCOM conducted mine clearance operations after reports suggested Iranian forces had lost track of the mines they had planted.

The infrastructure threats were escalatory and specific. The President repeatedly threatened to destroy Iranian power plants and oil facilities if Iran did not agree to unconditional surrender and the reopening of the Strait on American terms.

Operation Southern Spear and the Venezuela Oil Seizure

The Iran war did not occur in isolation from a broader pattern of resource-oriented military and political action. In January 2026, weeks before Operation Epic Fury began, the United States captured and arrested Nicolas Maduro of Venezuela as part of a campaign designated Operation Southern Spear. Following Maduro's removal, the United States enforced a comprehensive oil blockade of Venezuela and imposed tariffs on Venezuelan oil.

The interim government that replaced Maduro, led by Delcy Rodriguez, recognized American pressure while simultaneously defending Venezuela's right to maintain relations with Russia, China, Iran, and Cuba. By late January 2026, there were no substantive steps taken to reduce Venezuela's ties with American strategic competitors. The operation that removed Maduro did not remove Russian or Chinese influence from Venezuela. It removed Maduro.

The pattern of Venezuela and Iran together reveals something important about the nature of the resource strategy. Both nations held oil assets of strategic significance. Both nations had deep relationships with Russia. The military and political actions against both nations deepened those nations' reliance on Russia rather than weakening it, because the American actions removed their other strategic options without providing a credible American alternative.

The Insider Trading Allegations

Investigations into suspicious financial activity tied to the President's public statements about the Iran war produced findings that, if substantiated, would represent an additional dimension of the corruption documented in Chapter 2.

Reports documented approximately $580 million in market positions placed on falling oil prices approximately 15 minutes before the President announced the postponement of strikes on Iranian power plants on March 23, 2026. Reports documented approximately $950 million in similar market positions placed shortly before the President announced the two-week ceasefire on April 7, 2026. The total documented in suspicious positions correlated with presidential announcements reached approximately $1.5 billion.

These allegations have not been finally adjudicated. This book notes them as documented facts in the public record, not as established legal conclusions. What they represent, if the pattern is what it appears to be, is the most direct possible evidence of financial self-interest underlying the public statements of a President conducting a war. Under Chapter 2's analysis of the emoluments and self-dealing pattern, financial interest in policy outcomes that harm national security interests and benefit foreign adversaries is evidence of the corrupt motive underlying the broader conduct.

□ □ □

Section Six: The Global Consequences — Aid Measured in Human Cost

The Aid and Comfort framework, as established in Chapter 4 through the Cramer and Kawakita standards, requires that the aid be actual. The Iran war's consequences were not theoretical. They were measured in specific, documented, quantifiable human costs that extend across the globe and will continue to be felt for years.

The Strait of Hormuz and the Grocery Supply Emergency

The closure of the Strait of Hormuz did not merely affect the price of gasoline. The Strait is the transit point for more than just oil. The Gulf Cooperation Council states, the nations of Saudi Arabia, the United Arab Emirates, Kuwait, Qatar, Bahrain, and Oman, rely on the Strait for more than 80 percent of their caloric intake. When the Strait closed, their food supply closed with it.

By mid-March 2026, approximately 70 percent of the region's food imports were disrupted. Major retailers were forced to airlift staples by air to maintain inventory. Consumer prices for food spiked 40 to 120 percent. In Iran itself, food inflation reached 105 percent. Bread and cereals rose 140 percent in price. Oils and fats rose 219 percent.

The disruption extended far beyond the Middle East because the region is a critical hub for the chemical components of global agriculture. Approximately 50 percent of global urea and sulfur exports transit the Strait of Hormuz. Twenty percent of the liquefied natural gas used as feedstock for nitrogen fertilizers transits the same route. The war coincided with the Northern Hemisphere's spring planting season. Analysts from the UN World Food Programme warned that reduced fertilizer usage during planting season would lower yields for wheat, rice, and maize in the harvest that follows.

The Global Ripple

The consequences of the Strait closure rippled across every continent. In Egypt, higher oil prices strained public finances and traffic through the Suez Canal declined, producing approximately $10 billion in documented losses. In the Philippines, President Marcos declared a state of national energy emergency on March 24, 2026. Diesel prices hiked by nearly 39 percent. Government agencies implemented a four-day work week to conserve energy. The Philippine Peso fell to a record low. In Sri Lanka and Bangladesh, governments reintroduced fuel rationing and shortened work weeks for public employees. In Vietnam and Thailand, filling stations ran completely out of diesel.

These are not distant abstractions. These are documented, dated, country-specific consequences of a war launched by the President of the United States without congressional authorization during active negotiations. Each price spike, each rationing measure, each state of emergency declared in a country that had nothing to do with Iran's nuclear program, is the measurable human cost of the aid and comfort provided to Russia through the mechanism of Middle Eastern instability.

The European Energy Crisis

Europe was thrust into what analysts described as a second major energy crisis. The closure of the Strait disrupted Qatari LNG supplies, causing European natural gas benchmark contracts to spike 41 percent. European chemical and steel manufacturers imposed surcharges of up to 30 percent. Economists warned of permanent deindustrialization in energy-intensive sectors if the blockade persisted.

The European Central Bank postponed planned interest rate reductions in response to the inflationary pressures the war created. The economic burden fell disproportionately on European nations that had already strained their own finances through the support of Ukraine in its resistance to Russian military aggression.

Russia, whose economy runs primarily on energy exports, profited from every dollar of European energy price increase. Russia's strategic passivity in the Iran war, documented in Section Three, was not confusion or weakness. It was the behavior of a nation watching its primary geopolitical competitor consume itself in a war that delivered Russia its strategic objectives without Russian military cost.

□ □ □

Section Seven: The Transatlantic Rift — NATO Fracturing in Real Time

Chapter 6 documented the systematic deconstruction of NATO through statements and threats. The Iran war produced the actual fracturing that those statements had been designed to enable. The alliance did not merely show stress. It broke in specific, documented, bilateral ways that Russia's own doctrine had described as the objective.

The Spain Trade Severance

Spain refused to permit American military forces to use Spanish bases for operations related to the Iran strikes. Madrid's refusal was constitutionally and legally grounded: NATO is a defensive alliance, and the Iran war was an offensive operation launched by a NATO member without collective alliance authorization. Spain was not obligated under Article 5 to support an offensive American military operation against a non-NATO nation that had not attacked any NATO member.

The administration's response was the severance of all trade with Spain. Not sanctions. Not diplomatic protest. The complete termination of bilateral trade with a NATO ally and European Union member nation, in retaliation for that nation's constitutionally grounded refusal to participate in an unauthorized war.

Spanish Prime Minister Pedro Sanchez characterized the situation with a phrase that captured the essential dynamic: he would not applaud those who set the world on fire just because they show up with a bucket.

The UK, Italy, and the Coalition

The United Kingdom's offer to deploy aircraft carriers in support of the operation was dismissed by Washington with a characterization of the war as already won. Italian Prime Minister Giorgia Meloni publicly stated that Rome disagreed with American security priorities and sought a separate diplomatic path. The 41-nation UK-led coalition, assembled to provide at least nominal support for securing the Strait of Hormuz, declined to provide military forces, opting instead for sanctions support.

The President's documented response to allied restraint included statements about the Royal Navy that were characteristically personal and dismissive: You don't even have a navy. You're too old and you had aircraft carriers that didn't work.

These statements were made about the navy of the United States' oldest and most consequential military ally, the nation whose intelligence sharing relationship with the United States is the foundation of the Five Eyes intelligence partnership. They were made publicly, internationally, during an active military operation in which the support of that ally would have been strategically valuable. They caused documented diplomatic damage. And they advanced Russia's primary strategic objective of alliance dissolution with a directness that no amount of Russian information warfare could have produced as efficiently.

EU President Costa: Russia Is the Only Winner

European Union President Antonio Costa's assessment, made in documented public statements during the spring of 2026, deserves to stand as a conclusion to this section.

> *"Russia is the only winner of this crisis."* **European Union President Antonio Costa, spring 2026**

This was not a partisan American political statement. It was the assessment of the elected leader of the European Union, representing the collective judgment of twenty-seven European nations that had watched the Iran war unfold and had examined its consequences for their economies, their security, and their alliances.

Russia was the only winner. Not the United States, which consumed military resources and fractured its alliances. Not Israel, which faced expanded proxy threats from Hezbollah and Iranian-aligned forces whose operational autonomy increased after the decentralization of Iranian command following Khamenei's death. Not Iran, which saw its Supreme Leader killed, its military infrastructure destroyed, and its economy subjected to a blockade. Not the global economy, which suffered the consequences of the Strait of Hormuz closure in food prices, fuel costs, and industrial surcharges across every continent.

Russia. Which did not fire a shot. Which condemned the war in its strongest diplomatic language. And which collected tens of billions of dollars in additional oil revenue from the energy market disruption that the war produced.

□ □ □

Section Eight: The Intent Inference and the Legal Synthesis

The Kawakita standard permits a jury to infer treasonous intent from the totality of conduct. The Iran chapter presents that totality in its most concentrated form.

The JCPOA withdrawal produced a more nuclear-capable, more Russia-aligned Iran, as its opponents specifically predicted and documented before the withdrawal occurred. The maximum pressure campaign drove Iran deeper into Russia's strategic and economic orbit. The removal of American restraint on Israeli military operations produced the Twelve-Day War of 2025, which produced the conditions for the February 2026 conflict. The February 2026 war was launched during active negotiations, without congressional authorization, based on a stated justification that military briefers contradicted in classified congressional session.

The war produced: an oil price spike that delivered Russia a financial windfall measured in tens of billions of dollars; a drawdown of American precision-guided munitions that reduced American capacity to support Ukraine against Russian military aggression; a fracturing of NATO that advanced Russia's primary strategic objective; the severing of trade with Spain and the diplomatic alienation of the United Kingdom and Italy; a global food crisis whose consequences were felt from the Gulf to Southeast Asia to sub-Saharan Africa; and American public approval of the war at 37 percent, with 53 percent opposed, producing the domestic political division that Russia's own doctrine described as a primary tool of hybrid warfare.

Every outcome produced by this sequence of choices served Russia's documented strategic objectives. Every outcome was either foreseen by the officials who opposed the choices or described in advance by Russia's own published military doctrine. And the primary actor who consistently chose the path that produced these outcomes, over the available alternatives that would not have produced them, was the President of the United States.

A President genuinely seeking to contain Iran's nuclear threat would not have withdrawn from a verified nuclear agreement over the objections of his own Secretary of Defense. A President genuinely seeking regional stability would not have removed the restraint that historically prevented Israeli military operations

from producing the escalation cycles Russia's doctrine needed. A President genuinely seeking to protect American security interests would not have launched a war during active negotiations without congressional authorization, based on a stated justification his own military briefers contradicted. Under the Kawakita standard, the choice of the path that serves the enemy over the path that serves the nation, made consistently across eight years and multiple decision points, is the pattern from which treasonous intent is inferred. A jury is entitled to ask: if not treason, what is the explanation for a pattern this consistent?

> **THE WITNESSES:** *Secretary of Defense James Mattis testified before the Senate Armed Services Committee in October 2017 that the JCPOA was in the national security interest and recommended staying in it. Mattis's resignation letter and subsequent documented statements establish his opposition to the military posture that produced the Iran war escalation. The IAEA's May 2018 compliance report establishing Iranian compliance at the time of the JCPOA withdrawal is a primary source document. The congressional War Powers resolution votes, 47 to 53 in the Senate and 212 to 219 in the House, are documented in the congressional record with named senators and representatives establishing the constitutional violation on the record. Pentagon closed-session briefers who told Congress there was no imminent threat intelligence are documented through congressional accounts. EU President Costa's Russia is the only winner statement is documented in press conference records. European diplomatic communications expressing alarm about NATO fracturing are documented in allied governmental statements. The $580 million and $950 million market positions correlated with presidential announcements are documented in financial press reporting and are the subject of congressional investigation requests.*

□ □ □

The next chapter asks what happens when the instruments of betrayal documented in Chapters 2 through 7 are protected by the systematic dismantlement of every institution capable of exposing or prosecuting them. The Iran war produced the most concentrated cluster of overt acts in the entire record. Part VII documents the wall that was built around those acts to ensure they could not be reached.

□ □ □

PART III

THE THEFT OF THE REPUBLIC

Stewardship as Betrayal: Financial, Economic, and Social Destruction

Chapter Eight

The Financial Betrayal: The Ukraine Aid Freeze, Pentagon Funds, and the Impoundment Pattern

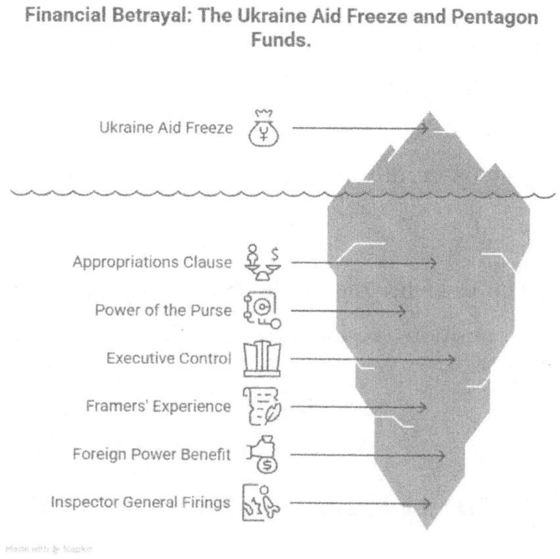

There is a line in the Constitution that most Americans have never read but that the Framers considered one of the most important safeguards against tyranny.

> *"No Money shall be drawn from the Treasury, but in Consequence of Appropriations made by Law."* — **Article I, Section 9, U.S. Constitution**

That line means this. The President of the United States cannot spend money that Congress has not authorized. He also cannot refuse to spend money that Congress has authorized. The power of the purse belongs to the legislature, not the executive. This is not a technicality. It is the foundational mechanism through which Congress checks the executive. An executive that controls the money without legislative check controls everything.

The Framers understood this from direct experience. They had watched the British Crown fund its preferred policies by bypassing Parliament. They were not going to let that happen in the new Republic. So they wrote the Appropriations Clause into the Constitution before they even got to the structure of the executive branch. Money first. Authority second.

This chapter is about what happens when a President uses control of the money not to advance the interests of the United States but to benefit the foreign power that the preceding chapters have established as a functional enemy. It is about what happens when the financial mechanism of executive power is turned against the nation it was designed to serve.

And it is about what happens when the people who are supposed to catch that happening are removed from their positions specifically because they caught it happening.

□ □ □

Section One: The 2019 Ukraine Aid Freeze — Breaking the Law to Help the Enemy

In the summer of 2019, the Office of Management and Budget issued an internal hold on $391 million in military assistance for Ukraine. The hold was quiet. It was implemented through administrative channels without public announcement. When congressional staff began asking questions, the explanations changed repeatedly, a pattern that is itself evidence of consciousness of guilt.

Ukraine, at that moment, was in active military conflict with Russia in its eastern territories. Russian-backed forces had been attacking Ukrainian lines in the Donbas region since 2014. The $391 million in assistance was not a foreign aid payment in the general sense. It was a specific military package, congressionally authorized with bipartisan support, that included Javelin anti-tank missiles, radar systems, training support, and military equipment, designed to give Ukrainian forces the capability to defend themselves against the Russian-backed offensive that was actively killing Ukrainian soldiers.

Congress had authorized the money. The Constitution required it to be spent. The White House withheld it anyway.

The Legal Finding

The Government Accountability Office, a nonpartisan congressional watchdog that exists specifically to evaluate whether executive branch conduct complies with the law, investigated the Ukraine aid freeze. Its January 2020 report reached a conclusion that was unambiguous in its legal language.

The OMB had violated the Impoundment Control Act of 1974. Not arguably violated. Not potentially violated. Violated.

The Impoundment Control Act was passed specifically in response to a previous presidency's attempt to exercise the same kind of unilateral control over congressional appropriations. Congress passed it to make clear, in the most explicit statutory language available, that the executive branch does not have the authority to refuse to spend funds that Congress has authorized. The GAO's January 2020 finding established, as a matter of documented legal fact, that the White House had broken that law.

The False Justification and the Sworn Testimony That Destroyed It

The stated justification for the Ukraine aid freeze was concern about Ukrainian corruption. That justification was given to the press, to Congress, and to allied governments. It was the public explanation for conduct that the GAO had found violated federal law.

Then the witnesses testified under oath. And the sworn testimony dismantled the justification with a consistency that four independent witnesses produced independently.

Ambassador William Taylor, the senior American diplomatic official in Ukraine during the period of the freeze, testified that no corruption concerns had been raised through normal diplomatic channels during the period in question. If corruption concerns were the real reason for the freeze, Ambassador Taylor, as the senior American official on the ground in Ukraine, would have been aware of those concerns. He was not, because they did not exist in the form the justification claimed.

Dr. Fiona Hill, the National Security Council's senior director for Europe and Russia and one of the most qualified Russia experts in the United States government, testified that the corruption pretext was not the actual reason for the hold. She was in the room. She had access to the internal deliberations. And she testified, under oath, that the stated justification did not reflect the actual reason.

Ambassador Gordon Sondland, who had donated one million dollars to the Trump inaugural committee and had been appointed European Union Ambassador specifically because of his political loyalty, testified about what the aid was actually conditioned on.

> *"Was there a quid pro quo? As I testified previously, with regard to the requested White House call and White House meeting, the answer is yes."*
> **— Ambassador Gordon Sondland, House Intelligence Committee testimony, November 2019**

A false justification for conduct that independently violated federal law is not a mistake. It is a cover-up. And a cover-up is the specific legal indicator of consciousness of guilt, the awareness that the underlying conduct was legally indefensible and required a false explanation to survive public scrutiny.

□ □ □

Section Two: What 55 Days Meant on the Battlefield — The Cramer Analysis

The Supreme Court's Cramer standard requires that the aid be actual, not theoretical. It is not enough to show that an act could potentially have helped an enemy. The act must have actually advanced the enemy's mission.

This is the legally essential question for the Ukraine aid freeze: did the freeze actually help Russia?

The answer requires us to leave the legal analysis for a moment and go to eastern Ukraine in the summer of 2019.

The Battlefield Reality

During the 55 days that the Ukraine aid freeze was in effect, from the time the hold was implemented until it was finally released under congressional and public pressure, Russian-backed forces in the Donbas did not pause their operations. They did not stand down while the administrative hold was processed. They continued to probe Ukrainian defensive lines. They continued to conduct artillery operations. They continued to press against the positions that Ukrainian forces were trying to hold with the resources they had.

The Javelin anti-tank missiles that Congress had authorized for Ukraine, specifically because Russian-backed forces were using armored vehicles against Ukrainian positions, were sitting in a warehouse in the United States while those armored vehicles operated against Ukrainian lines. The radar systems that would have allowed Ukrainian forces to detect and respond to incoming artillery were not delivered. The training support that would have improved Ukrainian tactical effectiveness was delayed.

Under the Cramer standard, Aid and Comfort is measured by the benefit received by the enemy. Russia received 55 days of operational freedom on the Ukrainian front lines, during which the weapons Congress had specifically authorized to constrain Russian-backed aggression were not on the battlefield. That is not potential aid. That is actual aid. It is measured in days of unhindered operational activity by the forces of the identified enemy.

Laura Cooper, the Deputy Assistant Secretary of Defense responsible for Ukraine policy, testified before Congress about something that made the actual-aid analysis even more concrete. Ukraine knew about the hold almost immediately after it was implemented. The signal of American unreliability was sent before a single Ukrainian soldier knew whether the weapons would arrive or not. The strategic damage of the freeze was not only the delayed weapons. It was the message the freeze sent to Ukraine, to Russia, and to every ally watching: that American military commitments could be conditional on political favors to the American President.

Under Cramer, aid is measured by what the enemy actually receives. Russia received 55 days of unhindered operational freedom on the Ukrainian front lines, plus a strategic signal that American military commitments to nations resisting Russian aggression were negotiable. That is actual aid. That is actual comfort. The weapons were delayed. The signal was immediate.

□ □ □

Section Three: The Pentagon Diversion — Military Readiness as a Political Instrument

The Ukraine aid freeze was not an isolated instance of executive control over congressionally appropriated national security funds. It was part of a pattern. And patterns, under the Kawakita standard, are the evidence from which treasonous intent is inferred.

In 2019, the same year as the Ukraine aid freeze, the administration redirected $3.6 billion in military construction funds from their congressionally authorized purposes to the construction of a border wall. The Department of Defense Inspector General documented the diversion. The funds came from military readiness programs, housing construction for military families, and infrastructure projects at bases around the world.

Congress had not authorized the redirection. The Constitution required congressional appropriation for any specific military expenditure. The money was moved anyway, without congressional authorization, based on the President's declaration of a national emergency that courts repeatedly found to be legally deficient.

What the Diversion Actually Cut

The $3.6 billion did not come from an undefined pool of excess military spending. It came from specific programs that had been specifically funded for specific purposes by the specific votes of specific members of Congress. Military readiness programs that kept combat units at operational effectiveness were cut. Housing construction for military families at bases across the United States and around the world was suspended. Infrastructure projects at overseas installations, including projects that supported the American military presence in Europe and the Pacific, were defunded.

In the context of this book's broader argument, the overseas infrastructure cuts carry specific significance. The American military presence in Europe, the forward-deployed forces, the bases, the infrastructure, the logistics networks, is the physical embodiment of the Article 5 commitment that Chapter 6 established as NATO's deterrence mechanism. Cutting the infrastructure that supports that presence does not merely delay construction projects. It signals to both allies and adversaries that American military commitment to European defense is subject to redirection for domestic political purposes.

Under the Haupt standard, an act performed with knowledge of the enemy's objectives, that advances those objectives, is an overt act of aid and comfort regardless of the stated justification. The stated justification for the Pentagon fund diversion was border security. The effect was the weakening of military readiness and the defunding of the infrastructure that supports the American military presence in Europe. The beneficiary of that weakening, in the context of the documented pattern established in preceding chapters, was Russia.

□ □ □

Section Four: The 2025 Reprise — When a Crime Repeated Is No Longer a Mistake

The 2019 Ukraine aid freeze was investigated. It produced a GAO finding of a legal violation. It produced sworn congressional testimony that dismantled the false justification. It produced an impeachment of the President of the United States. The Senate acquitted along party lines.

And then it happened again.

In early 2025, at the beginning of the second term, the administration suspended military assistance to Ukraine again. Not for 55 days this time. Indefinitely. Ukraine was no longer in a limited conflict in its eastern territories. Ukraine was engaged in a full-scale war against a Russian military invasion that had begun in 2022 and that had produced the largest European land war since World War II. The military assistance Congress had authorized for Ukraine in 2025 was specifically intended to help Ukraine defend against that invasion.

The suspension was implemented through executive action rather than legislation. Congress had authorized the assistance. The President declined to deliver it. The same constitutional structure that the GAO had found violated in 2019 was violated again, at larger scale, with larger strategic consequences, against a Ukraine that was now fighting for its territorial survival rather than for contested positions in a regional conflict.

The Kawakita Pattern

The Kawakita standard permits the inference of treasonous intent from the pattern of conduct over time. The relevant question is not whether any single act is individually sufficient to establish treasonous intent. The relevant question is whether the pattern, viewed as a whole, supports the inference that the conscious objective was to advance the enemy's mission.

A President who freezes military aid to a nation resisting Russian military aggression in 2019, is caught, investigated, and impeached for it, is acquitted along party lines, and then repeats the same conduct in 2025 at larger scale and with full knowledge of the legal conclusions the 2019 freeze had produced, is not making a mistake. A mistake is something you stop doing when you learn it is wrong. A strategy is something you repeat when it has been temporarily interrupted.

The 2019 freeze and the 2025 suspension are the same act, performed twice, by the same actor, against the same nation, for the benefit of the same adversary. The only difference is scale. Under Kawakita, the repetition of the same conduct after documented legal consequences is the strongest available evidence that the intent behind the conduct was conscious and deliberate rather than inadvertent.

A President who repeats an illegal act after being caught, investigated, impeached, and acquitted for it is not making a policy judgment. He is executing a

strategy. The strategy's consistent beneficiary across two instances, separated by years, is Russia. That consistency is the Kawakita inference of treasonous intent.

□ □ □

Section Five: The Inspector General Firings — You Remove the Smoke Detectors When You Are Planning a Fire

The inspectors general of the federal government are the internal oversight mechanism of the executive branch. They are independent officials, appointed through a formal process, whose statutory obligation is to investigate fraud, waste, and abuse within the agencies they oversee and to report their findings to both the executive branch and Congress. They are not merely bureaucrats. They are the institutional mechanism through which the separation of powers operates at the granular level of agency conduct.

Congress relies on inspector general reports to exercise its constitutional oversight function. When an executive branch agency is violating the law, when appropriated funds are being misused, when officials are exceeding their authority, the inspector general is the first line of detection. Without that detection, Congress cannot exercise oversight. Without congressional oversight, the executive branch operates without accountability.

Between April and May of 2020, the President fired or attempted to remove multiple inspectors general across the national security apparatus. The timing was not coincidental. It followed the GAO's finding that the Ukraine aid freeze had violated the Impoundment Control Act. It followed the first impeachment proceedings. It followed a period in which the inspector general system had been performing exactly the function it was designed to perform: detecting and reporting executive branch conduct that violated the law.

Michael Atkinson: Fired for Following the Law

Intelligence Community Inspector General Michael Atkinson was fired specifically because he had forwarded a whistleblower complaint about the Ukraine aid freeze to Congress. His legal obligation was clear. Federal whistleblower statutes required him to forward the complaint to the congressional intelligence committees. He did what the law required.

He was fired for it.

The legal significance of that firing is precise and important. Atkinson was not fired for poor performance. He was not fired for insubordination or misconduct. He was fired for performing his statutory legal obligation in a case that implicated the President's own conduct. The firing was the executive branch's attempt to use personnel power to prevent the operation of the legal oversight system that the Framers designed to keep the executive branch accountable to the law.

Steve Linick: Fired During an Active Investigation

State Department Inspector General Steve Linick was fired while his office was actively investigating the conduct of Secretary of State Mike Pompeo. The investigation concerned the alleged misuse of State Department resources for personal purposes. Linick had also been involved in producing records relevant to the first impeachment proceedings.

He was fired while the investigation was ongoing. The investigation did not conclude. The findings were not completed. The accountability mechanism was terminated before it could produce its output.

The Pattern and Its Legal Significance

The Atkinson and Linick firings were not isolated events. They were part of a documented pattern of inspector general removals across the national security apparatus during the same period in which the Ukraine aid freeze, the Pentagon fund diversion, and the Oval Office intelligence disclosure documented in Chapter 5 were subjects of congressional and investigative scrutiny.

The smoke detector analogy, used in the constitutional law analysis that informed this chapter's research, captures the legal significance precisely. You do not remove smoke detectors because you are concerned about false alarms. Smoke detectors produce false alarms occasionally, and the appropriate response to a false alarm is to investigate why it triggered and to adjust the detection parameters. You remove smoke detectors when you are planning a fire and you do not want it detected.

The inspector general firings, timed as they were to the period of maximum legal scrutiny of the conduct documented in this chapter, are consciousness of guilt evidence of the highest order. They are the executive branch's attempt to remove the institutional detection mechanism before it could complete its reporting function on conduct that the executive branch understood to be legally indefensible.

Under the Kawakita standard, intent is inferred from conduct. An administration that removes inspectors general during active investigations of its own conduct is an administration that knows its conduct will not survive scrutiny. That knowledge is the awareness of guilt. And awareness of guilt is the evidence of the intent the treason statute requires.

□ □ □

Section Six: The Legal Synthesis — When Usurpation of the Purse Becomes Adherence to the Enemy

The Ukraine aid freeze, the Pentagon fund diversion, the 2025 suspension, and the inspector general firings are individually serious legal violations. Each constitutes, on its own, documented evidence of executive misconduct that rises to the level of statutory and constitutional breach. The Impoundment Control Act was violated twice. The Appropriations Clause was violated. The inspection and oversight function of the federal government was systematically dismantled.

But this book is not making the case for statutory violations. It is making the case for treason. And the step from statutory violation to treason requires the legal synthesis that this section provides.

From Domestic Crime to Constitutional Crime

A President who withholds aid in defiance of a congressional appropriation is not exercising executive discretion. He is acting as a sole decision-maker in a constitutional republic that was designed, at every level of its structure, to prevent exactly that concentration of power. The Appropriations Clause, the Impoundment Control Act, the inspector general system, the congressional oversight function, all of these mechanisms exist to ensure that no single person in the executive branch can unilaterally control national security resources without legislative check.

When that usurpation of the legislative check delivers a strategic advantage to the nation's primary documented adversary, the domestic crime of impoundment becomes the constitutional crime of adherence to enemies. The mechanism is financial. The method is administrative. But the effect is military, and the beneficiary is Russia.

The method was financial. The effect was military. The beneficiary was Russia.

That three-part structure is the legal bridge between the Impoundment Control Act and Article III, Section 3. The Impoundment Control Act violation establishes the unlawfulness of the conduct. The military effect on Ukraine's defensive capacity establishes the actual aid under the Cramer standard. And the beneficiary, Russia, the nation whose primary strategic objective includes the weakening of Ukraine's military resistance to Russian aggression, establishes the enemy that received the aid and comfort.

The Cumulative Pattern

The financial betrayal documented in this chapter does not stand alone. It is part of the cumulative pattern that the Kawakita standard permits the jury to evaluate as a whole.

The Russia alignment documented in Chapter 5, the NATO deconstruction documented in Chapter 6, the Iran war nexus documented in Chapter 7, and the financial betrayal documented in this chapter all share the same structure. The act appears, on its surface, to be an executive policy decision within the scope of presidential authority. The stated justification is facially plausible. And then the sworn testimony dismantles the justification, the legal findings establish the violation, and the strategic beneficiary of the violation is consistently, without exception, Russia.

No single chapter in this book presents a case that is, by itself, beyond reasonable doubt. That is the nature of the cumulative pattern argument, and this book has acknowledged that from its Legal Introduction. The case is the pattern. The pattern is the proof. And the pattern, evaluated against the Cramer, Haupt, and Kawakita standards that this book has applied consistently across every chapter, points in one direction.

The power of the purse was given to Congress because the Framers understood that an executive who controls the money controls the nation's fate. When that control is exercised not in service of the nation but in service of its adversary, the domestic constitutional violation becomes the constitutional crime of treason. Not because the money was stolen. Because of who benefited when it was withheld.

> **THE WITNESSES:** *Ambassador William Taylor testified before the House Intelligence Committee that no corruption concerns had been raised through normal diplomatic channels during the period of the Ukraine aid freeze. Dr. Fiona Hill, National Security Council senior director for Europe and Russia, testified that the corruption pretext was not the actual reason for the hold. Ambassador Gordon Sondland confirmed the existence of a quid pro quo in sworn testimony. Laura Cooper, Deputy Assistant Secretary of Defense for Ukraine policy, testified that Ukraine knew about the hold almost immediately after it was implemented, establishing that the strategic signal of American unreliability was delivered before the military impact was felt. The Government Accountability Office's January 2020 report establishing the Impoundment Control Act violation is a primary-source public document. Intelligence Community Inspector General Michael Atkinson's firing, and the specific statutory obligation he was fulfilling when he forwarded the whistleblower complaint, is documented in the congressional record and in the written notification the President was required to provide. State Department Inspector General Steve Linick's firing during an active investigation is documented in State Department records and in the congressional correspondence surrounding his removal.*

□ □ □

The next chapter asks a question that this chapter's conclusion raises naturally. If the financial mechanism of executive power can be used as a weapon against the nation's own national security interests, what happens to the social infrastructure that keeps the nation resilient enough to defend itself? What happens to the population's health, housing, and economic security when the same pattern of resource misappropriation is turned on the domestic safety net?

The answer is documented in the numbers that Chapter 1 introduced and that the next chapter examines in their full legal and constitutional context.

□ □ □

Chapter Nine

Monetizing the Presidency: The Emoluments, the Crypto, and the Corruption Motive

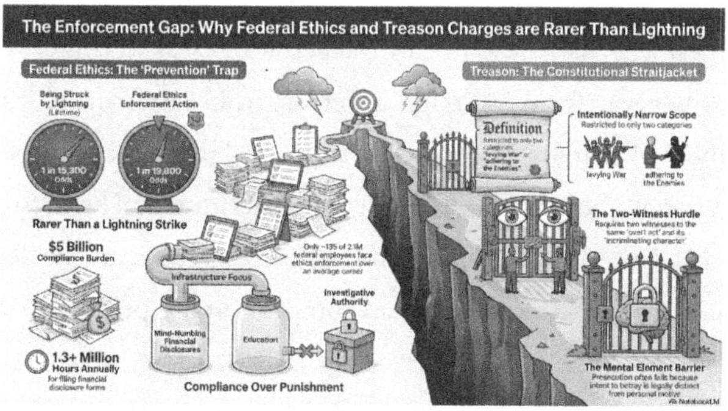

The Framers worried about a specific kind of corruption. Not the ordinary, petty corruption of an official taking a bribe for a favorable permit. They worried about something grander and more dangerous: a President whose personal financial interests were so entangled with foreign governments that his policy decisions could not be trusted to reflect the interests of the United States.

They had watched this happen. Not in the abstract. In the monarchies and court systems of Europe, foreign payments to officials were the standard mechanism through which foreign governments purchased influence over the policies of their adversaries and competitors. A minister who received annual payments from the French court was not merely taking a gift. He was acquiring a financial dependence on France's continued goodwill that corrupted every judgment he made about policy toward France.

The Framers wrote two provisions into the Constitution specifically to prevent this.

> *"No Person holding any Office of Profit or Trust under them, shall, without the Consent of the Congress, accept of any present, Emolument, Office, or Title, of any kind whatever, from any King, Prince, or foreign State."* — **Article I, Section 9, Foreign Emoluments Clause**

And in Article II, Section 1, they barred the President from receiving any emolument from the United States or any of the states beyond the fixed presidential salary established by Congress.

The reason for these provisions was not abstract ethics. It was strategic. A President who receives financial benefits from a foreign government has a financial interest in maintaining the goodwill of that government. That financial interest corrupts the President's judgment on every policy question involving that government. The corruption does not have to be explicit. There does not have to be a spoken agreement. The dependence itself is sufficient to corrupt, because the human mind naturally protects the sources of its financial security.

The Framers had watched this happen in European monarchies for centuries. They were not going to let it happen in America.

They tried.

□ □ □

Section One: The Hotel Era — When Foreign Governments Bought Rooms

During both terms, the Trump Organization continued to operate hotels, golf courses, and other commercial properties. The President did not divest from these businesses. He did not place them in a blind trust, which has been the standard practice through which modern presidents separated their private financial interests from their public duties. He placed them in a revocable trust managed by his sons, a trust he could access at any time, to which he remained financially connected, and whose revenues flowed to his family throughout his presidency.

The result was a documented pattern of foreign governmental patronage that began within days of the inauguration and continued through both terms.

The Documented Payments

The Saudi Arabian government booked large blocks of rooms at the Trump International Hotel in Washington, D.C. during periods when Saudi Arabia was actively seeking American diplomatic and military support for its foreign policy objectives, including the blockade of Qatar. Kuwaiti officials moved their annual national day reception from the Four Seasons Hotel, where they had traditionally held it, to Trump's Washington hotel following the inauguration. Documented stays and events by diplomatic missions from Malaysia, Turkey, the Philippines, and multiple other nations generated millions of dollars in revenue flowing to the President's family businesses while those governments' relationships with the United States were active matters of executive policy.

The financial conflict is not an allegation. It is documented in hotel financial records, diplomatic correspondence, and congressional investigative findings. This is not a conspiracy theory. It is a ledger entry.

Dismantling the Fair Market Value Defense

The most predictable defense to the emoluments analysis is this: they paid for the rooms, this is commerce, and charging a fair market rate for a hotel room is not a constitutional violation.

This defense fails, and it fails for a specific reason that goes to the heart of what the Emoluments Clause was designed to prevent.

The Emoluments Clause is triggered by the source of the payment, not the amount. The Framers did not write that no President shall accept a payment from a foreign sovereign in excess of fair market value. They wrote that no President shall accept any present, emolument, or title of any kind from any king, prince, or foreign state. Any. Of any kind.

The reason is precisely the dependence argument. Whether a foreign sovereign pays rack rate, premium rate, or below market rate for hotel rooms, the act of a foreign sovereign putting money into the President's pocket creates the financial relationship the Framers feared. The President now has a financial interest in that sovereign's continued goodwill. Whether the rate was fair or not is irrelevant to the constitutional concern.

Furthermore, the hotel bookings were frequently not ordinary market transactions at all. Many involved bookings of blocks of rooms that went partially or entirely unused, events moved from other venues specifically to direct money to the President's business, and diplomatic missions choosing Trump properties over comparable alternatives in circumstances where the choice of venue carried obvious political significance. This was not commerce. It was, in the language the Framers would have recognized, a present from a foreign state.

□ □ □

Section Two: The Domestic Emoluments — Stealing From the Taxpayer

The Foreign Emoluments Clause receives most of the attention in this chapter's analysis. But Article II, Section 1 contains a second prohibition that this book's opening draft identified and then set aside. The domestic emoluments clause deserves its own analysis, because it establishes something legally important about the pattern of financial self-dealing that runs through both terms.

The domestic emoluments clause bars the President from receiving any emolument from the United States or any of the states beyond the constitutionally established salary. The purpose is identical to the foreign emoluments clause: to prevent financial dependence on the source of the payment from corrupting the President's judgment. In the domestic context, the concern is that a President who profits from the federal government or from state governments has a financial interest in the decisions of those governments that corrupts his executive judgment.

The GSA Lease

The Trump International Hotel in Washington, D.C. occupies the Old Post Office building on Pennsylvania Avenue. The building is owned by the federal government and managed by the General Services Administration. The Trump Organization leased the building from the GSA before the 2016 election. After the election, the Trump Organization was simultaneously the President of the United States and the lessee of a federal government building, paying rent to an agency whose leadership the President appointed and whose budget the President's administration controlled.

The GSA continued the lease. Legal scholars across the political spectrum identified the arrangement as a potential domestic emoluments violation. The revenue flowing from the Trump Organization's operation of the hotel included profits generated by the very diplomatic missions, foreign governments, and political allies whose patronage was directly stimulated by the President's political position.

Why This Matters for the Treason Analysis

The domestic emoluments violation serves a specific function in this book's broader argument. It establishes what lawyers call consciousness of guilt about the financial self-dealing pattern as a whole.

A President who is willing to violate the domestic emoluments clause, the provision that prohibits him from enriching himself through his relationship with the federal government he controls, for the relatively modest financial benefit of a hotel lease, has already crossed the mental threshold required to betray the country for larger geopolitical gains. The smallness of the domestic violation actually makes it more legally significant, not less. It demonstrates that the financial self-interest is not merely opportunistic. It is habitual. It is a feature of conduct, not a one-time exception.

Under the Kawakita standard, intent is inferred from the pattern of conduct over time. A pattern of financial self-dealing that includes the domestic emoluments violation, the foreign emoluments violations, the crypto arrangements, and the specific policy decisions that correlate with those financial relationships, is the pattern from which the Kawakita inference of treasonous motive is drawn.

□ □ □

Section Three: The Crypto Dimension — Why the Second Term Was Worse

The second term introduced a form of financial conflict that the Framers could not have anticipated but would certainly have recognized. The mechanism is new. The danger is identical.

World Liberty Financial, a cryptocurrency venture connected to the Trump family, sold tokens to investors including entities linked to foreign sovereign wealth funds. Foreign sovereign wealth funds are not ordinary investors. They are governmental entities, direct extensions of foreign state financial power, whose investment decisions serve the strategic objectives of the governments that control them. When a foreign sovereign wealth fund purchases tokens in a Trump family cryptocurrency venture during a period when that foreign government's relationship with the United States is an active matter of presidential policy, the constitutional concern is not merely a conflict of interest. It is a payment from a foreign state to the President's family while the President is making decisions that affect that foreign state.

That is the Emoluments Clause in its most direct form.

Why Crypto Is Worse Than Hotels: Transparency and Opacity

The hotel era operated in the relative sunlight of the existing financial disclosure system. Hotel revenues eventually appear on tax returns. Property assessments are public records. Congressional investigators can subpoena financial records and trace the flow of foreign governmental money into the Trump Organization's accounts.

Cryptocurrency transactions operate differently. Token purchases can be made through wallets whose ownership is pseudo-anonymous. Transactions in decentralized finance protocols can be obscured through layered arrangements that make tracing the original source of funds significantly more difficult than tracing a wire transfer from a foreign governmental hotel booking. The opacity is not accidental. It is a structural feature of the technology. And that structural opacity makes the detection and prosecution of emoluments violations significantly harder.

The Valuation Manipulation: A Force Multiplier for Leverage

The hotel payment model was straightforward. A foreign government paid X dollars for hotel rooms or events. X dollars flowed to the Trump Organization. The President had a financial interest in the continued goodwill of the government that paid X dollars.

The cryptocurrency payment model is a force multiplier for that same dynamic. Here is how it works.

The Trump family holds a large stake in the World Liberty Financial token. The token's market value depends on demand. When a foreign sovereign wealth fund makes a large purchase of the token, two things happen simultaneously. The fund transfers money to World Liberty Financial in exchange for the tokens it receives. And the large purchase increases market demand for the token, which increases the token's price, which increases the value of the Trump family's existing holdings by a multiple of the purchase price.

A foreign sovereign wealth fund that purchases $10 million in Trump family tokens does not merely transfer $10 million to the family. If the purchase inflates the token's value sufficiently, the family's existing holdings could increase in value by $50 million, $100 million, or more. The financial benefit to the family is not limited to the purchase price. It is amplified by the market mechanics of the token itself.

This is not a financial technicality. It is the Emoluments Clause problem in its most dangerous modern form. A foreign government that can provide the President's family with $100 million in financial benefit through a $10 million token purchase has acquired an order of magnitude more leverage over the President's policy decisions than the hotel era ever produced.

The hotel model was a payment. The crypto model is a force multiplier. A foreign sovereign wealth fund that understands tokenomics can provide the President's family with financial benefits that dwarf any hotel booking, at a fraction of the transparency cost, with significantly less legal exposure under existing disclosure frameworks. The Framers feared the dependence that foreign payments create.

The crypto model creates that dependence at a scale the Framers could not have imagined.

The Ongoing Financial Stake

There is one more dimension of the crypto arrangement that distinguishes it from the hotel bookings. A hotel stay is a one-time transaction. The foreign government books the rooms, pays for the rooms, and the transaction is complete. There is no ongoing financial relationship between the foreign government and the Trump Organization that depends on the foreign government's continued support.

A token purchase creates a different kind of financial relationship. The foreign sovereign wealth fund that purchases a stake in World Liberty Financial has an ongoing financial interest in the token's value. The Trump family has an ongoing financial interest in the token's value. Both parties now share a financial stake whose value depends on the same underlying market conditions. The President's family and the foreign government are not merely in a historical transaction. They are in an ongoing financial partnership whose mutual benefit depends on conditions that presidential policy can influence.

The ongoing financial stake is the ongoing financial dependence. And the ongoing financial dependence is the ongoing corruption of presidential judgment that the Emoluments Clause was written to prevent.

□ □ □

Section Four: The Foreign Agent Bridge — From Conflict of Interest to Agency

The preceding sections have analyzed the financial entanglements under the Emoluments Clause and 18 U.S.C. section 208, which prohibits government officials from participating in matters in which they have a personal financial interest. Both of these frameworks address conflict of interest: the President's judgment is corrupted by his financial stake in the foreign government's goodwill.

But there is a third legal framework that this chapter needs to address, because it takes the analysis one significant step further. 18 U.S.C. section 219 makes it a federal crime for a United States government official to act as an agent of a foreign principal.

The Distinction Between Influence and Agency

A conflict of interest means that the President's judgment is corrupted by his financial relationships. He may make decisions that favor foreign governments because those governments are enriching his family. The causation is indirect: the financial relationship affects the judgment, and the corrupted judgment affects the policy.

Agency is different and more direct. An official who acts as an agent of a foreign principal is not merely influenced by that principal. He is working for that principal. He is taking direction, advancing objectives, making decisions on behalf of a foreign government within the institutions of the American government. The financial relationship is not merely corrupting his judgment. It is the payment in an employment relationship.

The legal question that section 219 raises in the context of this chapter is this: at what point does the pattern of financial entanglements documented in this chapter, combined with the pattern of policy decisions that consistently benefit the foreign governments from whom those entanglements derive, shift from conflict of interest to agency?

The answer is a factual question for a jury. But the framework for asking it is established in section 219. And the pattern documented in this chapter, a pattern in which financial relationships with foreign governments correlate specifically with policy decisions favorable to those governments, is the factual record on which that question is based.

The Quid and the Quo: A Timeline of Convergence

To establish the agency argument under section 219, and to establish the motive argument under the treason analysis, the chapter must do more than document financial inflows on one side and policy decisions on the other. It must establish the correlation between them.

The correlation is established through the timeline.

Saudi Arabia booked rooms at the Trump International Hotel during the period when Saudi Arabia was seeking American support for its blockade of Qatar. The Trump administration broke with decades of American policy and sided with Saudi Arabia against Qatar, a country that hosts the largest American military base in the Middle East. The sequence: payment, then policy reversal favorable to the payer.

The Russia sanctions relief of March 5, 2026, documented in Chapter 5, occurred at the precise moment when Russia was receiving maximum financial benefit from the Iran war's energy market disruption. The timing: the policy action that benefited Russia occurred at the moment of Russia's maximum financial exposure to American sanctions. The sequence: maximum financial benefit available, then sanctions relief delivered.

The World Liberty Financial token purchases from entities linked to foreign sovereign wealth funds occurred during a period in which those sovereign wealth funds' home governments' relationships with the United States were active matters of presidential policy. The sequence: investment creating financial dependence, then policy decisions affecting the investing governments.

None of these sequences constitutes a proven quid pro quo in the legal sense that would require direct evidence of an explicit agreement. That is not what this chapter argues. What this chapter argues is that the correlation between financial entanglements and favorable policy outcomes is the pattern from which the Kawakita inference of corrupt motive is drawn. The jury does not have to find a signed contract. It has to find that the pattern is not coincidence.

□ □ □

Section Five: The Intent Versus Motive Problem — Why 'I Was Just Making Money' Is Not a Defense

The most predictable defense to this chapter's argument is not the fair market value argument addressed in Section One. It is a more fundamental objection.

He was not trying to betray his country. He was trying to make money. The financial entanglements were not motivated by a desire to benefit Russia or Saudi Arabia or any other foreign government. They were motivated by ordinary commercial greed, by the instinct of a businessman to extract maximum financial benefit from every opportunity his position presented. That is not treason. That is the American entrepreneurial spirit, applied, inappropriately, to the presidency.

The legal answer to this defense comes from a 1948 federal court decision called Chandler v. United States, and from the Supreme Court's subsequent affirmation of the same principle in Kawakita v. United States. And it is one of the most important legal principles in this entire book.

The Chandler Principle

Douglas Chandler was an American citizen who had moved to Germany before World War II. During the war, he broadcast Nazi propaganda for the German government. He was prosecuted for treason.

His defense was sincere. He genuinely believed, or claimed to believe, that his broadcasts served the ultimate welfare of the United States by exposing the dangers of international communism and Jewish influence in American politics. He was not trying to help Germany win the war. He was trying, in his own mind, to help America understand the truth.

The court rejected his defense with language that has been central to American treason jurisprudence ever since.

> *"Whether Chandler was 'sincere' in what he did, whether he had the heart of a patriot, is a matter that may be sifted out at the last Great Judgment Seat."* — **Chandler v. United States, 1st Circuit (1948)**

The law of treason is not concerned with whether the defendant's heart was pure. It is concerned with whether the defendant's act objectively provided aid and comfort to an enemy. If the act provides that aid, the defendant's sincere belief that the act served the national interest is not a legal defense. The court is not the last Great Judgment Seat. It evaluates conduct, not intentions.

The Application to Commercial Motive

Chandler believed he was a patriot. The defense in the case this book presents will argue that the financial entanglements were motivated not by patriotism but by commerce, that the President was not trying to betray his country but to make money.

Under the Chandler standard, this distinction is legally irrelevant.

The question is not why the President entered into financial relationships with foreign governments. The question is whether those financial relationships objectively created the dependence on foreign governmental goodwill that the Emoluments Clause was designed to prevent, and whether policy decisions were made in a manner consistent with serving that dependence rather than serving the national interest.

If the objective consequence of the financial entanglements was to corrupt the President's policy judgment in favor of foreign governments whose interests conflicted with American national security interests, the motive behind the entanglements is as legally irrelevant as Chandler's sincere belief in the patriotic value of Nazi propaganda.

The defendant's heart is a matter for the last Great Judgment Seat. The law of treason is concerned with what the defendant did and who benefited from it.

The Psychological Component: Desperation as Vulnerability

There is a dimension of this analysis that the editorial research for this chapter identified and that deserves its own treatment, because it addresses a question that the Chandler standard raises but does not answer.

If the motive behind the financial entanglements was commercial rather than ideological, why would a billionaire president sell out his country's interests for hotel revenues and token sales?

The answer, which the financial press has documented through reporting on the Trump Organization's debt obligations and the financial pressures of its various business ventures, is that the relationship between wealth and financial security is not always linear. A highly leveraged real estate empire with significant debt service obligations, operating in a volatile market, can face acute cash flow pressures that a simpler balance sheet would not produce. A family business that depends on the continued perception of brand value and the sustained flow of high-margin revenue, including from foreign governments, faces financial vulnerabilities that create dependence on the sources of that revenue.

Financial desperation, or even financial anxiety, is the condition that makes a person most susceptible to foreign financial leverage. A monarch with a full treasury is harder to buy than a king with creditors at the door. The Framers understood this. The Emoluments Clause is not merely about protecting the Republic from a President who wants to sell it. It is also about protecting the Republic from a President whose financial vulnerabilities make him susceptible to being purchased by those who want to buy it.

Whether the Trump Organization's financial position created that vulnerability is a factual question that the financial disclosure records, the German Deutsche Bank loan documents, and the tax records that have been partially disclosed would answer more fully than this book can from public information alone. What this book argues is that the question is legally relevant and that the Emoluments Clause was written with exactly this scenario in mind.

□ □ □

Section Six: The Legal Synthesis — Financial Entanglement as Evidence of Treasonous Motive

This chapter has established four distinct legal arguments, each of which contributes to the overall treason analysis in a specific way.

The Foreign Emoluments Clause violations document the specific financial flows from foreign governments to the President's family businesses during both terms. The fair market value defense has been dismantled. The constitutional violation is not about the amount. It is about the relationship.

The domestic emoluments violation establishes the pattern of financial self-dealing as habitual rather than exceptional. A President who enriches himself through his relationship with the federal government he controls, for relatively modest financial benefit, has already crossed the threshold that makes larger betrayals psychologically and morally available.

The crypto dimension documents the escalation of financial entanglement in the second term, with specific analysis of how token purchases by foreign sovereign wealth funds create financial leverage that multiplies the financial benefit to the family, creates an ongoing financial partnership rather than a one-time transaction, and operates with significantly less transparency than the hotel era.

The section 219 foreign agent bridge asks the question that the combination of financial entanglements and correlated policy decisions raises: at what point does the pattern shift from conflict of interest to agency?

None of these arguments, standing alone, constitutes treason. The emoluments violations are independent constitutional violations with their own legal analysis. The corruption motive argument is evidence of the intent element of the treason charge, not a substitute for the overt act analysis established in preceding chapters.

Their specific role in this book is evidence of motive. The treason argument, to establish the Kawakita inference of treasonous intent, requires a showing that the pattern of conduct documented in Chapters 4 through 8 was not coincidental alignment with Russian and other foreign interests, but intentional conduct undertaken with the purpose of advancing those interests. Financial entanglement with the foreign governments whose interests are served by that pattern provides the corrupt financial motive that transforms a pattern of alignment from plausible coincidence into intentional conduct.

Under Haupt, intent is the variable that transforms an otherwise ambiguous act into a treasonous one. The financial entanglements documented in this chapter are the evidence of what that intent was. The President had a financial interest in maintaining the goodwill of the foreign governments whose interests consistently benefited from his policy decisions. The Framers wrote the Emoluments Clause because they understood that financial interest corrupts policy judgment. When that corrupted policy judgment produces outcomes that advance the mission of an identified enemy, the financial corruption becomes the motive for the treason.

THE WITNESSES: *The Saudi government hotel bookings are documented in congressional investigative findings, hotel financial records* *disclosed in emoluments litigation, and diplomatic correspondence. The Kuwait national day reception move is documented in State Department communications and press reporting. The World Liberty Financial token purchases and their connection to foreign sovereign wealth funds are documented in blockchain transaction records, financial press reporting, and congressional investigation requests. The GSA Old Post Office lease and its domestic emoluments implications are documented in GSA lease records, congressional oversight correspondence, and legal filings in emoluments litigation. The financial press reporting on Trump Organization debt obligations is documented in Deutsche Bank records disclosed in congressional subpoena proceedings and in investigative reporting confirmed by multiple sources.*

□ □ □

The financial chapter closes here. The corruption motive has been established. The financial entanglements with foreign governments are documented. The Chandler standard has been applied to the motive defense.

The next chapter asks what it looks like when the same pattern of resource misappropriation documented in Chapter 8 is turned not outward toward foreign policy but inward toward the domestic population. What happens to the social infrastructure of a nation when the executive branch treats the federal budget not as the people's money but as a political instrument? And what does the resulting domestic devastation mean for the nation's capacity to defend itself against the foreign adversaries documented in Part II of this book?

□ □ □

Chapter Ten

The Economic Front: De-Dollarization, Budget Collapse, and the Weaponization of Poverty

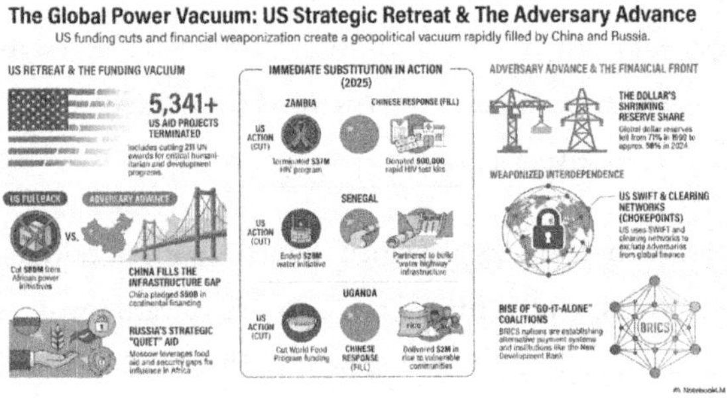

The Constitution requires that overt acts of treason actually give aid and comfort to the enemy. Under Cramer, the act must actually advance the enemy's mission. Every chapter in this book through Chapter 9 has documented acts whose connection to Russian benefit is direct: a presidential statement that gave Russia cover for its interference denial, a sanctions failure that reduced the cost of Russian election aggression, a battlefield aid freeze that gave Russian-backed forces 55 days of operational freedom, a NATO deconstruction that produced documented Russian military posture changes in the Baltic states.

This chapter argues something more sophisticated, and in some ways more legally significant.

It argues that domestic economic policy choices, choices about how to manage the dollar's global role, what to fund in the federal budget, and which populations to protect with social services, can satisfy the Cramer actual aid standard not through direct transfer to Russia but through the removal of the defensive infrastructure that protects the United States from Russian hybrid warfare.

The Gerasimov Doctrine does not merely describe what Russia will do to the United States. It describes what Russia needs the United States to do to itself. When domestic policy choices produce exactly the conditions that Russia's own published military doctrine identifies as the prerequisites for successful hybrid warfare against a Western democracy, and when those choices are made after the President has been briefed that those conditions are Russia's target, the Haupt standard applies. An act performed with knowledge of the enemy's objectives, that advances those objectives, is an overt act of aid and comfort regardless of the domestic policy label attached to it.

This chapter makes that case in three parts. The dollar's global dominance as a national security asset. The federal budget as the skeleton of American power. And the destruction of social services as the domestic execution of the Gerasimov playbook.

□ □ □

Section One: The Dollar — America's Greatest Strategic Weapon

Imagine you own the only gas station on a 500-mile highway. Every vehicle that wants to travel that road has to come to you. You set the price. You decide who gets fuel and who does not. You can refuse to serve troublemakers, and when you do, their economy effectively stalls on the side of the road. Your gas station is not just a business. It is power.

That is the United States dollar's role in the global economy.

Because the dollar is the world's reserve currency, the currency in which oil is priced, international contracts are settled, and foreign reserves are held, the United States has extraordinary strategic leverage that no other nation on earth possesses. The architecture operates through two specific mechanisms that military and intelligence strategists call the Panopticon Effect and the Chokepoint Effect.

The Panopticon Effect: Because the SWIFT messaging network handles more than 40 million international financial instructions daily, and because most of those instructions route through a handful of New York clearing banks, the United States can observe global financial flows with a comprehensiveness that no other nation can match. American intelligence has visibility into the economic activity of every nation whose financial institutions participate in the dollar-clearing system, which is virtually every nation on earth.

The Chokepoint Effect: Because most international dollar transactions clear through New York, the United States can cut any nation off from the global financial system by denying access to those clearing facilities. Iran, Russia, and North Korea have all experienced this in varying degrees. When the United States imposes systemic sanctions, it does not need military force to impose them. It only needs to instruct the New York clearing banks, and the target's economy is stranded.

This architecture is what makes American sanctions the most powerful non-military strategic tool in the history of international relations. And Russia has stated, publicly and repeatedly, that dismantling it is one of its primary strategic objectives.

"Russia did not want to give up the dollar as the reserve currency or means of payment, but it was forced to do it." — **Vladimir Putin, Russian President**

De-dollarization is other nations building their own gas stations. And every domestic policy choice that erodes the conditions under which dollar dominance is maintained advances Russia's primary stated objective.

The Weaponization Dilemma and How Specific Acts Accelerated It

The International Monetary Fund's documented data shows that the dollar's share of global reserves declined from 71 percent in 1999 to approximately 58 percent in 2024. That decline did not happen by accident. It happened because of policy choices that eroded the two foundations on which dollar dominance rests: the perceived neutrality of the dollar as a global public good, and the reliability of the United States as a stable financial partner whose commitments can be trusted.

The threat to default on United States debt through repeated debt ceiling crises is the most direct example. The dollar's reserve status rests on the full faith and credit of the American government. United States Treasury securities are the world's premier safe asset precisely because no one seriously believes the American government will default on them. When the President repeatedly threatened to allow a default as a political negotiating tactic, foreign central banks and reserve managers were required to evaluate, for the first time in the post-World War II era, whether U.S. Treasury securities were genuinely risk-free. Institutions that must provide absolute safety to their depositors cannot afford that uncertainty. The rational response to debt ceiling threats is to diversify reserves into assets whose safety does not depend on a political decision made in Washington.

Every time that diversification occurs, a portion of the demand for dollars that sustains the Chokepoint and Panopticon effects moves elsewhere. The gas station loses a customer. And lost customers, in the monetary hegemony model, are lost permanently because of the institutional inertia that makes switching costs so high. Once a foreign central bank has established reserve holdings in gold, yuan, or euros, the operational infrastructure, the accounting systems, the risk management frameworks, is sunk. The customer does not easily return.

Unpredictable tariff warfare produced the same effect through a different mechanism. When the United States imposes sweeping tariffs without strategic coherence, trading partners who cannot predict American commercial policy have a powerful incentive to build trade relationships, payment systems, and financial infrastructure that do not depend on dollar-denominated clearing. China's CIPS payment system, Russia's SPFS messaging alternative to SWIFT, and the BRICS Pay initiative are all responses, in part, to the perception that dollar-dependent financial infrastructure is vulnerable to American political unpredictability.

> *"America's economic strength is our greatest strategic asset. The dollar's reserve status is not separate from our national security. It is a component of it."* — **2022 U.S. National Security Strategy**

The President received the 2022 National Security Strategy. It told him explicitly that the dollar's reserve status is a component of national security. Every

subsequent policy choice that eroded that reserve status, the debt ceiling threats, the tariff unpredictability, the sanctions overreach that accelerated alternative payment system development, was made with knowledge of the national security cost. Under the Haupt standard, that knowledge is the evidence of intent.

□ □ □

Section Two: The Federal Budget — The Skeleton of American Power

A nation's federal budget is the structural skeleton of its power. Military strategists do not think of national power as merely the size of the army or the number of nuclear warheads. They think of it as the full spectrum of governmental capacity: military readiness, diplomatic presence, intelligence gathering, public health resilience, scientific capability, and the soft power projection that shapes the perceptions and allegiances of populations around the world.

Cut the skeleton, and everything collapses inward.

The Department of Government Efficiency, operating in the second term, oversaw the elimination of tens of thousands of federal positions across national security, intelligence, diplomatic, and regulatory agencies. The cuts were documented, specific, and consequential in ways that bear directly on the treason analysis in this book.

The USAID Vacuum: Where American Withdrawal Becomes Russian Advance

The United States Agency for International Development was effectively dismantled in 2025. Five thousand, three hundred and forty-one foreign aid projects were terminated. The programs that were eliminated had served a function that military strategists understand precisely: they created institutional presence, economic relationships, and popular goodwill in developing nations that competed directly with Russian and Chinese influence operations.

The connection between USAID cuts and Russian influence expansion is not theoretical. It is documented in country after country with specific dates and specific dollar amounts.

In South Africa, when the United States cut funding for HIV and AIDS programs in 2025, China stepped in within months with $3.49 million for prevention programs. The Chinese presence that replaced the American one came with the political obligations that Chinese foreign assistance routinely carries. In Zambia, after the United States terminated a $37 million HIV and AIDS program, China donated 500,000 test kits. In Senegal, the end of a United States water infrastructure initiative led to a Chinese-funded water highway project. In each case, the pattern was identical. American withdrawal created a vacuum. Chinese presence filled it. And the populations that experienced the transition drew the obvious conclusion about which nation's government cared about their welfare.

Russia's entry into these vacuums was less transactional and more strategic. In Nigeria, Russia expanded its influence specifically by praising the government's counterterrorism efforts while Washington issued condemnations. Russian state media amplified that contrast. In multiple Nigerian states, protesters waved Russian flags.

> *"We are waving the Russian flag because Tinubu's government is not listening to us. Russian presidents always support African nations' development, unlike other nations."* — **Lawal Kodo, 28-year-old protester in Kano, Nigeria, 2025**

That young man in Kano did not become a Russian asset through a recruitment operation. He became one through the consistent experience of American abandonment and Russian presence. USAID programs had made the American government visible, present, and useful in his community. When those programs disappeared, the American government became invisible. The USAID cut did not merely save money. It surrendered the territory of human allegiance that American soft power had spent decades acquiring.

Under the Cramer standard, the aid must be actual. Russia's documented expansion of influence in the specific communities where USAID programs were eliminated is the actual aid. It is measured in polling data, in flag-waving protests, and in the documented expansion of Russian media penetration in the Global South. The budget cut was the mechanism. Russia's strategic advance was the result.

The Intelligence and Cybersecurity Gaps

USAID was the most visible cut. It was not the most operationally dangerous one.

The Cybersecurity and Infrastructure Security Agency, the federal body responsible for defending American critical infrastructure against cyberattacks of the kind Russia has been documented to conduct, faced budget reductions that the cybersecurity professional community publicly described as alarming. The same Russian intelligence services whose SolarWinds attack penetrated the Treasury Department, the Commerce Department, and the Department of Homeland Security, documented in Chapter 4, continued their probing operations against American infrastructure throughout this period.

Cutting the defenders of the power grid while the identified enemy is actively probing the power grid is not fiscal responsibility. It is sabotage executed through a budget process.

State Department reductions eliminated embassy and consulate positions that gather human intelligence, maintain alliance relationships, and provide the diplomatic presence through which American interests are advanced and Russian influence is contested. The Centers for Disease Control and the National Institutes of Health saw reductions that weakened biosurveillance capacity, a national security function whose importance was formally recognized in national security doctrine after the September 11 attacks established that asymmetric threats, including biological ones, could damage the United States more effectively than conventional military force.

> *"Russians want to show that the West is failing; when there is a legal geopolitical vacuum, Russia moves in."* — **Shada Islam, Independent EU Analyst**

The Gerasimov Doctrine describes the destruction of an adversary's institutional capacity as a primary strategic objective of hybrid warfare. The federal budget cuts documented in this section destroyed institutional capacity across every

dimension that Gerasimov doctrine identifies: diplomatic presence, intelligence gathering, public health resilience, and soft power projection. A budget that executes the Gerasimov doctrine's strategic objectives is not merely bad fiscal policy. It is Aid and Comfort delivered through an appropriations process.

□ □ □

Section Three: The Weaponization of Poverty — Domestic Cuts as Gerasimov Execution

The 2022 National Security Strategy formally identifies domestic resilience, including economic security and public health, as a component of American national power. Military strategists understand something that domestic policy debates often obscure: a population that is hungry, sick, uneducated, and financially desperate is easier to radicalize, harder to mobilize for national defense, and more vulnerable to foreign influence operations.

This is not a theoretical observation. It is the explicit content of Russian hybrid warfare doctrine.

What the Gerasimov Doctrine Actually Says

General Valery Gerasimov, the Chief of the Russian General Staff, published the doctrine that bears his name in 2013. This book has cited it throughout as evidence of Russian hostile intent. But in this chapter, the specific content of the doctrine is more important than the general fact of its existence.

> *"The very 'rules of war' have changed. The role of nonmilitary means of achieving political and strategic goals has grown, and, in many cases, they have exceeded the power of force of weapons in their effectiveness."* — **General Valery Gerasimov, Russian Chief of the General Staff, 2013**

Gerasimov described a model in which the primary battlefield is not geographic territory but the social and psychological cohesion of the adversary population. The doctrine explicitly describes the exploitation of domestic social divisions, economic inequality, racial tension, and healthcare inequity as primary tools for weakening Western democracies without military engagement. It identifies a ratio of four nonmilitary actions to every one military action as the optimal formula for what it calls influence over destruction and inner decay over annihilation.

The Senate Intelligence Committee's Volume 2 report documented that Russian social media operations specifically targeted economically anxious communities, healthcare debates, and social justice movements. Not because these were random topics that happened to generate engagement. Because these were the vulnerabilities that Russian doctrine had identified as most susceptible to exploitation.

Russia does not need to invade a country to destabilize it. It needs the country to do the work itself.

The Policy Choices That Did the Work

During the period documented in this book, more than 25 million Americans lost Medicaid coverage. Federal housing assistance programs were reduced. The supplemental nutrition assistance program faced repeated legislative threats. Public school funding formulas were restructured in ways that deepened the resource disparities between wealthy and low-income communities. Opioid treatment programs, which had been one of the documented targets of Russian disinformation campaigns designed to deepen American healthcare despair, were defunded in multiple states following federal funding cuts.

The Russian disinformation infrastructure was simultaneously amplifying these developments. Senate Intelligence Committee findings documented that Russian social media operations specifically targeted communities experiencing healthcare cuts, using those cuts as evidence for the narrative that the American government had abandoned its citizens. When USAID disappeared from African communities, Russian state media amplified the abandonment. When American healthcare programs contracted, Russian social media amplified the despair.

This synchronization is the evidence of coordination or willful alignment that the editorial research for this chapter identified as legally significant. When a President's domestic policy choices consistently produce exactly the social conditions that Russian hybrid warfare doctrine identifies as necessary for successful influence operations, and when Russian information operations consistently amplify those conditions in the specific communities most affected by those policy choices, the Kawakita inference of treasonous intent applies to the domestic policy choices just as it applies to the foreign policy choices documented in preceding chapters.

The Force Multiplier Effect

The specific legal argument this chapter makes is not that cutting Medicaid is treason. That would prove too much. Domestic policy disagreements about the appropriate size and scope of social programs are legitimate political disputes that this book deliberately does not enter.

The legal argument is narrower and more precise. It is that domestic policy choices which predictably and documentably produce the specific social conditions that Russian hybrid warfare doctrine requires for successful operations against the United States, made by a President who has been briefed that those conditions are Russia's target, and made in the context of the comprehensive pattern of conduct documented in Chapters 4 through 9, become part of the Aid and Comfort analysis.

Under Haupt, the intent transforms the act. A domestic policy choice that would be merely contested if made by a President with no other connection to the pattern of Russian alignment documented in this book becomes legally significant when made by a President whose comprehensive conduct demonstrates the Kawakita inference of treasonous intent. The domestic cuts are not evidence of treason in isolation. They are evidence of the systemic dismantlement of every category of American defensive capacity that Russian doctrine identifies as the target.

□ □ □

Section Four: The Policy Defense Rebuttal — Why 'I Thought It Was Good Policy' Does Not Close the Case

This chapter anticipates the most fundamental objection to its entire argument, and it must address that objection directly before reaching the legal synthesis.

The objection is this: politicians cut budgets. Presidents change trade policies. Administrations restructure federal agencies. Economic policy disagreements are the ordinary substance of democratic politics. Calling economic policy choices treason is not a legal argument. It is the criminalization of political disagreement, exactly what the Framers wrote the Treason Clause to prevent.

This objection is serious and deserves a serious answer.

The Distinction the Law Draws

The Treason Clause was written to prevent the criminalization of political dissent. The Framers specifically did not want Congress or the executive to use the charge of treason to prosecute political opponents for holding unpopular views or advocating for losing policies. Ex parte Bollman, Cramer, and every major treason case since has enforced this protection through the high evidentiary bar of the two-witness rule and the requirement of an overt act that actually advances the enemy's mission.

The policy defense is legally available when the policy maker lacks knowledge that the policy advances an enemy's mission. A President who cuts foreign aid because he genuinely and sincerely believes that American resources are better deployed domestically, without knowledge that the cuts will advance Russian strategic objectives, is making a policy decision that this book does not call treason.

The legal distinction is created by knowledge. Specifically, by the briefings the President received.

The Intelligence Community Warnings

The 2022 National Security Strategy told the President, in the most explicit language available in an official government document, that domestic resilience is a component of national security and that the dollar's reserve status is not separate from national security but a part of it. This document was prepared by the President's own national security apparatus. It represented the institutional consensus of the intelligence and national security community about what threatens America.

The Gerasimov Doctrine, and its specific identification of economic inequality, healthcare inequity, racial tension, and social division as the primary targets of Russian hybrid warfare against Western democracies, was the subject of regular intelligence community briefings to the President. The Senate Intelligence Committee findings about Russian social media targeting of economically anxious communities were provided to the administration.

A President who receives these briefings and then pursues policies that predictably produce the exact social conditions the intelligence community has identified as Russia's hybrid warfare targets cannot claim the policy defense. He has been told that these policies advance the enemy's mission. The Haupt standard does not require that the President approved of the Russian benefit. It requires only that he performed the act with knowledge of the enemy's objectives. The briefings provided that knowledge.

The General and the Ammunition Dump

Consider an analogy. A military commander receives intelligence that the enemy plans to overrun his position by exploiting his unit's shortage of anti-tank ammunition. He receives a written operational assessment that explicitly identifies anti-tank ammunition as the critical vulnerability the enemy intends to target.

Then he orders his unit to destroy its own anti-tank ammunition reserves, characterizing the order as fiscal responsibility and logistics simplification.

When the enemy overruns the position using exactly the vulnerability the commander was warned about, the commander cannot claim the policy defense. He was warned. He knew. He ordered the destruction of the exact defensive asset the intelligence assessment had identified as the target. The policy label does not change the legal analysis.

That is the argument this chapter makes about the economic front. The 2022 National Security Strategy identified dollar dominance, institutional soft power, and domestic resilience as the defensive assets Russia's hybrid warfare is designed to erode. The policies documented in this chapter systematically eroded all three. The briefings that warned the President about Russian hybrid warfare objectives were the operational intelligence assessment. The policy choices that executed those objectives were the order to destroy the ammunition.

□ □ □

Section Five: The Cramer Scorecard — Quantifying the Aid and Comfort

The Cramer standard requires that the aid be actual. This chapter's final section does what the Cramer standard requires: it measures the actual benefit Russia received from the economic conduct documented in the preceding sections.

This is not a political accounting. It is a legal accounting, applying the Cramer standard to the documented outcomes of the economic policy choices this chapter has analyzed.

Russian Strategic Objective One: De-dollarization

Russia's stated objective is to reduce the dollar's reserve status and thereby weaken the American sanctions architecture that constrains Russian economic and military activity.

The documented result: the dollar's share of global reserves declined from 71 percent in 1999 to 58 percent in 2024, with the steepest portion of that decline occurring during and immediately following the period of maximum dollar weaponization threats, debt ceiling crises, and tariff unpredictability. The BRICS payment alternative framework advanced significantly. Saudi Arabia conducted oil sales in Chinese yuan, breaking the 50-year petrodollar arrangement that had been one of the foundational pillars of dollar reserve status.

The aid was actual. It was measured in percentage points of global reserve share.

Russian Strategic Objective Two: Isolation of the United States From Its Allies

Russia's published doctrine identifies the dissolution of Western alliances and the isolation of the United States from its traditional partners as a primary strategic objective. Chapter 6 documented the NATO deconstruction. This chapter documents the economic dimension of the same objective.

The documented result: the termination of 5,341 USAID projects created governance and economic vacuums in developing nations that China and Russia filled, shifting the allegiance calculations of those nations' populations and governments. Trade conflicts with European allies, including the Spain trade severance documented in Chapter 7, added economic fracturing to the military alliance fracturing documented in Chapter 6. The Global South, which had historically been contested territory between Western influence and Russian and Chinese influence, shifted measurably toward the Russian and Chinese axis following the USAID dismantlement.

The aid was actual. It was measured in flags waved in Kano, in Chinese water infrastructure in Senegal, in Russian security agreements in the Sahel.

Russian Strategic Objective Three: Domestic Unrest and Social Division in the United States

Russia's Gerasimov Doctrine identifies the exploitation of domestic social divisions, economic inequality, and healthcare inequity as the primary tools of hybrid warfare against Western democracies. The Senate Intelligence Committee documented that Russian information operations specifically targeted these vulnerabilities.

The documented result: 25 million Americans lost Medicaid coverage. Federal housing assistance contracted. The opioid crisis, which Russian disinformation operations had been targeting as a destabilization tool, deepened in communities where treatment programs were defunded. Russian social media operations amplified every domestic policy contraction, using the cuts as evidence for the narrative that the American government had abandoned its citizens. The Senate Intelligence Committee documented the specific Russian amplification campaigns targeting communities affected by healthcare and economic program reductions.

The aid was actual. It was measured in the Senate Intelligence Committee's findings about Russian information operation success in communities experiencing economic contraction.

Under Cramer, the aid must be actual. The dollar's decline in reserve share is actual. The USAID vacuum filled by Russia and China is actual. The documented Russian information operation success in communities affected by

domestic economic cuts is actual. Three of Russia's primary documented strategic objectives were measurably advanced by the economic conduct documented in this chapter. The act meets the constitutional standard. The method was economic. The effect was strategic. The beneficiary was Russia.

THE WITNESSES: *The 2022 National Security Strategy stating that dollar reserve status is a component of national security is a public governmental document. The IMF data documenting the decline in dollar reserve share from 71 to 58 percent is public data from a multilateral institution. Vladimir Putin's public statements about de-dollarization are documented in Russian presidential press releases and multiple major news organization archives. The USAID project termination count of 5,341 is documented in State Department records and congressional oversight findings. The South Africa HIV funding replacement by China is documented in Chinese government press releases and NGO reports. The Zambia, Senegal, and Nigeria cases are documented in United Nations agency reports, NGO findings, and press reporting confirmed by multiple sources. The Gerasimov Doctrine is a public document published in the Russian Military-Industrial Courier. The Senate Intelligence Committee's Volume 2 findings about Russian social media targeting of economically anxious communities are documented in the Committee's published report. The debt ceiling crisis market impacts and foreign central bank response are documented in Federal Reserve, IMF, and major financial institution reports.*

□ □ □

This chapter completes the economic dimension of the treason argument. The dollar's strategic power has been documented. The federal budget as the skeleton of American power has been documented. The weaponization of poverty as execution of the Gerasimov playbook has been documented. The policy defense has been rebutted. And the Cramer scorecard has quantified the actual aid.

The next chapter addresses the immunity question that sits at the center of any legal proceeding against a former president, and that the Supreme Court's 2024 ruling in Trump v. United States placed directly in the path of this book's entire argument.

□ □ □

PART IV

THE IMMUNITY DEFENSE

The Supreme Court's Shield and Its Constitutional Limits

Chapter Eleven

Trump v. United States (2024): The Immunity Ruling and the Treason Exception

In July 2024, the Supreme Court of the United States issued a ruling that legal scholars described as the most consequential expansion of presidential power since the founding of the Republic.

The case was Trump v. United States. The question was whether a former president could be criminally prosecuted for official acts taken while in office. The Court's answer, in a 6 to 3 decision written by Chief Justice John Roberts, was that presidents enjoy presumptive immunity for official acts and absolute immunity for acts taken in their core constitutional functions.

The dissents were unusually sharp.

"In every use of official power, the President is now a king above the law." **— Justice Sonia Sotomayor, dissenting**

"The decision has created a law-free zone around the presidency, transforming the office from the servant of the law into someone who stands above it." **— Justice Ketanji Brown Jackson, dissenting**

The majority opinion is now the law. And it is the most significant legal obstacle to any treason prosecution arising from the conduct documented in this book.

This chapter does four things. It explains what the ruling actually says. It presents the strongest constitutional arguments against applying it to treason. It documents why those arguments are supported by the Framers' own recorded words and the specific text of the Constitution. And it addresses, directly and without evasion, the arguments on the other side.

The conclusion this chapter reaches is not that the immunity ruling is irrelevant. It is that the ruling has not resolved the treason question and that five specific constitutional arguments support the position that the treason clause operates as a carve-out from any immunity doctrine the Court might construct.

□ □ □

Section One: What the Ruling Actually Says

Chief Justice Roberts established a three-tier framework for presidential immunity.

At the top, absolute immunity applies to the President's core constitutional functions. The majority opinion specifically identifies the Commander in Chief power, the pardon power, the appointment power, and the veto power. No criminal prosecution can reach conduct in these areas, period.

In the middle, presumptive immunity applies to other official acts, meaning actions taken within the outer perimeter of presidential authority. This immunity can theoretically be overcome, but the majority established a standard so high that the practical effect is near-absolute protection for most executive conduct.

At the bottom, no immunity applies to unofficial or private acts. A president who commits a private crime while in office can be prosecuted for it.

The majority also established a rule about evidence. Even when a former president is prosecuted for a non-immune private act, prosecutors cannot introduce evidence of immune official acts to prove liability. Chief Justice Roberts wrote that allowing such evidence would permit a prosecutor to do indirectly what he cannot do directly.

> *"That proposal threatens to eviscerate the immunity we have recognized. It would permit a prosecutor to do indirectly what he cannot do directly, invite the jury to examine acts for which a President is immune from prosecution to nonetheless prove his liability on any charge."* — **Chief Justice John Roberts, Trump v. United States majority opinion (2024)**

Even Justice Amy Coney Barrett, who joined the majority on the broader immunity framework, explicitly disagreed with the evidentiary rule. She argued that excluding official acts from evidence in related prosecutions would hamstring prosecutions for non-immune crimes, particularly bribery cases in which the official act is precisely the thing that was sold.

Justice Sotomayor identified the logical endpoint of the evidence exclusion rule with a hypothetical that has become one of the most cited passages in recent constitutional scholarship. If a President announces in an official speech his intent to murder a political rival and then hires a private hitman, the prosecutor cannot use the official speech to prove premeditation, because the speech is an immune official act. The private murder is prosecutable. The stated intent that preceded it is not evidence.

> *"That holding, which will prevent the Government from using a President's official acts to prove knowledge or intent in prosecuting private offenses, is nonsensical."* — **Justice Sonia Sotomayor, dissenting**

This is the ruling this chapter must address.

□ □ □

Section Two: The Text the Court Ignored — The Impeachment Judgment Clause

The strongest textual argument against applying the immunity ruling to conduct that constitutes treason is not found in the treason clause itself. It is found in a provision of Article I that the majority opinion declined to address in a way that resolves the question.

Article I, Section 3, Clause 7 of the Constitution states that judgment in cases of impeachment shall not extend further than to removal from office but that the party convicted shall nevertheless be liable and subject to indictment, trial, judgment, and punishment according to law.

Read that sentence carefully. It says that a President who is impeached and removed remains subject to criminal prosecution. It assumes, as a matter of constitutional design, that a former president who was convicted in an impeachment trial for conduct in office can then be criminally prosecuted for that same conduct.

Now ask: what kind of conduct is the Impeachment Clause designed to address? Article II, Section 4 provides the answer. The President, Vice President, and all civil officers of the United States shall be removed from office on impeachment for and conviction of treason, bribery, or other high crimes and misdemeanors.

Treason is named first. It is the first ground for impeachment listed in the Constitution. And the Impeachment Judgment Clause explicitly preserves criminal prosecution for the conduct that produces impeachment.

The logical structure is unavoidable. The Constitution names treason as the primary ground for impeachment. The Constitution explicitly preserves criminal prosecution after impeachment conviction. If the immunity ruling were read to immunize treason, it would render the Impeachment Judgment Clause an empty shell for the very offense the Constitution names first among the grounds for removal.

A constitutional interpretation that renders a specific provision meaningless for the specific offense that provision was most clearly designed to address is not a valid constitutional interpretation. Courts are required to give effect to every provision of the Constitution. The Impeachment Judgment Clause was written to ensure that presidents could be criminally prosecuted for the high crimes committed in office. Treason is a high crime. The Clause applies.

The Framers themselves said so. At the Philadelphia Convention, delegate James Wilson stated explicitly that if the President is himself a party to the guilt of treason, he can be impeached and prosecuted. Wilson was not speaking hypothetically. He was describing the constitutional design he was helping to create. His words are in the record of the Convention.

Legal scholar Michael Stern, analyzing the Convention records, noted that the high crimes and misdemeanors standard for impeachment was principally aimed at official misconduct, specifically conduct that envisions a President organizing a treasonous conspiracy under the authority of his office. The Framers contemplated, and deliberately designed for, a President who could be prosecuted for using official power to commit treason.

□ □ □

Section Three: The Private Act Distinction — When Profiteering Destroys Immunity

The Supreme Court explicitly held that unofficial or private acts receive no immunity whatsoever. That holding creates a second path around the immunity ruling that does not require overcoming the core functions absolute immunity at all.

Chapter 9 of this book documented the financial entanglements between the President's family businesses and the foreign governments whose interests consistently benefited from the policy decisions documented in Chapters 4 through 8. The emoluments violations, the crypto token purchases by foreign sovereign wealth funds, the hotel bookings by foreign diplomatic missions, the correlation between financial inflows and favorable policy outcomes, all of this establishes what Chapter 9 called the corruption motive.

For the immunity analysis, the corruption motive is not merely evidence of intent. It is the legal mechanism through which the acts themselves are reclassified from official to private.

A Merchant Is Not a Magistrate

When a President makes a foreign policy decision, not because he believes it serves the national interest, but because a foreign government has purchased tokens in his family's cryptocurrency venture, he is not performing an official act. He is performing a private transaction using the trappings of office.

The Supreme Court's majority opinion, in the very footnote that legal scholars have studied most carefully, acknowledged that while a pardon is a core constitutional act, accepting a bribe in exchange for the pardon is not immune. The majority wrote that taking a bribe is, obviously, no part of the executive process or function.

The principle that the footnote establishes applies beyond the pardon context. If the corrupt motive transforms the pardon from an official act to a non-immune private transaction for bribery purposes, the same principle applies to every policy decision whose apparent purpose was the advancement of the President's private financial interests rather than the national interest.

A President who sells the Qatar policy for Saudi hotel bookings is not performing a Commander in Chief function. He is performing a commercial transaction. A President who lifts Russia sanctions when his family cryptocurrency venture has received investments from Russian-aligned sovereign wealth funds is not performing a foreign policy function. He is performing a private financial transaction that uses the authority of his office as the mechanism of delivery.

Under the Court's own framework, the immunity dissolves when the act is private rather than official. And an act whose purpose is personal financial enrichment rather than public benefit is a private act regardless of the official mechanism through which it is executed.

Justice Barrett's Warning

Justice Barrett's partial dissent on the evidence exclusion rule identified precisely why this distinction matters for prosecution. She argued that the Constitution does not require blinding juries to the circumstances surrounding conduct for which Presidents can be held liable.

> *"To make sense of charges alleging a quid pro quo, the jury must be allowed to hear about both the quid and the quo, even if the quo, standing alone, could not be a basis for the President's criminal liability."* — **Justice Amy Coney Barrett, concurring in part and dissenting in part**

Barrett's point applies with full force to the financial corruption argument. If a prosecutor charges the President with the unofficial private act of accepting financial benefits from foreign governments in exchange for policy favors, the jury must be allowed to hear about both the financial inflows and the policy decisions that followed them. The policy decisions are the quo. The financial inflows are the quid. Neither makes sense as evidence without the other.

The corruption loophole that the private act distinction creates is not a loophole in the pejorative sense. It is the constitutional design functioning as intended. The Framers wrote the Emoluments Clause and the bribery ground for impeachment specifically because they understood that a President who monetizes his office is not governing. He is profiteering. And profiteering is a private act, regardless of the official position that makes it profitable.

□ □ □

Section Four: The Allegiance Argument — Why Treason Cannot Be an Official Act

The preceding two sections have addressed the immunity ruling through constitutional text and the private act distinction. This section addresses a structural constitutional argument that operates at a deeper level.

Treason cannot be an official act. Not because of what treason does. Because of what treason is.

Treason is the violation of the oath that creates the President's authority. It is the betrayal of the allegiance that gives official acts their legitimacy. The Presidential Oath, documented in Article II, Section 1, is the legal instrument through which the President is granted the authority to act officially. Every official act the President performs, every order issued, every pardon granted, every treaty negotiated, derives its legitimacy from the oath that established the President's allegiance to the United States.

When the President acts in service of a foreign enemy rather than the United States, he has not merely violated the oath. He has destroyed the allegiance that makes official action possible. And if the allegiance that authorizes official acts has been destroyed, the acts performed through official mechanisms in service of the foreign enemy are not official acts. They are the use of official mechanisms to commit the act that is constitutionally defined as the betrayal of those mechanisms.

The Contractor Analogy

Consider an analogy. A licensed contractor has legal authority to enter your property, use specialized tools, and construct things on your behalf. That license is the source of his authority. It grants him access and capability that he would not otherwise have.

If the contractor uses his contractor's license to gain access to your property and then helps a burglar case the house, he has not committed a licensed act. He has used the appearance of authority, granted by the license, to commit a betrayal. The license does not protect the betrayal. The license is precisely what makes the betrayal more serious, because it is the instrument through which trust was established and then violated.

The presidential oath is the President's license. It grants authority. It establishes allegiance. And it defines the one category of conduct that the authority can never be used to commit. When a President uses the powers of his office to advance the mission of a foreign enemy of the United States, he is not performing an official act. He is using official powers to commit the act that the Constitution most explicitly and specifically prohibits.

James Madison's Principle

James Madison anticipated this argument in Federalist No. 51 when he wrote that the structure of the Constitution assumes that power will be used for the purposes for which it was granted. A power used against the purposes for which it was granted is not an exercise of that power. It is an abuse of it.

The immunity doctrine was designed to protect the exercise of constitutional authority, specifically the President's ability to perform the duties his office requires without fear that every controversial decision will be criminalized by a successor administration with different policy preferences. That is a legitimate concern and a legitimate purpose.

But the immunity doctrine cannot logically extend to conduct that is not merely controversial but is the constitutional antithesis of authority. A power used to betray the nation is not a power used for the purposes for which it was granted. It is a power used against the most fundamental purpose for which it was granted. And Madison's principle, which predates the immunity ruling by more than two centuries, establishes that the abuse of power is not protected by the grant of power.

The President of the United States cannot officially betray the country, because officially requires the allegiance that treason destroys. The immunity doctrine protects official acts. Treason is not an official act. It is the constitutional definition of the betrayal of official duty. Extending immunity to treason would not protect the President's ability to govern. It would protect the President's ability to destroy governance itself.

□ □ □

Section Five: The Core Functions Wall — Even Absolute Powers Have Limits

The most difficult argument for this chapter to address is the majority's absolute immunity for core constitutional functions. The Commander in Chief power, the pardon power, and several other specifically named functions receive absolute protection. No criminal prosecution. No exceptions named.

This book has documented conduct in both of those areas. Chapter 3 documented the Commander in Chief function being used to deploy an armed mob against the Capitol and to withhold the National Guard's defense of that Capitol. Chapter 2 documented the pardon power being used to ratify the insurrection and to maintain a standing offer of immunity to a private army. If the immunity ruling is absolute for these functions, the argument that those specific acts can be prosecuted faces a significant obstacle.

This section presents the strongest available arguments that absolute immunity for core functions has limits, and that treason is among them.

The Pardon Power and Its Limits in Revolutionary History

The Framers' own generation drew explicit limits on executive pardon power in the context of treason and insurrection. The 1776 Constitutions of Virginia, Pennsylvania, and New York stripped the executive of the power to pardon individuals convicted of treason. In Virginia, Governor Patrick Henry was explicitly prohibited from granting mercy for treason, leaving that determination to the General Assembly.

The Framers who wrote the federal Constitution were the same generation that had enacted these state limitations. They were not operating in ignorance of the principle that treason is categorically different from ordinary crimes in its relationship to executive clemency. The absence of a similar limitation in the federal Constitution may reflect the impeachment mechanism's role as the check on presidential treason rather than a decision to grant unlimited pardon authority.

What is clear from the historical record is that no serious legal argument at the founding period contemplated a President who could pardon his own co-conspirators in a treasonous scheme, because the founding period understood the pardon power as an instrument of mercy for ordinary criminals, not a protective mechanism for the President's own criminal network.

No Man Shall Be the Judge in His Own Case

There is a principle so fundamental to the Anglo-American legal tradition that it predates the Constitution by centuries. No man shall be a judge in his own case. The principle, known by the Latin phrase nemo "judex" in causa sua, is one of the foundations of natural justice.

If the pardon power is absolute and unreviewable, and if a President can use the pardon power to protect co-conspirators in his own treason, the President has become the judge in his own case. He has used an official power to immunize the criminal network that served his treasonous objective. The absolute character of the pardon power, under this reading, would transform it from an instrument of mercy into an instrument of impunity for the President's own criminal enterprises.

This is an absurd result. Courts do not reach absurd results when a rational reading of the constitutional text is available. The rational reading is that the pardon power, like all presidential powers, is bounded by the oath that authorizes it. A pardon issued in service of treason is not an exercise of the mercy power. It is an exercise of the corruption power, and the oath does not authorize that.

The Take Care Clause as the Boundary

Article II, Section 3 requires the President to take care that the laws be faithfully executed. The word faithfully is not decorative. It is a substantive limitation on how the executive power may be used. A Commander in Chief who uses military authority to deploy an armed force against a constitutional process is not faithfully executing the laws. He is using the Commander in Chief power to destroy the laws he is obligated to execute.

The Take Care Clause functions as a constitutional outer boundary on executive power. Acts that violate the faithful execution requirement are not official acts in the full constitutional sense. They are what constitutional scholars call ultra vires acts, acts beyond the powers of the office, because the office's powers are defined by the oath and the Take Care Clause that require faithful service rather than betrayal.

□ □ □

Section Six: The Absurd Result Doctrine and 300 Years of Disqualification History

Courts are required to interpret constitutional provisions in ways that avoid absurd results. This principle, called constitutional avoidance, is one of the bedrock canons of judicial interpretation. When a reading of a constitutional provision would produce an outcome that no reasonable person could believe the Framers intended, courts look for a rational alternative reading.

The absurd result of applying the immunity ruling to treason is this: the Constitution creates an office called the presidency. It defines the oath that officer must swear. It defines treason as the highest crime the officer can commit. It establishes impeachment as the mechanism for removing an officer who commits treason. It explicitly preserves criminal prosecution for an officer who is removed. And then, under the immunity ruling as applied to treason, the criminal prosecution that the Constitution explicitly preserves becomes unavailable because the very conduct that made the officer impeachable was performed through official mechanisms.

The Constitution created an office that can destroy the Constitution itself without legal consequence. That is an absurd result.

The Framers did not intend that result. The historical record, spanning three centuries of American legal practice, proves they did not.

The Three-Hundred-Year Lineage of Loyalty and Disqualification

The research underlying this chapter documents a consistent trajectory in American law from the colonial period to the present: disloyalty to the constitutional order has never been treated as a protected exercise of governmental authority.

The New Haven Colony in 1656 provided the death penalty for anyone who would treacherously and perfidiously attempt the alteration and subversion of the frame of policy or fundamental government. The offense was not merely armed rebellion. It was the attempt to subvert the constitutional order from within, by those who had been entrusted with its operation.

The Revolutionary generation, in responding to Loyalist subversion, established the principle that loyalty to the constitutional order is a prerequisite for governmental authority. The mass confiscation of Loyalist estates, the disqualification statutes, the prohibitions on pardoning treasonous conduct, all of these mechanisms reflect a unified understanding that authority derives from allegiance, and that the betrayal of allegiance terminates the authority.

The 14th Amendment's Section 3 extended this principle to the constitutional text itself. Any person who has taken an oath to support the Constitution and then engages in insurrection or rebellion or gives aid or comfort to the enemies of the United States is disqualified from holding office. Senator Morrill explicitly confirmed during the congressional debates that the term civil officer includes the President.

The immunity ruling does not address Section 3. It cannot override Section 3. And Section 3, read alongside the treason clause and the Impeachment Judgment Clause, establishes the constitutional framework within which the immunity ruling must be interpreted. That framework has never, in three hundred years of American law, protected the exercise of governmental authority in service of the nation's enemies.

The Hamilton Principle

Alexander Hamilton wrote in Federalist No. 69 that a President, upon conviction of high crimes, would be removed and afterwards be liable to prosecution and punishment in the ordinary course of law. He wrote in Federalist No. 65 that the subjects of presidential impeachment are those offenses which proceed from the misconduct of public men, or, in other words, from the abuse or violation of some public trust. They are of a nature which may with peculiar propriety be denominated political, as they relate chiefly to injuries done immediately to the society itself.

Treason is the paradigmatic example of the injury Hamilton described: an injury done immediately to the society itself, committed through the abuse of a public trust. Hamilton's principle and the Impeachment Judgment Clause and Section 3 of the 14th Amendment and the Framers' recorded words at the Philadelphia Convention all point in the same direction.

The immunity ruling has not changed that direction. It has created an obstacle that requires navigation. This chapter has identified five paths around that obstacle, each grounded in constitutional text, historical practice, or the structural logic of the constitutional design itself.

The Constitution is not a suicide pact. A reading of the immunity ruling that immunizes treason, the one act the Constitution most explicitly prohibits, the one offense the Constitution names first as grounds for impeachment, the one crime whose prosecution is explicitly preserved by the Impeachment Judgment Clause, would transform the immunity ruling into precisely what it cannot be: a mechanism for destroying the constitutional order from within. The rational reading, the historically grounded reading, the reading that gives effect to every provision of the Constitution rather than allowing one provision to nullify the others, is that the treason clause operates as a constitutional carve-out from any immunity doctrine. The Framers who wrote both provisions in the same document did not intend one to nullify the other.

□ □ □

This chapter has addressed the most significant procedural obstacle to the treason argument this book makes. Five constitutional paths have been identified: (i) the Impeachment Judgment Clause as a textual limit on immunity for treason, (ii) the private act distinction as applied to conduct motivated by personal financial gain, (iii) the allegiance destruction argument establishing that treason cannot be an official act, (iv) the limits of absolute immunity for core functions derived from the oath and the Take Care Clause, and (v) the absurd result doctrine supported by three hundred years of American disqualification jurisprudence.

The immunity ruling is the law. This book does not pretend otherwise. But the treason question is not resolved by the immunity ruling. It is the question that the immunity ruling has left open, and the question that the Framers, the historical record, and the constitutional text all answer the same way.

□ □ □

PART V

THE ARCHITECTURE OF DECEPTION

Lies, Misrepresentations, and Consciousness of Guilt

A DETECTIVE STORY WORKS like this. Someone did something wrong. The detective does not have a confession. What the detective has is a pattern of clues, each of which points in the same direction. No single clue proves the crime. But the pattern, viewed as a whole, tells an unmistakable story.

Part V is the detective story inside the legal brief.

Every lie documented in the following chapters covers precisely one of the elements of the treason argument. The Russia relationship was concealed because the relationship was indefensible. The January 6 preparation was manufactured through lies and then denied because the preparation constituted an overt act of war. The NATO misrepresentations were designed to disguise the systematic dismantling of the alliance as negotiating toughness. The ceasefire denial enabled a massacre. The economic lies concealed harm that served identifiable adversary interests.

In criminal law, deliberate false statements about one's own conduct are admissible as evidence of guilty knowledge. The legal instruction a jury receives is this: if you find that the defendant made deliberately false statements about the conduct at issue, you may, but are not required to, infer that the defendant was conscious of guilt. The more elaborate the lie, the more specific the concealment, the stronger the inference.

The architecture of deception documented in Part V does not merely support the treason argument of Parts I through IV. It completes it. The lies are the proof that the actor knew.

Chapter Twelve

The Russia Lies: Misrepresentations, Obstruction, and the Architecture of Denial

The simplest lie is the flat denial. I did not do it. I was not there. I do not know that person.

In the law of evidence, lies are not merely moral failings. They are circumstantial evidence of consciousness of guilt. When a suspect lies about his whereabouts, the jury is permitted to infer that he has something to hide. When a defendant constructs a false narrative and maintains it across years and multiple legal proceedings, the jury is permitted to infer that the truth the narrative conceals would establish his guilt.

When a President lies about his relationship with a foreign adversary that his own intelligence community has unanimously documented as attacking American democracy, the inference is not merely that he is dishonest. It is that he is compromised. And when the lie actively prevents the defensive response to the attack, it is not only consciousness of guilt. It is the lie functioning as an act of aid and comfort in its own right.

This chapter documents three categories of lie, organized not chronologically but by legal function.

The business lies: the Trump Tower Moscow cover-up, designed to conceal the financial motive that Chapter 9 established as the engine of the Russia alignment.

The intelligence lies: the Manafort data transfer concealment and the Helsinki validation, in which the President publicly endorsed Russia's denial of its own interference operation at a global press conference.

The institutional lies: the witch hunt narrative and the Comey firing, which constituted what the Mueller Report documented as a two-phase campaign to obstruct the investigation into all of the above.

The Russia lies are not separate from the treason analysis. They are its connective tissue. The financial entanglements documented in Chapter 9 provided the motive. The policy shifts documented in Chapters 4 through 8 provided the overt acts. The lies documented in this chapter provide the final piece: the specific intent that the Kawakita standard permits the jury to infer from the totality of conduct.

Innocent people do not construct multi-year false narratives to explain conduct they believe was lawful.

□ □ □

Section One: The Business Lies — The Trump Tower Moscow Cover-Up

In 2016 and 2017, the flat denial was the response to every question about the relationship between the Trump campaign and Russia. Nobody from my campaign was in contact with Russians. I have nothing to do with Russia. I have no investments in Russia.

The documented record contradicts each of these statements specifically.

More than 140 contacts between Trump campaign officials and Russian nationals were documented in the Mueller investigation record. Trump Tower Moscow negotiations continued through at least June 2016, the same month as the Trump Tower meeting, while the candidate was publicly declaring no Russia business connections. The financial interest, the ongoing business deal requiring Russian governmental approval, was being actively concealed at the same moment it was most legally significant.

The Felix Sater Email and the Scale of the Motive

The Trump Tower Moscow project was not merely a real estate venture. The emails between Michael Cohen and Trump business associate Felix Sater documented the explicit political dimension of the deal and the explicit awareness of its relationship to the Russian government's support for the campaign.

> *"I think I can get Putin to say that at the Trump Moscow press conference... We can own this election... 2 boys from Brooklyn getting a USA president elected."* — **Felix Sater, email to Michael Cohen during Trump Tower Moscow negotiations**

Read that sentence carefully. The Trump Tower Moscow deal and the presidential campaign were, in Sater's documented understanding, part of the same integrated strategy. Russian governmental approval for the commercial deal and Russian electoral support for the campaign were not separate tracks. They were the same track. The financial interest and the political interest ran together.

The Cohen Guilty Plea and the Party Line

Michael Cohen, the President's personal attorney, pleaded guilty in 2018 to making false statements to Congress about the Trump Tower Moscow timeline. He had told Congress that negotiations ended in January 2016. In fact, they continued through June 2016.

But the guilty plea is not merely a chronological correction. Cohen explained, under oath, why he lied. He described adhering to a party line aimed at minimizing links between the Moscow project and Individual 1, the President. Cohen stated that when he initially denied business dealings to the press, the President responded: Why mention it if it is not a deal?

That instruction is the legal significance of the business lies. It establishes that the concealment was directed. The party line was established at the top. And the party line's purpose, in Cohen's own documented words, was to minimize the documented connection between the President's financial interests and the Russian government whose electoral support the campaign was simultaneously accepting.

Under the corrupt intent standard established in the Mueller investigation's legal framework, the triangle of evidence for establishing corrupt motive consists of financial interest, favorable policy statements, and concealment. The business lies are the documented apex of that triangle. The Trump Tower Moscow cover-up is not merely a false statement. It is the evidence that the concealment was intentional, directed, and designed to prevent the public and the investigating authorities from understanding the relationship between the President's financial interests and his Russia policy.

The Air Force One Statement

The Trump Tower Moscow cover-up was not the only documented instance of the President personally directing the construction of a false narrative. In July 2017, when the June 2016 Trump Tower meeting became public, the President personally dictated a statement released by his son claiming the meeting was primarily about Russian adoption policy.

The email chain arranging the meeting told a different story. The meeting had been arranged by Rob Goldstone, who wrote explicitly that the Russian government was offering official documents and information that would incriminate Hillary Clinton as part of Russia and its government's support for Mr. Trump.

> *"If it's what you say I love it especially later in the summer."* **Donald Trump Jr., email response to offer of Russian government assistance, June 3, 2016**

Adoption was not mentioned anywhere in the email chain. The lie was documented before it was told, by the emails that contradicted it. And the President personally dictated it. On Air Force One, using the authority and the communications infrastructure of the presidency, he constructed a false evidentiary record for a pending federal investigation.

That is not political spin. Under 18 U.S.C. section 1512(c)(2), it is obstruction of an official proceeding.

THE WITNESSES: *Michael Cohen's guilty plea to false statements to Congress is a public court record. Cohen's congressional testimony about the party line and the presidential instruction is documented in House and Senate committee transcripts. The Felix Sater emails are documented in the Mueller Report Volume I. The Air Force One statement and its contradiction by the email chain arranging the Trump Tower meeting are documented in the Mueller Report and confirmed by multiple White House sources including contemporaneous reporting.*

□ □ □

Section Two: The Intelligence Lies — From Polling Data to Helsinki

The business lies were designed to conceal financial motive. The intelligence lies were designed to conceal something more specific and more directly relevant to the treason analysis: the passage of American intelligence to a Russian intelligence asset, and the presidential validation of Russia's denial of its own attack.

The Manafort Data Transfer: Passing the Battlefield Map

In the summer of 2016, campaign chairman Paul Manafort met with Konstantin Kilimnik. The Senate Intelligence Committee, in its bipartisan five-volume report, assessed that Kilimnik was a Russian intelligence officer. Manafort shared internal campaign polling data with him. Detailed information about American voter demographics, strategic vulnerabilities, and the campaign's targeting analysis.

The lies about this transfer went in multiple directions. Manafort lied about the meeting. The campaign lied about the meeting. And the specific nature of the lie reflected a precise understanding of what the act actually was.

Internal campaign polling data is not merely private commercial information. In the context of an ongoing Russian information warfare operation targeting American voters, as documented by the unanimous January 2017 Intelligence Community Assessment, internal polling data is targeting intelligence. It identifies which voter populations are most susceptible to specific disinformation messages. It maps the vulnerabilities of the American democratic system at the granular level of individual congressional districts.

Passing that data to a Russian intelligence officer is not campaign strategy. It is the provision of a battlefield map to the opposing commander during an active intelligence operation against the United States.

The Senate Intelligence Committee called it a grave counterintelligence threat. Not a concerning finding. Not a troubling discovery. A grave counterintelligence threat. Those four words from a bipartisan committee controlled by Republicans are the institutional assessment of what the data transfer actually was.

The lie about it was the recognition that the act was criminal. You do not construct a false account of a meeting unless you understand that the truthful account of the meeting would establish that a crime was committed. Under the consciousness of guilt analysis, the specific content of the lie is evidence of the specific understanding of the guilt it was designed to conceal.

Passing internal campaign polling data to a Russian intelligence officer during an active Russian information warfare operation against the United States is not a campaign irregularity. It is the provision of targeting intelligence to the enemy. The lie about it was not political protection. It was the recognition that the act was criminal. Innocent people do not construct elaborate false accounts of meetings with Russian intelligence officers.

Helsinki: The Lie That Functioned as Propaganda

Perhaps no single act in this chapter is more legally significant than what happened in Helsinki, Finland, on July 16, 2018.

The President of the United States stood beside Vladimir Putin at a joint press conference and was asked directly whether he believed his own intelligence community's unanimous conclusion that Russia had ordered an influence campaign against the 2016 American presidential election, or whether he believed Putin's denial.

> *"President Putin says it's not Russia. I don't see any reason why it would be."* **President Donald Trump, Helsinki press conference, July 16, 2018**

This was not a diplomatic hedge. It was not a nuanced foreign policy statement open to multiple interpretations. It was a flat denial of the unanimous findings of the CIA, the NSA, the FBI, and every other component of the American intelligence community, delivered publicly, at a joint press conference with the leader of the nation conducting the attack, in the most high-profile diplomatic setting available.

Chapter 5 of this book analyzed the Helsinki statement through the Kawakita lens of aid and comfort, documenting how it gave Russia heart and courage to continue its operations. This chapter analyzes it through the lie lens: not only what it gave Russia but what it took from the United States.

When the President of the United States publicly endorses the denial of a foreign attack that is actively ongoing, he does not merely help the attacker. He disables the defense. A government that has been told by its own President that the attack is not happening cannot mount a coherent defense against it. Congressional sanctions will face a presidential veto. Cybersecurity budgets will face resistance. Intelligence community warnings will be dismissed. Public awareness campaigns will be contradicted from the Oval Office.

The Helsinki lie was not merely consciousness of guilt about the Russia relationship. It was the lie functioning as an instrument of the attack itself. By denying the attack, the President was ensuring its continuation. That is the Aid and Comfort of denial: not merely protecting the attacker from consequences, but actively preventing the American defensive response that would have stopped the attack.

Former CIA Director John Brennan, who had overseen the compilation of the January 2017 Intelligence Community Assessment, used a specific word when he characterized Helsinki.

> *"Donald Trump's press conference performance in Helsinki rises to and exceeds the threshold of high crimes and misdemeanors. It was nothing short of treasonous."* — **John Brennan, former CIA Director, July 16, 2018**

Brennan was not using the word loosely. He was making a specific legal characterization of a specific act by the person who held the most powerful public platform in the world.

> **THE WITNESSES:** *The January 2017 Intelligence Community Assessment establishing Russian interference with high confidence is a public primary source document. Vladimir Putin's public denial at Helsinki is on camera. The President's Helsinki statement is a public record. John Brennan's treasonous characterization is documented in his public Twitter post and subsequent interviews. Former DNI James Clapper and NSA Director Admiral Mike Rogers both publicly characterized the Helsinki statement as alarming and damaging to American national security.*

□ □ □

Section Three: The Institutional Lies — The Two-Phase Obstruction Campaign

The Mueller Report's Volume II documented eleven episodes of potential obstruction of justice. This section does not examine all eleven. It examines the two-phase structure of the obstruction campaign, because understanding the two phases is essential to understanding why the obstruction is relevant to the treason analysis rather than merely to an independent criminal charge.

Phase One: Shielding the Network

During the first five months of the administration, the President's obstructive conduct was focused primarily on protecting his subordinates and maintaining the public narrative that the Russia investigation was a politically motivated attack on his presidency. Because he believed he was not personally a target of the investigation, his primary strategy was to use the personal relationships and institutional authority of the presidency to halt specific criminal inquiries into specific individuals.

The Michael Flynn episode is the clearest example. On February 14, 2017, after engineering a private meeting by clearing the Oval Office of the Attorney General and senior advisors, the President told FBI Director James Comey:

> "I hope you can see your way clear to letting this go, to letting Flynn go. He is a good guy. I hope you can let this go."

Two weeks earlier, at a private dinner, the President had told Comey:

> "I need loyalty, I expect loyalty."

The legal significance of the sequence is specific. The loyalty demand established the quid. The Flynn request established the quo. The FBI Director's continued employment was being made contingent on his willingness to halt a specific criminal investigation into a specific individual who, if he cooperated with investigators, could provide information about the President's own conduct.

Flynn did cooperate, eventually. He was pardoned. The pardon pattern, documented in Chapter 2, is the Phase One obstruction campaign's logical conclusion: a standing offer of immunity to anyone willing to protect the President's secrets.

Phase Two: Direct Interference and the False Record

The firing of James Comey on May 9, 2017 was the pivot point from Phase One to Phase Two. When the President learned that a Special Counsel had been appointed to investigate the Russia matter, his reaction was documented by contemporaneous witnesses.

> *"Oh my God. This is terrible. This is the end of my Presidency. I'm fucked."*
> **President Donald Trump, upon learning of Special Counsel appointment, May 17, 2017, documented in Mueller Report**

That statement is legally significant beyond its emotional content. It establishes that the President understood the appointment of the Special Counsel as a direct threat to his presidency, not as the ordinary functioning of the legal system applied to conduct he believed was innocent. The response of a person who believes his conduct was lawful is frustration. The response of a person who understands that an independent investigation will reveal criminal conduct is panic.

Phase Two was characterized by increasingly direct attempts to terminate the investigation, construct false records, and manage witnesses.

In June 2017, the President ordered White House Counsel Don McGahn to have Special Counsel Robert Mueller removed, citing fabricated conflicts of interest. McGahn prepared to resign rather than carry out the order. Later, when the order became public, the President pressured McGahn to create an internal White House record denying that the order had ever been given. McGahn refused again.

The McGahn false record attempt is, in the Mueller investigation's legal analysis, an attempt to suborn false testimony from a key witness in the obstruction investigation itself. You do not ask your White House Counsel to create a false record of a conversation unless you understand that the truthful record of that conversation establishes a crime.

In June and July 2017, the President directed Corey Lewandowski, a private citizen with no governmental role, to deliver a message to Attorney General Jeff Sessions instructing Sessions to publicly limit the Special Counsel's investigation to future election interference only, not the 2016 campaign or its relationship with Russia. By using an outside intermediary who was not subject to Justice Department oversight, the President demonstrated, in the Mueller investigation's legal analysis, a consciousness of wrongdoing. He understood that a formal directive through governmental channels to limit the investigation of his own past conduct would be legally untenable.

The Witch Hunt Narrative as Legal Obstruction

The public campaign labeling the Russia investigation a witch hunt, a hoax, and a rigged investigation constitutes, under 18 U.S.C. section 1512(c)(2)'s broad application, obstruction by public pressure. This is not a free speech argument against political rhetoric. It is a legal argument about the use of the world's most powerful public platform to influence witnesses, potential jurors, and investigating officials.

The President called cooperating witnesses rats, using the specific language of organized crime witness intimidation. He praised non-cooperating witnesses like Paul Manafort and Roger Stone as brave, establishing a public signal that protection was contingent on silence. He attacked individual prosecutors and investigators by name. He characterized the investigation as an illegal, unconstitutional attempt to undermine his presidency.

The legal framework for evaluating this conduct is obstruction's nexus requirement: the act must have the natural and probable effect of interfering with an official proceeding. When a sitting President with the world's most visible platform uses that platform to characterize an active federal investigation as a witch hunt, to praise witness non-cooperation as bravery, and to call cooperating witnesses by the specific terminology that organized crime uses to threaten potential informants, the natural and probable effect on witnesses, investigators, and potential jurors is documented and foreseeable.

The President's admission to Russian Foreign Minister Lavrov and Ambassador Kislyak, in the Oval Office, that firing Comey had taken great pressure off the Russia investigation, links the institutional obstruction directly to the subject of the investigation. He told the foreign ministry representatives of the adversarial nation that his intelligence community had unanimously identified as the source of the attack on American democracy that he had relieved the pressure on the investigation into that attack.

That admission is the connective thread that runs through all three categories of lie documented in this chapter. The business lies concealed the financial motive. The intelligence lies disabled the defensive response and endorsed the attack. The institutional lies attempted to terminate the investigation before it could establish the connection between the financial motive, the intelligence assistance, and the policy alignment.

□ □ □

Section Four: The Lies as Connective Tissue — The Legal Synthesis

This chapter has documented three categories of lie and their specific legal functions. But the lies are more than individual instances of obstruction or false statements. They are the architecture of denial that holds the entire pattern together.

The Kawakita standard permits the inference of treasonous intent from the totality of conduct over time. That totality includes not only the overt acts of aid and comfort documented in Chapters 4 through 10 but also the conduct that surrounds and supports those overt acts. The construction and maintenance of a multi-year false narrative about the nature of the Russia relationship is evidence of the intent underlying the overt acts, because the intensity of the cover-up corresponds to the seriousness of what is being covered up.

If the Russia alignment were merely a series of unfortunate policy coincidences that happened to benefit Russia, there would be no need to lie about it. If the Trump Tower Moscow deal were an ordinary commercial venture unrelated to the political strategy of the campaign, there would be no need to construct a party line to conceal its timeline. If the Manafort data transfer were an innocent campaign meeting of no strategic significance, there would be no need to lie about it to multiple investigators. If the Trump Tower meeting were genuinely about adoption policy, there would be no need to personally dictate a false account of it aboard Air Force One.

The lies are not merely evidence of consciousness of guilt. They are evidence of the specific guilt that the overt acts established. Each lie tracks precisely the overt act it was designed to conceal. The Trump Tower Moscow lie conceals the financial motive. The Manafort meeting lie conceals the intelligence handoff. The Helsinki statement denies the attack. The witch hunt narrative attempts to terminate the investigation before it can connect the dots.

The architecture of denial is not a collection of independent lies. It is a coordinated structure designed to protect a coordinated pattern of conduct. Under the Kawakita standard, the intensity and coordination of the cover-up is evidence of the intent underlying the conduct being covered up. Under the obstruction framework, the cover-up is itself a crime. And under the treason analysis, the cover-up is the final overt act: the attempt to prevent the constitutional accountability mechanisms from exposing and stopping the treasonous pattern documented in this book.

The Special Counsel's non-exoneration finding captures the evidentiary state with precision: while the investigation did not conclude that the President committed a crime, it also did not exonerate him. What the investigation could not establish was the specific intent required for the specific charges brought within its jurisdictional scope. What this book has argued, across twelve chapters, is that the specific intent required for the treason clause is established by the pattern, including the pattern of lies, when evaluated against the Kawakita standard.

The financial entanglements provided the motive. The policy shifts provided the overt acts. The lies provided the intent. And the architecture of denial, maintained across years and multiple legal proceedings, is the strongest evidence available that the person who built it understood, precisely and fully, what the truthful account of the Russia relationship would establish.

THE WITNESSES: *The Mueller Report Volume II documents all eleven obstruction episodes in detail, with specific citations to witness testimony and documentary evidence. James Comey's contemporaneous memos about the loyalty dinner and the Flynn request are primary source documents. The Lewandowski intermediary order is documented in McGahn's congressional testimony and Mueller Report accounts. The Oval Office Lavrov admission that the Comey firing relieved pressure on the Russia investigation is documented in contemporaneous reporting confirmed by multiple sources including the President's own subsequent public statements. The Special Counsel's non-exoneration language is quoted directly from the Mueller Report.*

□ □ □

The next chapter assembles the legal opinion that is the culmination of this entire analysis. Every element documented in Chapters 2 through 12 converges in the legal conclusion: the allegiance, the enemy, the overt acts, the intent, the two-witness evidence, and the answer to the immunity question. The case will be stated, as this book has always intended, as a citizen's brief rather than a prosecutorial indictment. But the standard to which it will be held is the constitutional standard that the Framers wrote into Article III. That is the only standard that matters.

□ □ □

Chapter Thirteen

The January 6 Lies: The Big Lie as an Instrument of Insurrection

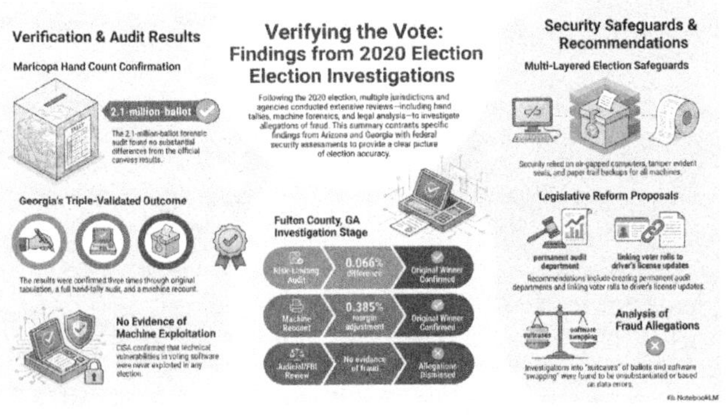

The Framers defined treason as levying war against the United States. Modern warfare is not waged solely with muskets and cannons. It is waged with information, with mobilization, with the radicalization of a population against its own government.

Before the first window was broken at the Capitol, before the first barrier was breached, the war had already begun. It was launched with a lie.

The stolen election narrative was not a political argument. It was information warfare. It was the ammunition used to build an army. It was the fuel that converted ordinary citizens who believed their country had been stolen into an assemblage that charged the seat of government. And before a single rioter ever reached the Capitol steps, the person who told the lie knew it was false.

That is the essential fact this chapter establishes. Not that the lie was wrong. Not that the lie was irresponsible. That the lie was knowingly, documentably, adjudicably false, and that its teller knew it was false while telling it, and that he deployed it anyway to manufacture the assemblage that Chapters 2 and 3 of this book document as levying war.

Chapter 3 proved that the assemblage was recruited, armed, directed, and sustained. This chapter proves the mechanism through which the assemblage was manufactured in the first place. The Bollman standard requires an assemblage of persons for the purpose of executing a treasonable design. The Big Lie was the manufacturing process.

□ □ □

Section One: The Pre-Deployed Weapon — Premeditation Before the Election

The stolen election narrative is commonly understood as a reaction to the November 2020 election results. The votes came in. Trump lost. He claimed fraud. The sequence, in the public understanding, runs in that order.

The documented record establishes the opposite sequence.

Months before the November 2020 election, the President began publicly claiming that the only way he could lose the election was if it were rigged. He made these claims repeatedly, specifically, and publicly, across interviews, rallies, and social media posts, during the spring and summer of 2020 when no votes had been cast and no results existed to dispute.

His campaign experts told him in early November that his chances of success were very bleak, approximately five to ten percent. Steve Bannon, on audio recording dated October 31, 2020, described the strategy: he is just going to say he is a winner. That does not mean he is a winner. He is just going to say he is a winner.

On election night, before the mail-in ballot count was anywhere near complete, before any state had certified its results, before any court had reviewed any evidence, the President declared victory and called the ongoing counting process a fraud on the American public.

His campaign manager Bill Stepien had warned him specifically about the red mirage effect: that mail-in ballots, which Democratic voters disproportionately used because of the pandemic, would be counted later, creating the appearance of an early Trump lead that would narrow as the full count proceeded. Trump knew this. He had been told. And he declared fraud anyway, before the count that would have explained the shift was complete.

Why Premeditation Matters Legally

This sequence is not merely interesting historical context. It is evidence of the specific intent the treason analysis requires.

A person who believes he was genuinely defrauded reacts to documented evidence of fraud. He investigates specific instances. He pursues legal remedies based on specific claims about specific ballots or specific precincts. His legal arguments improve as the evidence accumulates.

A person who deploys a false narrative as a strategic weapon pre-positions that narrative before the evidence exists to support it. He makes the claim before any evidence is available. His legal arguments do not improve as courts review the evidence, because there is no evidence to improve them. And his response to every legal rejection is not to revise the claim based on the court's findings but to attack the court for its political affiliation.

The pre-election claims are the evidentiary record of premeditation. They establish that the stolen election narrative was not a reaction to evidence of fraud. It was a pre-deployed weapon, constructed before the election occurred, for the specific purpose of refusing to accept a result that the President's own advisors had told him was the likely outcome.

A person who constructs a fraud narrative before any votes are counted and then refuses to revise that narrative despite 60 court rejections, despite his own Attorney General calling it nonsense, despite his own campaign data team's assessment, is not reacting to evidence of fraud. He is executing a pre-designed strategy of refusal. The premeditation of the lie is the strongest available evidence that the lie was intentional. And an intentional lie that manufactures an armed assemblage directed at a constitutional process is an overt act of war.

□ □ □

Section Two: The Adjudicated Falsity — What 60 Courts, Audits, and a $787 Million Settlement Prove

The stolen election narrative was litigated in more than 60 federal and state courts. It was examined by Republican-appointed judges, by judges Trump himself had appointed, by state courts and federal courts across every jurisdiction where fraud was alleged. Every court that examined the specific evidence rejected it.

This is not the result of partisan judicial bias. These were courts operating under different procedural rules, different evidentiary standards, and different political compositions. The consistency of the rejection, across 60 different legal forums, is itself evidence about the quality of the underlying claim. Legal claims that fail in 60 consecutive court proceedings have not been rejected by a biased system. They have been rejected because they lack the evidentiary foundation that courts require.

State-Level Results

In Georgia, Secretary of State Brad Raffensperger's team conducted multiple recounts, a full hand recount of all five million ballots cast, and an audit. Every count confirmed Biden's margin. Raffensperger, a Republican who had supported Trump's election campaigns, publicly stated that the results were accurate.

In Arizona, the Republican-controlled state senate sponsored the Cyber Ninjas audit, a months-long, painstaking review of 2.1 million Maricopa County ballots conducted by an organization that had promoted election conspiracy theories. The final report confirmed that Joe Biden had won the county. The audit actually increased Biden's margin by 360 votes. Cyber Ninjas subsequently shut down after facing contempt fines for failing to release public records related to its own review.

In Michigan, a Republican-led state Senate investigation found no evidence of widespread fraud sufficient to change the outcome. In Pennsylvania and Wisconsin, Republican-appointed judges rejected every legal theory presented to them.

The Fox News Settlement: Private Knowledge of Public Falsity

The $787.5 million defamation settlement between Dominion Voting Systems and Fox News Network established something beyond the corporate liability of a media company. The discovery process that preceded the settlement produced Fox's internal communications, and those communications revealed what Fox's executives and hosts privately understood about the claims they were publicly amplifying.

> *"Sidney Powell is a bit nuts. Between us, I've been pushing back on this all along."* — **Tucker Carlson, private text message, disclosed in Dominion Voting Systems v. Fox News litigation**

Tucker Carlson's private text is not an isolated instance. The discovery record documented that multiple Fox hosts and executives privately characterized the specific fraud claims as crazy and insane while those same claims were being given prominent airtime because Fox's executives feared that covering the story accurately would lose viewers to competitors who were amplifying the narrative.

The settlement does not directly establish Trump's personal knowledge of the falsity of the claims. But it establishes, as a matter of public record, that the claims about voting machine manipulation were known to be false by the people most prominent in promoting them. In the context of the broader documented record, including the campaign data team's private assessments, the Attorney General's repeated private statements that the claims were nonsense and bullshit, and the sixty court rejections, the private knowledge of falsity within the broader ecosystem surrounding the President is evidence that the ecosystem's leaders understood what the courts were confirming.

The Raffensperger Call: Solicitation of Election Fraud

On January 2, 2021, the President of the United States called Georgia Secretary of State Brad Raffensperger. The call was recorded.

During the call, Raffensperger and his team rebutted each specific fraud claim in real time with documentary evidence. As each claim was raised and contradicted, the President continued making the claims. The recording is a document in which both the false assertions and their factual refutation appear in the same conversation, simultaneous, with the President continuing to assert claims that were being specifically contradicted in the moment he was asserting them.

But the legal significance of the Raffensperger call is not merely that false claims were made to a state official. The call contained a specific request. Find 11,780 votes, the President said. One more than Biden's margin.

That request is not a policy dispute about election administration. It is not a request for a recount or an audit or a legal review. It is a request for a specific number of votes, a number that did not exist in the certified results, to be found by an official whose job is to certify those results. Under Georgia criminal law and federal law governing election fraud, soliciting a public official to alter certified election results is a felony. The Raffensperger call is documented solicitation of election fraud by the President of the United States.

> **THE WITNESSES:** *All 60-plus court decisions are public documents available in the federal and state court record systems. The Cyber Ninjas audit report is a public document published by the Arizona State Senate. The Michigan Senate Oversight Committee report is a public document. The Fox News internal communications were produced in discovery in Dominion Voting Systems v. Fox News and excerpted in publicly filed court documents. The Raffensperger call was recorded and has been published in full by multiple news organizations and confirmed by both parties on the call.*

□ □ □

Section Three: The Eastman Memo — When Legal Advice Becomes Criminal Conspiracy

John Eastman was a constitutional law professor with distinguished academic credentials. He wrote a memo. The memo proposed a legal theory.

In subsequent legal proceedings, Eastman acknowledged that he understood his theory was unlikely to succeed in court. He specifically told Vice President Pence's counsel Greg Jacob that the Supreme Court would reject his theory by a vote of nine to zero.

A legal theory its own author concedes would fail nine to zero in the Supreme Court is not legal advice. It is a pretext. And the legal system has now determined that it was more than a pretext.

The Federal Court's Crime-Fraud Ruling

In June 2022, Federal District Judge David Carter issued a ruling in the litigation over Eastman's emails that has become one of the most significant judicial findings in the entire January 6 legal record.

Judge Carter found that it was more likely than not that Eastman and Donald Trump had committed obstruction of justice and had engaged in a conspiracy to defraud the United States. Based on that finding, Judge Carter applied the crime-fraud exception to attorney-client privilege and ordered Eastman to turn over his emails to the January 6 Select Committee.

The crime-fraud exception to attorney-client privilege operates as follows. Attorney-client privilege exists to protect genuine legal advice and the confidential communications between lawyer and client that enable that advice. The exception strips that protection when the communications were made in furtherance of a crime or fraud. If a lawyer and a client are not seeking legal advice but are planning a crime, the privilege does not apply.

Judge Carter's application of the crime-fraud exception to the Eastman communications means that a federal court found, as a factual matter, that the Eastman memo was not legal advice pursued in good faith. It was the planning document for a criminal conspiracy.

The crime-fraud exception is the legal system's way of saying: this was not lawyering. This was plotting. When a federal judge applies the crime-fraud exception and orders attorney-client privileged communications produced, the judge has made a specific factual finding that the client and the lawyer were using the appearance of legal advice to plan a crime. The Eastman memo was not a shield.

It was a sword. And it was wielded in furtherance of the conspiracy to defraud the United States that the Mueller investigation documented as the legal standard for the conduct surrounding January 6.

The Eastman Disbarment

In 2026, the California Supreme Court disbarred John Eastman. The disbarment proceedings reviewed his conduct in connection with the January 6 effort and found it constituted professional misconduct of the most serious kind. An attorney who contributes to a criminal conspiracy to overturn a democratic election does not retain the license that the state grants him to practice law.

The disbarment is not, in isolation, a finding of criminal guilt. It is a professional accountability determination by the highest court of his licensing state. But it adds to the documented record of institutional findings, the 60 court rejections, the federal crime-fraud ruling, the House Select Committee referrals, that the conduct surrounding January 6 was not aggressive legal advocacy. It was documented misconduct in furtherance of a specific anti-constitutional purpose.

□ □ □

Section Four: The Mobilization Order — December 19, 2020

Chapter 3 of this book documented how the December 19, 2020 tweet served as the recruitment mechanism for the militia groups that formed the armed assemblage of January 6.

This chapter addresses the same tweet from a different analytical angle: not as a recruitment mechanism but as the moment when the information warfare campaign became operational mobilization.

On December 19, 2020, four days after the Electoral College had formally certified Biden's victory, the President posted: Big protest in D.C. on January 6th. Be there, will be wild.

The words be there, will be wild, read against the background of two months of stolen election propaganda, meant something specific to the groups who received them. The January 6 Select Committee documented what happened immediately after the tweet was posted.

Proud Boys leader Enrique Tarrio sent a message to the organization's leadership channel: the call is out. Turns out the President has called for a massive protest on the 6th. The Proud Boys established the Ministry of Self Defense encrypted operational planning channel within days of the tweet. Tactical planning began: maps of Washington identifying police positions, designated entry points, communications protocols, and formation strategies for a group that was arriving not to attend a rally but to execute an operational plan.

The Oath Keepers began recruiting military-experienced members specifically for January 6 operations. The encrypted communications channels of multiple militia organizations, later reviewed in the seditious conspiracy trials, documented that these groups understood the December 19 tweet as a directive from their Commander in Chief, not as a generic invitation to a political rally.

The Causal Chain the Convictions Establish

Twelve jury verdicts in the seditious conspiracy trials of the Proud Boys and Oath Keepers have established, as a matter of proven legal fact, that the groups that attacked the Capitol were operating as organized forces executing a coordinated plan to prevent the constitutional certification process.

In those trials, the Department of Justice established the evidentiary chain from the President's communications to the operational planning of the convicted groups. The Proud Boys leaders did not arrive at the Capitol on January 6 because they spontaneously decided to attend a protest. They arrived because the man who had spent two months telling them the election was stolen from him had told them to be there, at a specific place, on a specific date, for something wild, and they had spent the preceding weeks planning what wild would look like.

The seditious conspiracy convictions do not establish the President's personal criminal liability. They were not his trial. But they establish, as a matter of proven legal fact, the factual predicate that connects the lie to the levying of war. The assemblage that Bollman requires was manufactured by the information warfare campaign this chapter documents. The convictions of the assemblage's leaders are the legal confirmation that it was a treasonous assemblage.

A man who tells an army a lie that makes them willing to fight, mobilizes them to a specific location on a specific date, and directs them toward a constitutional target, is not merely a liar. He is a commander who used information as a weapon to manufacture the force he then deployed.

The President told the lie. The lie radicalized the base. The President mobilized the base. The base formed the army that attacked the Capitol. The foot soldiers of the Proud Boys and the Oath Keepers have been convicted of seditious conspiracy for the attack those twelve jury verdicts describe. They believed the lie. They acted on the mobilization. The man who told the lie and issued the mobilization order has not yet faced a treason proceeding. This book argues that the twelve jury verdicts are the factual predicate that such a proceeding would require.

> **THE WITNESSES:** *The December 19 tweet is a public document. The Proud Boys Ministry of Self Defense planning channel communications were produced in the federal seditious conspiracy trials and are documented in the court records of United States v. Tarrio et al. The Oath Keepers operational planning is documented in United States v. Rhodes et al. The January 6 Select Committee's Final Report documents the connection between the December 19 tweet and the militia group response. Twelve federal jury verdicts in the seditious conspiracy cases are public court records.*

□ □ □

Section Five: The Seditious Feedback Loop — How the Lie Became the War

The Big Lie did not exist in a vacuum. It operated as a feedback loop between the President's public communications and the militia groups' operational planning, each reinforcing the other in a cycle that escalated from political rhetoric to armed insurrection.

The Architecture of Radicalization

Starting in the spring of 2020, the President's pre-emptive claims that the election would be rigged established the foundational premise. By election night, when he declared victory before the count was complete and called the ongoing counting a fraud on the American public, that premise was activated into a specific grievance. Through November and December, every court rejection was reframed not as a legal determination that the evidence was insufficient but as evidence of the system's corruption. Every state official who certified accurate results was characterized as an enemy of democracy. Every piece of contradicting evidence was dismissed as part of the conspiracy.

This is the standard architecture of radicalization. You establish a narrative that makes all contradicting evidence into confirmation. Court rejections prove the courts are corrupt. Audit confirmations prove the auditors are compromised. Attorney General statements that the claims are nonsense prove the Attorney General is a traitor. Once the framework is established, nothing can refute it, because the framework has already pre-classified all refutation as part of the conspiracy.

The militia groups operating within this information environment did not need to independently verify the fraud claims. Their Commander in Chief had told them the election was stolen. The evidence confirming it was everywhere in the information ecosystem they inhabited. The legal and factual rebuttals were not evidence against the claim; they were evidence of how deep the conspiracy ran.

The 1776 Returns Battle Plan

In the weeks before January 6, a document called 1776 Returns circulated in the networks connected to the planning of the day. The document was a tactical plan for occupying the Capitol and adjacent federal buildings. It was premised explicitly on the assumption that the President would invoke the Insurrection Act and that the occupation would be legally protected and militarily supported by the executive branch.

The document reveals something legally significant about the mental state of the people who attacked the Capitol. They were not acting as a mob that lost control. They were acting as a force that believed it had authorization. They believed their Commander in Chief had told them the election was stolen, had summoned them to Washington, had told them to be wild, and had implied that he would invoke the legal mechanism that would make their occupation lawful.

This belief was based on the lie. The lie was the authorization. When the President told two months of stolen election narrative and then told the assembled crowd to march to the Capitol and fight like hell, the people who had been radicalized by the lie understood that as a command from the person whose authority they were there to vindicate.

The Feedback Loop's Legal Significance

The feedback loop between the lie and the assemblage is the causal mechanism that connects the information warfare to the levying of war. The Bollman standard requires an assemblage of persons for the purpose of executing a treasonable design. The design was to prevent the certification of the electoral results. The assemblage was the crowd that assembled in Washington on January 6. The lie was the mechanism that made the assemblage possible.

Without the lie, there is no assemblage. Without the assemblage, there is no levying of war. The lie and the overt act of treason are causally inseparable. The information warfare campaign was the first act of the war. January 6 was its kinetic execution.

□ □ □

Section Six: The Lie as an Overt Act — Synthesis

This chapter's final section makes the argument that the editorial analysis of this chapter identified as its most important contribution: the Big Lie itself, not merely as consciousness of guilt or as context for the overt acts documented in Chapter 3, but as an overt act of information warfare that, under the modern definition of hostile action established in Chapters 4 and 7, satisfies the constitutional standard.

Chapter 4 of this book established that under the Gadahn precedent and the Gerasimov Doctrine, hostile action against the United States does not require kinetic military force. It requires sustained, documented hostile action with the intent to harm American institutions, infrastructure, or lives. The Pentagon and NATO have formally recognized that cyber warfare and information warfare operations against critical infrastructure constitute acts of war.

American democracy's critical infrastructure includes its elections. The constitutional certification process is the specific mechanism through which the transfer of power that the Framers designed and that John Adams executed in 1801 occurs. An information warfare campaign specifically designed to delegitimize that infrastructure, to prevent that process from operating, and to manufacture an armed assemblage that would physically disrupt it, is an attack on American critical democratic infrastructure.

The Gerasimov Doctrine specifically describes the degradation of public trust in democratic institutions as a primary tool of hybrid warfare against Western democracies. The Big Lie was the domestic application of exactly the strategic framework that Russia's own military doctrine describes as warfare. It was waged against the American people by an American president using the most powerful communication platform in the world.

This observation does not establish that the Big Lie was coordinated with Russia or that it was executed in service of Russia's specific objectives. The Russia alignment is documented in Chapters 4 through 10. This chapter's observation is different: that the Big Lie, evaluated under the modern understanding of warfare that the preceding chapters have established, was itself a weapon of information warfare deployed against American democratic infrastructure.

The lie manufactured the army. The army levied the war. The lie and the war are causally inseparable. And a person who deploys a known falsehood as a weapon to manufacture an armed assemblage directed at a constitutional process has not merely lied about politics. He has committed, in the words of the Constitution's own definition, an overt act of levying war against the United States.

"The simplest definition of treason is this: using power you were trusted with to destroy the thing you were trusted to protect. The stolen election lie was

the mechanism. The Capitol was the target. The Constitution was the thing being destroyed." — **The constitutional argument of this chapter**

The next chapter is the Legal Opinion that assembles every element documented in this book into the citizen's brief for which this entire analysis has been building.

□ □ □

Chapter Fourteen

The NATO and Foreign Policy Lies: Misrepresenting the Alliance Destruction

There is a technique in communication and intelligence called inoculation. Before a damaging truth can spread, you get ahead of it with a more appealing counter-narrative. You establish in the audience's mind a story that makes the truth look like a lie when it eventually arrives.

The inoculation has to be deployed early, consistently, and with enough emotional resonance that it preemptively discredits the truth before the truth becomes visible. It is not enough to deny. You have to establish a counter-identity so firmly that the contradicting evidence looks like an attack rather than a correction.

This is not a new technique. It is the mechanism behind effective propaganda campaigns in every era of modern history. And it was deployed, with precision, around the single most damaging fact pattern in the entire Russia alignment documented in Chapters 4 through 8.

> *"I'm tougher on Russia than anyone."* **President Donald Trump, repeated across interviews, rallies, and social media posts, 2017 through 2019**

That was the inoculation narrative. It was deployed consistently, across years, across platforms, across contexts. And it was deployed specifically because the underlying pattern of conduct, the CAATSA sanctions non-implementation, the Helsinki submission, the intelligence sharing with Russian officials in the Oval Office, the Ukraine aid freeze, the NATO deconstruction documented in Chapter 6, was precisely the opposite of toughness.

The inoculation was not a response to criticism. It was a preemptive defense against a truth that the documented record of the preceding chapters establishes was being concealed. This chapter documents the specific lies that formed the inoculation strategy, their specific legal functions, and the specific legal framework that makes them relevant to the treason analysis rather than merely to a political accountability argument.

□ □ □

Section One: The NATO Funding Lie — Broadcasting the Enemy's Narrative

The repeated claim that the United States pays for NATO while European allies do not pay their fair share is factually wrong in a way that is documentable, specific, and legally significant beyond mere inaccuracy.

NATO does not operate as a common military budget that member nations contribute to proportionally. Each member nation funds its own military, with a benchmark goal of spending two percent of gross domestic product on defense. The United States military budget is large because United States global strategic interests, extending far beyond Europe to the Pacific, the Middle East, and every ocean and air corridor the American economy depends on, require a large military. The size of the American defense budget reflects American global ambitions and American strategic interests, not European free-loading.

This is not a matter of interpretation. It is documented in NATO's own financial reporting and confirmed by every credible defense economist who has examined the question. Secretary of Defense James Mattis, while serving in the administration, never endorsed the characterization of European allies as freeloaders. The uniformed military leadership never endorsed it. The intelligence community never endorsed it. The lie was not supported by any official within the national security apparatus whose job it was to evaluate it.

Why the Lie Was Deployed

The lie served a specific strategic function that the inoculation framework explains. It recast the alliance from a mutual defense arrangement in which American participation serves documented American strategic interests, which it does, into a protection racket in which America was being exploited by ungrateful allies who refused to pay what they owed.

That reframing is precisely Russia's preferred characterization of NATO. It is the narrative Russia needs its adversaries to believe in order to justify its own aggression, undermine allied solidarity, and erode the Article 5 collective defense guarantee that is the primary deterrent against Russian military expansion.

The Russian Federation has spent decades funding disinformation campaigns designed to convince European and American publics that NATO is an expensive, exploitative, and obsolete arrangement that serves American imperial interests rather than the mutual security of its members. The President of the United States delivered that narrative to the American public through the most credible possible source: the Commander in Chief himself.

The Broadcaster Precedents and Why They Apply

The World War II treason cases established a legal principle that this book has cited in previous chapters in other contexts. In the case of Mildred Gillars, known as Axis Sally, an American citizen was convicted of treason for broadcasting Nazi propaganda from Germany. Her broadcasts were designed to demoralize American forces and undermine American alliance cohesion. The court found that speech in service of an enemy's strategic objectives, delivered with the intent to advance the enemy's mission, constitutes an overt act of aid and comfort regardless of whether any physical weapon was used.

The Axis Sally precedent establishes a specific legal principle for this chapter's argument. If a private citizen broadcasting NATO is bad for American interests from a German radio station can be convicted of treason for serving the enemy's narrative, then the President of the United States delivering Russia's preferred NATO narrative from the Oval Office and from rally stages before tens of thousands of Americans achieves the same strategic objective with infinitely more power and credibility.

A private broadcaster has limited reach and limited credibility. The President of the United States has the most powerful public platform on earth and the institutional credibility of the most powerful office in the world. When that platform and that credibility are used to deliver the enemy's narrative to the American public, the broadcaster precedent applies with greater, not lesser, force.

Under the Gadahn precedent established in Chapter 4, speech in service of an enemy's strategic objectives can constitute an overt act of aid and comfort. Under the Axis Sally broadcaster precedent, the propagation of the enemy's preferred narrative about American alliances is an overt act when performed with knowledge of the enemy's objectives. The NATO funding lie was Russia's preferred narrative. The President delivered it to the American public with the authority of his office. The broadcaster precedents apply.

□ □ □

Section Two: The G7 Re-Admission Lie — Acting as Russia's Advocate

In 2018, and repeatedly in subsequent years, the President advocated publicly and within the G7 forum for Russia's readmission to the group from which it had been expelled in 2014.

Russia was expelled from what was then the G8 following its illegal annexation of Crimea, a violation of Ukrainian sovereignty, international law, and the commitments Russia had made in the 1994 Budapest Memorandum, in which Russia had specifically agreed to respect Ukraine's territorial integrity in exchange for Ukraine surrendering its Soviet-era nuclear weapons.

The President's stated reason for advocating Russia's readmission was pragmatic: Russia should be at the table. The G7 was a meeting of the leaders of the world, and excluding Russia was counterproductive.

This framing contained a specific lie. Russia was not excluded because of a diplomatic disagreement or a procedural dispute. It was excluded because it had used military force to seize sovereign territory belonging to a nation that had surrendered its nuclear deterrent based on Russia's own security guarantees. The exclusion was the sanction. The readmission would have been the reward for the violation.

The Legal Significance of G7 Advocacy

When the President of the United States argues, within a multilateral forum designed to coordinate Western policy toward Russia, that Russia's conduct should be excused and its exclusion from that forum should be ended, he is not conducting diplomacy. He is acting as Russia's lawyer.

The distinction matters legally because diplomatic engagement with Russia, including discussions about how to manage the relationship, is a legitimate exercise of executive foreign policy authority. Advocating within a Western coalition forum for the termination of the specific sanctions architecture that was Russia's primary economic consequence for violating international law is not diplomacy. It is advocacy on behalf of the adversary against the collective position of every American ally.

Every other G7 leader refused to support Russian readmission. The unanimous allied position was that Russia's readmission was contingent on compliance with international law regarding Ukraine. The American President was the sole voice within the forum arguing for Russia's rehabilitation without compliance. He was not mediating between positions. He was taking Russia's side against the position of every nation in the alliance.

Under the adherence treason standard established in Chapter 5, adherence to an enemy requires association with the enemy's venture, participation in it as something the actor wished to bring about, and seeking by his actions to make it succeed. Advocating within a Western forum for the termination of the sanctions that constitute the enemy's primary economic consequence for documented hostile action against the United States and its allies is participation in the enemy's diplomatic objective. It seeks to make the enemy's mission succeed.

□ □ □

Section Three: The Toughness Inoculation — The Javelin Defense and Why It Fails

The most commonly deployed defense against the Russia alignment argument in this book is specific and deserves a specific answer. The defense goes like this: the President gave Ukraine Javelin anti-tank missiles. Barack Obama refused to provide lethal weapons to Ukraine. Trump provided them. That proves he was tougher on Russia than his predecessor, and the toughness narrative was not inoculation. It was accurate.

This argument is worth addressing directly because it is not entirely without factual foundation. The Javelin decision was real. It was a departure from the Obama administration's position. And it served as the factual anchor for the toughness inoculation.

Why a Single Weapons System Does Not Establish Toughness

The legal question is not whether any specific action that could be characterized as tough was taken. The legal question is whether the pattern of conduct, evaluated as a whole under the Kawakita standard, demonstrates the consistent conscious objective of advancing Russia's mission.

The Kawakita standard does not evaluate individual acts in isolation. It evaluates the totality. And the totality of the Ukraine relationship is not captured by the Javelin decision.

It is captured by the Javelin decision alongside the 2019 Ukraine aid freeze that withheld $391 million in congressionally authorized military assistance while Russian-backed forces operated against Ukrainian lines, alongside the 2025 suspension of military assistance that the Government Accountability Office found violated the Impoundment Control Act for the second time, alongside the public pressure on Ukraine to negotiate on terms that European allies uniformly described as favorable to Russia.

Providing one weapons system while simultaneously dismantling the alliance structure that makes those weapons effective is not toughness. It is a token gesture designed to provide cover for the larger strategic pattern. The Javelin missiles required American training to use effectively. That training was part of the military assistance package that the 2019 freeze suspended. The weapons were provided. The training and the broader assistance that made the weapons operationally effective were frozen at the moment they were most needed.

The toughness inoculation worked because it contained a grain of factual truth. The best inoculations always do. A completely false claim is easier to refute than a misleading one. The Javelin decision was real. It was used to establish the toughness narrative. And then, eighteen months later, while Russian-backed forces were operating against Ukrainian lines, the congressionally authorized military assistance that would have included training, radar systems, and equipment was sitting in a warehouse because the President had frozen it to extort a political favor. The inoculation was the Javelins. The betrayal was the freeze.

□ □ □

Section Four: The Ukraine Corruption Pretext — A False Justification in Four Testimonies

The official justification for the 2019 Ukraine aid freeze was concern about Ukrainian corruption. This justification was given to the press, to Congress, to allied governments, and to the public. It was the stated reason for conduct that the Government Accountability Office subsequently found had violated the Impoundment Control Act.

Then the witnesses testified. And the sworn testimony dismantled the justification with a completeness that four independent witnesses, each with specific direct knowledge of the decision-making process, achieved by converging on the same account.

The Four Testimonies

Ambassador William Taylor, the senior American diplomatic official in Ukraine during the freeze, testified that no corruption concerns had been raised through normal diplomatic channels during the period of the hold. If genuine concern about Ukrainian corruption were the reason for the freeze, Ambassador Taylor would have been aware of those concerns. His testimony established that the stated reason was not communicated through the standard channels through which genuine policy concerns are expressed.

Dr. Fiona Hill, the National Security Council's senior director for Europe and Russia and one of the most qualified Russia policy experts in the United States government, testified that the corruption pretext was not the actual reason for the hold. She was present in the internal deliberations. She knew what the actual reason was. And she testified, under oath, that the stated justification did not reflect it.

Ambassador Gordon Sondland, who had donated one million dollars to the Trump inaugural committee and had been appointed European Union Ambassador through his political relationship with the President, provided the clearest and most unambiguous testimony about what the hold was actually conditioned on.

> *"Was there a quid pro quo? As I testified previously, with regard to the requested White House call and White House meeting, the answer is yes."*
> **— Ambassador Gordon Sondland, House Intelligence Committee, November 2019**

The Government Accountability Office, in its January 2020 report, found that the Office of Management and Budget had violated the Impoundment Control Act by withholding the congressionally appropriated funds. The GAO found the violation regardless of what justification was offered, because the law does not permit the executive branch to substitute its policy preferences for congressional appropriation decisions.

Four witnesses. Four independent accounts. One consistent conclusion. The stated justification was false. The real condition for the aid was political. The political action benefited Russia by withholding military assistance from a nation Russia was actively attacking. And the false justification was the inoculation that was deployed to make the political condition invisible.

The Pattern Across Both Terms

The corruption pretext did not appear only in 2019. It was deployed as a recurring justification across both terms wherever Ukraine policy was involved. When military assistance was suspended in 2025, the stated justification involved concerns about Ukrainian governance. When diplomatic pressure was applied to Ukraine to negotiate on terms favorable to Russia, the public framing involved Ukrainian accountability and burden-sharing.

Under the Kawakita standard, a justification that is deployed repeatedly across different instances of the same conduct is not a policy position. It is a strategic narrative. The consistency of the Ukraine corruption pretext across years and across different instances of the same underlying conduct is the pattern from which the Kawakita inference of deliberate intent is drawn.

□ □ □

Section Five: The DNC Server Lie — The Purest Form of Aid and Comfort

The most legally elegant example of the foreign policy lie as aid and comfort is the claim that Ukraine, not Russia, hacked the Democratic National Committee server in 2016.

This theory, which circulated in pro-Russian internet forums and was amplified by Russian state media, claimed that the DNC hack attributed to Russian military intelligence by the unanimous January 2017 Intelligence Community Assessment was actually conducted by Ukrainian actors attempting to frame Russia. The President raised this theory in conversations with Ukraine, in press statements, and, according to the testimony of Fiona Hill and other witnesses, in private meetings with his own national security officials who uniformly told him the theory was false and was itself a Russian intelligence fabrication.

What the Theory Does

The DNC server theory performs two simultaneous operations for Russia.

First, it exonerates Russia for the 2016 interference operation that the unanimous Intelligence Community Assessment concluded Putin personally ordered. By attributing the hack to Ukraine, it removes the established factual predicate for the sanctions and the investigative focus that Russia's election interference had generated. Russia had been sanctioned, its officials had been expelled, its operations had been investigated, and its culpability had been documented by every American intelligence agency. The server theory, if believed, erases all of that.

Second, it implicates Ukraine, the nation that was simultaneously resisting Russian military aggression in its eastern territories and whose military effectiveness depended on American assistance and alliance solidarity. A Ukraine that hacked American political organizations to frame Russia is a Ukraine that is not a reliable American partner, not a nation deserving of military assistance, and not a cause around which Western alliances should cohere.

The theory exonerates the enemy. It incriminates the ally. It serves Russia's strategic objectives at every dimension simultaneously.

Why the President Was Told It Was False

The theory was not merely contested. It was specifically and directly refuted by the American intelligence community. Fiona Hill testified before the House Intelligence Committee that she had told the President directly that the server theory was a fictional narrative that had been perpetrated and propagated by the Russian security services themselves. She told him this. He continued promoting the theory.

A President who has been told by his own intelligence officials that a specific claim is a Russian intelligence fabrication designed to shift blame from Russia to an American ally, and who continues to promote that claim publicly, is not making a policy judgment. He is making a choice. And under the Chandler standard established in Chapter 5, the objective consequence of that choice, shielding Russia from accountability and implicating its victim, is what the law evaluates. The motive for the choice, the internal justification, is legally secondary.

To lie in order to shield an enemy from accountability for a documented attack on American democracy is the definition of providing aid and comfort. The DNC server lie used the authority of the presidency to validate a Russian intelligence fabrication. It exonerated Russia for a proven hostile act. It implicated an American ally in that same act. And it was promoted after the President had been told, by his own intelligence officials, that it was false. That is not inoculation. That is adhesion to the enemy's mission.

> **THE WITNESSES:** *The Intelligence Community Assessment's unanimous conclusion that Russian military intelligence conducted the DNC hack is the primary source document. Fiona Hill's testimony that she told the President the server theory was a Russian intelligence fabrication is documented in House Intelligence Committee transcripts. The President's continued promotion of the theory after receiving this briefing is documented in press statements and the July 25, 2019 Zelensky call transcript released by the White House. The Sondland quid pro quo testimony is documented in House Intelligence Committee transcripts.*

□ □ □

Section Six: The Legal Synthesis — Strategic Cover for Strategic Betrayal

The foreign policy lies documented in this chapter served a unified strategic function. They were not independent instances of political spin. They were the cover narrative for the pattern of conduct documented in Chapters 4 through 10.

The inoculation narrative established a public identity of toughness that made the documented pattern of Russia alignment appear impossible. The NATO funding lie recast the alliance deconstruction of Chapter 6 as fiscal responsibility rather than strategic capitulation. The G7 re-admission advocacy positioned the dismantlement of the sanctions architecture as pragmatic diplomacy rather than Russia advocacy. The Javelin toughness narrative provided a factual anchor for the inoculation while the 2019 freeze and the 2025 suspension were executing the actual betrayal. The Ukraine corruption pretext provided a false justification for conduct that four witnesses testified under oath had a completely different actual motivation. And the DNC server lie used the presidential platform to validate a Russian intelligence fabrication and implicate Russia's victim in Russia's crime.

The pattern of lies tracks the pattern of overt acts with precision. Each lie corresponds to a specific overt act that it was designed to conceal. That correspondence is not accidental. It is the architecture of a deliberate deception campaign designed to allow the conduct to continue without triggering the institutional and political accountability that exposure would have produced.

Under the Kawakita standard, intent is inferred from the totality of conduct. The totality includes not only the overt acts but the lies that were constructed to conceal them. A person who tells the truth about his conduct does not need an inoculation narrative. A person who constructs a systematic cover narrative that tracks precisely the overt acts being concealed has demonstrated, through the architecture of the deception itself, the awareness that the underlying conduct required concealment.

That awareness is the specific intent the treason analysis requires.

The foreign policy lies are not peripheral to the treason analysis. They are the connective tissue between the financial motive documented in Chapter 9, the overt acts documented in Chapters 4 through 8, and the intent that the Kawakita standard permits the jury to infer from the totality of conduct. The inoculation strategy was not a communications decision. It was an architecture of denial built specifically to prevent the exposure of a documented pattern of strategic betrayal.

□ □ □

Chapter Fifteen

The Iran Ceasefire Denial: The Most Documented Lie in the Record

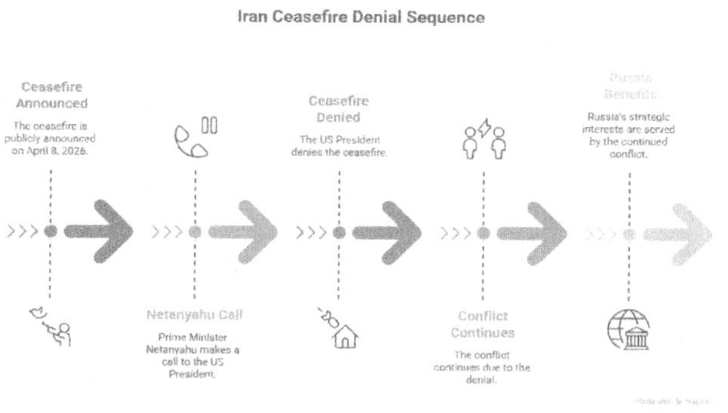

Of all the lies documented in Part V of this book, the Lebanon ceasefire denial of April 8, 2026 is the most specifically documented, the most clearly witnessed, and the most immediately consequential.

It is the lie that most cleanly satisfies the two-witness constitutional requirement for treason. It is the lie whose consequences were most immediate and most countable. And it is the lie that, in the context of this book's central argument, most precisely served the identified enemy's documented strategic interests.

This chapter is not a policy argument. It is a legal analysis of a specific documented act with a specific documented causal chain, specific identified witnesses, and a specific and quantifiable benefit to Russia that satisfies the Cramer actual aid standard.

The chapter does this in four steps. First, documenting what was announced. Second, documenting what was denied. Third, documenting what happened as a direct result. Fourth, establishing why the continuation of the conflict that the denial enabled served Russia's primary strategic objectives and therefore constitutes aid and comfort to the identified enemy under the constitutional standard this book has applied throughout.

□ □ □

Section One: What Was Announced — The Ceasefire That Was Real

On April 8, 2026, Pakistani Prime Minister Shehbaz Sharif made an announcement to the world.

Pakistan had been serving as the mediating nation in the negotiations between the United States, Iran, and their respective allied parties over the 2026 Iran war that had begun on February 28 when Operation Epic Fury launched its initial strikes. The mediation had been conducted with full diplomatic participation from multiple nations. It was not a backroom arrangement. It was a formal multilateral process.

Sharif announced that a ceasefire had been reached. It was effective immediately. And critically, it included all fronts of the conflict, including Lebanon.

Lebanese President Joseph Aoun welcomed the announcement and praised the mediation efforts of Pakistan, Egypt, and Turkey. His welcome was not cautious or qualified. It reflected his understanding, based on the specific communications he had received through diplomatic channels, that Lebanon was included.

Hezbollah announced a pause in its attacks against Israel. The announcement was made in direct reliance on the ceasefire's Lebanon inclusion. Hezbollah stopped shooting because Hezbollah understood, based on the announcement by the mediating nation, that it was covered.

Iran, the United States, and Israel all initially indicated they would suspend strikes. President Trump cited Iran's 10-point framework as a basis for ongoing negotiation, signaling that the comprehensive announcement Pakistan had made was consistent with the diplomatic framework the administration understood to be in place.

The ceasefire was real. It was announced. It was acted upon. Hezbollah stopped shooting. That is a documented fact established by contemporaneous diplomatic records, public statements from heads of state and government, and the specific behavioral change of Hezbollah, which suspended its operations.

□ □ □

Section Two: What Was Denied — The Reversal That Followed the Netanyahu Call

Within hours of the Pakistan announcement, the denial began.

Prime Minister Netanyahu said the ceasefire did not include Lebanon. President Trump said Lebanon was not included in the deal because of Hezbollah's presence. Vice President Vance walked back the comprehensive framing that Pakistan's announcement had established, characterizing the overall arrangement as a fragile truce rather than a comprehensive ceasefire. The White House said Lebanon had never been part of the deal.

Iran said the opposite. France said the opposite. Pakistan, as the mediating nation, said the opposite.

> *"Lebanon was fully included in the ceasefire."* **French President Emmanuel Macron, April 8, 2026**

France was not a disinterested bystander. France had been actively involved in the regional diplomatic process. Macron was not speculating about what Pakistan had intended to announce. He was stating his direct understanding of the negotiated terms. His statement was made publicly, on the record, on the same day as the denial.

On April 9, 2026, CBS News reported that diplomats confirmed that President Trump had initially included Lebanon in the ceasefire, and that even Israel had acknowledged these terms before the position shifted following a tense phone call between Netanyahu and Trump. Multiple diplomats. On the record through a credible news organization. Confirming Lebanon's inclusion as an established fact of the negotiation that was subsequently reversed.

The documentary record establishes a specific sequence. Lebanon was included. Trump knew Lebanon was included. Israel initially acknowledged the terms. Netanyahu called. The position shifted. Lebanon was excluded. And Operation Eternal Darkness began.

The reversal was not a clarification of a misunderstanding. There was no ambiguity in Pakistan's announcement or in France's confirmation or in the diplomatic record that CBS reported. The reversal was a change of position that followed a specific phone call between the Israeli Prime Minister and the American President, and it removed the ceasefire protection that Hezbollah had already relied upon in halting its attacks.

□ □ □

Section Three: The Two-Witness Requirement — Heads of State as Constitutional Witnesses

Article III, Section 3 of the Constitution requires no person to be convicted of treason unless on the testimony of two witnesses to the same overt act or on a confession in open court.

The legal question this chapter must answer is whether the Lebanon ceasefire denial constitutes an overt act that meets the two-witness standard.

It does. And it meets that standard with a redundancy that leaves no reasonable interpretive space.

Who the Witnesses Are

French President Emmanuel Macron made a public statement on April 8, 2026 confirming that Lebanon was fully included in the ceasefire. He was not repeating what he had heard from a news report. He was stating his direct understanding of the diplomatic terms that had been negotiated with France's participation in the regional process. His statement is on the record, contemporaneously made, and by a head of state of a major ally with direct diplomatic involvement in the negotiations.

Pakistani Prime Minister Shehbaz Sharif made the comprehensive ceasefire announcement in his capacity as the mediating nation's head of government. He announced that all fronts were included, including Lebanon, based on his direct knowledge of the negotiated terms. He was not a third-party observer. He was the mediator. His announcement was made in his official capacity, based on direct firsthand knowledge of what had been agreed.

Multiple diplomats, confirmed by CBS News on April 9, provided contemporaneous corroboration that Lebanon had been included in the initial agreement and that the shift in position followed the Netanyahu call. These were not anonymous sources providing opinion. They were participants in or briefed on the actual negotiations.

Why These Witnesses Satisfy the Constitutional Standard

The two-witness rule was designed to prevent treason prosecutions from proceeding on the word of a single, potentially biased or mistaken accuser. The Framers understood that a person's life and liberty should not be forfeited based on one person's testimony about an act whose character the witnesses had not directly observed.

The witnesses here are not one person. They are the heads of state of France and Pakistan, multiple diplomatic sources corroborated through credible news reporting, and the behavioral record of Hezbollah itself, which halted attacks in direct reliance on the inclusion they had been told was real. Each of these witnesses is independent of the others. Each has specific direct knowledge of the negotiated terms. Each has documented their account contemporaneously. And each account is consistent.

The President of France and the Prime Minister of Pakistan are not anonymous sources. They are heads of state with direct diplomatic knowledge of what was negotiated. Their testimony would be admissible in any court in any jurisdiction in the world. The constitutional requirement for two witnesses to the same overt act is met here with a redundancy that would satisfy the most rigorous application of the Cramer standard. The overt act is documented. The witnesses are documented. The two-witness rule is satisfied.

> **THE WITNESSES:** *The witnesses to the ceasefire's Lebanon inclusion are: French President Emmanuel Macron, public statement April 8, 2026; Pakistani Prime Minister Shehbaz Sharif, official mediating announcement April 8, 2026; multiple unnamed diplomats confirmed by CBS News*

through reporting published April 9, 2026; the behavioral record of Hezbollah, which halted attacks in direct reliance on the announced inclusion; and Lebanese President Joseph Aoun, who publicly welcomed the announcement based on his understanding of its terms. The subsequent denial by President Trump is on the public record in his own statements, including his interview with PBS News Hour in which he stated Lebanon was not included because of Hezbollah.

□ □ □

Section Four: Black Wednesday — The Causal Chain to the Massacre

On the same day that the denial was issued, Israel launched Operation Eternal Darkness.

The operation involved approximately 50 fighter jets delivering approximately 160 munitions across Lebanon in a 10-minute window. One hundred targets struck simultaneously. The strikes hit densely populated civilian areas of Lebanon including Beirut neighborhoods such as Ain al-Mreisseh, Basta, and Barbour, where civilian populations had no more warning than the time it took for a bomb to fall from altitude.

At least 357 people were killed. Over 1,200 were injured. Lebanon called it Black Wednesday.

The Causal Chain

The causal chain is direct and documented and requires no inference.

Hezbollah halted its attacks against Israel on the morning of April 8 in direct reliance on Pakistan's announcement that Lebanon was included in the ceasefire. That reliance was reasonable. The mediating nation had made a specific announcement. France had confirmed it. Lebanon's President had welcomed it. Hezbollah ceased fire.

The denial of Lebanon's inclusion was then issued following the Netanyahu call. The removal of the ceasefire protection that Hezbollah had relied upon to halt its attacks created a window of military vulnerability. Hezbollah had stood down. Israel then launched Operation Eternal Darkness.

The denial of Lebanon's inclusion did not merely misrepresent diplomatic terms. It removed the defensive posture that a genuine ceasefire would have maintained. By announcing the ceasefire in terms that led Hezbollah to stand down, and then denying those terms after Hezbollah had already ceased fire, the denial functioned as a trap. Hezbollah halted in good faith. The denial of the good faith created the opening. Operation Eternal Darkness filled it.

The Human Cost

Three hundred and fifty-seven dead in 10 minutes. A funeral struck in the Beqaa Valley, killing 10 mourners. Three girls killed in Adloun. A surgeon operating on an 11-month-old infant at the American University of Beirut Medical Center, who arrived alone at the emergency room amid the chaos, to relieve pressure in the child's head. Hospitals flooded with more than 70 critically injured patients simultaneously, rendering the medical golden hour, the 60-minute window for life-saving intervention in trauma cases, mathematically impossible to honor.

The military doctrine used in the operation was specifically designed to overwhelm emergency response capacity. By striking 48 distinct geographic zones simultaneously, the operation saturated radar, emergency networks, and hospital intake systems. The speed was calculated. The simultaneous breadth was calculated. The effect was calculated. And the lie was what made it possible.

□ □ □

Section Five: The Strategic Beneficiary — Why Russia Needed the War to Continue

The treason analysis requires more than a documented lie with documented consequences. It requires that the lie provide aid and comfort to the enemy identified in Chapter 4. And the editorial analysis this book has undertaken for every chapter in Part V requires this chapter to make that connection explicit.

This section makes it.

What a Comprehensive Ceasefire Would Have Done

A comprehensive ceasefire on April 8, 2026 that included Lebanon and held across all fronts would have produced a specific set of strategic consequences. The Strait of Hormuz, effectively closed since the Iranian blockade that had produced the 94 percent collapse in tanker traffic documented in Chapter 7, would have been on a path to reopening. Global oil prices, which had surged toward $100 per barrel and were projected to rise further if the closure continued, would have stabilized and declined as the market anticipated the restoration of normal transit.

American military resources, the precision-guided munitions, the Patriot interceptors, the naval assets, the intelligence community bandwidth, consumed by Operation Epic Fury in the Iran theater, would have been available for redeployment. European allies, who had been forced into a second major energy crisis by the Strait of Hormuz closure, would have had relief from the inflationary pressure that the war had imposed on their economies.

And Russia, which had been collecting a financial windfall from the energy market disruption that Chapter 7 documented as a direct benefit of the Iran war's continuation, would have seen that windfall begin to diminish.

What the Denial Preserved

The denial of Lebanon's inclusion in the ceasefire ensured that the war continued. Operation Eternal Darkness was not merely a military operation against Hezbollah. It was the action that transformed a potential comprehensive peace into a continued conflict. By enabling the operation through the denial of Hezbollah's ceasefire coverage, the denial guaranteed that the Iran war's consequences, including the Strait of Hormuz closure, the energy market disruption, the oil price spike, and the American resource diversion, would persist.

Russia's documented strategic interests in the continuation of the Iran war are addressed in Chapter 7. The war produced an oil price windfall that delivered tens of billions in additional revenue to the Russian economy. It consumed American military resources that would otherwise be available for the European theater where Russia is engaged in active warfare. It fractured NATO in the specific ways the Gerasimov Doctrine described as primary objectives of Russian hybrid warfare. And it maintained the global attention diversion that reduced domestic American and allied political pressure to respond to Russian aggression in Ukraine.

The denial of Lebanon's ceasefire inclusion preserved every one of these strategic benefits to Russia for the additional weeks during which the Lebanon conflict continued after Black Wednesday. The oil prices that Russia was collecting windfall revenues from did not fall. The American resources did not redeploy. The NATO fracturing did not heal. Russia continued to benefit from the continuation of the conflict.

The Cramer Actual Aid Analysis

Under the Cramer standard, the aid must be actual. The Strait of Hormuz's continued closure following Black Wednesday is documented in commodity market records and shipping industry data. Russia's continued oil revenue windfall during the period following the denial is documented in energy market analysis and Treasury Department assessments. The American resource diversion that continued during the weeks of the Lebanon conflict is documented in Pentagon records and congressional testimony about munitions drawdowns.

The denial of Lebanon's ceasefire inclusion is the most specifically timed act of aid to Russia documented in this book. The ceasefire would have ended the conflict's most significant contribution to Russian strategic objectives. The denial extended those contributions. The beneficiary is documented. The benefit is documented. The act is documented.

A comprehensive ceasefire on April 8, 2026 would have lowered oil prices, freed American military resources, relieved allied economic pressure, and ended the conflict that was delivering Russia a strategic windfall. Russia needed the war to continue. The denial of the ceasefire ensured it did. The bombs fell on Lebanon. The strategic benefit flowed to Moscow. The lie was not merely a diplomatic deceit. It was a mechanism to prolong a war that served the enemy's economic

and strategic interests, deployed through the mechanism of diplomatic perfidy, enabled by the authority of the American presidency.

□ □ □

Section Six: Perfidy — The Weaponization of American Credibility

There is a specific term in international law for the act of using the appearance of a protected status, such as a ceasefire, to gain a military advantage over an adversary who has relied on that protection in good faith. The term is perfidy. Under the laws of armed conflict, perfidy is prohibited as a war crime because it destroys the basic premise on which protected status operates. If ceasefires can be used as traps, parties will never trust them. If surrender flags can be used to set ambushes, parties will never surrender. The prohibition on perfidy is the prohibition on using the mechanisms of peace as weapons of war.

The Lebanon ceasefire denial meets the functional definition of perfidy. The ceasefire was announced. Hezbollah relied on it in good faith and stood down. The protection was then denied. The standing down created a military opening. The opening was exploited. Three hundred and fifty-seven people died.

The Broader Damage to American Diplomatic Power

Beyond the immediate harm, the perfidy of the Lebanon ceasefire denial inflicted a specific and lasting damage on the United States that is strategically significant independent of the body count.

The United States' diplomatic power, its ability to negotiate agreements, broker ceasefires, and mediate conflicts, rests on the credibility of the American presidential word. When other parties to a negotiation agree to terms that the American President endorses, they do so in reliance on the American President's commitment being real. That reliance is the foundation of American diplomatic leverage. It is why other nations come to Washington when they need mediation rather than going to Moscow or Beijing.

The Lebanon ceasefire denial destroyed that credibility in the specific theater where it was exercised. If the American President commits to ceasefire terms and then reverses that commitment following a call from an ally, allowing a massacre to proceed against parties who had already stood down in reliance on the commitment, then every future party to a U.S.-mediated negotiation must ask: is this commitment real, or will it be reversed the next time a U.S. ally makes a phone call?

That question weakens American diplomatic power across every arena in which it operates. It is not a temporary diplomatic setback. It is the destruction of a national security asset, because American diplomatic credibility is as much a component of American national security as any weapons system or intelligence capability.

Under the economic front analysis of Chapter 10, this book established that the destruction of American national security assets through deliberate conduct, performed with knowledge of the enemy's objectives and their benefit from that destruction, constitutes aid and comfort under the Haupt standard. The weaponization of American credibility through diplomatic perfidy is the destruction of a national security asset. Russia, whose primary strategic interest in the Middle East theater was the continuation of the conflict and the sustained reduction of American diplomatic and military effectiveness, benefited from that destruction directly.

□ □ □

Section Seven: The Legal Synthesis — The Lie with the Body Count

The Lebanon ceasefire denial is the most tightly documented overt act in this book's entire treason analysis. It satisfies every legal element the preceding chapters have established as necessary.

The allegiance element is established by the oath documented in Chapter 2. The enemy element is established by the Cramer hostile purpose standard and the Gadahn functional definition documented in Chapter 4. The overt act element is established by the documented denial of Lebanon's ceasefire inclusion, confirmed by two heads of state and multiple diplomatic sources. The two-witness requirement is satisfied by France's Macron and Pakistan's Sharif, both heads of state with direct diplomatic knowledge, corroborated by multiple diplomatic sources and Hezbollah's own behavioral record. The actual aid element under the Cramer standard is satisfied by the documented continuation of the conflict's strategic benefits to Russia that the denial preserved. And the intent element under the Kawakita standard is established by the pattern documented in Chapters 4 through 14, of which this act is the most precisely timed and most directly consequential.

The two-witness rule is satisfied. The actual aid standard is satisfied. The causal chain is direct and documented. The strategic beneficiary is identified and documented. And the immediate human cost is 357 people dead in 10 minutes on a day that could have been the day the Lebanon war ended.

The two-witness requirement is met by heads of state. The causal chain to the massacre is established by the timeline of the airstrikes. The strategic beneficiary of the continued chaos was the adversary whose interests the President had consistently advanced across two terms. This was not a miscommunication. It was a trap set with the authority of the American presidency. It resulted in the deaths of 357 people and the preservation of a conflict status quo that served the enemy. This is the lie with the body count. And in the legal framework of this book, it is an overt act of aid and comfort delivered through the mechanism of diplomatic perfidy.

□ □ □

Chapter Sixteen

The Economic and Domestic Lies: Misrepresenting National Harm

When a doctor tells a patient they have nothing to worry about, and the doctor knows that is not true, we do not call that a political disagreement. We call it malpractice. The patient's ability to seek treatment, to protect themselves, to prepare for what is coming, has been taken from them by the lie.

The economic and domestic lies documented in this chapter are a form of national malpractice. They concealed from the American public the real consequences of policies whose strategic effects, as documented in Chapters 9 and 10, advanced the interests of the identified enemy. A public that does not know it is being harmed cannot act to stop the harm. That is the function of the lie.

But this chapter's legal argument is more specific than the malpractice analogy suggests. These lies were not merely political malpractice, the failure of a government to be honest with its citizens about inconvenient truths. They were information warfare operations that disabled the country's ability to defend itself, thereby aiding the adversary. They concealed threat vectors that the enemy was actively exploiting. They inoculated the public against the policy corrections that an honest accounting would have produced. And in doing so, they removed the early warning systems that a democracy relies on to protect itself from the exact categories of harm the Gerasimov Doctrine targets.

□ □ □

Section One: The COVID Lie — Disabling the National Defense

On February 7, 2020, the President of the United States told journalist Bob Woodward, in a recorded conversation, that COVID-19 was deadly stuff and more deadly than even your strenuous flus. He said it goes through the air. He understood the airborne transmission mechanism. He understood the lethality. He had been told by National Security Advisor Robert O'Brien on January 28 that the virus would be the gravest national security threat he would face in his presidency. He had been told by Deputy National Security Advisor Matthew Pottinger that it was comparable to the 1918 Spanish Flu pandemic, which killed between 50 and 100 million people globally.

On the same day as the February 7 Woodward recording, the President's public communications continued to characterize the virus as manageable and mild. On February 2 he had told the public that the United States had pretty much shut it down. On February 26 he predicted there would soon be zero cases. He likened the virus to seasonal flu.

The Woodward recordings established, as a matter of contemporaneous audio record, that the gap between private knowledge and public statement was not a matter of evolving scientific understanding or appropriate caution about uncertain facts. The President told Woodward on March 19: I wanted to always play it down. I still like playing it down, because I don't want to create a panic.

He played it down. He knew it was deadly. He played it down anyway.

The National Security Dimension

The 2022 National Security Strategy, which the President received and which this book has cited throughout as the authoritative statement of what the intelligence community had told him about the relationship between domestic resilience and national security, explicitly identifies public health as a component of national power. A biological threat that kills over a million Americans and produces the largest economic disruption since the Great Depression is a national security event.

By lying about the nature of the threat, the President disabled the national defense response. He prevented the mobilization of resources at the scale and speed the threat required. He prevented the implementation of containment strategies that public cooperation would have made possible. He prevented the public vigilance necessary to mitigate the attack. A population that has been told there is no serious threat does not take the precautions that slow transmission, protect the vulnerable, or preserve the economic activity that a functioning national defense requires.

The result was a pandemic response that was chaotic, delayed, and catastrophically under-resourced in its critical early weeks, because the person who controlled the information about the threat had chosen to conceal it.

The Russia Connection

Russia's Gerasimov Doctrine, which Chapter 4 established as Russia's published declaration of hostile intent against Western democracies, specifically identifies the exploitation of internal crises and healthcare failures as primary tools of hybrid warfare. The doctrine describes the degradation of public trust in government institutions, the amplification of social divisions, and the exploitation of healthcare failures as the specific conditions through which Western democracies are weakened without military engagement.

During the COVID pandemic, Russian state media and Russian-affiliated social media operations ran documented disinformation campaigns specifically targeting American pandemic response. Russian active measures amplified vaccine misinformation, attacked public health institutions, and promoted the political divisions that the pandemic had exposed. Senate Intelligence Committee findings documented the specific Russian operations targeting American pandemic-related social divisions.

The President's public messaging during the pandemic aligned with the Russian disinformation campaigns in specific and documented ways. Both minimized the threat. Both attacked public health institutions and the scientists who ran them. Both amplified social division around pandemic response measures. Whether this alignment was coordinated or merely served Russia's objectives through the mechanism of compatible messaging, the effect was identical: the American pandemic response was weakened, social trust was eroded, and the domestic instability that Russia's doctrine identified as its objective was produced.

The Woodward tapes establish the knowledge element. On February 7, 2020, the President knew COVID-19 was deadly and airborne. He then told the public the opposite. The lie disabled the national defense response to a biological threat. Russia was actively exploiting that threat through information warfare operations. A President who lies about a biological threat vector that his own national security staff has characterized as the gravest threat he faces, while Russia actively exploits American chaos around that threat, has provided aid and comfort through the mechanism of domestic information warfare.

□ □ □

Section Two: The Tariff Lie — Financing the Fracture

The claim that tariffs imposed on Chinese imports are paid by China is specifically, universally, and thoroughly contradicted by economic analysis from the Federal Reserve, the International Monetary Fund, the Congressional Budget Office, and every mainstream economic research institution that has examined the question.

Tariffs are taxes on imports. They are paid by the American importers who purchase the goods, and they are passed on to American consumers in the form of higher prices. This is not contested among economists. Peer-reviewed studies on the 2018 tariffs concluded they resulted in complete pass-through to U.S. domestic prices. By the end of 2018, tariffs were costing U.S. consumers and firms an estimated $3 billion per month in added tax costs and $1.4 billion per month in deadweight welfare losses. The Congressional Budget Office estimated that the 2025 tariff expansion would reduce the size of the U.S. economy, increase inflation by an average of 0.4 percentage points annually, and reduce household purchasing power.

China's exporters responded to the tariffs by redirecting trade to other markets. Chinese exports to Africa grew by 29.3 percent and to ASEAN nations by 17.8 percent. The tariffs did not stop Chinese exports. They rerouted them while imposing the full cost of the resulting price increases on American households.

Why the Lie Mattered Strategically

The legal argument about the tariff lie is not primarily that the policy was wrong. Policy disagreements are legitimate. The legal argument is that the lie was the mechanism that allowed the policy to continue.

Without the lie, the American public would have understood that the trade war was a domestic tax on American consumers, not a penalty on China. A public that understood the economic reality would have demanded a different cost-benefit analysis of the trade war's strategic consequences. And the trade war's strategic consequences, beyond the domestic economic cost, included the fracturing of Western economic alliances documented in Chapter 10.

European allies, Canadian allies, and Asian trading partners who were also targeted by American tariffs during the same period were forced to evaluate whether their economic relationships with the United States could be relied upon. The tariff policy, presented to the American public as a tool for punishing China and restoring American economic strength, was simultaneously a policy that drove U.S. trading partners to develop dollar-independent payment systems, alternative trade relationships, and economic architectures that reduced their dependence on the dollar-based financial system that is documented in Chapter 10 as America's primary strategic economic asset.

Russia benefited from this fracturing in the specific ways Chapter 10 documents. The degradation of the dollar's reserve status reduces the effectiveness of American sanctions, which are Russia's primary economic constraint. The fracturing of Western economic alliances reduces the coordinated economic pressure on Russia that multilateral sanctions require. And the domestic economic disruption produced by the tariff policy feeds the social instability that Russia's doctrine identifies as the condition it needs for successful hybrid warfare.

The tariff lie was not merely an inaccurate description of trade economics. It was the political mechanism that allowed a policy to continue that was simultaneously imposing domestic economic costs on American households and fracturing the Western economic alliances through which American strategic power is exercised. Without the lie, the policy would have faced the democratic accountability that accurate information would have produced. The lie protected the policy. The policy served the enemy's interests. The lie that protected the policy is therefore part of the architecture of the betrayal.

□ □ □

Section Three: The Efficiency Pretext — The Cover for Dismantlement

Chapter 10 documented what the Department of Government Efficiency actually did: it eliminated tens of thousands of federal positions across national security, intelligence, diplomatic, and regulatory agencies. It effectively dismantled USAID, terminating 5,341 foreign assistance programs. It reduced the Cybersecurity and Infrastructure Security Agency. It cut State Department positions that gather human intelligence and maintain alliance relationships.

The public explanation for all of this was efficiency. Fiscal responsibility. The elimination of waste. The government was too big, too expensive, and too slow, and the DOGE cuts were the corrective.

This was the cover story. It was a lie in the specific legal sense: it was a false explanation for conduct that had a different actual purpose.

What Was Actually Cut

Fiscal responsibility does not explain the specific pattern of what was cut. Genuine fiscal responsibility, applied to a federal budget of multiple trillions of dollars, would target the largest expenditures first. It would not prioritize, above all other targets, the specific agencies whose institutional function is to detect and respond to exactly the threats this book has documented.

USAID was not cut because it was inefficient. It was cut despite the fact that, as Chapter 10 documented, every dollar of USAID spending in developing nations generates documented returns in American strategic influence, allied partnership, and competitive advantage against Chinese and Russian influence operations. The specific documented result of the USAID cuts was the expansion of Russian and Chinese influence in the specific communities where USAID programs had operated.

The Cybersecurity and Infrastructure Security Agency was not cut because its work was wasteful. CISA's specific mission is defending the exact infrastructure, election systems, power grids, financial networks, that Russian intelligence services have been documented to probe and attack. Cutting the defenders of the power grid while the identified enemy is probing the power grid is not efficiency. It is sabotage executed through a budget process.

The Pretext as Evidence of Intent

The efficiency pretext is legally significant in the same way that the Ukraine corruption pretext documented in Chapter 14 is legally significant. When the stated reason for a specific action is demonstrably false, and the real consequence of that action consistently advances the identified enemy's strategic objectives, the false justification is evidence of consciousness of guilt about the real purpose of the action.

Four witnesses testified that the Ukraine aid freeze had nothing to do with Ukrainian corruption. The DOGE cuts have a different evidentiary structure, but the same logical architecture. The stated reason, efficiency, cannot explain why efficiency cuts prioritized the specific agencies whose function is to defend against Russia's documented offensive capabilities. A genuine efficiency program does not systematically dismantle the specific institutional defenses against a specific identified adversary while leaving other government spending untouched.

The pattern of what was cut is the evidence. The efficiency pretext is the lie that was used to make the pattern invisible to the public whose oversight is the ultimate check on executive power.

□ □ □

Section Four: The De-Dollarization Silence — Disarming the Sentry

The Federal Reserve, the Treasury Department, and the International Monetary Fund all have documented, in official publications and congressional testimony, the risk that unpredictable tariff policy, aggressive sanctions use, and withdrawal from multilateral institutions pose to the dollar's reserve currency status.

Treasury Secretary Janet Yellen warned publicly that the aggressive use of financial sanctions creates a desire for targeted nations to find non-dollar alternatives. The dollar's share of global foreign exchange reserves fell from 72 percent in 2001 to 57.8 percent at the start of 2025. Moody's downgraded the U.S. credit rating in May 2025, citing political polarization and attacks on the independence of the Federal Reserve.

These warnings were not communicated to the American public as part of the policy debate about tariffs and trade. The de-dollarization risk, which the Federal Reserve has estimated could cost the United States hundreds of billions in additional annual borrowing costs if the dollar's reserve share falls significantly, was not presented to the American public as one of the strategic consequences of the trade and sanctions policies they were being asked to support.

Why the Silence Is Evidence

This is not a conventional lie in the form of a false statement. It is a lie of omission, a concealment of a known material risk from the people whose democratic participation in policy formation depends on having accurate information about the consequences of that policy.

The legal significance of the omission is the same as the legal significance of the commission in the other sections of this chapter. A public that does not know it is bearing the cost of the de-dollarization risk cannot act to stop it. A Congress that is not informed about the dollar's reserve share erosion cannot legislate the corrections that would slow it. A Federal Reserve that is publicly undermined and whose independence is attacked cannot exercise the institutional credibility that the dollar's safe asset status depends on.

By concealing the de-dollarization risk while pursuing policies that accelerated it, the administration removed the early warning systems that a democracy relies on to course-correct. The sentry who was supposed to be watching for the erosion of America's primary strategic economic asset was disarmed by the concealment of what that sentry was supposed to be watching for.

The Cramer Actual Aid Analysis

Under the Cramer standard, the aid must be actual. The dollar's reserve share erosion is documented in IMF data. Russia's stated primary strategic objective of de-dollarization is documented in Vladimir Putin's own public statements, quoted in Chapter 10. The specific economic mechanisms through which de-dollarization reduces Russian strategic vulnerability to American sanctions are documented in Treasury and Federal Reserve analysis.

The concealment of the de-dollarization risk from the public prevented the democratic accountability that would have produced corrective action. That corrective action, if taken, would have slowed or reversed the dollar's reserve share decline. The decline serves Russia's primary strategic economic objective. The concealment that enabled the decline to proceed without democratic correction is therefore aid to the enemy under the Cramer actual aid standard.

□ □ □

Section Five: The Legal Synthesis — Information Warfare Against the American Public

The four categories of economic and domestic lie documented in this chapter share a common structure that elevates them from political deception to information warfare.

Each lie concealed a threat vector that the identified enemy was actively exploiting. The COVID lie concealed a biological crisis that Russia was exploiting through documented information warfare operations designed to maximize American social division and institutional distrust. The tariff lie concealed the domestic cost of a policy that was simultaneously fracturing the Western economic alliances Russia's doctrine identifies as its primary strategic obstacle. The efficiency pretext concealed the systematic dismantlement of the specific institutional defenses against Russian intelligence operations. The de-dollarization silence concealed the erosion of the primary strategic economic asset whose defense depends on democratic accountability and institutional credibility.

In each case, the lie operated not only as a shield for past conduct but as a mechanism that allowed harmful conduct to continue. The COVID lie prevented the public response that would have mitigated the pandemic's harm. The tariff lie provided the political cover that kept the trade war alive. The efficiency pretext allowed the DOGE dismantlement to proceed without the congressional and public scrutiny that accurate information would have generated. The de-dollarization silence allowed the reserve share erosion to continue without democratic correction.

Under the Haupt standard, an act performed with knowledge of the enemy's objectives that advances those objectives is an overt act of aid and comfort. The President received the 2022 National Security Strategy. He was briefed on the Gerasimov Doctrine. He was told by his own national security staff about the COVID threat, the de-dollarization risk, and the strategic consequences of the DOGE cuts. He made the choice, in each instance, to conceal the truth from the public whose democratic participation is the ultimate check on executive conduct.

A democracy's primary defense against the Gerasimov Doctrine's model of hybrid warfare is an informed public that can recognize threats and demand responses to them. A President who systematically conceals the threats that Russia's doctrine targets from the public that could force a response has not merely lied about domestic policy. He has disabled the defense. The lie was the weapon. The American public was the target. And the beneficiary of a public that cannot see the threat coming is the adversary that is delivering it.

The next chapter is the Legal Opinion. Every element established across seventeen chapters of evidence converges in the citizen's brief for which this entire analysis has been building. The allegiance. The enemy. The overt acts. The two-witness evidence. The intent. The immunity exception. The connective tissue of lies, both foreign and domestic. All of it assembled into the legal argument that this book was written to make.

□ □ □

Chapter Seventeen

The Unified Architecture: What the Pattern of Lies Reveals

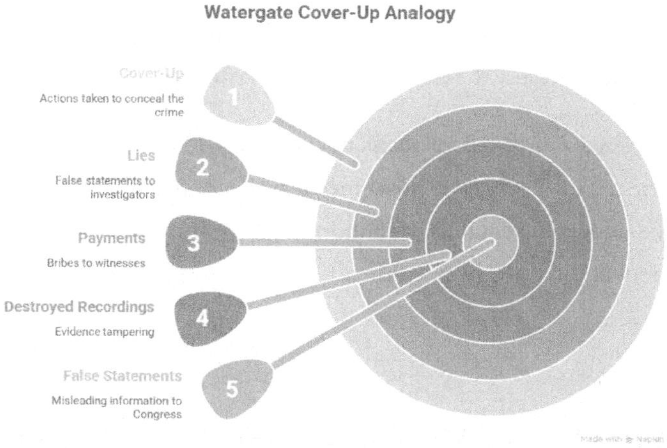

In the summer of 1972, investigators discovered that members of the Nixon administration had broken into the headquarters of the Democratic National Committee at the Watergate Hotel in Washington, D.C.

What happened next revealed something important about guilt.

The break-in itself was a serious crime. But it was the cover-up, the lies to investigators, the payments to witnesses, the destroyed recordings, the false statements to Congress, that established beyond any remaining doubt that the principals knew what they had done was indefensible. Innocent people do not construct elaborate cover-ups. They call the police.

There is one precise way in which the analogy to Watergate breaks down, and it breaks down in the direction that makes the conduct documented in this book more serious, not less. The Watergate burglars lied to hide a crime. The President in this case lied to continue one.

The Watergate comparison has been made so often in American political discourse that it has lost some of its evidentiary precision. So let this book make the comparison with that precision restored.

The analogy is not that the conduct documented in this book is similar in scale or significance to Watergate, though the argument of this book is that it vastly exceeds Watergate in both. The analogy is structural. The cover-up reveals the crime. The cover-up is the proof that the underlying conduct was understood, by the person who committed it, to require concealment because the truth was legally catastrophic.

The pattern of lies documented in Chapters 11 through 15 functions like the Watergate cover-up in the treason analysis. It is not merely evidence of additional crimes. It is the proof that the underlying conduct was understood, by those who committed it, to be exactly as serious as this book argues it is.

□ □ □

Section One: The Kawakita Link — Why the Lie Proves the Intent

This book has applied the Kawakita standard throughout its analysis of the overt acts documented in Chapters 4 through 10. The standard is simple and powerful: treasonous intent may be inferred from the totality of conduct over time. The jury does not need a confession. The jury does not need a signed agreement between the President and a foreign adversary. The jury needs the pattern. The pattern speaks for itself.

Part V of this book adds something to that pattern that is, in some respects, more legally significant than any single overt act documented in Part II through Part IV.

It adds the lies.

Under the Kawakita standard, the totality of conduct includes not only the overt acts themselves but the reaction to those acts. The reaction is evidence of the awareness of what the acts were. And the awareness of what the acts were is the specific intent the treason analysis requires.

The Metric of Intent

Here is the legal principle stated as plainly as it can be stated.

A President who accidentally aligns his foreign policy with a foreign adversary's interests makes a mistake. When the mistake is discovered, he acknowledges it. He corrects course. He does not need to construct a false narrative to explain conduct he believed was legitimate.

A President who intentionally aligns his foreign policy with a foreign adversary's interests commits a betrayal. When the betrayal begins to come into view, he lies. He constructs a cover narrative. He fires the investigators. He attacks the witnesses. He characterizes the investigation as a witch hunt. He deploys every mechanism of denial available to prevent the truth from reaching the accountability structures that were designed to respond to it.

The difference between the accidental alignment and the intentional betrayal is the lie.

A mistake does not require a cover-up. A crime does.

Under the Kawakita standard, intent is the variable that transforms an ambiguous act into a treasonous one. The lie is the metric of that intent. A President who accidentally benefits a foreign adversary admits the mistake when confronted. A President who intentionally benefits that adversary constructs a lie to conceal it. The architecture of denial documented in Chapters 11 through 15 is not peripheral to the treason argument. It is the most direct evidence of the intent the treason argument requires.

□ □ □

Section Two: The Map of Concealment — Every Lie Tracks Its Overt Act

Look at what was lied about.

The Russia relationship was concealed because it was indefensible. The multi-year campaign to deny the nature and depth of the Russia alignment, the flat denials, the party line about Trump Tower Moscow, the Helsinki endorsement of Putin's denial, the witch hunt narrative used to obstruct the investigation, was constructed because the underlying relationship, documented in Chapters 4 through 8, was exactly what this book argues it was.

The January 6 preparation was manufactured through lies and then denied because the preparation constituted an overt act of war. The false narratives about the Trump Tower meeting and the election fraud that manufactured the assemblage are documented in Chapter 13. The obstruction campaign that attempted to terminate the investigation before it could fully map the preparation is documented in Chapter 12. The lies track the overt acts in Chapter 3 with precision.

The NATO misrepresentations disguised the systematic dismantling of the primary defense against the identified enemy. The NATO funding lie recast the alliance deconstruction as fiscal responsibility. The G7 re-admission advocacy was framed as pragmatic engagement. The lies are the cover for the conduct documented in Chapter 6.

The Ukraine aid freeze was given a false justification because the real reason, benefiting Russia at the expense of a nation Russia was attacking, while extorting a political favor for the President's personal benefit, was legally catastrophic. Four witnesses testified under oath that the corruption pretext was false. The lie is the cover for the conduct documented in Chapters 5 and 8.

The ceasefire denial enabled a massacre and preserved regional instability that served Russian strategic objectives. The lie is the cover for the conduct documented in Chapter 15.

The map of concealment and the map of the treason argument are identical. Every element of the treason case has a corresponding lie designed to cover it. That is not coincidence. That is the architecture of guilt.

There is also something worth noting about the specific character of many of these lies. Most were public. They were made from the Oval Office, from press conferences, from rally stages, from social media platforms with tens of millions of followers. A public lie witnessed by millions satisfies the Article III two-witness requirement many times over. The ceasefire denial was made on international television before every head of state in the world. The witch hunt narrative was broadcast on every major news network. The I'm tougher on Russia than anyone inoculation was repeated at hundreds of public events. The lies were not private. They were performed. And a lie performed before millions of witnesses is documented with a redundancy that no treason prosecution in American history has previously enjoyed.

The Financial Motive the Lies Also Protected

The architecture of concealment protected more than just the Russia relationship and the overt acts. It protected the financial motive documented in Chapter 9.

Chapter 9 established that the financial entanglements between the President's family businesses and the foreign governments whose interests consistently benefited from his policy decisions are the evidence of motive in the treason analysis. The emoluments violations, the crypto arrangements, the hotel bookings by foreign diplomatic missions, all created documented financial relationships between the President and the foreign governments he was serving.

If the truth of the Russia relationship had been admitted, those financial flows would have been examined in the light of what they were: payments from foreign governments to the President's family businesses during the same periods in which those governments were receiving policy benefits that served their interests and damaged American national security interests.

The Russia lie protected the Russia relationship. The Russia relationship served the financial interest. The financial interest was the motive for the Russia relationship. The architecture of concealment protected the entire structure simultaneously.

□ □ □

Section Three: The Operational Lie — The Cover-Up Was Also the Weapon

There is a dimension of the lie architecture documented in Chapters 11 through 15 that goes beyond the Watergate cover-up analogy. The Watergate cover-up was purely defensive. It was designed to prevent discovery of what had already happened. The lies documented in Part V were not only defensive. Several of them were operational. They were not only hiding the past. They were enabling the future.

The Inoculation Strategy

The I'm tougher on Russia than anyone narrative, documented in Chapter 14 as the inoculation strategy, was not merely a shield against past criticism. It was a pre-positioned narrative that made every future allegation of Russia alignment appear to be a politically motivated lie. By establishing the counter-narrative before the evidence was fully visible, the inoculation ensured that the evidence, when it arrived, would be received in a context that had been pre-designed to discredit it.

That is not cover-up as rear-guard defense. That is information warfare conducted against the American public to protect an ongoing course of conduct that continued across two terms. The inoculation narrative was deployed as an operational tool to allow the Russia alignment to proceed without triggering the institutional response that exposure would have produced.

The NATO Misrepresentation as Active Dismantlement

The NATO funding lie, documented in Chapter 14, was not merely a false explanation for what had already happened. It was the justification mechanism that allowed the systematic dismantlement of Chapter 6 to proceed without congressional intervention.

Chapter 6 documents that Congress had passed legislation specifically prohibiting presidential withdrawal from NATO without congressional authorization, because Congress had determined that Russia's primary strategic objective was NATO's dissolution and that executive discretion over that question could not be trusted. The NATO funding lie provided the political cover that prevented the public and their congressional representatives from recognizing that the dismantlement was proceeding in a direction that served the primary objective of the nation this book has established as a functional enemy.

Without the lie, the dismantlement might have been stopped by the institutional mechanisms that were designed to stop exactly this kind of conduct. The lie was not just concealing the dismantlement. The lie was the mechanism that made the dismantlement possible.

The Ceasefire Denial as Active Harm

The Lebanon ceasefire denial documented in Chapter 15 is the clearest example of the operational lie. It was not concealing something that had already happened. It was enabling something that was about to happen.

Hezbollah had halted. The denial removed the ceasefire protection that the halt had relied upon. Israel launched Operation Eternal Darkness. Three hundred and fifty-seven people died. The denial was not a cover story for a past act. It was the mechanism through which the future act became possible.

This is the lie used as a weapon. Not defensively, to hide conduct from accountability. But offensively, to remove a protection so that a harm could be inflicted and a conflict could be prolonged that served the identified enemy's strategic interests.

The lies documented in Part V were not only a shield. They were a sword. The inoculation protected the Russia alignment as it continued. The NATO misrepresentation enabled the systematic dismantlement by providing the political cover Congress needed to act but did not receive. The ceasefire denial enabled a massacre by removing the protection Hezbollah had relied upon in standing down. The operational lie is not just evidence of consciousness of guilt. It is itself an overt act of the treasonous design.

□ □ □

Section Four: The Jury Instruction — Consciousness of Guilt

Federal courts give a specific jury instruction when a defendant has made false statements about the conduct at issue in a criminal case. The instruction is called the Consciousness of Guilt instruction. It is a recognized evidentiary principle in American criminal law.

The instruction tells jurors that while false statements are not proof of guilt in themselves, and while no jury is required to draw any inference from a false statement, the jury may consider the defendant's false statements in determining whether the defendant acted with the knowledge and intent required for the charge.

The specific language of the instruction captures something important about how guilt works in the real world. Evidence that a defendant made deliberately false or misleading statements about matters relevant to the charged conduct is something you may consider in determining whether the defendant understood that his conduct was criminal. You are not required to draw this inference. But you may.

Why This Instruction Applies to the Treason Charge

The false statements documented in Part V are not peripheral to the treason charge. They do not concern unrelated matters. They do not involve personal conduct having no bearing on the elements of the crime.

They concern precisely the elements of the treason charge.

The Russia relationship lie concerns the enemy, the adherence, and the intent elements. The January 6 lies concern the overt act of levying war and the preparatory conduct that preceded it. The NATO misrepresentations concern the aid and comfort provided to the identified enemy through the systematic deconstruction of the primary deterrent against that enemy. The Ukraine corruption pretext concerns the specific illegal act of impounding congressionally authorized military assistance from a nation the enemy was attacking. The ceasefire denial concerns the specific overt act documented in Chapter 15.

Every false statement documented in Part V is directly connected to a specific element of the charge this book presents. Every false statement satisfies the nexus requirement of the Consciousness of Guilt instruction. And together, they satisfy something more important: they establish, as a matter of documented behavioral fact, that the person who made them understood what the true account of his conduct would establish.

The Standard the Law Sets

Federal courts have distilled the conditions for consciousness of guilt evidence into four requirements. The statement must be demonstrably false or misleading. It must have been made prior to formal proceedings, suggesting a preemptive narrative shift rather than litigation strategy. It must reflect a specific intent to mislead rather than an accidental error or memory failure. And it must concern matters that are directly related to the specific charges at issue.

The lies documented in Part V satisfy all four conditions. They are demonstrably false, as established by sworn testimony, court findings, governmental audit reports, and the documentary record. They were made prior to formal proceedings and in many cases before any formal investigation had been initiated, indicating preemptive narrative construction rather than litigation response. The multi-year sustained pattern of consistent denial, inoculation, and obstruction establishes specific intent to mislead rather than inadvertent error. And every lie tracks a specific element of the treason case.

The Consciousness of Guilt instruction is the legal system's recognition that the architecture of denial is itself evidence. It does not create a conviction. It does not substitute for the overt act evidence, the witness testimony, or the documented record of Russian benefit. But it is the final piece of the Kawakita inference.

A President who unwittingly benefits a foreign adversary admits the error when confronted with the evidence. A President who intentionally benefits that adversary lies to cover it up. The lies documented in Part V are the behavioral signature of the second category. They are the proof that the betrayal was knowing, deliberate, and calculated to succeed. In a treason prosecution, the Consciousness of Guilt instruction would ask the jury to consider whether the sustained architecture of denial, built precisely around the elements of the charge, is the behavior of a person who understood that the truth would establish the charge. The answer that the pattern of lies provides is the answer that Kawakita permits the jury to draw.

□ □ □

Section Five: The Architecture as the Argument — What the Pattern Proves

This chapter has established four things about the lies documented in Part V.

First, under the Kawakita standard, the lies are the metric of intent. The totality of conduct that Kawakita permits the jury to evaluate includes the reaction to the overt acts, and the reaction documented in Chapters 11 through 15 is the reaction of a person who understood that the overt acts required concealment.

Second, the map of concealment and the map of the treason argument are identical. Every element of the case has a corresponding lie. That correspondence is the architecture of guilt, and the precision of that correspondence is more probative than any single piece of evidence in the record.

Third, several of the lies were operational rather than merely defensive. The inoculation narrative enabled the Russia alignment to continue. The NATO misrepresentation provided the political cover for the systematic dismantlement. The ceasefire denial enabled a massacre. The lie was not only concealing the treasonous design. In several specific instances, it was executing it.

Fourth, the Consciousness of Guilt instruction, applied to the specific false statements documented in Part V, provides the jury with a specific legal framework for treating the architecture of denial as evidence of the intent the treason charge requires.

Taken together, these four points establish something about the treason argument that no single overt act can establish on its own. They establish, as a matter of sustained behavioral record, that the person at the center of this analysis understood what his conduct was, understood that it could not survive honest scrutiny, and constructed an architecture of denial specifically designed to prevent honest scrutiny from reaching it.

The Watergate comparison is apt. The cover-up was the proof. In Watergate, the cover-up proved corruption. In this analysis, the cover-up proves treason.

Not because the lies are themselves treason. But because the lies reveal the understanding of the person who told them. And the understanding of a person who has betrayed his country is the understanding that the truth must be kept from a nation whose response would be, justly and constitutionally, to hold him accountable.

The Framers wrote the treason clause into the Constitution not because they believed presidents would inevitably betray their countries. They wrote it because they understood that the greatest danger to a republic is not the enemy at the gates. It is the person inside the gates who opens them, and then lies about having done so.

Every element this book has established across sixteen chapters converges in the citizen's brief for which this entire analysis has been building. The allegiance. The enemy. The overt acts. The two-witness evidence. The intent. The immunity exception. The connective tissue of lies. All of it assembled into the legal argument that this book has been written to make.

□ □ □

PART VI

THE IRAN WAR: FEBRUARY 28 THROUGH APRIL 12, 2026

From Unauthorized War to Broken Ceasefire: The Real-Time Documented Record

Everything in Parts I through V is history. Documented, verified, and legally analyzed, but history nonetheless.

Part VI is happening now.

In 43 days, from February 28 through April 12, 2026, the theoretical arguments of the earlier chapters became concrete, documented, witnessed reality. An unauthorized war launched during active negotiations. A congressional override defeated by seven votes. Russia receiving sanctions relief at the moment of maximum financial benefit from the war. A ceasefire whose Lebanon provisions were denied in real time by diplomats who were present, enabling the largest single-day massacre of the Lebanon conflict. The most explicit NATO withdrawal threat in the alliance's history. And public statements about negotiation progress, military objectives, and ceasefire terms specifically contradicted by foreign governments, military briefers, and diplomatic sources with contemporaneous documentation.

The 43 days are not background. They are the overt acts.

Chapter Eighteen

The Unauthorized War: February 28, 2026 and the Constitutional Violation

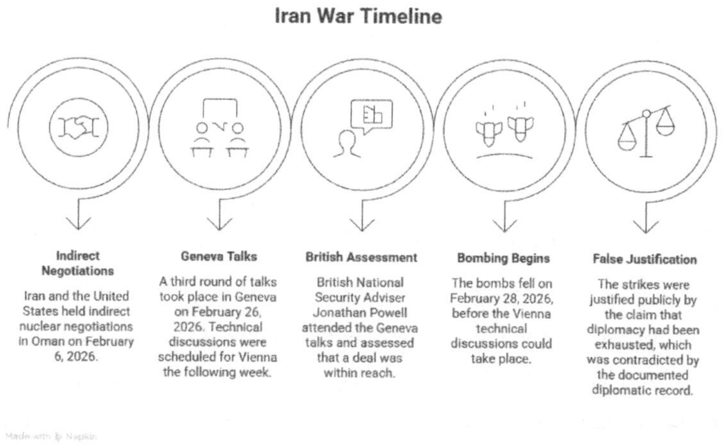

In 43 days, from February 28 through April 12, 2026, the theoretical arguments of the earlier chapters became concrete, documented, witnessed reality. An unauthorized war launched during active negotiations. A congressional override defeated by six votes in the Senate and seven in the House. Russia receiving sanctions relief at the moment of maximum financial benefit from the war. A ceasefire whose Lebanon provisions were denied in real time by diplomats who were present, enabling the largest single-day massacre of the Lebanon conflict. The most explicit NATO withdrawal threat in the alliance's history. And public statements about negotiation progress, military objectives, and ceasefire terms specifically contradicted by foreign governments, military briefers, and diplomatic sources with contemporaneous documentation.

The 43 days are not background. They are the overt acts.

□ □ □

At approximately 1:00 in the morning on Saturday, February 28, 2026, ship-launched Tomahawk cruise missiles and air-launched munitions from United States Air Force and Navy jets began striking targets in Iran. The strikes targeted nuclear facilities, military infrastructure, government sites, and leadership. Iranian state media confirmed the death of Supreme Leader Ayatollah Ali Khamenei on March 1, declaring 40 days of mourning. Satellite imagery confirmed severe damage to his compound.

The strikes were launched without a declaration of war. Without an Authorization for Use of Military Force. Without any formal congressional approval. Without even the 48-hour notification required by the War Powers Resolution of 1973. And without any evidence, presented to Congress or the public, of the imminent threat that would have justified the President's inherent authority to repel sudden attacks.

> *"The Congress shall have Power to declare War."* **Article I, Section 8, Clause 11, U.S. Constitution**

Congress did not declare war. Congress was not consulted. Congress was not notified in advance. The President of the United States launched a major combat operation against a sovereign nation, killing its head of state, during active negotiations, based on a stated justification that his own military advisors contradicted in classified briefings to Congress.

□ □ □

Section One: War During Negotiations — The Timeline That Destroys the Justification

The Iran war did not begin because diplomacy failed. The Iran war began while diplomacy was working.

On February 6, 2026, Iran and the United States held indirect nuclear negotiations in Oman. The Omani Foreign Minister, Badr al Busaidi, who facilitated those talks, reported significant progress. On February 26, 2026, a third round of talks took place in Geneva. The Omani mediator again reported significant progress and announced that technical-level discussions had been scheduled for Vienna the following week.

British National Security Adviser Jonathan Powell attended the Geneva talks and assessed afterward that a deal was within reach. He described Tehran's offers as surprisingly significant. The Vienna technical discussions were scheduled for March 2, 2026. The bombs fell on February 28.

The administration publicly said it was not thrilled with the pace of diplomatic progress. And then, 48 hours after a round of talks that an allied national security official assessed had produced a deal within reach, the strikes began.

The Vienna technical discussions never happened. The Omani mediating process was destroyed by the strikes that began before the next scheduled meeting. Diplomacy did not fail before the war began. The war was launched before diplomacy could succeed.

The False Justification

The strikes were justified publicly by the claim that diplomacy had been exhausted. That claim was specifically contradicted by the documented diplomatic record. The Omani mediator said significant progress had been made. The British National Security Adviser said a deal was within reach. Technical discussions were scheduled for the following week.

A false justification for a major military action launched during active negotiations is not merely a rhetorical error. It is the same pattern documented throughout Part V of this book. The public statement and the documented reality are different. A President who launches a war during negotiations that an allied official assessed had produced a deal within reach, and publicly claims diplomacy was exhausted, is lying about the reason for the war.

Under the treason framework, the question that false justification raises is the same question the framework always asks: who benefits from the documented reality rather than the stated justification?

□ □ □

Section Two: No Imminent Threat — The Pentagon Tells Congress the Truth

The legal framework for presidential military action without congressional authorization is narrow and specific. The President may repel sudden attacks against the United States or American forces without waiting for Congress to act. That is the imminent threat exception, and it is the constitutional basis the administration publicly invoked for the February 28 strikes.

The White House cited a cumulative effect of Iranian activities that made an attack feel based on fact. The public statement claimed an imminent and direct threat to American forces and interests.

In classified briefings to Congress, Pentagon officials told a different story. A Pentagon source told Congress in closed-door briefings that there was no intelligence suggesting Iran was planning to attack American forces first. No evidence of Iran preparing an imminent attack. No intelligence that the threat the public justification described had materialized or was about to.

The Brennan Center for Justice, in a contemporaneous legal analysis, concluded that Trump acted unilaterally and lawlessly, without congressional authorization and absent any imminent threat to the United States.

The public statement said imminent threat. The classified military briefing said no such threat existed. This is the same structure as every lie documented in Part V of this book. Two stories: one for the public, one for the people who actually know the facts. And the same legal inference applies here that applies throughout the treason analysis: a false justification for conduct whose real reason was something else is consciousness of guilt about the real reason.

THE WITNESSES: *The February 26 Geneva talks and the Omani mediator's assessment of significant progress are documented in contemporaneous reporting from multiple international news organizations and* *confirmed by the Omani Foreign Ministry. British National Security Adviser Jonathan Powell's assessment that a deal was within reach is documented in UK governmental reporting and press statements. The Pentagon classified briefing to Congress contradicting the imminent threat public justification is documented through congressional accounts cited in national security reporting. The Brennan Center for Justice legal analysis is a public document.*

□ □ □

Section Three: The Khamenei Assassination — Burning the Bridge to Peace

Among those killed on the first day of the Iran strikes was Ayatollah Ali Khamenei, the Supreme Leader of the Islamic Republic of Iran, who had held that position since 1989.

The assassination of a nation's head of state during a strike that the striking nation publicly justified as a response to an imminent military threat is not a routine military operation. It is a strategic decision with consequences that extend far beyond the military objectives of the strikes themselves.

Removing the Supreme Leader in the opening hours of a conflict removes the single individual most capable of making the political decision to accept terms and end the conflict. Iran's system of government is structured around the Supreme Leader's authority to authorize major strategic decisions, including the decision to negotiate and to accept a ceasefire. With Khamenei dead and the constitutional succession machinery damaged by the strikes, Iran had no institutional mechanism for making the strategic choices that would end the war quickly.

The succession crisis that followed confirmed this. Executive authority moved to an interim council. The Assembly of Experts, the body responsible for selecting a new Supreme Leader, had its facilities in Qom and Tehran damaged in the strikes. The process of selecting Mojtaba Khamenei, the late leader's son, as the new Supreme Leader did not conclude until March 11, leaving Iran without a constitutionally settled leadership for 10 days.

The Strategic Consequence: A War That Could Not End Quickly

The Khamenei assassination was a bridge-burning act in the specific military strategic sense. By killing the person most capable of making Iran's strategic decision to accept terms, the first day's strikes guaranteed that the war would last longer than it would have if leadership continuity had been preserved.

A war that lasts longer consumes more American military resources, more American precision-guided munitions, more Patriot interceptors, more naval assets, for a longer period. It produces more energy market disruption. It generates more oil price elevation. It maintains for a longer period all of the strategic consequences documented in Chapter 7 as benefiting Russia.

The decision to target leadership decapitation in the opening hours of the strikes was not militarily necessary to destroy Iran's nuclear facilities. It was an escalation choice. And the escalation choice that guaranteed a prolonged conflict was made at the moment when diplomacy had produced a deal within reach that would have resolved the nuclear question without a war at all.

A President who launches a war during negotiations that an allied official assessed had produced a deal within reach, justifies it with a false imminent threat claim, and opens the war with the assassination of the one leader most capable of making the political decision to end it quickly, has not made a series of poor policy judgments. He has made a series of choices that guaranteed the war would be prolonged, that the prolonged war would consume American military resources and produce energy market instability, and that both of those consequences would directly benefit the identified enemy whose financial and strategic position depends on exactly those conditions.

□ □ □

Section Four: The Why of the War — Oil, Subservience, Expansion, and Russia

The public justifications for the Iran war shifted across the 43 days. Imminent threat. Preventing nuclear weapons. Regime change. Neutralizing the existential threat to Israel. Each justification arrived after the previous one had been contradicted by the documented record. Together they form a pattern of post-hoc rationalization that the treason framework recognizes as consciousness of guilt about the real motivations driving the war. This section documents those real motivations from the public record, including the President's own statements.

American Subservience to Israeli Initiative

The most direct documented statement about the war's actual initiation came not from a critic but from the Secretary of State himself. Secretary of State Marco Rubio stated publicly that the strikes were triggered by Israel's plan to launch an attack, leaving Trump with no choice but to join.

> *"Israel's plan to launch [an] attack" left Trump with "no choice but to join."*
> **Secretary of State Marco Rubio, documented public statement, 2026**

Read that admission carefully. The Secretary of State of the United States said the President of the United States had no choice. Not that the President evaluated the situation and determined military action was in the American national interest. Not that the intelligence community assessed an imminent threat requiring immediate response. That Israel planned to attack, and the President joined because he had no choice.

This is not a minor diplomatic nuance. It is the Secretary of State publicly acknowledging that American military power, deployed without congressional authorization at the cost of American treasure and the lives of military personnel, was subordinated to an ally's unilateral decision to go to war. Israel is a sovereign nation with its own strategic interests, its own territorial ambitions, and its own regional agenda. Those interests do not automatically align with American national interests. A President who deploys American military assets because an ally left him no choice has not exercised Commander in Chief authority. He has surrendered it.

This was also not the first time. The February 28, 2026 strikes were the second joint American and Israeli military operation against Iran in nine months. The Twelve-Day War of June 2025 had been the first. The pattern of American military assets being repeatedly deployed in coordination with Israeli operations, without congressional authorization and without the constitutional process the Framers established to ensure wars serve American interests, is a pattern of subordination rather than alliance.

The Greater Israel Context and Netanyahu's Documented Endorsement

Understanding what Israeli strategic interests were driving the war requires understanding what Israeli leadership had publicly stated about its regional goals. In August 2025, Prime Minister Netanyahu was asked directly whether he felt a connection to the vision of Greater Israel, the concept of Eretz Yisrael HaShlema referring to unified Israeli sovereignty from the Jordan River to the Mediterranean Sea. His answer was: Very much.

Arab governments condemned this statement as proof of colonial delusions and expansionist intent. It was not an isolated remark. Hardline members of the Israeli cabinet had used the ongoing conflicts to entrench control over the West Bank and Gaza, framing military operations as advancing permanent Israeli sovereignty. The 1982 Yinon Plan, a documented Israeli strategic framework, argued that Israel's security depended on the fragmentation of neighboring Arab states into smaller ethnic and confessional groupings. Destabilizing Iran, the central pillar of regional resistance to Israeli territorial expansion, serves this documented strategic framework by removing the military and diplomatic capability of the nation most positioned to oppose Israeli regional expansion.

The legal argument this book makes is specific. The treason claim is against Trump, not Israel. The relevance of Israeli strategic objectives is that Rubio's documented admission establishes that American military power was deployed in response to an ally's initiative rather than American national interest. A President who bypasses the constitutional war power process and subordinates American military assets to a foreign government's strategic agenda, while that deployment simultaneously serves the financial and strategic interests of the identified enemy, has satisfied the constitutional elements this book has established across eighteen chapters.

Trump's Oil Seizure Motivation: The President's Own Words

The financial motivation for the Iran war is documented in Trump's own public statements with a specificity that no other motivation in this chapter can match. He said it himself.

On March 30, 2026, the President stated explicitly that the United States could take the oil in Iran. He expressed a direct interest in taking the Strait of Hormuz over from Iran. By April 12, after negotiations had failed to produce the terms he demanded, he announced a naval blockade to stop all ships from entering or leaving Iranian ports and to intercept ships that paid tolls to Iran. He threatened to obliterate all of Iran's oil wells and power plants if they did not agree to American terms and reopen the Strait.

These statements are not ambiguous or metaphorical. The President of the United States said the United States could take another nation's oil. This followed the pattern established in Venezuela, where the capture of President Nicolas Maduro earlier in 2026 had been accompanied by the diversion of Venezuelan oil shipments, establishing what the documented record describes as a sequential resource seizure strategy applied to two nations.

Senator Lindsey Graham provided the strategic framing explicitly. He stated publicly that the United States was going to make a ton of money on the Iran war. He noted that Venezuela and Iran together held 31 percent of the world's oil reserves and that an American partnership with those reserves would be China's nightmare and a good investment. The private financial motivation documented in Chapter 9 and the public strategic framing offered by Graham converge on the same conclusion: the war's primary stated purpose was resource seizure and the weaponization of energy supply against China, not the imminent threat or nuclear prevention justifications offered to the public and contradicted by the classified record.

The Nuclear Pretext Contradicted and Iran's Military Reality

When the oil seizure strategy encountered Iran's actual military resistance, the public justification shifted to nuclear prevention. The administration began characterizing Iran as the worst terrorist state and claiming Iran was rebuilding a nuclear program that required military destruction.

The International Atomic Energy Agency reported no evidence of an ongoing nuclear weapons program in Iran. The same structure as the imminent threat claim: a public justification specifically contradicted by the international monitoring institution whose entire purpose is to determine whether such programs exist.

The administration also claimed Iran's military had been destroyed. Iran's actual military performance contradicted this claim. Iran employed a mosaic defense strategy, a decentralized command structure in which regional centers continued operating independently after top leadership was eliminated. Iranian retaliatory strikes on American military bases in Saudi Arabia and the United Arab Emirates caused significant damage, with some bases rendered all but uninhabitable. The military that was supposed to have been destroyed was conducting effective retaliatory operations against American positions throughout the 43 days.

The sequence of post-hoc justification shifts is the pattern of consciousness of guilt that Part V of this book established as the architecture of denial. The oil seizure goal was stated publicly and then became politically untenable as the war's costs became apparent. The nuclear pretext was deployed as the replacement justification despite being contradicted by the IAEA. The destroyed military claim was made despite Iran's documented military effectiveness against American positions. Each justification arrived to replace the previous one after that one had been contradicted. That is not the behavior of a President who launched a war for the reasons he stated. It is the behavior of a President who launched a war for reasons he could not state publicly and then constructed successive false justifications as each previous one failed.

Russia as the Primary Strategic Beneficiary

The war was framed as being against Iran and designed to contain China. The documented primary beneficiary was Russia.

Iran and Venezuela together accounted for approximately 17 to 18 percent of China's total oil imports as of late 2025. Russia was already China's largest single oil supplier at 17.5 percent. By disabling Iranian and Venezuelan supply through military operations and blockade, the war forced Chinese refineries that had built their business models on discounted sanctioned oil from Iran and Venezuela to transition to Russian heavy grades. Russia absorbed the displaced supply, strengthening the most important trade relationship insulating the Russian economy from the full effect of Western sanctions.

The oil price effects were the largest energy disruption since the 1970s. Brent crude surpassed $100 per barrel for the first time in four years and peaked at $126 per barrel, rising faster than during any other conflict in recent history. Russia's net revenue increased because rising prices more than compensated for any decline in physical export volume. External analysis documented that Russia earned an extra $150 million per day from the conflict's oil price effects.

Russia leveraged the conflict strategically. Moscow used the Strait of Hormuz closure to validate its long-standing argument that maritime energy routes are unreliable due to American military interference. Russia explicitly promoted the Power of Siberia 2 pipeline as the only safe and reliable option for Chinese energy supply, offering China its geography and nuclear umbrella as the guarantee of supply stability that maritime routes could no longer provide. The war that was publicly described as China's nightmare drove China deeper into energy dependence on Russia.

On March 13, 2026, the Trump administration temporarily lifted restrictions on the sale of Russian oil, citing the need to stabilize global energy prices. The policy provided Russia with an eased regulatory environment for its oil sales during the precise period when prices were at their peak. The sanctions relief that Chapter 5 documented as the pattern of Russian alignment was extended to Russia during the conflict that Russia was the primary beneficiary of financially.

Secretary Rubio said Trump had no choice but to join Israel's attack. Trump said the United States could take Iran's oil. Graham said it would make a ton of money and be China's nightmare. The IAEA found no nuclear weapons program. Iran's military was not destroyed. Brent crude peaked at $126 per barrel. Russia absorbed China's displaced Iranian oil supply and earned $150 million per day in additional revenue. Moscow used the Strait closure to sell China on permanent pipeline dependence from Russia. The Trump administration then granted Russia sanctions relief during the height of the price surge. The Framers gave Congress the war power specifically to prevent a President from launching wars for personal, financial, or foreign-government-driven reasons without asking whether the war served American interests. That question was

never asked before the bombs fell. The documented answer, assembled from the public record, is that the war served Israeli territorial objectives, Trump's documented oil seizure ambitions, and Russia's primary strategic and financial interests simultaneously.

□ □ □

Section Five: The Congressional Attempt — Six Votes in the Senate, Seven in the House

The constitutional check did not fail entirely. It came within six votes in the Senate and seven in the House of succeeding.

Senators Tim Kaine, a Democrat from Virginia, and Rand Paul, a Republican from Kentucky, introduced a War Powers resolution requiring congressional authorization for any further military action in Iran. Representatives Ro Khanna, a Democrat from California, and Thomas Massie, a Republican from Kentucky, introduced a companion measure in the House. These were bipartisan efforts, Democrats and Republicans together, asserting that the Constitution meant what Article I, Section 8 says about the war power.

The Senate defeated the measure 47 to 53. Six votes. Rand Paul was the lone Republican to cross party lines and support the constitutional check. John Fetterman of Pennsylvania was the only Democrat to cross party lines and oppose it. The House defeated its version 212 to 219. Seven votes.

> *"Trump's military attack on Iran is illegal and unconstitutional. It was not approved by Congress and holds dangers for all Americans."* — **Senator Ed Markey, February 28, 2026**

The closeness of these votes is legally significant in a specific way that goes beyond their immediate political failure.

The administration knew before the first strike was launched that congressional authorization would be difficult to obtain. The bipartisan character of the opposition, Republicans and Democrats together asserting the constitutional war power, told the administration that the votes for prior authorization might not exist. By launching the strikes before congressional consultation, the President did not merely exercise his military authority. He preempted a constitutional check that might have stopped the war before it started.

Starting the shooting before asking for permission the administration knew would be hard to get is not a procedural irregularity. It is the deliberate bypass of the institutional mechanism that exists to prevent exactly the kind of unauthorized war this chapter documents.

The Witnesses the Congressional Record Creates

The bipartisan Senate and House votes are legally significant beyond their political consequences. Senators Kaine and Paul, Representatives Khanna and Massie, are witnesses on the public record establishing three documented facts.

First, that the war was launched without congressional authorization and that knowledgeable bipartisan groups of legislators believed it required such authorization. Second, that the constitutional check specifically designed to require that authorization was operative and available and was bypassed. Third, that the vote totals, 47 to 53 in the Senate and 212 to 219 in the House, establish that a meaningful and bipartisan portion of the legislative branch regarded the war as unconstitutional.

These are not anonymous sources. They are named senators and representatives whose public votes and public statements are in the congressional record. The constitutional violation is documented there, in the most public possible forum, by the officials whose authority Article I, Section 8 invests with the war power.

> **THE WITNESSES:** *The February 26 Geneva talks and the March 2 Vienna technical discussions that were superseded by the strikes are documented in Omani Foreign Ministry statements and confirmed by UK governmental reporting. Jonathan Powell's within reach assessment is documented in UK press reporting. The 47 to 53 Senate vote is documented in the Senate legislative record, with Rand Paul confirmed as the lone Republican supporter. The House 212 to 219 vote is documented in House*

legislative records. The Pentagon classified briefing contradicting the imminent threat public justification is documented in congressional accounts. The Russian $150 million per day additional revenue from the oil price spike is documented in Atlantic Council and Treasury analysis.

□ □ □

Section Six: The Legal Synthesis — Unauthorized War as Overt Act

Chapter 7 analyzed the Iran war as a whole through the lens of the treason framework. This chapter narrows the analysis to the specific overt act of the unauthorized initiation of the war, because that specific act is legally distinct from the war's consequences in a way that matters for the treason analysis.

The unauthorized initiation of the Iran war satisfies the Cramer actual aid standard in its most direct form. The war was launched without the congressional authorization the Constitution requires. The false imminent threat justification was contradicted by the classified military briefing to Congress. The diplomatic process that was producing a deal within reach was destroyed by strikes that began before the next scheduled meeting. And the strategic beneficiary of the war that resulted, Russia, received $150 million per day in additional oil revenue and the diversion of American military resources from the European theater.

The Youngstown analysis that Chapter 6 applied to NATO and Chapter 8 applied to the Ukraine aid freeze applies here with full force. When the President acts in direct contravention of Article I, Section 8's assignment of the war power to Congress, his authority is at its lowest ebb. He is not exercising executive discretion. He is usurping a legislative power that the Constitution assigns specifically to the branch designed to ask whether a war serves the national interest before authorizing it.

The usurpation of that power, to launch a war whose consequences predictably and documentably served Russia's primary strategic objectives, performed at the precise moment when diplomacy had produced a deal within reach that would have resolved the nuclear question without a war, is the overt act this chapter establishes.

The next chapter documents what happened to the constitutional ceasefire that might have ended the 43 days before the worst of them arrived.

□ □ □

Chapter Nineteen

The Negotiation Lies: Talking Peace While Escalating War

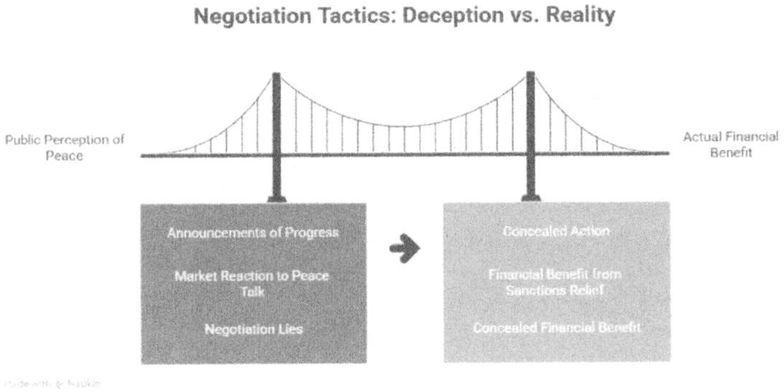

There is a technique used by negotiators, con artists, and magicians alike. While one hand makes an obvious, reassuring gesture that draws every eye in the room, the other hand does the actual work. The misdirection is the point. The visible action is designed to prevent the audience from seeing the consequential one.

During the 40 days of the Iran war, the American people were shown the right hand. The President announced that objectives were nearly complete, that peace was close, that there were very good talks with Iran, and that a deal was coming soon. Markets moved on those announcements. Oil prices fell when investors believed peace was near. The American public exhaled.

The left hand was the March 5 sanctions relief. A quiet decision, announced one week into the war, that lifted American sanctions on Russian oil exports to India at the precise moment those sanctions were most valuable as a constraint on the identified enemy and at the precise moment Russia was profiting most from the war's oil price spike.

This chapter documents both hands. The negotiation lies that managed the public's perception of the conflict. The sanctions relief that delivered the financial benefit those lies were designed to conceal. And the legal analysis that establishes why their coordination, their precise timing, and the absence of any innocent explanation for either one satisfies the aid and comfort standard under the Cramer and Haupt analysis this book has applied throughout.

□ □ □

Section One: The Negotiation Lies — What Was Said and What Was Real

During the 40 days of the Iran war, the American public received a consistent and reassuring message from the White House.

> *"The objectives are nearly complete. Peace is close. There are very good talks with Iran. A deal is coming soon."* **President Donald Trump, repeated communications during the Iran war, February through April 2026**

The Iranian government's consistent message was different.

Iranian officials stated publicly and on the record that there were no serious talks. They denied that the conversations Trump described as very good had taken place. One senior Iranian official put it plainly: the peace talks the American President was describing existed only in his statements, not in any diplomatic reality the Iranian government recognized.

This is not a matter of competing diplomatic interpretations or different characterizations of the same conversations. The contradiction is categorical. The President said talks were occurring and were progressing. The other party to those alleged talks said they were not occurring at all.

When the President of the United States and the government of the nation he claims to be negotiating with give categorically incompatible accounts of whether negotiations are taking place, one of them is lying. The Iranian government had no incentive to deny negotiations that were actually occurring. Denying them would have removed whatever diplomatic leverage Iran might derive from appearing to negotiate. Iran's denial was therefore against its own diplomatic interest and is accordingly more credible as an accurate account of the diplomatic reality.

What the Lies Accomplished in the Oil Markets

Oil prices are one of the most sensitive economic instruments on the planet. They move in real time on perceptions of risk, stability, and supply. During a military conflict involving the Middle East, they move on every announcement about whether the conflict is escalating or de-escalating.

During the 40 days of the Iran war, oil prices moved precisely in correspondence with the administration's peace announcements. When Trump said talks were going well, prices fell. When the conflict continued despite those announcements and Iran denied the talks, prices rose. The pattern was consistent, measurable, and documented in commodity market records.

The most dramatic single instance occurred on March 23, 2026. Trump announced he was postponing strikes on Iranian power plants for five days and described major points of agreement that had supposedly been reached. Oil prices fell sharply on global markets as investors anticipated de-escalation.

Iran denied that any talks had taken place.

The sequence is legally precise. The President made a specific, dramatic claim about military restraint and diplomatic progress. That claim moved global oil markets. Iran flatly denied the claim. The market movement was therefore produced by a claim the other party says was false. And the market movement, specifically the temporary price dip followed by the resumption of the high-price conflict status quo, served Russia by maintaining the volatile, elevated price environment in which Russia was collecting its oil windfall.

This is not theoretical. Oil prices fell when peace seemed near. Oil prices rose when conflict continued. Russia's revenues are directly correlated with oil prices. The fake peace announcements were the mechanism that managed the domestic American political temperature, kept the public from revolting at the gas pump, and sustained the conflict and its oil price effects for the duration of the 43 days.

> **THE WITNESSES:** *Trump's quoted statements about very good talks, objectives nearly complete, and peace being close are documented in White House communications and press conference records during the Iran war period. The Iranian government's denials that serious talks were occurring are documented in Iranian Foreign Ministry statements and confirmed by international news organizations covering the conflict. The March 23 strike postponement announcement and the sharp oil price decline that followed are documented in commodity market records. Iran's simultaneous denial of the talks is documented in contemporaneous news reporting.*

□ □ □

Section Two: The Smoking Gun — March 5, 2026 and the Sanctions Relief

On March 5, 2026, exactly one week into the Iran war, the President of the United States announced that Russia would be temporarily allowed to export its oil to India without American sanctions.

That announcement is the most precisely timed act of aid in the documented record of this book.

The legal analysis requires understanding three things about what happened on March 5 and why its timing is the evidence that the Haupt standard establishes as proof of intent.

What American Sanctions on Russian Oil Were Doing

Following Russia's 2022 invasion of Ukraine, the United States and its allies imposed sanctions on Russian oil exports as part of a comprehensive economic pressure campaign. The sanctions were designed to constrain the revenue flows that funded Russia's military at the moment Russia needed that funding most.

The sanctions were working. They had been constraining Russian oil revenues and reducing the financial resources available to a military engaged in active warfare in Ukraine and, under Russia's own doctrine, conducting hybrid warfare against the United States and its allies. The sanctions were the economic weapon that the United States had spent years building into its most effective tool for constraining Russian aggression without direct military confrontation.

They were the velvet rope keeping Russia out of the full financial benefit of global oil markets at the moment Russia most needed that benefit.

What the Iran War Did to Oil Prices

The Iran war, launched on February 28, 2026, caused the largest disruption to global energy supply since the 1970s. The effective closure of the Strait of Hormuz produced a 94 percent collapse in tanker traffic. Brent crude surpassed $100 per barrel for the first time in four years and peaked at $126 per barrel, rising faster than during any other conflict in recent history.

Russia, as one of the world's largest oil exporters, was positioned to receive a massive financial benefit from those price spikes. Every dollar added to the price of a barrel of oil translated directly into additional revenue for Russia. External analysis documented that Russia was earning an extra $150 million per day from the conflict's oil price effects.

American sanctions on Russian oil were the one constraint on Russia's ability to fully capitalize on those high prices. The sanctions limited where Russia could sell its oil and constrained the volume it could move to the markets where prices were highest.

The India Mechanism

The March 5 announcement was specifically targeted. The sanctions relief allowed Russia to export its oil to India without American sanctions. This was not a generic loosening of the sanctions architecture. It was a specific authorization for a specific trade flow at the specific moment that trade flow would generate maximum financial benefit to Russia.

India was a significant and growing market for Russian oil. Many Indian refineries had built business models around discounted sanctioned oil from Russia. The sanctions had been constraining this trade. Lifting them at the moment global prices had peaked allowed Russia to sell into the Indian market at high prices, converting the full benefit of the Iran war's oil price spike into Russian government revenue.

The sanctions were lifted precisely when they were most valuable as a constraint. At the precise moment Russia was profiting most from a conflict that American military action without congressional authorization had created. The one economic tool most capable of limiting Russia's windfall from the war was removed one week after the war began.

The Cramer Standard Applied

Under the Cramer standard, the central question in the treason analysis is whether the specific act actually advanced the enemy's mission. This requires identifying the enemy's mission and establishing that the act provided material advancement of that mission.

Russia's mission, as documented throughout this book, has two primary components. The first is active military warfare against Ukraine, a U.S. partner nation. The second is the hybrid warfare campaign against the United States and its democratic institutions that Russia's own Gerasimov Doctrine describes as the primary strategic objective of Russian military and intelligence operations. Both components of Russia's mission require continuous, substantial funding. The Russian military does not operate for free. The hybrid warfare operations do not operate for free. The revenue that finances both components flows primarily from energy exports.

Lifting sanctions that constrain Russian energy export revenues at the moment those revenues are at their peak directly and immediately advances Russia's mission under the Cramer standard. The financial resources that were being constrained by the sanctions flow to the military that uses them to conduct the operations. The act of removing that constraint is the act of providing those resources. It is as direct as it gets.

The Haupt Standard Applied

The Haupt standard establishes that the timing of an act is evidence of the intent behind it. When an act is performed at the precise moment it benefits the enemy most, the timing is not a coincidence. It is the evidence that the act was performed for the purpose of benefiting the enemy at that moment.

The March 5 sanctions relief was not performed during a period of normal oil prices when its effect on Russian revenues would have been modest and its policy rationale could plausibly have been energy market management. It was performed one week into a war that had caused oil prices to surge toward $126 per barrel. At that specific moment, the sanctions were at their maximum value as a constraint on Russian revenue, because Russia was positioned to earn maximum additional revenue from the high prices. And the act of lifting the constraints at that specific moment converted the maximum available Russian windfall from potential to actual.

The Haupt standard asks: does the timing reveal the intent? The timing here reveals that the sanctions were lifted at the precise moment lifting them would do the most good for Russia and the most harm to the American sanctions strategy. There is no other way to explain why that specific moment was chosen.

On March 5, 2026, one week into an unauthorized war that had driven oil prices to their highest level in four years, the President of the United States lifted sanctions on Russian oil exports. Russia was the primary financial beneficiary of the war those sanctions would have constrained. The sanctions were lifted at the precise moment they were most valuable as a weapon and most needed as a constraint. Under Cramer, that act advanced Russia's mission directly and immediately. Under Haupt, the timing proves the intent. There is no innocent explanation.

□ □ □

Section Three: The Coordination — How the Two Hands Worked Together

The negotiation lies and the sanctions relief are legally significant individually. Together, they are a coordinated pattern that the Kawakita standard permits the jury to evaluate as a unified course of conduct.

The Misdirection Function of the Peace Announcements

The fake peace announcements served a specific and measurable function in relation to the sanctions relief. They managed the domestic American political temperature.

If the American public had understood that the war was not progressing toward peace, that Iran denied the talks, and that Russia was collecting $150 million per day in additional oil revenue from the conflict, the political pressure to end the war and restore the sanctions would have been substantial. The peace announcements prevented that political response by creating the impression that the war was nearly over and a deal was close.

They also directly depressed oil prices through market psychology, giving the American public temporary relief at the gas pump and reducing the domestic political cost of a war that was delivering a sustained financial windfall to Russia. When prices fell on a peace announcement, Americans felt the relief. When prices rose again as the conflict continued and Iran denied the talks, the cycle repeated, with the next peace announcement providing the next temporary relief.

The peace announcements were not failed diplomacy. They were the cover for the conflict's continuation. They were the right hand that kept the audience's eyes from the left hand's work.

The Absence of Innocent Alternatives

The legal analysis requires examining whether there is an innocent explanation for the combination of these two acts. There is not.

If the goal of the March 5 sanctions relief was to lower global oil prices and provide relief to American consumers at the gas pump, there were alternatives that did not simultaneously put money into Russia's pocket. The Strategic Petroleum Reserve exists specifically to be released in energy market emergencies. Diplomatic pressure on OPEC nations to increase production is a standard tool of American energy policy. Coordination with allied nations on demand reduction or strategic reserve releases could have addressed the price spike without benefiting Russia.

The administration chose the one policy option that simultaneously addressed the oil price issue and delivered a financial windfall to Russia. Among all the available tools for managing the oil price spike produced by the Iran war, the one that was selected was the one that most directly benefited the identified enemy at the moment the identified enemy most needed the benefit.

Under the Haupt standard, when the only action taken from among multiple available options is the one that benefits the enemy, the choice of that specific option over all others is evidence of the intent to benefit the enemy.

The Pattern Across the 43 Days

The March 5 sanctions relief and the negotiation lies do not stand alone in the 43-day record. They are two instances of a pattern.

Chapter 18 documented the false imminent threat justification for starting the war. The classified military briefing said no imminent threat existed. The public statement said the opposite. The war started. Oil prices spiked. Russia benefited.

The negotiation lies maintained the war's continuation by preventing the domestic political pressure that would have ended it sooner. Iran denied the talks. The war continued. Oil prices stayed elevated. Russia kept collecting.

The March 5 sanctions relief removed the financial constraint on Russia's ability to capitalize on the elevated prices. Russia earned maximum revenue from the conflict at the moment the sanctions would have been most effective at constraining it.

The March 23 strike postponement announcement manipulated markets by temporarily depressing prices, managed the domestic temperature, and was contradicted by Iran before prices resumed their elevated level.

Each act in the sequence served Russia. Each act was accompanied by a public statement that contradicted the documented reality. Each act followed the pattern of consciousness of guilt that Part V of this book established as the architecture of denial.

□ □ □

Section Four: The Legal Synthesis — Aid and Comfort at Maximum Value

The legal conclusion this chapter supports is specific and grounded in the documented public record.

The negotiation lies satisfy the consciousness of guilt analysis established in Chapter 16. They are demonstrably false, contradicted by the other party to the alleged negotiations. They were deployed to prevent the domestic political accountability that accurate information about the conflict would have generated. They are connected directly to the acts they were designed to conceal, specifically the continuation of a war whose primary financial beneficiary was Russia.

The March 5 sanctions relief satisfies the Cramer actual aid standard. The act advanced Russia's mission directly and immediately by removing the financial constraint that had been limiting Russia's ability to capitalize on the oil price windfall produced by the war. The act provided a material benefit, documented in the $150 million per day additional revenue, to a military engaged in active warfare against a U.S. partner nation and in hybrid warfare against the United States itself.

The March 5 sanctions relief satisfies the Haupt timing-as-intent standard. The act was performed at the precise moment it would generate maximum benefit to Russia and maximum harm to the American sanctions strategy. The timing eliminates any innocent explanation for the choice of that specific moment, from among all moments available for a policy adjustment, to lift the constraint.

The coordination between the peace announcements and the sanctions relief satisfies the Kawakita cumulative inference standard. The pattern of conduct, evaluated as a whole, reveals a consistent course of action that benefited Russia at every decision point: starting the war, maintaining it through false peace announcements, removing the financial constraint on Russia's windfall, and manipulating markets through specific false claims about diplomatic progress.

> ***The American soldiers who flew missions over Iran during those 40 days were not told that their Commander in Chief was simultaneously engineering a financial windfall for the adversary that funds the forces arrayed against America's allies in Europe. The American families watching gas prices were not told that the very good talks their President described had been flatly denied by the other side. They were told a story. It was reassuring and patriotic and full of optimism about deals coming soon. It was, according to the documented record, a lie. And at the other end of the chain of consequences those lies created, sat Russia, collecting its money. Under the constitutional standard that has defined treason since the founding of this Republic, that is aid and comfort to an enemy. Delivered through the mechanism of fake peace, at the moment of maximum value, while American families held their breath.***

The 43 days documented are the most recent entries in the record this book has assembled across the chapters in this book. The Legal Opinion chapter assembles them all.

□ □ □

Chapter Twenty

The Lebanon Ceasefire Denial: The Most Documented Lie in the Record

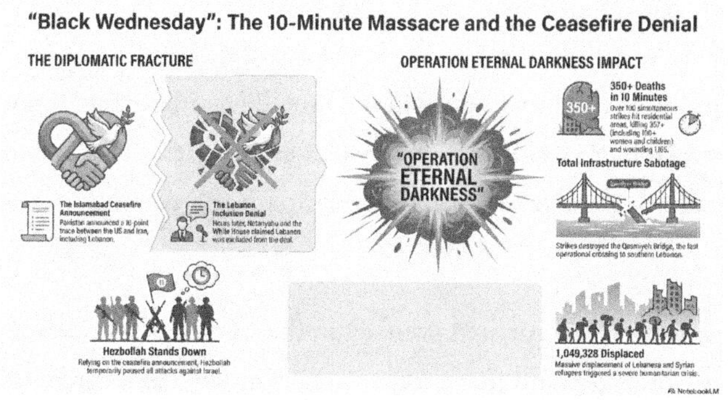

Imagine a burning building. The fire alarm has sounded. The residents inside have heard it, trusted it, and begun moving toward the exits in an orderly way. The evacuation is working. And then someone cuts the alarm. Not because the fire is out. Because they want the residents to stop moving.

The residents, hearing silence, assume the danger has passed. They stop. The fire, which was always real, reaches them where they stand.

On April 8, 2026, the ceasefire was the alarm. Lebanon was a building full of people who heard it, trusted it, and stopped. The denial was the hand that cut the wire. The fire was 50 Israeli fighter jets delivering 100 strikes in 10 minutes across a nation whose defenders had just laid down their weapons in good-faith reliance on a peace they were told existed.

Three hundred and fifty-seven people died on that day. Lebanon called it Black Wednesday. The world called it a massacre. The mediating nation, the French President, and multiple diplomats on the record all confirmed the same thing: Lebanon had been included in the ceasefire before the hand cut the wire.

Chapter 15 of this book established the legal framework for analyzing a ceasefire denial as a constitutional overt act. It developed the two-witness standard, the causal chain analysis, the perfidy argument, and the Russia strategic beneficiary connection in the context of the broader treason analysis this book has built.

This chapter is different from Chapter 15 in one essential way. Chapter 15 was analysis applied to documented events. This chapter is the documented events themselves. The witnesses are not described in the abstract. They are named heads of state whose public statements are in the international record. The body count is not a legal abstraction. It is confirmed by hospital records, governmental casualty reports, and the testimony of surgeons who operated on the wounded in real time. The causal chain is not an inference from circumstantial evidence. It is a sequence of events dated, timed, and recorded by independent nations, news organizations, and diplomatic communications across the world.

This is the most tightly documented overt act in this book. The fire alarm was cut. The building burned. And the hand that cut the wire belongs to the record.

□ □ □

Section One: The Announcement — What the Mediator Said

Pakistani Prime Minister Shehbaz Sharif, the leader of the nation that had conducted the ceasefire mediation between the United States, Iran, and their respective allied parties, announced to the world on April 8, 2026 that a ceasefire had been reached. It was effective immediately. It covered all fronts. It included Lebanon.

The Pakistani announcement was the most authoritative statement available about what had been agreed, because Pakistan was the mediating nation. The mediator is not a secondary source or an outside observer. The mediator is the party who conducted the negotiation, who communicated the terms to each side, and who announced the result.

When the mediating nation says Lebanon was included, that is not an interpretation of the ceasefire terms. That is a report of the ceasefire terms from the party whose job was to negotiate and communicate them.

Lebanon's President Joseph Aoun welcomed the announcement and praised the mediation efforts of Pakistan, Egypt, and Turkey. His welcome was not cautious. It reflected his specific understanding, based on the diplomatic communications he had received through official channels, that Lebanon was covered.

Hezbollah announced a pause in attacks against Israel. The announcement was made in direct reliance on the ceasefire's Lebanon inclusion. Hezbollah did not announce a conditional pause or a temporary review of its position. It announced a pause in accordance with the ceasefire it understood to cover Lebanon. Hezbollah stopped shooting.

Iran, the United States, and Israel all initially indicated they would suspend strikes. President Trump cited Iran's 10-point framework as a basis for ongoing negotiations, signaling that the comprehensive ceasefire Pakistan had announced was consistent with the diplomatic framework the administration understood to be in place.

The ceasefire was real. It was announced by the mediator. It was accepted by Lebanon. It was acted upon by Hezbollah. And then, within hours, it was denied.

□ □ □

Section Two: The Denial — What the White House Said

Less than 24 hours after President Trump had called Iran's 10-point framework a workable basis on which to negotiate, the White House reversed course.

Press Secretary Karoline Leavitt described the 10-point plan as fundamentally unserious, unacceptable, and completely discarded. She said it had been literally thrown in the garbage by President Trump and his negotiating team.

Prime Minister Netanyahu said Lebanon was not covered by the agreement. He insisted that the fight against Hezbollah was separate and ongoing.

President Trump said Lebanon was not in the deal because of Hezbollah. Vice President Vance called the overall arrangement a fragile truce, walking back the comprehensive framing that Pakistan's announcement had established. The White House said Lebanon had never been part of the deal.

Iran said the opposite. France said the opposite. Pakistan, as the mediating nation, had already said the opposite in its official announcement of the ceasefire terms.

> *"Lebanon was fully included in the ceasefire."* — **French President Emmanuel Macron, April 8, 2026**

On April 9, 2026, CBS News spoke to diplomats, described in the plural, who agreed that initially President Donald Trump had included Lebanon in the ceasefire, and even Israel had acknowledged these terms before the position shifted.

The documentary sequence is precise. Lebanon was included. Trump initially acknowledged the terms. Israel initially acknowledged the terms. A phone call occurred between Netanyahu and Trump. The position shifted. Lebanon was excluded. And Operation Eternal Darkness began within hours of that exclusion.

□ □ □

Section Three: The Constitutional Standard — Competent Witnesses Under Article III

Article III, Section 3 of the Constitution requires that no person shall be convicted of treason unless on the testimony of two witnesses to the same overt act, or on a confession in open court.

The legal question this section answers is whether the Lebanon ceasefire denial satisfies that standard. It does, and it satisfies it with a redundancy that few treason cases in American history have enjoyed.

The Overt Act

The overt act is the denial of Lebanon's inclusion in the ceasefire terms that the mediating nation had announced and that multiple parties had accepted and acted upon. The act is specific. It is dated. It is documented in governmental statements, press secretary communications, diplomatic cables reported through credible news organizations, and the behavioral response of Hezbollah, which had halted its attacks in direct reliance on the announced inclusion.

The First Witness: Prime Minister Shehbaz Sharif

Shehbaz Sharif is the Prime Minister of Pakistan. He is the head of government of the nation that served as the mediating party in the ceasefire negotiations. His knowledge of Lebanon's inclusion in the ceasefire terms is firsthand. He was not briefed on the terms by a secondary source. He was the mediator. He conducted the negotiations. He communicated the terms. He announced them to the world.

His competence as a witness under Article III is not merely his official position. It is his direct, firsthand knowledge of the specific fact at issue: that Lebanon was included in the negotiated ceasefire terms. He announced that fact officially, in his governmental capacity, on April 8, 2026. His testimony would be admissible in any court in any jurisdiction in the world.

The Second Witness: President Emmanuel Macron

Emmanuel Macron is the President of France. France was not a neutral bystander to the ceasefire negotiations. France had been actively involved in the regional diplomatic process and had its own direct engagement with the parties and the mediating framework. Macron stated publicly, on the record, on April 8, that Lebanon was fully included in the ceasefire. He subsequently condemned the Israeli strikes as indiscriminate and expressed full solidarity with Lebanon.

His competence as a witness is established by his direct diplomatic engagement with the ceasefire framework and his public, on-the-record, contemporaneous statement about the terms. His testimony is independent of Sharif's. France and Pakistan are different nations with different diplomatic interests and different relationships with the parties to the conflict. Their accounts converge on the same factual conclusion: Lebanon was included.

Corroboration: The Diplomatic Sources and the Behavioral Record

The CBS News diplomatic sources, described in the plural, provide a third independent account that Lebanon's inclusion was the initial agreed position of both the United States and Israel before the position shifted following the Netanyahu call. These are not anonymous tips or speculation. They are participants in or recipients of the actual diplomatic communications, speaking through a credible news organization on the record.

The behavioral record of Hezbollah, which halted its attacks in direct reliance on the announced inclusion, provides a fourth form of corroboration. Hezbollah's halt was a costly action. It exposed Hezbollah to exactly the military vulnerability that Israel exploited in Operation Eternal Darkness. Hezbollah would not have halted unless it believed, based on the communications it had received, that Lebanon was covered. The halt is documented proof that Hezbollah understood Lebanon to be included. And the halt was the direct cause of the vulnerability the denial exploited.

The President of Pakistan, the mediating nation, announced Lebanon's inclusion as established fact. The President of France confirmed it publicly. Multiple diplomats confirmed to CBS News that it was the initial agreed position. And Hezbollah halted its attacks in direct reliance on it, exposing itself to the attack that followed. The Article III two-witness requirement is satisfied here with a redundancy that would meet the most rigorous application of the Cramer standard. The overt act is documented. The witnesses are heads of state with direct firsthand knowledge. The two-witness rule is not merely satisfied. It is satisfied beyond any reasonable interpretive doubt.

□ □ □

Section Four: Black Wednesday — The Causal Chain to the Massacre

On April 8, 2026, while the denial was being processed by the world's diplomatic community and while Hezbollah had halted its attacks in reliance on the ceasefire's Lebanon inclusion, Israel launched Operation Eternal Darkness.

The operation involved approximately 50 fighter jets delivering strikes across Lebanon within a 10-minute window. One hundred targets struck simultaneously. The strikes hit densely populated civilian areas of Lebanon including central Beirut neighborhoods, the Beqaa Valley, and southern Lebanon. This was the bloodiest single day of the entire conflict.

The Causal Chain

The causal chain runs in a straight line and requires no inference to follow.

One. The ceasefire was announced by the mediating nation and included Lebanon. Two. Hezbollah halted its attacks in direct reliance on that inclusion. The halt was the behavioral consequence of the announcement. Three. The denial of Lebanon's inclusion was issued following the Netanyahu call, removing the ceasefire protection that Hezbollah had relied upon in standing down. Four. Israel launched Operation Eternal Darkness within hours of the denial, exploiting the military vulnerability that Hezbollah's halt had created. Five. At least 357 people died.

Without the lie, step four could not have happened in the form it took. Without the lie, Hezbollah would not have stood down. Without the standdown, Israel would not have had the military window that the operation exploited. The lie created the vulnerability. The vulnerability was exploited. Three hundred and fifty-seven people died.

The denial of Lebanon's inclusion was not merely a misrepresentation of diplomatic terms. It was the mechanism through which a military window was created and through which that window was then used to conduct the largest single-day massacre of the Lebanon conflict.

The Human Cost

Three hundred and fifty-seven people dead in 10 minutes. The strikes hit a funeral in the Beqaa Valley, killing 10 mourners. Three girls were killed in Adloun on the southern coast.

At Hiram Hospital in Tyre, Doctors Without Borders staff were injured and the facility was severely damaged. Hospitals in Beirut were flooded with more than 1,200 casualties simultaneously.

A surgeon at the American University of Beirut Medical Center documented operating on an 11-month-old infant who arrived at the emergency room alone, without parents, to relieve pressure in the child's head. The surgeon described a triage of despair characterized by mass crush injuries and traumatic amputations, with doctors forced to prioritize those with even a marginal chance of survival over the dying.

Lebanon's government declared it Black Wednesday and accused Israel of conducting a massacre. The UN Security Council convened in emergency session. More than 20 nations condemned the strikes. The international credibility of the American presidency, used to announce a ceasefire and then within hours to deny it, was the instrument through which this outcome became possible.

> *"The greatest threat to any ceasefire in the region remains Israel, which prefers ambiguous ceasefire deals."* — **Andreas Krieg, King's College London, Al Jazeera, April 8, 2026**

Perfidy: The Weaponization of Trust

The international law of armed conflict contains a specific prohibition on a specific category of act. Perfidy is the use of the appearance of a protected status, such as a truce or ceasefire, to create a military vulnerability in an adversary who has relied on that protected status in good faith.

The Lebanon ceasefire denial meets the functional definition of perfidy with precision. The ceasefire was announced. Hezbollah relied on it in good faith and halted its attacks. The protection was then denied. The standdown created a military window. The window was exploited. Three hundred and fifty-seven people died.

Beyond the immediate harm, the perfidy inflicted a specific and lasting damage on something this book has documented throughout as a critical American national security asset:

the credibility of the American presidential word. If the President of the United States commits to ceasefire terms and then reverses that commitment, allowing a massacre to proceed against parties who had already stood down in reliance on the commitment, every future party to a U.S.-mediated negotiation must ask: is this commitment real, or will it be reversed the next time an ally makes a phone call?

That question, once raised in the minds of every future negotiating partner, weakens American diplomatic power across every arena in which it operates. American diplomatic credibility is as much a component of American national security as any weapons system. The weaponization of that credibility through perfidy is the destruction of a national security asset.

> **THE WITNESSES:** *The ceasefire announcement by Prime Minister Sharif is documented in Pakistani governmental communications and confirmed by Iranian Foreign Ministry statements. Macron's Lebanon was fully included statement is a public record. The CBS News diplomatic sources confirming initial US and Israeli acknowledgment of Lebanon's inclusion are documented in CBS reporting of April 9, 2026. The White House press secretary's literally thrown in the garbage statement is a public record. Trump's initial workable basis characterization and its reversal are documented in reporting from Fox News and NBC News. The 357 death count is confirmed by Lebanese health ministry records, UNHCR reporting, and multiple international news organizations. The surgeon's account of the 11-month-old infant is documented in AUBMC medical staff testimony reported internationally.*

□ □ □

Section Five: The Strategic Beneficiary — Why Russia Needed the Ceasefire to Fail

The treason analysis requires establishing who benefited from the overt act. The immediate tactical beneficiary of the ceasefire's collapse was Israel, which gained the military window Operation Eternal Darkness exploited. The strategic beneficiary of the Lebanon conflict's continuation was Russia.

What a Comprehensive Ceasefire Would Have Done

A comprehensive ceasefire on April 8, 2026, covering all fronts including Lebanon, and holding across all parties, would have begun the process of de-escalating the broader Iran war. The Strait of Hormuz, effectively closed and driving global oil prices toward their peak, would have been on a path toward normalization. The military and diplomatic attention of the United States, consumed by the Middle East theater, would have begun its reorientation toward the European theater where it was needed to support Ukraine.

For Russia, every one of those consequences was negative. Lower oil prices would have reduced the financial windfall that Chapter 19 documented Russia collecting at $150 million per day. American military resource reorientation toward Europe would have increased the deterrent pressure on Russia's Ukraine operations. And a successful American-mediated peace in the Middle East would have restored the diplomatic credibility and the international standing that Russia's strategic interests depend on degrading.

What the Denial Preserved

The denial of Lebanon's inclusion ensured that the war continued. Black Wednesday reignited regional fury and threatened to collapse the entire ceasefire framework. Iran paused Strait of Hormuz traffic in response to the continued Israeli attacks in Lebanon, threatening to restart the full-scale conflict on its first day of theoretical ceasefire.

Oil prices, which had crashed 15 percent in minutes when the ceasefire was announced, rebounded above $120 within 24 hours as traders realized the Strait remained functionally closed. By keeping the conflict alive through the denial, the ceasefire's collapse preserved the oil price environment that was delivering Russia its financial windfall.

Russia and China used their UN Security Council positions to veto a resolution that would have reopened the Strait of Hormuz to all nations. Both had already secured toll-free passage from Iran while Western shipping paid $1 to $2 per barrel in Iranian tolls plus insurance premiums that had reached 2.5 to 5 percent of hull value. The continued closure of the Strait benefited Russia and China simultaneously, while imposing costs on every Western economy dependent on Middle Eastern energy.

The Strategic Distraction Value

Chapter 18 documented that the Iran war consumed American precision-guided munitions, Patriot interceptors, and naval assets from stockpiles built to deter Russian aggression in Europe. Every day the Lebanon conflict continued and the Iran war remained unresolved was another day those resources were unavailable for the European theater where Russia was conducting its primary military operations.

The sources analyzing Russia's strategic position during the period characterize its interest in the continuation of the conflict through a specific framing: the logic of perpetual war in the Middle East serves Russia's interests by ensuring the United States remains distracted and resource-drained. Russia's primary strategic goal, keeping the United States distracted and resource-drained, was preserved by the lie that extended the Lebanon conflict past the April 8 ceasefire that should have ended it.

A comprehensive ceasefire on April 8 would have lowered oil prices, freed American military resources for the European theater, and restored American diplomatic credibility in the region. Russia needed none of those outcomes to occur. The denial of Lebanon's ceasefire inclusion ensured they did not. The oil prices remained elevated. The American resources remained pinned. The diplomatic credibility was destroyed by the perfidy. Three hundred and fifty-seven people paid with their lives for a lie whose strategic beneficiary sat in Moscow, counting its oil revenues.

□ □ □

Section Six: The Legal Synthesis — The Lie with the Body Count

The Lebanon ceasefire denial is the most tightly documented overt act in this book. It satisfies every constitutional requirement the treason analysis has established across twenty chapters.

The overt act is the denial of the Lebanon inclusion. It is specific, dated, documented in governmental communications from multiple independent nations, and directly connected to the military exploitation that followed.

The two-witness requirement is satisfied by the Prime Minister of Pakistan and the President of France, two heads of state with direct firsthand knowledge of the negotiated terms, corroborated by multiple diplomatic sources and by Hezbollah's own behavioral record of halting in reliance on the announced terms.

The causal chain is direct. The announcement created the standdown. The denial removed the protection the standdown relied upon. The removal of protection created the military window. The military window was exploited in Operation Eternal Darkness. Three hundred and fifty-seven people died.

The actual aid element under the Cramer standard is satisfied by the documented continuation of the conflict's strategic benefits to Russia: the oil price maintenance above $120 per barrel, the continued American military resource consumption in the Middle East theater, the continued diversion from the European theater, and the diplomatic credibility destruction that weakened America's standing across every future negotiation.

The Haupt intent element is established by the pattern documented across twenty chapters. The Lebanon ceasefire denial did not occur in isolation. It was one act in a sustained course of conduct whose consistent direction was the service of Russia's primary strategic objectives, the documented pattern from which the Kawakita inference of treasonous intent is drawn.

And the perfidy element, while not a formal element of the constitutional treason standard, is legally relevant to the specific intent analysis. A President who uses the credibility of the American presidency to create a good-faith standdown by an adversary and then reverses the commitment that produced the standdown, allowing a massacre to proceed against parties who had already ceased fire, has not made a diplomatic mistake. He has made a deliberate choice. The deliberateness of that choice, established by the sequence of events and the specific timing of the reversal following the Netanyahu call, is the evidence of the intent the treason analysis requires.

This was not a miscommunication. It was not a diplomatic fumble. The ceasefire was announced by the mediating nation. Lebanon was included. Trump

called the 10-point framework a workable basis. Israel acknowledged the terms. Hezbollah stopped shooting. Then a phone call happened. Then the White House said the plan was literally thrown in the garbage. Then Israel struck Lebanon 100 times in 10 minutes. Three hundred and fifty-seven people died. Russia kept collecting its $150 million per day. And the American diplomatic credibility that had underwritten the ceasefire was destroyed as the instrument through which the trap had been set. That is not foreign policy. Under the constitutional standard that has defined treason since the founding of this Republic, that is aid and comfort delivered through the mechanism of deception, at the cost of 357 lives, in service of the adversary whose interests this book has documented throughout.

The 43 days of Part VI are complete in the documented record. The Legal Opinion chapter assembles everything this book has established across twenty chapters into the citizen's brief for which this entire analysis was written.

□ □ □

Chapter Twenty-One

The NATO Threat: From Deconstruction to Announced Destruction

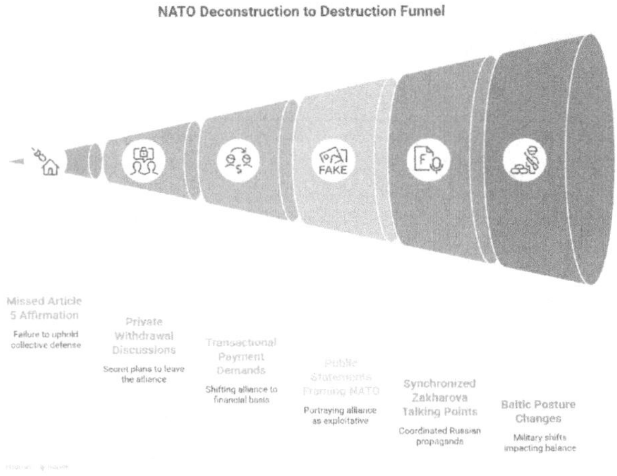

There is a difference between slowly weakening a dam and standing at the base of it with a sledgehammer, announcing to everyone downstream that you are ready to swing.

The missed Article 5 affirmation in 2017. The private withdrawal discussions documented in John Bolton's memoir. The transactional payment demands. The years of public statements framing the alliance as a protection racket in which America was being exploited. The synchronized Zakharova talking points. The Baltic posture changes that

NATO commanders assessed had already shifted the military balance. They were all covered in Chapter 6 of this book which documented the slow weakening of NATO.

This chapter is the sledgehammer announcement.

On April 9, 2026, the President of the United States told the world he was beyond reconsideration on withdrawing from NATO. The Secretary of State said the United States would have to reexamine whether the alliance still served its purpose. The White House press secretary said the allies had failed a test. And the NATO Secretary General, standing at a White House press conference, declined multiple times to deny that a withdrawal threat had been made.

Russia's primary stated strategic objective, documented in its military doctrine, in Putin's public statements, and in the intelligence community's assessment of Russian objectives, is the dissolution of NATO. On April 9, 2026, the President of the United States publicly announced he was considering exactly that outcome.

This chapter establishes why that announcement satisfies the constitutional treason standard's requirement of actual aid and comfort.

□ □ □

Section One: Why Allies Refused — The Unlawful Order Context

The administration characterized the NATO allies' refusal to join the Iran war as betrayal. The legal and constitutional context of that refusal is essential to understanding what the withdrawal threat actually meant.

When the United States launched strikes on Iran on February 28, 2026, it did so without consulting NATO allies, without any collective defense justification under Article 5, without any UN Security Council authorization, and without any international legal framework that European governments recognized as valid. The war was not self-defense under the UN Charter. It was not a response to an attack on a NATO member. It was a unilateral American decision to initiate a major combat operation against a sovereign nation that had not attacked the United States or any NATO member.

NATO allies declined to join. Several, including the United Kingdom, declined to allow American forces to use their bases to launch attacks against Iran. European leaders noted publicly and consistently that they had not been consulted, that the war had no legal basis they could recognize, and that they had concerns about escalation into a wider conflict that would trigger their own defensive obligations.

What the Refusal Actually Was

The allies were not failing NATO. They were describing what NATO is.

NATO is a defensive alliance. Its mutual defense commitment under Article 5 is triggered by an armed attack against a member nation, not by a member nation initiating an armed attack against a non-member. The Washington Treaty does not obligate member nations to join offensive military operations that individual members undertake unilaterally. It obligates them to respond if a member is attacked.

Iran had not attacked the United States. Iran had not attacked any NATO member. The United States attacked Iran. NATO's legal framework provides no obligation for other members to participate in that attack.

European leaders were not abandoning the alliance. They were upholding the international legal framework that the alliance was created to protect. They were declining to participate in what they assessed, correctly under international law, as an illegal offensive war launched without UN authorization, without an Article 5 trigger, and without the congressional authorization that the American Constitution requires for declarations of war.

The Significance of the Refusal for the Withdrawal Threat

The legal context of the refusal matters because it establishes what the withdrawal threat was actually punishing. The President did not threaten to withdraw from NATO because allies had failed to defend a member under attack. He threatened to withdraw because allies had refused to join an illegal offensive war. He was threatening to destroy the world's most powerful defensive alliance because its members would not commit what he was asking them to commit.

NATO allies refused to join the Iran war because the war was illegal under international law. They were not abandoning the United States. They were upholding the law. When the President threatened to withdraw from NATO in response to that refusal, he was not defending American interests. He was demanding that allies break international law with him, and threatening to hand Russia its primary strategic objective if they refused. That is not alliance management. Under the constitutional standard this book has applied throughout, that is the use of presidential power to advance the enemy's mission.

□ □ □

Section Two: The Explicit Threat — What Was Said and When

The withdrawal threat was not a private communication, a leaked diplomatic cable, or an anonymous source's account of a closed-door meeting. It was made publicly, repeatedly, and at the highest levels of the American government. The documented record is unambiguous.

The President

On April 1, 2026, the President stated publicly that he was beyond reconsideration on withdrawing from NATO. He called the alliance a paper tiger. He told reporters he believed he could make the withdrawal decision himself without Congress.

> *"NATO WASN'T THERE WHEN WE NEEDED THEM, AND THEY WON'T BE THERE IF WE NEED THEM AGAIN."* **President Donald Trump, TruthSocial post in all capitals, April 9, 2026, following a two-hour meeting with NATO Secretary General Rutte at the White House**

The social media post followed a two-hour meeting with NATO Secretary General Mark Rutte at the White House on April 9. Rutte declined, multiple times at the subsequent press conference, to deny that Trump had threatened withdrawal during that meeting.

The Secretary of State

Secretary of State Marco Rubio stated on Fox News that the administration would have to reexamine whether or not this alliance that has served this country well for a while is still serving that purpose. He argued that NATO had become a one-way street. He stated explicitly that if NATO is just about defending Europe but allies deny the United States basing rights when needed, that is not a very good arrangement.

The Rubio statement carries a specific legal irony documented in the research. Section 1250A of the National Defense Authorization Act for fiscal year 2024, the statute that prohibits the President from unilaterally withdrawing from NATO, was co-sponsored by Senator Tim Kaine and then-Senator Marco Rubio. The man who co-authored the law prohibiting unilateral NATO withdrawal was now the Secretary of State arguing that the alliance needed to be reexamined.

The Press Secretary and Ambassador

White House Press Secretary Karoline Leavitt characterized the Iran war as a test the alliance failed, stating that member states had turned their backs on the American people. Ambassador to NATO Matthew Whitaker stated that the President was evaluating and reevaluating everything and that the U.S. could not indefinitely guarantee European security without benefit for America.

What Allied Leaders Said

The allied response to the withdrawal threat documented the seriousness with which it was received by the nations whose security architecture it threatened.

> *"Creating daily doubt regarding security commitments serves to hollow out the alliance's value from within."* **French President Emmanuel Macron, April 2026**

German Chancellor Friedrich Merz described the rift as a transatlantic stress test. NATO Secretary General Rutte admitted the President was clearly disappointed with many NATO allies and that their discussion had been very frank and very open.

From the United States Senate, the bipartisan response was equally direct. Senate Minority Leader Chuck Schumer vowed that the Senate would not vote to leave NATO and abandon allies just because Trump was upset they would not join his reckless war of choice. Senators Thom Tillis and Jeanne Shaheen, co-chairs of the Senate NATO Observer Group, warned that any president attempting withdrawal was fulfilling Vladimir Putin and Xi Jinping's greatest dreams. Senators Mitch McConnell and Chris Coons issued a joint statement reminding the administration that the only time NATO has invoked Article 5 was in response to an attack on America, after September 11.

THE WITNESSES: *All quotes from Trump, Rubio, Leavitt, and Whitaker are from documented public statements in April 2026, available in press conference records, social media archives, and news organization reporting. Macron's daily doubt quote is documented in French governmental communications and international press coverage. The Tillis-Shaheen and McConnell-Coons statements are documented in congressional records. The Rutte press conference refusal to deny the withdrawal threat is documented in video and transcript records of the April 9 White House press conference.*

□ □ □

Section Three: The Propaganda Force Multiplier — Speaking the Enemy's Language

The President called NATO a paper tiger.

That phrase is not original to Donald Trump. It is the language that Russian and Soviet propagandists have used to describe NATO for seventy years. It is the specific characterization that Russian state media repeats when arguing that the alliance is a hollow structure that would collapse under pressure. It is precisely the message that Russia's information warfare operations have been trying to plant in Western publics for decades.

Chapter 14 of this book applied the broadcaster precedents from the World War II treason cases to the NATO funding lie. In those cases, American citizens were convicted of treason for broadcasting propaganda that served the enemy's strategic narrative, even though the broadcasts were verbal rather than physical acts. The Axis Sally standard established that speech in service of an enemy's strategic objectives, delivered with the authority that the speaker's position conveys, constitutes an overt act of aid and comfort.

The President of the United States calling NATO a paper tiger is not a private opinion. It is the most powerful public platform in the world delivering the enemy's preferred characterization of the enemy's primary strategic obstacle to a global audience. It is not merely aligned with Russian propaganda. It is Russian propaganda delivered with the credibility and authority that no Russian propagandist could ever achieve.

Analyst Stefano Stefanini, a former Italian Ambassador to NATO, stated the consequence precisely: Trump does not need to leave NATO to undermine it. By just saying he might, he has already eroded its credibility. And Ian Bremmer of the Eurasia Group noted that if allies cannot trust the United States to honor Article 5, the alliance is already broken in the way that matters most.

The paper tiger characterization is the information warfare dimension of the withdrawal threat. It does not merely announce a policy. It validates the enemy's narrative, demoralizes the alliance, and signals to every adversary of NATO that the deterrent credibility it took 70 years to build is now the subject of doubt from the President of its most powerful member.

□ □ □

Section Four: The Statutory Violation — Congress Already Said No

The withdrawal threat was not only a strategic betrayal. It was a threatened violation of a specific federal statute.

Section 1250A of the National Defense Authorization Act for fiscal year 2024 explicitly prohibits the President from suspending, terminating, denouncing, or withdrawing the

United States from the North Atlantic Treaty without specific legislative consent. The law requires either a two-thirds Senate supermajority providing advice and consent for withdrawal, or a separate act of Congress passed by both chambers.

The President told reporters he believed he could make the decision himself without Congress. He said he did not need Congress for that decision.

This is the same pattern documented in Chapter 18's analysis of the unauthorized Iran war. The constitutional and statutory mechanisms that the Framers and Congress designed to prevent a President from taking major unilateral actions that serve foreign adversaries rather than American national interests were treated as obstacles to be bypassed rather than constraints to be honored. The war was launched without the congressional authorization Article I requires. The NATO withdrawal was threatened in defiance of the statute Congress specifically passed to prevent exactly this kind of unilateral action.

Jim Townsend of the Center for a New American Security stated that the United States is closer to a break than it has ever been and that there will be no return to business as usual. The statutory prohibition has not been tested in court because formal withdrawal has not yet occurred. But the public announcement of intent to withdraw in defiance of the statutory prohibition is itself legally significant. It is the announcement that the constitutional sentry, the congressional check on presidential power to destroy the alliance that deters the identified enemy, is being disregarded.

□ □ □

Section Five: The Actual Aid — Why the Announcement Was Enough

Under the Cramer standard, the aid provided to the enemy must be actual. The question is whether the withdrawal threat provided real, material benefit to Russia even without formal withdrawal occurring.

The answer is yes. And the evidence is in Russia's strategic position on April 9, 2026.

What Russia Needed on April 9

On April 9, 2026, Russia was operating under the following strategic conditions. Western sanctions, maintained through allied coordination, were constraining Russian energy revenues and military procurement. Ukraine was receiving allied military assistance that was limiting Russian military advances. NATO's Article 5 collective defense guarantee was the primary deterrent preventing Russia from extending its military operations into NATO member territory. And Russia's own military doctrine had identified NATO dissolution as the primary strategic objective that would fundamentally alter the balance of power in Russia's favor.

A United States withdrawal from NATO would have been, in the assessment of every allied leader and security analyst in the documented record, the single greatest strategic victory in Russian military history since the Cold War. It would have eliminated the primary deterrent preventing Russian military expansion into the Baltic states, Poland, and the rest of the NATO eastern flank. It would have collapsed the sanctions coordination architecture that depends on transatlantic political cohesion. And it would have validated, in the most dramatic possible way, Russia's 70-year argument that NATO was an artificial and unsustainable construct that would eventually collapse under its own contradictions.

What the Announcement Delivered

The President's public announcement on April 9 that withdrawal was beyond reconsideration delivered real, material strategic benefit to Russia without formal withdrawal occurring. It told the Kremlin that its primary strategic objective was under active consideration by the American President. It told NATO allies that the Article 5 guarantee they were relying on for their defense planning might not be honored. It told Russia's neighbors who were not NATO members that the deterrent that had kept them safe was potentially about to disappear. And it told every military planner in Russia's defense establishment that the alliance's most important asset, the credibility of American commitment, had been placed in doubt by the President himself.

The Kawakita standard asks whether the act gave the enemy heart and courage to continue. The April 9 announcement gave Russia's leadership the most credible signal it had ever received from an American President that its primary strategic objective was achievable. That is not a metaphorical benefit. It is the actual, material strategic relief that the Cramer standard requires.

A Bargaining Chip You Keep Hidden

There is a specific legal detail about the April 9 announcement that distinguishes it from a legitimate diplomatic pressure tactic. A bargaining chip is kept hidden. You reveal it to extract a concession. If the President had privately communicated to NATO allies that their continued refusal to support American military objectives would jeopardize American security commitments, that would be coercive diplomacy with a specific, identifiable, reciprocal objective.

Instead, the President publicly announced the consideration of withdrawal in all capitals on social media after a meeting with the NATO Secretary General, demanded no specific concession in exchange, and provided Russia with the public declaration that its primary strategic objective was under active consideration. No concession was requested. No terms were offered. No policy change by allies would have reversed the announcement. The announcement was the message. And the beneficiary of the message was Moscow.

Under Haupt, intent is inferred from the timing. The announcement was not made during a peacetime budget debate. It was made during a major war, at the moment the alliance was strained, and precisely when Russia needed to believe that the West would fracture. The President did not just weaken the dam. He stood at its base, held up the sledgehammer, and told the world he was ready to swing. For the enemy waiting downstream for 70 years for exactly this moment, that announcement was all the aid they needed.

□ □ □

Section Six: The Legal Synthesis — Announced Destruction as Overt Act

The NATO withdrawal threat of April 2026 satisfies the constitutional treason standard through four independent legal pathways.

First, the Cramer actual aid standard is satisfied by the real, material strategic benefit Russia received from the public announcement that its primary strategic objective was under active consideration by the American President. The benefit did not require formal withdrawal to be actual. The announcement itself changed Russia's strategic calculus, signaled to NATO allies that the Article 5 guarantee was in doubt, and delivered the psychological and political relief that an adversary under allied pressure most needed at the moment of maximum allied cohesion.

Second, the Haupt timing-as-intent standard is satisfied by the precision of the moment chosen for the announcement. The threat was made during an active war, at the moment NATO was strained by a dispute over an illegal American military action, and at the precise moment Russia's strategic position would benefit most from a signal of American alliance ambivalence. The timing reveals the intent.

Third, the broadcaster precedent established in Chapter 14 applies to the paper tiger characterization. The President of the United States delivered the enemy's preferred propaganda characterization of the enemy's primary strategic obstacle to a global audience with the credibility that no Russian propagandist could match. That is an overt act of information warfare in service of the enemy's strategic narrative.

Fourth, the threat to withdraw in defiance of the specific statute Congress passed to prevent exactly this unilateral action establishes the same pattern of constitutional sentry bypass documented in Chapter 18's analysis of the unauthorized Iran war. The law exists to prevent a President from destroying the alliance that deters the identified enemy. The announcement that the law would be disregarded is itself evidence of the intent to remove the deterrent.

The dam analogy this chapter opened with captures the legal conclusion. Chapter 6 documented the slow weakening. This chapter documents the announced destruction. The Kawakita standard permits the jury to evaluate the totality of conduct. The totality runs from the 2017 missed Article 5 affirmation through the seven years of public statements, private discussions, and strategic degradation, to the April 9 announcement that withdrawal was beyond reconsideration. That totality, evaluated as a unified course of conduct, is the overt act.

Russia's primary strategic objective is the dissolution of NATO. The President of the United States announced he was beyond reconsideration on withdrawing from NATO. The Secretary of

State said the alliance needed to be reexamined. The NATO Secretary General refused to deny the withdrawal threat had been made. Senators from both parties called it the fulfillment of Putin's greatest dream. And the man who co-authored the law prohibiting unilateral NATO withdrawal was now the Secretary of State arguing for reexamination. Under the constitutional standard this book has applied across twenty-one chapters, that is aid and comfort to the identified enemy, delivered through the mechanism of public announcement, at the moment of maximum strategic value to Russia and maximum strategic damage to the alliance the Framers' oath was designed to preserve.

□ □ □

Chapter Twenty-Two

The Cumulative Record: 43 Days as a Case Study in Treasonous Pattern

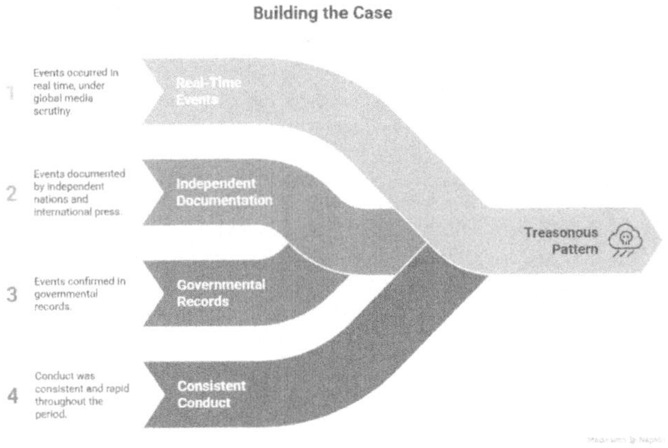

Prosecutors in major criminal cases often describe their evidence as a mosaic. No single tile tells the whole story. But step back and look at all of them together, and the picture becomes unmistakable.

Legal cases often rely on reconstructing the past from fragments, assembling a picture from documents years old, memories subject to dispute, and witnesses whose credibility can be attacked. Part VI required no reconstruction. The events occurred in real time, under the lights of global media, while the world watched. Every tile in this mosaic was laid in public, witnessed by independent nations, documented in governmental records, and confirmed in the international press within hours of occurring.

This distinction matters because it removes the shield of ambiguity. When a pattern of conduct is this dense, this rapid, this consistent, and this documented, the legal question changes. The question is no longer only whether the President intended to betray his country. The question becomes how he could not have intended it.

□ □ □

Section One: The Tiles — What the 43 Days Contain

In 43 days, from February 28 through April 12, 2026, the following occurred in documented, dated, witnessed sequence.

An unauthorized war was launched on February 28 during active diplomatic negotiations, based on a stated imminent threat justification that the administration's own military briefers contradicted in classified congressional session. The Geneva talks two days earlier had produced an assessment by the British National Security Adviser that a deal was within reach. The Vienna technical discussions scheduled for March 2 never happened. The bombs fell instead.

Congressional efforts to reassert the constitutional war power were defeated by six votes in the Senate and seven in the House, along broadly partisan lines, with bipartisan minority support from Senators Kaine and Paul and Representatives Khanna and Massie establishing the constitutional violation on the formal legislative record.

Russia received sanctions relief on its oil exports on March 5, one week into the war, at the precise moment of maximum Russian financial benefit from the energy market disruption the war had caused. Brent crude had surged toward $126 per barrel. Russia was earning an estimated $150 million per day in additional revenue. And on March 5, the one constraint on Russia's ability to capitalize on those prices was lifted.

False claims of peace progress moved global oil markets throughout the conflict. Trump announced objectives were nearly complete, that talks were going well, that a deal was coming. Iran denied the talks. On March 23, Trump announced a postponement of strikes on Iranian power plants and described major points of agreement. Oil prices fell sharply. Iran denied the talks. Prices rose again. Russia continued collecting.

A ceasefire was announced on April 8, acknowledged by the mediating nation as including Lebanon. Hezbollah halted its attacks in direct reliance. The administration denied Lebanon's inclusion within hours. Israel launched Operation Eternal Darkness. Three hundred and fifty-seven people died in 10 minutes. The largest single-day massacre of the Lebanon conflict occurred precisely because defenders had stood down based on a ceasefire they were told included them.

The most explicit NATO withdrawal threat in the alliance's history was issued in early April, using as its stated justification that allies had constitutionally declined to join an unauthorized war the President had started without their input or consultation. Russia's primary strategic objective, the dissolution of NATO, was publicly announced as under active consideration by the American President. The NATO Secretary General declined to deny the withdrawal threat at the subsequent press conference.

□ □ □

Section Two: The Elimination of Coincidence — Why Accident Cannot Explain This

Defense attorneys in complex cases almost always argue that a pattern of events is a series of coincidences. The bad judgment argument. The policy error argument. The diplomatic fumble argument. These defenses work when the events are separated by time, when innocent alternative explanations are plausible, and when the pattern is not too dense to be attributed to incompetence.

The 43 days eliminate every one of those defenses.

The Probability Argument

Consider each act individually and ask whether accident is a plausible explanation.

Is it plausible that a President accidentally starts an unauthorized war during active negotiations that an allied official assessed had produced a deal within reach? It is uncomfortable as a policy judgment, but not impossible as an accident.

Is it plausible that he simultaneously, one week later, lifts sanctions on the enemy who is profiting from the oil price spike produced by that war? Plausible as an independent energy policy decision. Less plausible as a coincidence with the war.

Is it plausible that he lies about the state of peace negotiations throughout the conflict, producing oil market movements that specifically benefit that enemy, while Iran publicly and repeatedly denies the negotiations he describes? Implausible as an accident.

Is it plausible that he threatens to withdraw from the alliance that is the enemy's primary strategic target, using as justification that allies refused to join the illegal war that produced the oil price spike from which the enemy is profiting? At this point the mathematical probability of coincidence does not approach zero. It reaches zero.

The Kawakita standard permits the jury to infer treasonous intent from the totality of conduct. The 43 days provide a totality so complete, so rapid, and so consistently directional that the inference is not permitted. It is compelled. Every act in the sequence served Russia. Every justification for every act was contradicted by the documented record. Every alternative explanation requires the simultaneous coincidental occurrence of independent errors that all happened to benefit the same adversary at the same moment.

The density of the 43 days is not background to the treason argument. It is the treason argument. When every act in a six-week period benefits the identified enemy, when every public justification for every act is contradicted by the classified or diplomatic record, and when the acts chain together into a sequence that each makes the next more effective, the only rational explanation for the pattern is that the pattern was intended.

□ □ □

Section Three: The Strategic Convergence — How the Acts Fed Each Other

The 43 days are not merely a list of bad acts. They are an integrated sequence in which each act made the next more effective and in which the combined effect delivered maximum strategic benefit to Russia. Understanding how the acts connected to each other is essential to understanding why their simultaneity is the proof of intent.

The Chain Reaction

The war caused the oil price spike. Brent crude surged from pre-war levels toward $126 per barrel. Russia, already the world's largest oil exporter, was positioned to collect windfall revenues from every dollar added to the price of a barrel. But American sanctions were constraining Russia's ability to fully capitalize on the high prices.

The March 5 sanctions relief removed that constraint. It allowed Russia to export its oil to India, the specific market where the displaced Iranian supply had created the greatest demand, at the precise moment global prices were highest. The war created the opportunity. The sanctions relief delivered the financial benefit the opportunity made possible.

The peace lies sustained the war. If the American public had understood that Iran denied the negotiations Trump was describing, that the conflict was not nearly over, and that Russia was collecting $150 million per day from the continued conflict, political pressure to end the war would have been substantial. The fake peace announcements managed the domestic political temperature, kept the war politically sustainable in the United States, and sustained the conflict and its oil price effects for the duration of the 43 days.

The Lebanon ceasefire denial extended the regional conflict. A comprehensive ceasefire on April 8 would have stabilized the Strait of Hormuz, lowered oil prices, and freed American military resources for the European theater. The denial of Lebanon's inclusion ensured the conflict continued. Three hundred and fifty-seven people died. Russia's oil windfall continued. American military resources remained pinned.

The NATO withdrawal threat punished the allies who tried to limit the cycle. NATO allies had refused to join an illegal war. Their refusal was constitutionally and legally correct. By threatening to destroy NATO in response to that refusal, the President simultaneously validated Russia's 70-year argument that NATO was unsustainable, signaled to Russia's neighbors that the deterrent protecting them was in doubt, and punished the specific nations who had declined to participate in the war whose continuation was serving Russia's financial interests.

The Machine's Output

Evaluated as an integrated sequence rather than a list of individual acts, the 43 days produced a specific and documented set of outputs for Russia. Approximately $150 million per day in additional oil revenue during the conflict. Removal of the sanctions that had been constraining that revenue at the moment of maximum price. Continued American military resource consumption in the Middle East theater rather than the European theater. The public announcement that Russia's primary strategic objective, NATO dissolution, was under active consideration by the American President. And the destruction of American diplomatic credibility through the Lebanon ceasefire perfidy, weakening the United States' ability to serve as the effective mediator whose mediation might have ended the conflict sooner.

Each output served Russia. Each act in the sequence produced one or more of those outputs. And the acts were separated by days, not months or years, occurring at a pace that leaves no room for the gradual accumulation of unintended consequences that might explain a pattern of policy errors.

□ □ □

Section Four: The Speed — What 43 Days Tells Us About Intent

Forty-three days is a remarkably compressed timeframe for the volume of conduct documented in Part VI. The entirety of Parts I through V covers the better part of a decade, from the 2016 campaign through the end of the first term and into the second. The events of Part VI occur in six weeks.

The speed itself is evidence.

A pattern of conduct that develops over years can be attributed to the gradual accumulation of policy decisions, diplomatic relationships, and institutional drift. Each individual step can be justified on its own terms, in the context of the moment it was taken, without reference to the long-term pattern it was contributing to. The defense that each act was reasonable at the time it was taken has at least some plausibility when the acts are separated by months and years.

When unauthorized war, sanctions relief for the enemy, fake peace negotiations, a ceasefire denial enabling a massacre, and a NATO withdrawal threat all occur within six weeks, that defense disappears. The pace eliminates the possibility that each act was an independent response to independent circumstances. The circumstances of each act were created by the preceding acts. The war created the oil price spike that the sanctions relief capitalized on. The sanctions relief created the revenue windfall that the peace lies sustained. The peace lies sustained the conflict that the ceasefire denial extended. The ceasefire denial extended the conflict that the NATO withdrawal threat punished allies for refusing to join.

The acts did not merely happen to occur in 43 days. They happened in 43 days because each required the preceding act to be effective and because each created the conditions that made the next act necessary. This is not the speed of a series of independent decisions. This is the speed of an integrated strategy executing itself.

□ □ □

Section Five: The Witness Inventory — The Richest in the Record

Part VI has something that Parts I through V, for all their documented strength, cannot fully match. The witnesses are heads of state and diplomatic officials of independent nations, bipartisan members of Congress, and military briefers in classified session. They have no U.S. domestic political stake in the narrative. Their accounts are contemporaneous, documented in the international press within hours of the events they describe, and independent of each other.

The Real-Time Advantage

The events of Parts I through V occurred over years. Documents can be destroyed. Memories fail. Witnesses who were present in private meetings can be attacked for their political motivations. The long time elapsed between events and their documentation creates space for ambiguity.

The events of Part VI were documented in real time. The ceasefire announcement was made publicly, by the mediating nation's head of government, on April 8. Its denial was made publicly, by the American President and the White House press secretary, on April 8. The military exploitation of the window the denial created began within hours. The casualty counts were confirmed by hospital records the same day. The NATO withdrawal threat was made at a public White House press conference. The Secretary General's refusal to deny it was recorded on video.

There are no memory lapses to exploit. There are no destroyed documents to argue. There is no time elapsed during which alternative narratives could be constructed. The real-time documentation of the 43 days is the evidentiary advantage that distinguishes Part VI from every other section of this book.

The Witnesses

Pakistani Prime Minister Shehbaz Sharif announced Lebanon's ceasefire inclusion as established fact. He is the head of government of the mediating nation. His knowledge of the negotiated terms is firsthand. He was the mediator. His account carries the highest possible diplomatic authority about the content of an agreement he personally conducted.

French President Emmanuel Macron confirmed Lebanon's inclusion publicly on the day of the announcement. He is the head of state of a major allied nation with direct diplomatic engagement in the regional process. His account is independent of Sharif's and converges on the same factual conclusion.

Lebanese President Joseph Aoun acted in reliance on the ceasefire's inclusion of Lebanon. His government's response is itself evidence of the diplomatic reality as Lebanon understood it. The behavioral record of Hezbollah halting its attacks corroborates the diplomatic record at the level of military conduct.

CBS News diplomatic sources, described in the plural, confirmed that Trump had initially included Lebanon in the ceasefire and that even Israel had acknowledged the terms before the reversal. These are participants in the actual diplomatic communications, documented through a credible news organization.

Senators Tim Kaine and Rand Paul, Representatives Ro Khanna and Thomas Massie, are on the formal legislative record establishing that the war was launched without the constitutional authorization their bipartisan votes sought to require. Their votes are in the congressional record. Their public statements are documented.

Pentagon closed-session briefers are on the record through congressional accounts that no imminent threat intelligence existed to justify the unilateral launch of the war. The administration's military briefers contradicted the administration's public justification in the most protected forum available to them.

NATO Secretary General Mark Rutte declined at a formal public press conference, multiple times, to deny that Trump had threatened withdrawal. That silence, in that context, by the head of the alliance in question at a press conference specifically about that alliance, is evidentiary in a way that exceeds many explicit statements.

The two-witness constitutional requirement for treason has never been more clearly satisfied in this record than in the 43 days of Part VI. The witnesses are not anonymous sources or politically motivated domestic partisans. They are heads of state, diplomatic officials of independent nations, bipartisan legislators, and military briefers. Their accounts are contemporaneous, documented in real time, and independent of each other. They are the constitutional witnesses the Framers required. They are present in the record.

□ □ □

Section Six: The Legal Synthesis — The Complete Picture

The Kawakita standard permits the jury to infer treasonous intent from the totality of conduct over time. The 43 days of Part VI provide the most concentrated totality in this book. They are the period when the pattern that Parts I through V documented across a decade accelerated into real-time execution.

The unauthorized war satisfies the overt act requirement and the congressional bypass establishes the usurpation of the war power that the Framers specifically designed as the check on presidential war-making for private or corrupt purposes.

The March 5 sanctions relief satisfies the Cramer actual aid standard. It provided material financial benefit to the identified enemy at the precise moment those sanctions were most valuable as a constraint. It satisfied the Haupt timing-as-intent standard. It occurred at the moment of maximum benefit to Russia and maximum harm to the American sanctions strategy.

The peace lies satisfy the consciousness of guilt analysis. They are demonstrably false, contradicted by the other party to the alleged negotiations. They are connected directly to the continuation of the conflict that benefited Russia. And they satisfy the operational lie standard established in Chapter 16: they were not only concealing past conduct but actively enabling the continuation of the conduct being concealed.

The Lebanon ceasefire denial satisfies the two-witness requirement with the redundancy documented in Chapter 20. It satisfies the causal chain requirement: the denial created the military window, the window was exploited, 357 people died. It satisfies the actual aid requirement: Russia's continued oil windfall was preserved by the continuation of the conflict the denial extended.

The NATO withdrawal threat satisfies the Kawakita heart and courage standard. It gave Russia's leadership the most credible signal it had ever received from an American President that its primary strategic objective was achievable. It satisfies the propaganda force multiplier standard established in Chapter 14: the paper tiger characterization delivered the enemy's narrative with presidential authority.

Evaluated individually, each act satisfies constitutional standards. Evaluated as the integrated sequence this chapter has documented, they do something more. They eliminate the coincidence defense. They establish the machine. They prove the intent not through any single act but through the convergence of all of them in 43 days, each feeding the next, each serving the same adversary, each accompanied by a public statement that the documented record contradicts.

> **The mosaic is complete. Unlike a mosaic where the artist places each tile with deliberate care over months and years, the 43 days were a flood: a flood of unauthorized violence, a flood of financial benefit to the enemy, a flood of lies to keep it all running, and a flood of strategic damage to the alliance the Framers' oath was designed to preserve. In that flood, the individual tiles merged into a single image. A President using the chaos of war to serve the strategic interests of the adversary he had been aligned with for years. The pattern is not background to the treason argument. The pattern is the treason argument.**

□ □ □

PART VII

THE ASSAULT ON THE REPUBLIC'S DEFENSES

Silencing, Intimidating, Corrupting, and Dismantling the Institutions That Stand Between Democracy and Tyranny

BEFORE A GOVERNMENT CAN betray its people, it must first dismantle the institutions designed to prevent betrayal. This is not a theory. It is the documented pattern of every authoritarian consolidation in modern history.

The free press is discredited, so that when the conduct is reported, the public has been prepared to disbelieve it. The judiciary is packed or delegitimized, so that legal accountability becomes impossible. The legislature is intimidated or hollowed out, so that the constitutional tools of oversight and impeachment cannot be effectively deployed. Witnesses are intimidated or rewarded for silence. Investigators are removed.

Part VII documents each step of this sequence in the record before us. The legal argument is this: when the conduct alleged in Parts I through VI is simultaneously protected by the destruction of every institution capable of exposing or prosecuting it, the destruction itself becomes part of the treasonous pattern. It is not separate from the treason. It is the wall built around it.

Chapter Twenty-Three

Silencing the Witnesses: The Assault on the Free Press

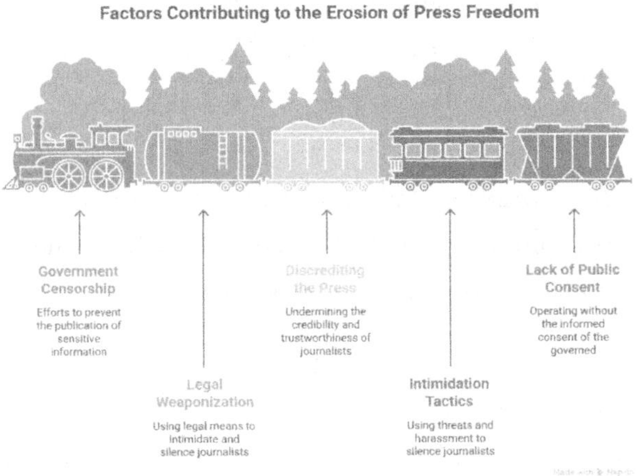

In 1971, the Nixon administration went to federal court to stop the New York Times and the Washington Post from publishing the Pentagon Papers, a secret government study documenting years of official deception about the Vietnam War. The administration argued that publication would harm national security. The newspapers argued that the public had a right to know.

The Supreme Court ruled 6 to 3 in favor of the newspapers.

> *"The press was to serve the governed, not the governors. The Government's power to censor the press was abolished so that the press would remain forever free to censure the Government."* **Justice Hugo Black, New York Times Co. v. United States (1971)**

That principle is the structural foundation of the First Amendment in a democracy. A free press is not merely a consumer good. It is a constitutional mechanism of accountability, the institutional witness whose function is to make it impossible for the government to operate in secret without the risk of public exposure.

When that mechanism is systematically discredited, intimidated, and legally weaponized, the constraint disappears. Conduct that would otherwise be exposed, investigated, and prosecuted can continue in the darkness the silencing creates.

This chapter is not about press freedom as a value, though it is that. It is about press freedom as a national security asset, the specific national security asset whose dismantlement was necessary to allow the conduct documented in the preceding chapters to proceed without the ultimate check: the informed consent of the governed.

□ □ □

Section One: The Press as National Security Sentry

This book has used a consistent metaphor throughout its analysis of the economic, diplomatic, and institutional damage documented in Parts I through VI. The sentry was disarmed. The early warning system was blinded. The check was bypassed.

The free press is the most important sentry of all. It is the one that every other check depends on.

The intelligence community can assess a threat. But if the President suppresses the assessment, the public never learns of it. Congress can subpoena documents. But if the documents are destroyed or classified beyond congressional access, the record is lost. Courts can adjudicate. But cases must be brought, and cases are built from reporting that exposed the underlying conduct.

The free press is the mechanism that moves information from closed government spaces into the public domain where democratic accountability operates. Without that mechanism, the inspector general's findings go unnoticed. The whistleblower's disclosure reaches no one. The congressional testimony generates no public pressure. The pattern of overt acts documented in this book remains invisible to the citizens whose democratic participation is the ultimate check on the power of the officials they elect.

A President who is conducting a sustained course of conduct that he understands would be exposed and stopped if the public knew about it has a specific interest in disabling that mechanism. He does not need to destroy the press to eliminate the check. He needs only to make enough people distrust the reporting that the reporting cannot generate the accountability response that accurate information would otherwise produce.

That is precisely what the enemy of the people campaign accomplished. And it accomplished it in precise alignment with the objectives of the identified enemy's own published doctrine.

□ □ □

Section Two: Enemy of the People — Speaking the Enemy's Language Again

The phrase enemy of the people has a specific history that is not rhetorical accident.

It was used by Soviet authorities to justify the imprisonment and execution of those who questioned the government. It was used by Nazi Germany to identify groups targeted for state persecution. In both cases, the function of the phrase was identical: to prepare the public to disbelieve, and to approve the silencing of, anyone who challenged the official narrative. The phrase was not an insult. It was a category. Once a person or institution was placed in that category, whatever they said or documented could be dismissed without engagement, because they were by definition serving the enemy rather than reporting the truth.

Beginning in 2017, the President of the United States applied this category to the American news media. CNN, the New York Times, the Washington Post, NBC, ABC, and CBS were repeatedly characterized as enemy of the people, fake news, and the opposition party across thousands of public statements over eight years, at press conferences, at rallies, on social media, and in interviews.

> *"The FAKE NEWS media (failing @nytimes, @NBCNews, @ABC, @CBS, @CNN) is not my enemy, it is the enemy of the American People!"* **President Donald Trump, tweet, February 17, 2017**

> *"Just stick with us, don't believe the crap you see from these people, the fake news. And just remember: What you're seeing and what you're reading is not what's happening."* **President Donald Trump, speech to the Veterans of Foreign Wars national convention, 2018**

The historian Timothy Snyder identified the constitutional significance of this rhetoric precisely: to abandon facts is to abandon freedom. If nothing is true, then no one can criticize power, because there is no basis upon which to do so.

The Gerasimov Alignment as Overt Act

Chapter 14 of this book applied the broadcaster precedents from the World War II treason cases to the NATO funding lie. The Axis Sally standard established that speech in service of an enemy's strategic objectives, delivered with the authority that the speaker's position conveys, constitutes an overt act of aid and comfort.

The Gerasimov Doctrine, Russia's published hybrid warfare manual, states explicitly that information technology is becoming one of the most promising types of weapons, used covertly not only against critically important informational infrastructures, but also against the population of a country. The doctrine identifies the erosion of free media and the destruction of internal trust mechanisms as primary tools for destabilizing Western democracies. Russia does not need to defeat NATO militarily if it can paralyze the democratic nations of the West by destroying their citizens' trust in the institutions that hold their governments accountable.

The enemy of the people campaign produced precisely the information environment that the Gerasimov Doctrine describes as its objective. It did so using the specific language, enemy of the people, that authoritarian systems have used for a century to silence accountability mechanisms. It did so from the most powerful public platform on earth, with the credibility and authority that no Russian propagandist could achieve.

NATO Secretary General Jens Stoltenberg described hybrid warfare as the dark reflection of our comprehensive approach: where the West uses a combination of military and non-military means to stabilize countries, hostile powers use the same combination to destabilize them. The enemy of the people campaign was hybrid warfare against American democratic institutions, delivered by the President of the United States, in alignment with the published doctrine of the identified enemy, from the Oval Office.

Under the Gadahn precedent established in Chapter 4, speech in service of an enemy's strategic objectives can constitute an overt act of aid and comfort. Under the Axis Sally broadcaster precedent established in Chapter 14, delivering the enemy's preferred narrative about American institutions from the most credible possible platform is an overt act. The enemy of the people campaign delivered Russia's preferred narrative about American media, systematically and over eight years, from the presidency itself. That is not protected political speech. Under the constitutional standard this book has applied throughout, it is an overt act of information warfare in service of the identified enemy's documented strategic doctrine.

□ □ □

Section Three: The Reality Winner Prosecution — Obstruction of the Treason Record

Reality Winner was a National Security Agency contractor. In 2017, she leaked a classified document to The Intercept. The document was a specific intelligence assessment of Russian military intelligence interference in American election systems, the specific subject matter of the treason analysis documented in Chapter 3 of this book.

Winner stated her motivation directly:

> *"My only intent was that maybe one person could restore the foundation of truth and integrity in a really tumultuous year."* **Reality Winner, on her motivations for the disclosure**

She was prosecuted under the Espionage Act. She received a sentence of more than five years in federal prison, at the time the longest sentence ever imposed for a federal whistleblower. Her defense was legally constrained by the Espionage Act's structure: under the statute, the question of whether her disclosure served the public interest is legally irrelevant. The law provides no public interest defense. The only question is whether classified information was disclosed without authorization.

Winner herself identified the specific irony of her situation:

> *"I helped the United States government kill people. I was good at it. But then I shared some information with the American people, and the US government felt that was a much worse thing to do than killing scores of people."* **Reality Winner**

Trevor Timm, Executive Director of the Freedom of the Press Foundation, stated the legal significance directly: Reality Winner alerted the public about a critical threat to election security. It continues to be a travesty that sources of journalists are prosecuted by the Justice Department under the Espionage Act.

The Legal Inversion

The Espionage Act was enacted to protect the United States from foreign espionage. Its function is to punish the disclosure of national security information to foreign adversaries. Reality Winner did not disclose information to a foreign adversary. She disclosed to an American news organization information about a foreign adversary's hostile actions against the United States.

Her prosecution inverted the statute's function. The law designed to punish the disclosure of information to foreign adversaries was used to punish the disclosure of information about foreign adversaries. The mechanism of accountability, a whistleblower exposing foreign hostile action against the United States, was prosecuted under the law designed to protect the nation from exactly the foreign hostile action she was exposing.

The prosecutorial message sent to every government official with knowledge of Russian hostile action against the United States was specific and documented: disclosure carries a federal criminal sentence. The law will not protect you if you tell the truth. The law will punish you.

Thomas Drake, an NSA whistleblower who was himself prosecuted under the Espionage Act before charges were reduced, captured the systemic message in a single sentence: Do not tell truth to power. We'll hammer you.

The chilling effect on the reporting that documents the overt acts of this book is not speculative. It is the documented, intended consequence of the prosecution. When the witnesses to the treason are told by the government that their testimony will result in imprisonment, the institutional witness is silenced not by force but by law. The law became the weapon. The statute designed to protect national security was deployed to protect the cover-up of the conduct that threatened national security.

THE WITNESSES: *The Reality Winner prosecution record is a public federal court document. The Espionage Act under which she was charged is 18 U.S.C. sections 793 and 798. Her stated motivations are documented in press interviews and public statements. The Trump 2017 enemy of the American people tweet is a public social media record. Justice Black's concurrence in New York Times Co. v. United States is a public Supreme Court document. Gerasimov's statement about information technology as a weapon is from his published 2013 article in the Russian military journal Voyenno-Promyshlennyy Kuryer.*

□ □ □

Section Four: The Institutional Escalation — From Rhetoric to Policy

The rhetorical campaign against the press was the first phase. In the second term, the assault became institutional. Federal power was deployed in specific, documented ways to translate the enemy of the people framing into structural suppression.

Federal Communications Commission Actions

Federal Communications Commission actions threatened broadcast licenses of news organizations reporting critically on administration conduct. The regulatory power of the FCC, whose mandate is to serve the public interest through the broadcast spectrum, was weaponized as an instrument of political intimidation against precisely the broadcast outlets whose First Amendment function is to report on the government that was threatening them. This is not the application of broadcast regulation. It is the use of broadcast regulation as a tool of political coercion against constitutionally protected speech.

Press Pool Exclusion

Specific wire services and news organizations were excluded from White House press pool access while outlets perceived as favorable were retained. The practical consequence of press pool exclusion is that the excluded organization cannot cover the President at events that are only open to credentialed pool members. It is not censorship of a specific story. It is the denial of the institutional access through which stories are produced. It is prior restraint achieved through accreditation rather than court order.

Federal Defamation Litigation Threats

Federal defamation litigation threats were directed at media organizations whose coverage was unfavorable. The purpose of such threats is not always to win in court. The purpose is often the litigation cost itself, the financial burden that defending against a defamation suit imposes on a news organization, particularly one serving a specialized beat with limited resources. This is financial attrition against the institutional witnesses whose reporting documents conduct the litigation is designed to suppress.

The USAID Information Vacuum

USAID funded international press freedom programs in dozens of countries. The dismantlement of USAID, documented in Chapter 10 as a component of the broader institutional deconstruction, terminated those programs. The practical consequence was documented in real time: the removal of American-funded independent journalism support created information vacuums in developing nations that Russian state media moved immediately to fill.

The USAID press freedom programs were not merely foreign aid. They were the international extension of the First Amendment principle: the belief that free societies are stronger than societies in which governments control information. Dismantling those programs simultaneously weakened the American commitment to that principle globally and strengthened the Russian state media alternative that the Gerasimov Doctrine depends on. It was the global application of the domestic enemy of the people strategy: remove the independent information source, let the state-aligned alternative fill the vacuum.

□ □ □

Section Five: The Legal Synthesis — Blinding the Republic

The assault on the free press documented in this chapter is not a separate crime alongside the treason documented in Parts I through VI. It is the necessary condition for the treason. It is the mechanism through which the architecture of denial was enforced and the overt acts were allowed to continue without the ultimate check.

A President who has nothing to hide welcomes press scrutiny as a mechanism of vindication. When false reporting is published, the remedy in a democratic system is accurate reporting, not the delegitimization of the institution. A President who characterizes the entire American news media as enemy of the people is not responding to specific inaccuracies. He is preemptively discrediting the institutional witness that is most likely to expose and document his conduct.

The treason analysis requires establishing that the overt acts were committed with the intent to betray the nation. One of the strongest available forms of evidence of that intent is the systematic effort to prevent the discovery of the overt acts. The enemy of the people campaign is precisely that systematic effort, applied not to individual pieces of evidence but to the entire institutional mechanism through which evidence reaches the public.

The Reality Winner prosecution is the most direct legal expression of this systematic effort. The law was used not to punish an act that harmed American national security but to punish an act that exposed harm to American national security caused by a foreign adversary. The inversion of the statute's purpose is itself evidence of the consciousness of guilt that the prosecution was designed to protect.

The Gerasimov alignment is the most constitutionally significant element of the legal analysis. When the President of the United States deploys, over eight years, the specific rhetoric and the specific institutional strategy that Russia's own hybrid warfare doctrine identifies as the mechanism for destabilizing Western democracies, the legal standard established in Chapter 14 applies. Speech in service of an enemy's strategic objectives, delivered with presidential authority, is an overt act of aid and comfort. The enemy of the people campaign meets that standard.

The treason documented in the preceding chapters required a specific enabling condition: the silencing of the witnesses. The journalists who documented the Russia alignment, the whistleblowers who disclosed the foreign hostile action, the news organizations whose reporting built the evidentiary record this book relies on, all of them were targeted. The targeting was not random. It was directed at precisely the institutional mechanisms most capable of exposing and stopping the conduct this book analyzes. By blinding the republic, the President ensured the betrayal could proceed in the information darkness the silencing created. That is not press criticism. Under the constitutional standard this book has applied throughout, it is the cover for the treason, and the cover is part of the crime.

The allegiance. The enemy. The overt acts across two terms and the 43 days of Part VI. The lies that provided the intent evidence. The silencing of the witnesses that enabled the conduct to continue. Every element the constitutional standard requires is present in the documented record. The citizen's brief that this book was written to present is ready to be stated.

□ □ □

Chapter Twenty-Four

Intimidation and Bribery: The Corruption of Allegiance

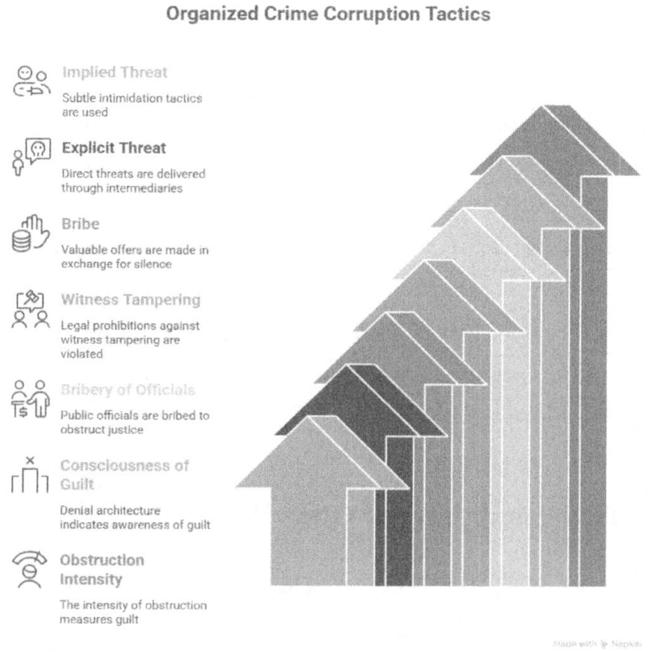

In organized crime, there is a hierarchy of tools for maintaining silence. At the bottom is the implied threat, the look, the casual reference to what happens to people who talk. In the middle is the explicit threat, the message delivered through intermediaries with plausible deniability. At the top is the bribe, the offer of something valuable in exchange for silence, protection, or active assistance.

All three tools appear in the documented record of this book. And all three are federally criminal. 18 U.S.C. section 1512 prohibits tampering with witnesses, victims, and informants. 18 U.S.C. section 201 prohibits bribery of public officials. These are not treason charges. They are the scaffolding around the treasonous conduct, and their systematic deployment is the strongest available evidence that the underlying conduct was understood to be legally indefensible.

Chapter 16 of this book established the Consciousness of Guilt standard: the architecture of denial is itself proof that the person who built it understood that the truth would establish the charge. This chapter documents the most explicit available expression of that consciousness. You do not bribe the witness if you are innocent. You do not fire the investigator if you have nothing to hide. You do not pardon the co-conspirator if there was no conspiracy. The intensity of the obstruction is the measure of the guilt.

□ □ □

Section One: The Intimidation of Officials — Removing the Investigators

The pattern of removing officials who documented or reported conduct relevant to the treason record is systematic, documented, and consistent across both terms. It is not a series of personnel decisions that happen to share a common direction. It is a directed campaign against the oversight function whose institutional purpose is to expose exactly the conduct this book analyzes.

The Comey Firing and the Oval Office Admission

The firing of FBI Director James Comey in May 2017 established the template. Comey was overseeing the investigation into Russian interference and potential coordination with the Trump campaign. He was fired.

What happened immediately afterward is the legally significant element. The President met with Russian Foreign Minister Sergei Lavrov and Ambassador Sergei Kislyak in the Oval Office. During that meeting, the President told them that firing Comey, whom he called a nut job, had relieved great pressure he faced regarding the Russia investigation.

The connection between the firing of the FBI Director and the relief of pressure on the Russia investigation is not an inference. It is a statement. And the statement was made to the officials of the nation whose relationship with the United States is the subject of the investigation that was relieved. That sequence, fire the investigator, tell the subject of the investigation you fired him, is not personnel management. It is documented obstruction communicated directly to the party whose interest in the investigation being stopped aligns with the President's own.

When the special counsel was subsequently appointed, the President's documented reaction was panic, captured in the Mueller Report: Oh my God. This is terrible. This is the end of my Presidency. That is not the reaction of a person who believes the investigation will exonerate him. It is the reaction of a person who understands that an independent investigation will reveal what he has done.

Sally Yates: Removed for Warning About Compromise

Sally Yates was the Acting Attorney General of the United States. She warned the White House that National Security Advisor Michael Flynn was potentially compromised by the Russian government because he had lied about his contacts with Russian Ambassador Kislyak. She was warning the President that his National Security Advisor was a national security risk.

She was fired.

The White House said she had betrayed the Department of Justice by refusing to enforce a travel ban executive order she had determined was unlawful. That is the stated justification. The documented sequence is different. She identified a national security risk connected to the Russia relationship that is central to the treason analysis. She was removed. The risk she identified, Flynn's undisclosed contacts with Russia, subsequently became a central element of the Mueller investigation.

Lieutenant Colonel Vindman: Removed for Truthful Testimony

Alexander Vindman served as the Director for European Affairs on the National Security Council. He testified before Congress about the Ukraine aid freeze, providing the specific firsthand account of what he had witnessed that corroborated the four-witness pattern documented in Chapter 14. His testimony was under oath. It was truthful by his account and consistent with the other witnesses.

He was escorted out of the White House. His twin brother, who also served on the NSC and had no role in the testimony, was removed simultaneously. Vindman filed a lawsuit alleging an intentional, concerted campaign of unlawful intimidation and retaliation by Trump allies to punish him for his testimony.

The twin brother's removal is the detail that removes any possible innocent explanation for the sequence. If the removal were simply a personnel decision about Vindman's conduct, it would not extend to a family member who played no role in the testimony. The extension to the family member is the statement about the nature of the retaliation.

The Systematic IG Purge

The inspectors general of the federal government are the official internal oversight mechanism of the executive branch. Their institutional function is precisely to identify and report exactly the categories of misconduct documented in this book. In a period of weeks in 2020, multiple inspectors general were fired across national security agencies.

Among them was Intelligence Community Inspector General Michael Atkinson. Atkinson had received and properly processed the whistleblower complaint about the Ukraine aid freeze that initiated the first impeachment inquiry. He followed the law. He forwarded the complaint through the legally required channels.

> *"The inspector general did exactly what the law required. He was fired for it."* **Senator Chuck Schumer, April 2020**

The systematic removal of the oversight officials who are the internal witnesses to executive branch misconduct is the organized crime hierarchy applied to federal government. At the bottom, the implied threat to any official considering reporting. In the middle, the explicit retaliatory firings that make the threat credible. And at the top, the bribe that the pardon section documents.

THE WITNESSES: *The Comey firing is documented in the Mueller Report and confirmed by Trump's own public statements in the NBC Lester Holt interview in which he acknowledged firing Comey regardless of the DOJ recommendation. The Oval Office Lavrov admission is documented in contemporaneous reporting confirmed by the White House's own readout. The Yates firing is documented in contemporaneous White House communications. The Vindman removal and twin brother firing are documented in public reporting and confirmed by Vindman's public statements and subsequent lawsuit. The Atkinson firing is documented in the President's own letter and the subsequent confirmation hearings.*

□ □ □

Section Two: The Pardon as Bribe — The Architecture of Protection

18 U.S.C. section 201(b) defines bribery as offering anything of value to a person to influence their conduct. A presidential pardon is something of value. It is freedom itself. When a pardon is offered in a pattern that consistently rewards non-cooperation with investigations into the President's own conduct, and when the pardoned conduct is specifically the conduct most relevant to the treason record, the pattern is legally probative of corrupt intent regardless of whether any explicit quid pro quo was articulated.

The pardon power is constitutional. Using it systematically to reward witnesses who protect the pardoner from investigation is not an exercise of the pardon power. It is its corruption.

But the pardons documented in this section were not merely rewards for past silence. They were something more legally significant. A pardon issued after the fact is a reward. A pattern of pardons issued for witnesses who refused to cooperate is a standing offer. It signaled to every future participant in the schemes documented in Part VI of this book that the President had the power and the will to shield them from federal prosecution. The pardons documented here were advertising. They told every official in the national security apparatus, everyone who knew about the Iran war's true motivations, the cease-fire denial, the sanctions relief, that loyalty to the President would be rewarded with the most powerful form of legal protection available.

Paul Manafort: The Complete Transaction

Paul Manafort was Trump's campaign chairman. He was convicted of eight counts of financial fraud and tax evasion and pleaded guilty to two counts of conspiracy. The Senate Intelligence Committee's bipartisan finding that Manafort shared internal campaign polling data with Konstantin Kilimnik, assessed as a Russian intelligence officer, is the most damaging single finding in the five-volume bipartisan Russia investigation record. The committee called it a grave counterintelligence threat.

Manafort did not testify against Trump in any significant way. His cooperation with the special counsel was eventually assessed as incomplete and misleading. When his cooperation effectively ended, the charges against him were not reduced through a cooperation agreement. They were eventually resolved by presidential pardon.

The sequence is the complete transaction. Manafort provided targeting intelligence to a Russian agent. That was the overt act of aid and comfort. He refused to provide complete testimony about the full extent of that act and its connections to the campaign. That was the service to the person most damaged by full disclosure. The pardon was the payment. The sequence, treasonous act, silence, pardon, is the complete arc of a corrupt arrangement that began with the handing over of a battlefield map to the enemy's intelligence officer and ended with the beneficiary of that silence receiving a full presidential pardon.

Roger Stone: Silence Before Prison, Commutation as the Contract

Roger Stone was convicted of seven felony counts including obstruction of justice, witness tampering, and lying to Congress. His crimes were committed in connection with the Russia investigation. The evidence established his coordination with the Trump campaign about WikiLeaks, which the Mueller Report identified as the conduit for Russian-stolen Democratic Party emails.

Stone maintained, publicly and consistently, that he would never roll on the President. His sentence was commuted in July 2020, days before he was scheduled to report to prison. He was fully pardoned in December 2020.

The timing of the commutation is the legal document of the transaction. Stone was convicted. He was sentenced. He maintained his silence about the full extent of his coordination. His prison reporting date arrived. Days before he had to report, the sentence was commuted. The message to every potential witness in any current or future investigation was specific and unmistakable: maintain silence, and the President will act before you have to go to prison. The commutation was not mercy. It was the delivery of a promised payment at the contractually specified moment.

Trump publicly praised Stone's bravery and guts for refusing to flip. The praise is the public acknowledgment of the transaction's terms. The bravery that was praised was the specific conduct of refusing to cooperate with investigators into the President's own conduct. The praise is the advertisement for the standing offer.

Michael Flynn: The Pardon Before Sentencing

Michael Flynn pleaded guilty to lying to FBI agents about his contacts with Russian Ambassador Kislyak, specifically his discussions about sanctions during the presidential transition, the period when a new administration is legally prohibited from conducting foreign policy. Flynn initially cooperated with the Mueller investigation. He withdrew his cooperation.

Trump's personal counsel left a voicemail for Flynn's lawyer stating that a decision to cooperate would be viewed as reflecting hostility toward the President and would affect any consideration of a pardon. That voicemail is the quid pro quo articulated explicitly. Maintain loyalty, receive pardon. Cooperate, receive hostility. Flynn withdrew his cooperation. He was pardoned in November 2020.

The voicemail removes the ambiguity that the legal standard allows in assessing pardon patterns. It is not merely a pattern from which corrupt intent can be inferred. It is the explicit articulation of the arrangement whose terms the pardon then fulfilled.

Paul Manafort passed targeting intelligence to a Russian agent, maintained silence about the full extent of that conduct, and received a full pardon. Roger Stone coordinated with the Russian conduit, lied to Congress to protect the President, maintained public silence about his full knowledge, and received a commutation days before his prison reporting date followed by a full pardon. Michael Flynn discussed sanctions with the Russian Ambassador during the transition and received a pardon after his counsel was told that cooperation would affect pardon consideration. This is not the exercise of executive mercy. This is the architecture of protection. Freedom itself was offered as the payment for silence about conduct whose full disclosure would have established the evidence chain this book has documented.

□ □ □

Section Three: The Standing Offer — What the Pardons Told Part VI Officials

The pardons of Manafort, Stone, and Flynn were completed in the first term. Part VI occurred in the second term. The legal significance of the connection between them is the standing offer the pardons created.

Every official who participated in or had knowledge of the Iran war's actual motivations, the sanctions relief decision, the Lebanon ceasefire denial, the NATO withdrawal threat, and every other act documented in Chapters 18 through 22 was operating in a legal environment that the pardons had already defined. The message of the first-term pardons to second-term participants was documented in the pattern: maintain loyalty, protect the President's secrets, and the President will protect you from the law.

The officials most likely to document and disclose the conduct of Part VI, the national security staff who knew the real motivations for the Iran war, the diplomatic officials who knew Lebanon had been included in the ceasefire, the military briefers who knew no imminent threat existed, were all operating in an environment where the cost of disclosure had been established by the Reality Winner prosecution and the benefit of silence had been established by the Manafort, Stone, and Flynn pardons.

The architecture of protection created in the first term was the enabling condition for the conduct of the second term. By establishing that silence would be rewarded and disclosure would be punished, the President constructed a system in which the officials most capable of exposing the overt acts of Part VI had documented reason to understand the consequences of either choice.

□ □ □

Section Four: The Legal Synthesis — The Architecture of Protection as the Final Proof

Chapter 16 of this book established the Consciousness of Guilt standard through the Kawakita analysis. The architecture of denial is the strongest available evidence that the person who built it understood that the truth, if known, would establish the charge. The lies documented in Part V are the architecture of denial. The intimidation and bribery documented in this chapter are its enforcement mechanism.

The legal principle is simple and ancient. Innocent people do not bribe witnesses. They have no reason to. Innocent people do not fire investigators who are closing in. They welcome the investigation as vindication. Innocent people do not pardon co-conspirators who maintained silence rather than testify. They have no co-conspirators whose silence requires payment.

Every element of the obstruction documented in this chapter points in the same direction. Every firing was of an official who was documenting or threatening to document the specific conduct most relevant to the treason charge. Every pardon was of a person whose silence protected the specific conduct most relevant to the treason charge. Every retaliatory action was directed at the specific individuals whose testimony would have most advanced the accountability record.

The precision of the targeting is itself the evidence. Arbitrary personnel decisions and random pardons do not display this level of consistent direction toward a single goal. The systematic removal of oversight officials, the systematic prosecution of whistleblowers who disclosed foreign hostile action, the systematic pardoning of witnesses who refused to cooperate, form a coherent architecture whose consistent direction is the suppression of the specific evidence most relevant to the treason analysis this book presents.

Under the Haupt standard, timing is evidence of intent. The timing of the pardons, delivered at the precise moments that protected the most valuable witnesses at their most critical junctures, establishes the intent behind them. Under the Kawakita standard, the totality of conduct reveals the purpose that any single act might obscure. The totality of the obstruction conduct reveals a purpose that cannot be explained by any innocent account of the underlying conduct.

Innocent people do not construct an architecture of protection. They do not bribe witnesses with the most powerful form of legal immunity available. They do not fire inspectors general who are doing exactly what the law requires. They do not remove officials who warn about national security risks connected to the conduct under investigation. The intensity and precision of the obstruction documented in this chapter is the measure of the guilt it was designed to protect. The architecture of protection is not separate from the treason argument. It is the final proof of the treasonous intent the Kawakita standard requires. A person who understood that the documented record of his conduct was legally indefensible constructed a system to make sure that record could never be fully assembled. This book has assembled it anyway.

□ □ □

Chapter Twenty-Five

The Assault on the Judiciary: Dismantling the Referee

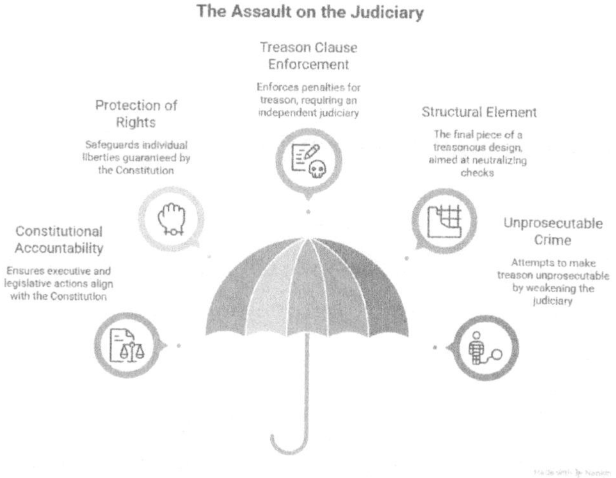

A basketball game without a referee is not a sport. It is a brawl. The rules still exist. The lines are still painted on the floor. But without someone to enforce them, the stronger team simply does whatever it wants.

The federal judiciary is the referee of the constitutional system. It is the institution that determines whether executive action falls within the law, whether congressional oversight has legal authority, and whether rights guaranteed by the Constitution are actually protected. Without it, the rules still exist on paper. But without enforcement, they do not constrain.

Article III of the Constitution establishes the federal judiciary in Section 1. Section 3 of Article III defines treason. They are in the same Article because the Framers understood that the judiciary and the treason clause are components of the same design. You cannot enforce the treason clause without an independent judiciary. An attack on the judiciary is an attack on the mechanism of constitutional accountability, including accountability for treason.

This chapter documents the assault on that mechanism. It is the final structural element of the treasonous design documented in this book: the neutralization of the constitutional check that makes the treason clause enforceable. A treason clause without a functioning independent judiciary is a rule written on paper with no referee to enforce it. The Framers understood that. They put both provisions in the same Article. The assault on Article III's Section 1 is an assault on Article III's Section 3. It is the attempt to make the highest crime in the Constitution unprosecutable.

□ □ □

Section One: The Delegitimization Campaign — Poisoning the Jury Pool

The strategy of delegitimizing the judiciary was not a reaction to specific adverse rulings. It was a preemptive operation designed to prepare the public to disbelieve any ruling that checked executive power.

By characterizing judges as partisan actors, Obama judges versus Trump judges, Bush judges versus Clinton judges, the President sought to establish in the minds of his supporters a framework in which every adverse ruling is proof of political bias rather than legal judgment. This framework eliminates the possibility of an independent check. If every adverse ruling is by definition illegitimate, and if every favorable ruling is by definition correct, then the judiciary can never actually constrain the executive. The referee has been defined in advance as always wrong when he calls a foul against the home team.

In 2018, after the President publicly characterized a federal judge who had ruled against an administration immigration policy as an Obama judge, Chief Justice John Roberts issued a statement remarkable for its directness. Chief Justices do not typically respond to presidential criticism of the courts. Roberts responded.

> *"We do not have Obama judges or Trump judges, Bush judges or Clinton judges. What we have is an extraordinary group of dedicated judges doing their level best to do equal right to those appearing before them. That independent judiciary is something we should all be thankful for."* **Chief Justice John Roberts, November 21, 2018**

The President attacked Chief Justice Roberts on social media in response.

That exchange is the documented institutional crisis in its most concentrated form. The Chief Justice of the United States identified the attack on judicial independence as institutionally dangerous. The President responded by escalating the attack. The delegitimization campaign was not retreating from institutional criticism. It was advancing against the highest judicial authority in the country.

The legal function of this campaign in the treason analysis is specific. The Consciousness of Guilt standard documented in Chapter 16 established that the architecture of denial is built to protect conduct that the architect understood to be legally indefensible. The delegitimization of the judiciary is the preemptive layer of that architecture. If the courts are discredited before they can rule, their rulings cannot generate the accountability response that legitimate judicial decisions produce. The jury pool has been prejudiced against the referee before the referee can call the foul.

□ □ □

Section Two: Structural Manipulation — The Garland Blockade and the Cannon Case

The assault on the judiciary was not limited to rhetoric. It extended to the structural manipulation of the courts themselves, reshaping the composition and assignment of federal judges in ways that served the specific interest of limiting judicial accountability for the conduct this book documents.

The Garland Blockade and the Court Composition

In March 2016, Supreme Court Justice Antonin Scalia died. President Obama nominated Merrick Garland, a widely respected federal appellate judge, to fill the vacancy. Senate Majority Leader Mitch McConnell refused to hold hearings, citing a principle that no Supreme Court nominee should be confirmed in a presidential election year. The seat remained vacant for 11 months.

Following the 2016 election, Neil Gorsuch was confirmed to the seat within months. The principle that had justified blocking Garland was not applied to Gorsuch. In 2020, with weeks remaining before the presidential election, Justice Ruth Bader Ginsburg died. The Senate confirmed Amy Coney Barrett to her seat eight days before the election, directly contradicting the stated principle that had prevented Garland's consideration four years earlier.

The practical consequence of this structural manipulation was a Supreme Court whose composition produced the Trump v. United States (2024) immunity ruling, which this book analyzed in detail in Chapter 11. The court that created the primary procedural obstacle to any treason prosecution was composed in part through a process that applied contradictory standards to achieve a specific political composition. The referee was appointed through a process designed to produce a specific outcome rather than an impartial arbiter.

The Cannon Case: Judicial Forum Shopping as a Weapon

The classified documents case, in which the President was indicted under the Espionage Act for the willful retention of national defense information, was filed in the Southern District of Florida and assigned to Judge Aileen Cannon, a Trump appointee who had received her appointment during the final weeks of the first term.

Judge Cannon's rulings in the case were described by legal scholars across the political spectrum, including conservative scholars with no partisan interest in the outcome, as legally unprecedented and favorable to the defendant in ways that exceeded the conventional scope of judicial discretion. Her management of the case produced significant delays. She ultimately dismissed the indictment on the grounds that the special prosecutor lacked proper appointment authority, a legal theory that conservative legal scholars widely rejected.

The 11th Circuit Court of Appeals subsequently issued an opinion criticizing the legal basis for her initial rulings. But the dismissal stood, and the case was never reinstated.

The structural lesson is precise. The judicial system that would adjudicate a treason claim was shaped by the same political operation that the treason argument targets. The appointment process that produced the judges, the filing strategy that assigned the cases to those judges, and the immunity ruling produced by the restructured Supreme Court all operate as components of a single system designed to ensure that the legal accountability mechanisms cannot reach the specific conduct this book analyzes. It is not merely that the referee was attacked rhetorically. The process by which referees are selected was manipulated to ensure that the most important calls would be made by referees who had been appointed by the person whose conduct they would adjudicate.

□ □ □

Section Three: The Second Term — Contempt as Policy

In the second term, the assault on judicial authority moved from delegitimization and structural manipulation to direct defiance. The administration adopted a legal theory that the judiciary lacked authority to constrain core executive functions, and it translated that theory into specific institutional conduct.

The Review Before Compliance Doctrine

Executive directives in the second term instructed federal agencies to review judicial injunctions before compliance in categories of cases the administration characterized as touching core executive power. The practical effect of a review before compliance doctrine is the interposition of executive judgment between a court order and its enforcement. An injunction that must be reviewed before agencies comply is not an injunction that constrains executive action. It is a suggestion that the executive may accept or reject based on its own assessment of whether the court had authority to issue it.

This is not a legal argument. Courts have procedures for challenging their own authority, including direct appeal. The review before compliance doctrine bypasses those procedures and substitutes executive self-assessment for judicial determination. It is the executive branch declaring itself the arbiter of whether court orders apply to it, which is the equivalent of a defendant in a civil case deciding whether the judgment against him is enforceable.

The War Powers and NATO Statute Defiance

When courts were presented with challenges to the unauthorized Iran war under the War Powers Resolution, and to the NATO withdrawal threat under the 2024 statutory prohibition on unilateral withdrawal, the Department of Justice filed appeals specifically designed to delay enforcement until the underlying issues became moot. The war ended. The NATO withdrawal, while threatened, did not formally occur. The mootness doctrine extinguished the cases.

This is a specific and documented litigation strategy: take actions that courts may find unlawful, appeal any adverse ruling through every available mechanism to delay enforcement, and ensure that the actions are sufficiently complete before enforcement could be ordered that mootness eliminates the cases. The courts' authority is formally respected while its practical effect is nullified. The referee calls the foul. The appeals delay the free throw until the game is over.

The Marbury v. Madison Repudiation

Administration officials made public statements in the second term questioning whether courts have authority to constrain executive action in areas characterized as core executive functions. These statements did not merely challenge specific rulings. They challenged the foundational principle of Marbury v. Madison, established in 1803, that the federal courts have authority to review and constrain executive action for consistency with the Constitution.

Marbury v. Madison is the constitutional foundation of judicial review. Without it, the courts retain no authority to tell the executive branch that its actions exceed its constitutional authority. The statements questioning this principle were not legal arguments made in court where they could be adjudicated. They were public declarations designed to undermine the public's understanding of the judiciary's role, reinforcing the delegitimization campaign while simultaneously signaling to executive branch officials that compliance with judicial orders was a matter of presidential discretion rather than legal obligation.

Marbury v. Madison established in 1803 that the Constitution means what it says regardless of what the executive branch would prefer it to mean. An executive branch that publicly questions whether courts can constrain core executive functions is not making a legal argument. It is announcing the end of constitutional government as the framework that governs executive conduct. When that announcement is made by an administration whose conduct this book establishes may satisfy the constitutional definition of treason, the announcement is the final element of the architecture of protection: the removal of the last referee capable of calling the foul.

□ □ □

Section Four: The Legal Synthesis — Why the Treason Clause Requires a Referee

The attack on the judiciary documented in this chapter serves a specific function in the treason analysis. It is the attempt to remove the peaceful mechanism through which constitutional accountability operates.

The Constitution provides three remedies when a President commits treason: impeachment by Congress, prosecution by the Department of Justice, and adjudication by the federal courts. This book has documented attacks on all three. Chapter 24 documented the intimidation of officials and the pardoning of witnesses who protected the President from congressional oversight and DOJ investigation. Chapter 23 documented the attack on the press that is the public mechanism for generating the political will to exercise those accountability mechanisms. This chapter documents the attack on the courts that would adjudicate the result.

The systematic nature of the assault is the final evidence of intent. A President who accidentally oversteps his authority submits to the correction when the courts identify it. He does not delegitimize the courts in advance, manipulate the appointment process to produce friendly referees, file appeals to delay enforcement until mootness eliminates the cases, and issue public statements questioning whether courts have authority over executive action. That pattern of conduct is the behavior of a person who understood in advance that the courts' legitimate exercise of their constitutional function would constrain conduct he intended to engage in.

The Framers put the Treason Clause in Article III, alongside the judiciary they established, for a reason. They understood the relationship between the two provisions. The clause that defines the highest crime is contained in the same article that establishes the institution that would adjudicate it. A Treason Clause without an independent judiciary capable of enforcing it is parchment. It is a rule with no referee.

By attacking the independence of the judiciary, by manipulating the appointment process, and by adopting a policy of contempt toward court orders and the foundational principle of judicial review, the President sought to ensure that no referee would be left on the floor to call the foul. The attack on Article III Section 1 is the attack on the enforceability of Article III Section 3. They are the same attack. And documenting it is the final structural element of the citizen's brief this book has presented.

A tyrant's first step is always to silence the judge. The Framers knew this because they had read their history. They wrote the Judiciary into the Constitution before they wrote anything else in Article III. And then they wrote the Treason Clause in the same Article, because they understood that the crime and the remedy belong together. You cannot have one without the other. The documented assault on the federal judiciary is not a separate controversy about judicial philosophy or Senate confirmation procedures. It is the final piece of the architecture of protection that this book has assembled across twenty-five chapters. It is the attempt to eliminate the referee before the final call has to be made.

THE WITNESSES: *Chief Justice Roberts' 2018 statement is a public record published by the Supreme Court press office. The Garland vacancy and subsequent confirmation history is documented in Senate records. The 11th Circuit's criticism of Judge Cannon's initial rulings is documented in the public court opinion in In re Trump. The Marbury v. Madison principle of judicial review is established in the 1803 Supreme Court opinion Marbury v. Madison, 5 U.S. 137. The Trump v. United States (2024) immunity ruling is the published Supreme Court opinion.*

Twenty-five chapters of documented record. The allegiance. The enemy. The overt acts across two terms and the 43 days of Part VI. The lies. The silencing of the witnesses. The intimidation of officials. The corruption of allegiance through bribery. The assault on the judiciary. All of it, assembled now into the citizen's brief for which this book was written.

□ □ □

Chapter Twenty-Six

The Institutional Surrender: When Constitutional Actors Abandon Their Posts

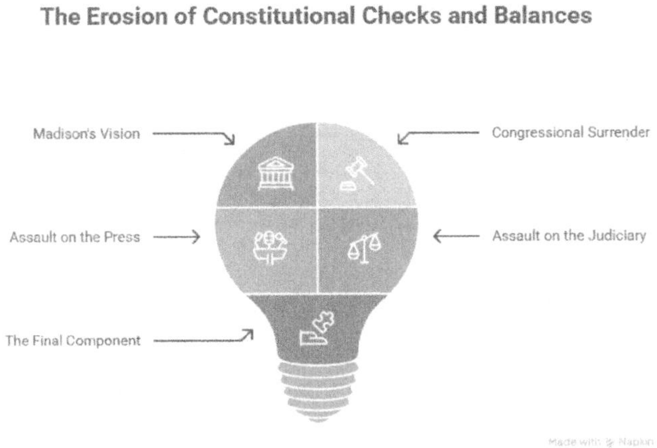

James Madison was a genius. But he was also a realist. He knew that the constitutional system he helped design would only work if the people who operated it actually wanted it to work.

> *"Ambition must be made to counteract ambition. The interest of the man must be connected with the constitutional rights of the place."* **James Madison, Federalist No. 51**

What Madison meant was this. Congress will check the President because members of Congress have an institutional interest in preserving legislative power. The judiciary will check both because judges have an interest in preserving judicial independence. The system relies on human ambition, specifically the ambition of the other branches, to function as a brake on executive overreach. Each branch defends its constitutional territory not from virtue but from self-interest. That is the design.

What Madison did not anticipate was the Congress that would voluntarily surrender its power. Not through ignorance. Not through incapacity. But through a calculated decision that political loyalty to a President was more valuable than the constitutional authority of the legislature. When the ambition of the legislative branch is subordinated to the ambition of the executive, the counterweight disappears. The brake lines are cut.

This chapter documents the surrender of the legislative branch. It is the final component of the architecture of protection this book has assembled across the preceding chapters. Chapter 23 documented the assault on the press that silenced the witnesses. Chapter 25 documented the assault on the judiciary that neutralized the referee. This chapter documents the surrender of the body with the constitutional authority to stop the conduct in the first place.

The assault on the press silenced the witnesses. The assault on the judiciary neutralized the referee. The surrender of Congress removed the last institution with the constitutional authority to call the game.

□ □ □

Section One: The War Power Surrender — Handing Over the Sword

The Constitution gives Congress, and Congress alone, the power to declare war. The War Powers Resolution of 1973 was passed specifically to codify this constitutional principle and prevent the kind of executive overreach that had characterized the Vietnam War.

It requires the President to notify Congress within 48 hours of committing forces to hostilities and to obtain congressional authorization within 60 days.

The Iran war was launched on February 28, 2026, without notification and without authorization. Chapter 18 documented this constitutional violation in detail. The question this chapter addresses is what Congress did when it had the opportunity to assert its constitutional authority in response.

When the War Powers resolution came to a vote in the House, Speaker Mike Johnson used the institutional power of the speakership to lobby Republican members to vote against it. The resolution failed by seven votes. The constitutional check existed. Congress chose not to use it.

Johnson's stated reasoning was documented in his own words:

> *"The idea that we would take the ability of our commander in chief, the president, take his authority away right now to finish this job, is a frightening prospect to me."* **Speaker Mike Johnson, on the War Powers resolution vote**

This statement requires precise legal analysis. The War Powers resolution did not propose to take the President's authority away. It proposed to require the President to obtain the congressional authorization the Constitution requires before conducting a major military operation. Johnson was not describing a constitutional problem with the resolution. He was describing his preference for executive primacy over the specific constitutional arrangement the Framers established when they wrote the war power into Article I rather than Article II.

The Speaker's Constitutional Oath

Johnson's role requires specific analysis because he is not merely a congressional leader. He is a constitutional officer. As Speaker of the House, he is second in the line of succession to the presidency. He took an oath to support and defend the Constitution of the United

States. That oath is substantively identical to the presidential oath examined in Chapter 2 of this book.

Before becoming Speaker, in December 2020, Johnson had signed an amicus brief supporting a Texas lawsuit seeking to invalidate the certified election results of Georgia, Michigan, Pennsylvania, and Wisconsin. On January 6, 2021, he and colleagues issued a statement objecting to the slates of electors. The legal theory in the amicus brief was the same theory that the Eastman memo operationalized in the scheme to prevent the constitutional transfer of power.

The pattern is consistent. The constitutional mechanisms of accountability were available. In each instance, Johnson chose not to use them. He chose, instead, to use his constitutional office to prevent those mechanisms from functioning. When the Speaker of the House uses his office to defeat a measure designed to enforce the Constitution's war power provision, he has not merely made a political choice. He has breached the structural design the Constitution established. The ambition of the House to defend its own war power was sacrificed for the political convenience of the executive. An unauthorized war, one of the overt acts documented in Chapter 18, was allowed to continue without the constitutional check designed to stop it.

□ □ □

Section Two: The Appropriations Surrender — Handing Over the Purse

The power of the purse is Congress's most powerful constitutional tool. No money shall be drawn from the Treasury without congressional appropriation. That provision gives Congress ultimate control over every function of the federal government. An executive branch that cannot spend money cannot do anything. The appropriations power is the legislative branch's most reliable check on executive action.

The Department of Government Efficiency's elimination of congressionally appropriated programs represents the most systematic assault on the appropriations power in the documented record.

The Timeline

In January 2025, the President issued a temporary pause on USAID funding. In February 2025, Speaker Johnson expressed full support for DOGE, stating it was uncovering hidden expenditures that Congress had been unaware of. In March 2025, Secretary of State Marco Rubio announced the cancellation of 5,200 contracts and the formal dissolution of USAID. By July 2025, USAID was officially merged into the State Department after more than 80 percent of its programs were canceled.

Programs that Congress had funded through the lawful legislative process were eliminated through executive action without statutory authority. Congress had not passed legislation repealing these programs. The statutes authorizing them were still on the books. The appropriations that funded them had been enacted by Congress. They were eliminated anyway, through executive action, without legislative repeal.

Nicholas Enrich, a former USAID official who witnessed the process, described it as a wrecking ball executed by unqualified personnel replacing decades of expertise. House Democratic Whip Katherine Clark characterized the Republican majority's acquiescence as voting to hand a blank check to Elon Musk.

The National Security Consequence

The specific national security consequence of the appropriations surrender is documented in Chapter 10 of this book. USAID's elimination created influence vacuums in developing nations across Africa, Latin America, and Asia that Russian and Chinese operations moved immediately to fill. The programs that were eliminated had provided the specific institutional presence that limited Russian and Chinese information operations, diplomatic influence, and strategic positioning in the developing world.

Under Madison's theory of competing ambitions, a Congress that does not use its constitutional tools is not merely failing politically. It is failing constitutionally, and its failure enables the conduct that those tools were designed to prevent. The appropriations surrender enabled a foreign policy consequence that serves the identified enemy's strategic objectives. The power of the purse was surrendered, and the beneficiary of that surrender was the adversary identified in this book.

□ □ □

Section Three: The Oversight Surrender — Two Impeachments, Two Failures

Impeachment is the Constitution's primary mechanism for congressional accountability of the executive. Article II, Section 4 provides that the President shall be removed from office on impeachment for and conviction of treason, bribery, or other high crimes and misdemeanors. Two impeachments were brought. Both failed. Not because the evidence was insufficient, but because the political calculus of a sufficient number of senators treated party loyalty as more important than constitutional responsibility.

The First Impeachment: Ukraine

The first impeachment arose from the Ukraine aid freeze, the conduct the Government Accountability Office found violated the Impoundment Control Act, the conduct that withheld military assistance from a nation Russia was attacking while the President sought a political favor for his personal benefit. Four witnesses testified under oath to the specific factual pattern. The GAO finding was documentary confirmation of the legal violation.

The Senate acquitted along party lines. The witnesses who had testified at personal and professional risk, who had then been removed from their positions in retaliation for their testimony, watched the constitutional accountability mechanism fail because 51 senators decided that party loyalty outweighed the documented evidence of a law violation that the GAO had confirmed independently of any witness testimony.

The Second Impeachment: January 6

The second impeachment arose from the January 6 insurrection. The House of Representatives voted 232 to 197 to impeach. In the Senate, 57 senators voted to convict, including seven Republicans who crossed party lines. The vote was a majority. It represented the most bipartisan conviction vote in a presidential impeachment trial in American history.

But 57 is not 67. Two-thirds of 100 is 67. The constitution requires a supermajority. The 57 to 43 vote failed to reach that threshold. The majority of the United States Senate, including senators from both parties, found the conduct impeachable. The constitutional mechanism failed because 43 senators calculated that protecting the President from conviction was worth more than the constitutional accountability the evidence supported.

The Legal Significance of the Failures

The legal significance of these failures is not that the President was innocent. It is that the constitutional remedy for high crimes and misdemeanors has been effectively disabled by partisanship. When impeachment fails not because the evidence is insufficient but because the political calculus of a sufficient number of senators treats party loyalty as more important than constitutional responsibility, the mechanism has been converted from a constitutional process into a partisan one. Its deterrent function has been eliminated.

A President who observes two impeachments, one for documented violation of the Impoundment Control Act and one for an armed attack on the Capitol, and watches both fail along party lines, receives a specific signal about the actual risk of the constitutional accountability mechanism. That signal is that the mechanism will not operate against a sufficiently popular president with a sufficiently loyal party base. That signal changes the rational calculation of every future official who is considering whether to use or to abuse the powers of the presidency.

□ □ □

Section Four: The Legal Synthesis — The Final Piece of the Architecture

The treason analysis in this book relies on the existence of a constitutional system capable of responding to betrayal. The Framers designed that system with three branches, each capable of checking the others. They specifically placed the treason clause in Article III, the judicial article, because they understood that the crime requires an independent tribunal to adjudicate it. But they gave the primary enforcement power to the political branches: Congress through impeachment, and the executive through prosecution.

This book has documented the assault on the press that silenced the witnesses to the overt acts. It has documented the assault on the judiciary that compromised the institution designed to adjudicate the accountability claim. This chapter has documented the surrender of the legislative branch, the body with the most immediate and powerful constitutional tools to stop the conduct in the first place.

Each element of the architecture of protection serves the same function: the neutralization of the specific institutional mechanism most capable of stopping the overt acts and holding the actors accountable. The press is silenced so the overt acts cannot be documented and communicated to the public that would demand accountability. The courts are compromised so the legal accountability claim cannot proceed. Congress surrenders so the oversight, funding, and impeachment powers cannot be used to constrain the conduct.

The result is a constitutional system in which the treason clause exists as text but has been stripped of its enforcement mechanisms. The rules are still on paper. The lines are still painted on the floor. But the referee has been attacked, the witnesses have been silenced, and the institutional actors with the power to call the game have decided that political loyalty is more important than constitutional fidelity.

Madison assumed that ambition would counteract ambition. He did not anticipate that one branch would voluntarily surrender its ambition to another. The surrender of Congress is not a separate constitutional crisis. It is the enabling condition for the treason this book documents. Without a functioning Congress, the overt acts of Parts I through VI could proceed without the institutional resistance the Framers designed. The architecture of protection is complete. The witnesses are silenced. The courts are compromised. The legislature has surrendered. The Republic, as the Framers designed it, has been left defenseless. The Legal Opinion is this book's response to that condition. It is the citizen's brief that the institutional failure makes necessary. When the institutions fail, the citizens must act. This book is that act.

THE WITNESSES: *Madison's Federalist No. 51 is a public primary document. Speaker Johnson's War Powers statement is documented in congressional press records. Johnson's December 2020 amicus brief is a public* *court filing. The House impeachment vote of 232 to 197 on the second impeachment is documented in the congressional record. The Senate conviction vote of 57 to 43 is documented in the congressional record. The GAO's Impoundment Control Act finding on the Ukraine aid freeze is documented in GAO Decision B-331564. Nicholas Enrich's wrecking ball characterization is documented in press interviews. The USAID timeline is documented in State Department communications and congressional testimony.*

□ □ □

Chapter Twenty-Seven

The Unified Assault: What the Pattern of Institutional Destruction Reveals

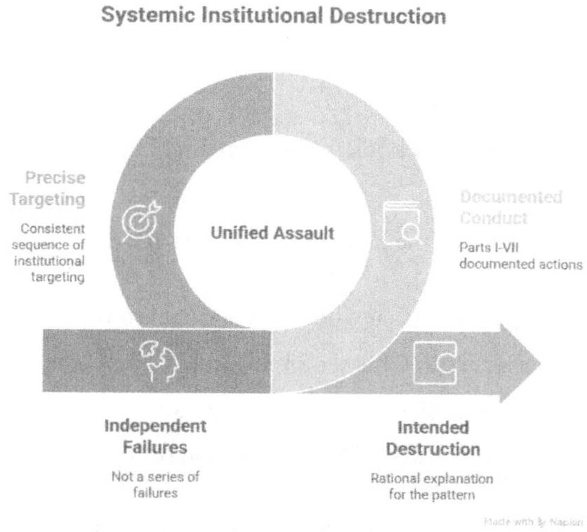

We have now traveled through seven Parts of documented conduct. Parts I and II established the overt acts of levying war and adhering to enemies. Part III documented the theft of the Republic through financial, economic, and social harm. Part IV addressed the immunity defense. Part V built the architecture of deception. Part VI documented 43 days of real-time overt acts. And Part VII has shown us the systematic destruction of every institution that would detect, expose, or prosecute the conduct documented in the earlier Parts.

It is time to step back and look at the mosaic from a distance.

The individual tiles have been placed with precision across twenty-six chapters. This chapter frames what the completed picture shows. And what it shows is not a series of independent failures, diplomatic fumbles, and policy errors. It is a sequence. A directed, documented, consistent sequence of institutional targeting whose direction is so precise and whose beneficiaries are so consistently the same that the only rational explanation for the pattern is that it was intended.

□ □ □

Section One: The Sequence of Institutional Destruction

When historians study how authoritarian power consolidates, they find a consistent sequence. It is not always exactly the same. The order varies. The pace varies. The specific methods vary. But the targets are always the same, because the targets are the only things that stand between a leader who wants unconstrained power and the acquisition of that power.

The sequence documented in this book is the following. Every step is documented with specific, witnessed, dated evidence in the preceding chapters. The sequence is not theoretical. It is the factual record of the period this book covers.

1. **Discredit the press.** So that when the conduct is reported, the public has been prepared to disbelieve it. Chapter 23 documented this step across eight years of enemy of the people characterizations, the Reality Winner prosecution, FCC license threats, and the USAID press freedom program dismantlement.

2. **Intimidate the witnesses.** So that those with direct knowledge of the conduct are deterred from coming forward. Chapter 24 documented this step through the retaliatory firings of Yates, Vindman, and the systematic IG purge, and through the pardons that rewarded silence and punished cooperation.

3. **Remove the investigators.** So that the institutional capacity to examine the conduct has been dismantled before it can be fully deployed. The Comey firing, the IG purge, the DOJ pressure, and the obstruction campaign documented in Chapter 12 collectively dismantled the investigative capacity most positioned to expose the overt acts.

4. **Delegitimize and manipulate the courts.** So that when the conduct reaches the judiciary, the institution has been compromised in its capacity to adjudicate it. Chapter 25 documented this step through the Obama judge campaign, the Garland blockade, the Cannon assignment, and the second-term contempt-as-policy doctrine.

5. **Neutralize the legislature.** So that the constitutional tools of impeachment, appropriations, and oversight cannot be effectively deployed. Chapter 26 documented this step through Johnson's war power defeat, the DOGE appropriations surrender, and the two failed impeachments.

6. **Claim immunity.** So that even if all other mechanisms fail, the conduct is placed beyond legal reach. Chapter 11 documented this step through the Trump v. United States (2024) immunity ruling, which the Supreme Court partially granted, creating the primary procedural obstacle that any treason prosecution would need to navigate.

The incompetence defense fails against this sequence. Incompetence produces random failures that vary in direction and target. This sequence is directionally consistent. Every step targets a specific institutional check. Every step benefits the same actors. Every step removes a specific obstacle to the specific conduct documented in Parts I through VI. Incompetence does not produce this level of precision. Intent does.

□ □ □

Section Two: The Constitutional Synthesis — Dismantling as Levying War

The Framers designed the Constitution with one overriding understanding: power unchecked produces tyranny. Every structural feature of the constitutional system, the separation of powers, the Bill of Rights, the independent judiciary, the free press, the treason clause itself, is a component of an integrated system designed to make tyranny structurally difficult. These components work together. Each one reinforces the others. The free press exposes what the inspector general finds. The inspector general forwards what the whistleblower reports. The whistleblower is protected by the courts that enforce the law. The courts are funded and constituted by the legislature. The legislature is accountable to the people who are informed by the free press.

When all components of that system are simultaneously under assault, when the press is discredited, witnesses are intimidated, investigators are removed, courts are delegitimized, the legislature is neutralized, and immunity is claimed, the system is not merely stressed. It is being dismantled. The integrated defense of the constitutional order has been systematically disabled.

And the dismantling of the constitutional system is not merely a governance failure. It is, under the analysis this book has built across seven Parts, an assault on the Republic itself. The Constitution is the United States in its structural form. To dismantle the Constitution is to levy war against the United States. The sequence documented in this chapter is not a list of separate crimes. It is the method of the treason.

The Framers did not limit the treason clause to men with muskets. They wrote it to cover every form of assault on the constitutional order. The most dangerous assault on a constitutional republic is not the one that comes from outside with guns. It is the one that comes from inside with paperwork. It fires the inspectors general. It pardons the witnesses. It claims presidential immunity. It uses the levers of constitutional government to dismantle the constitution those levers were designed to serve. That is levying war. And the sequence documented in this book is the method through which it was waged.

□ □ □

Section Three: The Final Inference — What the Destruction Proves

In a treason trial, a jury would hear all of this. They would hear twenty-six chapters of documented overt acts, a documented architecture of lies covering precisely those acts, and a documented sequence of institutional destruction targeting every institution capable of adjudicating those acts.

The jury instruction on consciousness of guilt would apply not merely to the individual lies of Part V but to the entire architecture of institutional destruction documented in Part VII.

The Kawakita standard permits the jury to infer treasonous intent from the totality of conduct. The totality assembled in this book includes not only the overt acts and the lies but the systematic destruction of the specific institutions most capable of exposing and stopping those acts. A person who had nothing to hide would have no reason to build the architecture documented in Chapters 23 through 26. A person who intended to commit the overt acts documented in Parts I through VI would have every reason to build exactly that architecture.

Innocent actors do not dismantle the institutions designed to hold them accountable. A person who is confident their conduct was lawful does not remove the inspectors general, discredit the press, fire the FBI director, lobby against the war powers resolution, reward the witnesses who stayed silent, and then claim immunity from prosecution. Each one of those actions could, in isolation, receive an innocent explanation. Together, in a sequence that precisely targets every institutional check on executive power, they cannot.

The pattern of institutional destruction is, like the pattern of lies documented in Part V, the proof that the actor knew. The proof that what was being done was understood, by the person doing it, to be what this book argues it is. A sustained and coordinated course of conduct serving the interests of an identified foreign adversary, carried out through the abuse of the most powerful office in the constitutional system, and concealed behind an architecture of denial whose precision and consistency is itself the evidence of the intent behind the conduct it was designed to protect.

This book has assembled the citizen's brief. It has placed every tile in the mosaic. It has connected every overt act to the constitutional standard, every lie to its legal function, every institutional assault to the mechanism it was designed to disable. The picture that emerges from the completed mosaic is not ambiguous. It is the picture of a constitutional system under deliberate assault from the inside, by the official sworn to protect it, in service of the adversary whose interests run directly contrary to the nation's. The Legal Opinion states that case in the form the Constitution requires.

□ □ □

PART VIII

"The truth is rarely pure and never simple." – Oscar Wilde

Chapter Twenty-Eight

The Defense Case

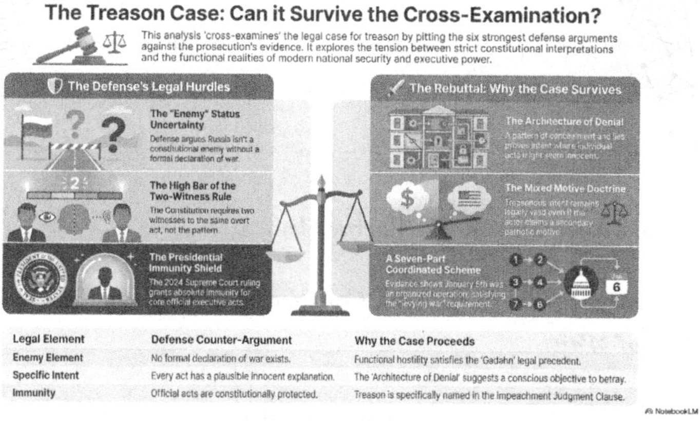

What the Other Side Would Argue, and Why It Fails

The Six Strongest Arguments Against This Book's Legal Conclusion, Addressed Directly

There is an old saying among trial lawyers: if you don't know the other side's best argument, you don't know your own case.

That principle applies here. This book has spent twenty-six chapters building a legal argument. The Legal Introduction acknowledged honestly that the argument has weak points, that the enemy element is legally contested, that the two-witness rule is demanding, that conviction is a distant prospect, and that the immunity ruling in Trump v.

United States (2024) creates significant procedural obstacles. Those concessions were not rhetorical humility. They were legal honesty.

This chapter takes that honesty one step further. It identifies the six strongest arguments a competent defense attorney would make against every major element of this book's case. It states each argument in its strongest form. And then it addresses each one directly, because a legal argument that cannot survive scrutiny of its weakest points is not a legal argument. It is a verdict dressed up as analysis.

Think of this chapter as the cross-examination that the argument must survive before it earns the right to go to the jury. The prosecution presents its case. The defense tests it. What is left standing after that test is the argument worth making.

Six arguments survive the test, in weakened or qualified form. None of them closes the case. Here is each one, stated honestly, addressed directly.

□ □ □

I. The Defense Argument on the Enemy Element

Defense Argument: Russia Is Not a Constitutional Enemy Because There Is No Declaration of War

This is the defense's strongest single argument, and it deserves the most serious treatment.

The Constitution's treason clause was written in 1787, in a world where enemies were nations that had formally declared war. The Framers understood enemy the way the 18th century understood it: armies on a battlefield, flags raised, diplomatic relations severed. Russia and the United States have an embassy in Moscow and an embassy in Washington. They have ambassadors. They have treaties. They have ongoing diplomatic communications. No court has ever formally declared Russia a legal enemy under Article III. No Congress has issued a declaration of war.

A defense attorney would argue, with some force, that applying the treason clause to a nation with which the United States maintains formal diplomatic relations stretches the constitutional text beyond what the Framers intended and beyond what any court has sanctioned.

Think of it this way. Imagine two neighbors who are locked in a bitter property dispute. They have filed lawsuits against each other, they are competing for the same zoning variance, and each one is quietly lobbying the city council to harm the other's interests. They are adversaries in every meaningful sense. But they still nod at each other in the driveway. They still share a fence. A court asked to apply a law designed for declared enemies might hesitate to extend it to neighbors who are still, technically, speaking.

Why This Argument Does Not Close the Case

The Gadahn indictment, while never resulting in a conviction because Gadahn was killed in a drone strike in 2015 before trial, established that the Department of Justice concluded the treason clause could reach a non-state actor engaged in sustained hostile operations, without any declaration of war. Adam Gadahn had produced and appeared in al-Qaeda propaganda videos. Al-Qaeda has never been a nation-state. No diplomatic relations existed to sever. No Congress declared war. Yet the DOJ determined that al-Qaeda's hostile purpose and hostile action against the United States satisfied the functional standard for an enemy under Article III. Because there was no conviction and no judicial ruling on the merits, the Gadahn indictment is not binding precedent. What it established is that the nation's chief law enforcement authority, applying the constitutional text, concluded the functional standard extended beyond formally declared enemies. That conclusion supports the argument here. It does not settle it.

The Intelligence Community Assessment of January 2017 did not conclude that Russia was a geopolitical competitor or a difficult negotiating partner. It concluded, with the highest confidence rating the intelligence community uses, that Russia engaged in a sustained campaign of hostile action against the United States, specifically targeting its election infrastructure, its democratic institutions, and its alliance structures. That is not diplomatic tension. That is hostile purpose, documented by the agencies of the federal government itself.

The diplomatic relationship exists because adversarial relationships require management through channels, not because the adversarial relationship does not exist. The United States designated Iran a state sponsor of terrorism while maintaining back-channel communications. It treated the Soviet Union as an enemy throughout the Cold War while maintaining an embassy in Moscow. Diplomatic contact has never been the legal standard for enemy status under the functional doctrine.

The enemy argument is the book's most legally contested element. The defense argument identifies a genuine uncertainty that a jury would have to resolve. But the resolution of that uncertainty is a jury question, not a threshold that forecloses the argument before it reaches a jury.

□ □ □

II. The Defense Argument on Specific Intent

Defense Argument: Every Act in This Book Has an Innocent Alternative Explanation

This is the defense's second-strongest argument, and it is the one that will resonate most with readers who are not already persuaded.

A good defense attorney does not need to prove innocence. She needs only to create reasonable doubt. And the way to create reasonable doubt about a complex pattern of conduct is to offer a plausible innocent explanation for each piece of that pattern, one at a time.

The Helsinki statement? A diplomatic preference for engagement over confrontation. A President who believed, however naively, that a direct relationship with Putin would produce better outcomes than public confrontation.

The Ukraine aid freeze? A legitimate policy concern about corruption in Ukraine, which is a real and documented problem, and about burden-sharing with European allies, which is a legitimate policy debate.

The NATO funding demands? A genuine belief that European allies were free-riding on American defense spending, a concern that has been expressed by American officials of both parties for decades.

The pardon of Roger Stone, Paul Manafort, and Michael Flynn? An exercise of the absolute presidential pardon power, combined with a belief that the prosecutions were politically motivated.

The defense will say: none of these acts, evaluated individually, required a treasonous motive. Each has a plausible innocent explanation. Specific intent to betray the country cannot be inferred from a series of acts that are each individually explicable without it.

Here is the analogy the defense would use. A doctor who prescribes opioids to ten patients is not necessarily a drug dealer. Each prescription might be individually justified. The pattern only becomes suspicious when you notice that every one of the ten patients paid cash, none of them had X-rays on file, and the doctor's brother-in-law ran a pill mill two towns over. The pattern is evidence. But the defense will argue that the pattern here does not rise to that level, that the innocent explanations are genuinely plausible, and that reasonable doubt is reasonable doubt.

Why This Argument Does Not Close the Case

The law's response to this argument comes from the broadcaster treason cases of World War II. In Chandler v. United States (1948) and Best v. United States (1949), courts established what legal scholars characterize as a mixed motive inference: a patriotic motive does not negate a treasonous intent. If an actor has the conscious objective of helping the enemy succeed, the requisite mental state for treason is present, even if the actor also believed, sincerely or insincerely, that his actions would ultimately benefit the United States.

The specific intent question is not: did he have a plausible innocent explanation ready? The question is: what was the conscious objective of the act?

And here is where the architecture of denial documented in Part V becomes the book's most powerful evidence of intent. Innocent explanations do not require construction. A President who delayed military aid because of a genuine corruption concern would, when confronted with the GAO's finding that the delay violated federal impoundment law, acknowledge the error and correct course. He would not fire the officials who raised the concern, construct an alternative narrative, pressure a foreign government to announce an investigation of a political rival as public justification, and then have his associates stonewall a congressional inquiry into the whole episode.

That sequence, documented and uncontested in the public record, is not the behavior of a person with an innocent explanation. It is the behavior of a person who understood that the true explanation could not survive scrutiny.

The public record answers the innocent explanation argument directly. A President who unwittingly benefits a foreign adversary admits the error when confronted with the evidence. A President who intentionally benefits that adversary lies to cover it up. The sequence documented in the Ukraine episode is the behavior of the second category.

The innocent explanation argument is strongest when applied to any single act. It collapses when applied to the pattern. The consistent direction of the conduct, the consistent beneficiary of the conduct, and the consistent architecture of concealment built around the conduct together constitute the totality of conduct from which the Kawakita inference is drawn. In Kawakita v. United States (1952), the Supreme Court held that treasonous intent may be inferred from a consistent pattern of directionally beneficial conduct toward an identified enemy, evaluated in its totality rather than act by act. That inference applies here.

□ □ □

III. The Defense Argument on the Two-Witness Rule

Defense Argument: Foreign Officials and Television Audiences Are Not Constitutional Witnesses

The two-witness rule is the Constitution's most demanding evidentiary requirement. It was designed specifically to prevent treason convictions based on inference, circumstance, or the word of a single accuser. The Constitution requires two witnesses to the same overt act, not two witnesses to two different pieces of the same pattern.

A defense attorney would argue that this book, for all its documentation, has not identified two witnesses to any single overt act who could testify in a properly constituted proceeding. Foreign heads of state cannot be compelled to testify. International television audiences are not witnesses in the constitutional sense. Congressional testimony about what a witness heard in a classified briefing is not the same as eyewitness testimony to the overt act itself.

The analogy here is a security camera that recorded a crime but whose footage cannot be authenticated because the camera's manufacturer went out of business. Everyone can see what happened. But the evidentiary rules that protect defen-

dants from false accusations also, in this case, protect the person on the tape. The two-witness rule was designed to be demanding. In this case, it is.

Why This Argument Does Not Close the Case

The Legal Introduction to this book made this concession honestly and directly: this book does not claim to fully satisfy the two-witness requirement for every overt act it documents. That concession stands.

What the book demonstrates, chapter by chapter, is the witness categories from which the two-witness requirement could be satisfied in a properly constituted proceeding. The January 6 overt act, the most publicly witnessed event in modern American political history, was observed by hundreds of members of Congress, by the Vice President of the United States, by the Capitol Police, by journalists, by the participants themselves, and by millions of television viewers. The Select Committee documented testimony from participants who described receiving instructions, coordinating the assemblage, and understanding the purpose of the breach.

For the Russia alignment overt acts, the Senate Intelligence Committee's five-volume bipartisan report documents the testimony of intelligence officials, campaign personnel, and foreign contacts, each of whom testified to specific acts. The question of which witnesses could satisfy the same overt act requirement for specific acts is a question for a grand jury and a trial court, not a question that forecloses the argument at the level of citizen analysis.

The two-witness argument is the defense's most technically sound point. The book acknowledges it honestly. What the book demonstrates is sufficient witness evidence, at the level of a citizen's brief, to submit the question to a properly constituted proceeding. The rest is for the jury.

□ □ □

IV. The Defense Argument on Presidential Immunity

Defense Argument: Trump v. United States (2024) Immunizes Every Act in This Book

This is the defense's most procedurally powerful argument, and it deserves an honest assessment.

In June 2024, the Supreme Court held in Trump v. United States that a former president is absolutely immune from criminal prosecution for acts within his core constitutional functions, and presumptively immune for all other official acts. The Court's majority opinion, written by Chief Justice Roberts, held that a President's communications with the Department of Justice, his exercise of the pardon power, and his discussions with the Vice President about the certification of the election are all within or close to the core constitutional functions that absolute immunity protects.

A defense attorney would argue, with substantial force, that most of the overt acts documented in this book are official acts. The Helsinki statement was made at an official diplomatic summit. The Ukraine aid decision was an exercise of executive foreign policy authority. The pardon decisions were exercises of the constitutional pardon power. The NATO funding demands were made in the context of official alliance negotiations. If each of these is immunized, the treason case loses most of its evidentiary foundation.

Here is the analogy that captures the immunity problem. Imagine a bank security guard who is paid to protect the vault. The bank's employee handbook says the guard has absolute authority to decide who enters the vault during business hours. The guard uses that authority to let his accomplices in after closing. The immunity argument says: the authority was real, the act was within the authority, and you cannot prosecute the act without questioning the authority itself. The Supreme Court, in the Trump immunity case, came uncomfortably close to accepting that argument.

Why This Argument Does Not Close the Case

Chapter 11 of this book addresses the immunity ruling in full. The chapter develops what it calls the textual absurdity argument: treason is the first offense named in the Impeachment Judgment Clause. The Framers placed it there specifically. A constitutional reading that grants absolute immunity for the first offense the Constitution specifically names as grounds for removal from office produces a textual absurdity that no honest reading of the constitutional structure can sustain.

Justice Sotomayor's dissent, joined by Justice Jackson, made the structural argument directly:

> *"The President of the United States is the most powerful person in the country, and possibly the world. When he uses his official powers in any way, under the majority's reasoning, he now will be insulated from criminal prosecution." —Justice Sonia Sotomayor, dissenting, Trump v. United States, 603 U.S.___ (2024)*

The immunity ruling also created an evidentiary exception that the book's argument survives. The Court held that evidence of immunized acts cannot be used to prove guilt for non-immunized acts. But it did not hold that the non-immunized acts themselves disappear. The January 6 assemblage, as a private act not performed in the President's official capacity, is the clearest candidate for the non-immunized category. The financial entanglements, as private business transactions conducted through family enterprises, are another. The Citizen's Judgment chapter addresses the specific immunity analysis for each category of overt act.

The immunity argument is the most significant procedural obstacle the book acknowledges. It does not eliminate the legal case. It narrows the path to a properly constituted prosecution. The citizen's analysis is not bound by the procedural constraints of a criminal proceeding. The constitutional argument stands regardless of whether the procedural path to prosecution is currently open.

□ □ □

V. The Defense Argument on the Levying War Prong

Defense Argument: January 6 Was a Riot, Not a Levying of War

The defense will argue that January 6, 2021, however disturbing, was a riot, not a levying of war in the constitutional sense. A riot is a crime. Seditious conspiracy is a crime. Obstruction of an official proceeding is a crime. Dozens of participants have been convicted of these crimes. But a riot, even a violent one at the seat of government, is not automatically an act of war against the United States.

Ex parte Bollman (1807) required an assemblage of persons organized for the purpose of executing a treasonable design. The defense will argue that the crowd at the Capitol on January 6 was not organized in the legal sense, that participants had diverse and often incoherent motivations, that no single person directed a unified military-style operation, and that calling it a levying of war stretches the constitutional standard beyond what the Framers intended.

The analogy is a flash mob that gets out of hand. The organizer sends a message, the crowd gathers, things escalate beyond what anyone planned, and chaos follows. A flash mob gone wrong is not a military operation. The defense will argue that what happened on January 6 was closer to the flash mob than to the armed insurrection the treason clause was designed to address.

Why This Argument Does Not Close the Case

The Select Committee's two-year investigation documented something more specific than a flash mob. It documented a seven-part scheme: a coordinated pressure campaign on the Vice President to reject electoral votes, a coordinated fake elector scheme in seven states, a coordinated effort to pressure the Department of Justice to declare the election fraudulent, a coordinated delay of National Guard deployment when the breach occurred, and an assemblage at the Ellipse that was organized, promoted, and directed at the Capitol during the active certification.

The legal question under Ex parte Bollman is not whether every participant had a unified understanding of the treasonable design. It is whether the assemblage was organized for the purpose of executing one. The Bollman decision itself involved participants who had varying levels of understanding of Burr's conspiracy. What mattered was that the assemblage as a whole was directed toward a treasonable objective, and that the person who directed it understood and intended that objective.

Seditious conspiracy convictions against Oath Keeper leaders established in federal court that the January 6 assemblage was not spontaneous. It was organized. The question of whether that organization rose to the level of a levying of war is a question the jury would answer with the full evidentiary record before it.

The levying of war argument faces genuine legal uncertainty. The Bollman standard requires a treasonable design, not merely a criminal one. Whether

the specific intent to overturn the constitutional transfer of power satisfies that requirement is a jury question that the Select Committee's documented record of the seven-part scheme makes submissible.

□ □ □

VI. The Defense Argument on the Book Itself

Defense Argument: This Book Is Political Advocacy, Not Legal Analysis

The most sweeping defense argument is not about any specific element of the treason case. It is about the nature of this book.

A defense attorney would argue that this entire volume, whatever its legal citations and constitutional framing, is a political document dressed in legal language. She would point to the title, which declares that a legal case exists. She would point to the rhetorical force of the evidence chapters, which present contested interpretations as documented facts. She would argue that any reader who finishes this book persuaded of the conclusion was persuaded before the legal analysis began, and that the legal analysis merely provided a framework for convictions already held.

She would cite the standard the Legal Introduction itself invoked: the difference between a legal brief and a political screed is the willingness to acknowledge what the evidence does not establish. And she would argue that this book, taken as a whole, does not consistently maintain that distinction.

The analogy she would use is a documentary film about a disputed historical event. The filmmaker has access to all the same evidence as a disinterested historian. But the filmmaker makes choices: which documents to feature, which witnesses to interview, which context to provide and which to omit. The resulting film may be accurate in every frame and still be advocacy rather than scholarship. The defense argument is that this book is a documentary, not a history.

Why This Argument Does Not Close the Case

The honest response is this: every legal brief is advocacy. The function of a brief is to present the strongest available case for one side, subject to the obligation of candor toward the tribunal. This book is a citizen's brief. It does not pretend otherwise.

What distinguishes this brief from political advocacy is not the absence of a conclusion. It is the quality of the reasoning that connects the evidence to the conclusion. The Legal Introduction established the constitutional standard with full rigor, including its weaknesses. This chapter has addressed the strongest defense arguments directly, including the ones that identify genuine legal uncertainties. The two-witness concession in the Legal Introduction remains. The enemy element concession remains. The immunity obstacle acknowledgment remains.

A political screed does not make those concessions. It asserts the conclusion and marshals evidence in support. This book makes the concessions because the argument is stronger for them. A juror who is told honestly that the case has weak points, and who evaluates the strong points after understanding the weak ones, is a juror whose verdict means something.

Abraham Lincoln, who was himself a lawyer before he was a President, put it simply:

> *"No man has a good enough memory to be a successful liar." — Abraham Lincoln*

The corollary for legal argument is equally simple. No argument is strong enough to survive if it requires the reader to ignore what the evidence does not establish. This book has not asked that. It has built its case on what the evidence does establish, acknowledged what it does not, and submitted the question to the reader's honest evaluation.

The political advocacy argument is the defense's most rhetorical point and its least legally substantive one. Every serious legal argument about a contested subject can be characterized as advocacy. The question is whether the argument is honest, rigorous, and grounded in the evidentiary record. The reader is the judge of that.

□ □ □

VII. What Survives the Cross-Examination

Six arguments. Each stated in its strongest form. Each addressed directly. Here is what survives.

The enemy element is the weakest point in the case, and the book says so. The functional enemy doctrine is a doctrine developed in the circuit courts and recognized by legal scholars, not yet ratified by the Supreme Court. A jury might reject it. A court might decline to extend Gadahn to a sovereign nation-state. That uncertainty is real and it is acknowledged.

The specific intent element is significantly strengthened by the architecture of denial. The mixed motive doctrine answers the innocent explanation argument for each individual act. The pattern of concealment, built precisely around the elements of the charge, answers it for the pattern as a whole.

The two-witness rule is demanding and the book does not claim to fully satisfy it for every overt act. It identifies the witness categories that could satisfy it in a properly constituted proceeding. The January 6 overt act, the most publicly witnessed event in modern American political history, presents the strongest case for satisfaction of the rule.

The immunity ruling narrows the procedural path to prosecution. It does not eliminate the constitutional argument. The textual absurdity of immunizing the first offense named in the Impeachment Judgment Clause is a genuine interpretive problem that the Supreme Court's majority opinion did not resolve.

The levying of war argument faces genuine legal uncertainty about whether the January 6 assemblage satisfies the Bollman treasonable design requirement. The seven-part scheme documented by the Select Committee makes the question submissible to a jury. Whether the jury answers it in favor of the argument is a question this book cannot answer, and does not pretend to answer.

And the political advocacy argument, the sweeping claim that this is a brief dressed as analysis, fails on the evidence. The concessions are real. The uncertainties are acknowledged. The reader has been asked to evaluate the argument on its merits, not to accept its conclusion.

What survives cross-examination is a case that a competent prosecutor, with the full investigative resources of the federal government and the full evidentiary record of the Senate Intelligence Committee, the January 6 Select Committee, the Government Accountability Office, and the Intelligence Community, could take to a grand jury and present to a trial jury.

That is what this book argues. That is what the evidence supports. That is what the cross-examination has left standing.

The defense has been heard. The case proceeds to the Citizen's Judgment.

□ □ □

PART IX

"We the People are the rightful masters of both Congress and the Courts, not to overthrow the Constitution but to overthrow the men who pervert the Constitution." – Abraham Lincoln

Chapter Twenty-Nine

CITIZEN'S JUDGMENT

LEGAL OPINION

A Citizen's Constitutional Brief

IN THE MATTER OF THE CONSTITUTIONAL ACCOUNTABILITY OF

DONALD J. TRUMP

Article III, Section 3, Constitution of the United States

QUESTION PRESENTED

Does the documented record assembled across twenty-seven chapters of this book establish probable cause to believe that Donald J. Trump committed treason under Article III, Section 3 of the Constitution of the United States?

OPINION OF THIS CITIZEN'S BRIEF: Yes.

The standard applied here is not guilt beyond a reasonable doubt. That standard belongs to a trial jury. The standard of this brief is the legal threshold for indictment: whether the totality of the documented facts, evaluated against the constitutional elements of Article III, Section 3, supports the conclusion that probable cause exists to believe each required element has been established.

The answer, on each element, follows.

□ □ □

I.

FINDING OF FACT: THE ALLEGIANCE

The Constitution requires that the defendant owe allegiance to the United States.

Finding: This element is satisfied without ambiguity and beyond any reasonable contest.

Donald J. Trump is a natural-born citizen of the United States. He swore the Presidential Oath of Office on January 20, 2017, and again on January 20, 2025. The oath of office is the specific, documented, constitutional instrument through which the fiduciary duty of the President to the Republic is established and recorded. He held the highest office of trust in the constitutional system. He owed the highest allegiance that office creates.

No element of the treason framework is more clearly satisfied. This finding requires no inference, no pattern analysis, and no contested legal argument. The allegiance element is established by the documented fact of birth, the documented fact of citizenship, and the documented fact of the oath.

□ □ □

II.

CONCLUSION OF LAW: THE FUNCTIONAL ENEMY

The Constitution requires that the defendant adhere to an enemy of the United States.

The Defense Position: The defense will argue that Russia is not an enemy because Congress has not formally declared war. They will cite the traditional requirement, established in cases like Ex parte Bollman and United States v. Greathouse, that enemies are subjects of a foreign power in a state of open, declared hostilities. Under this argument, diplomatic relations between the United States and Russia preclude the enemy designation.

This argument fails for four reasons, each of which is independently sufficient.

First, the Gadahn precedent. In United States v. Adam Gadahn (2006), the Department of Justice determined that an American citizen who provided material support and propaganda services to al-Qaeda qualified for treason prosecution. Al-Qaeda had not been granted diplomatic recognition by the United States. Congress had not declared war against al-Qaeda. Al-Qaeda was an enemy because it was conducting sustained documented hostile operations against the United States. The functional definition of enemy, derived from the Gadahn analysis, is hostile conduct, not formal declaration.

Second, Russia's own doctrine. The Gerasimov Doctrine, Russia's published military framework, explicitly describes ongoing hybrid warfare against the United States and Western democracies as an active strategic operation of the Russian armed forces. Russia has published its declaration of hostile intent. Its intelligence services have operationalized that declaration through election interference, cyber attacks on federal agencies, and information warfare campaigns documented by the unanimous January 2017 Intelligence Community Assessment. A nation that has published its doctrine of war against the United States and actively implemented that doctrine cannot claim the protection of formal diplomatic courtesy.

Third, the logic of the age. The Framers wrote the treason clause in an era when wars were declared and enemies wore uniforms. They did not anticipate a world in which the most dangerous attacks on a nation's sovereignty and democratic infrastructure come through fiber optic cables and social media algorithms rather than through cannon fire. To freeze the definition of enemy at the eighteenth-century understanding of declared war is to render the treason clause incapable of addressing the most significant category of hostile action the twenty-first century has produced. Courts do not read constitutional provisions to produce absurd results. Reading enemy to exclude nations that have published their doctrine of hybrid warfare against the United States and have been unanimously assessed by the intelligence community as implementing that doctrine produces an absurd result.

Fourth, the comparative case. Russia, a nation-state with a standing army, nuclear weapons, an established intelligence service, and a published military doctrine of hostile action against the United States, presents a stronger case for enemy status than al-Qaeda, a non-state terrorist organization, presented in the Gadahn analysis. If the functional enemy definition encompasses al-Qaeda, it encompasses Russia.

Conclusion of Law: Russia meets the functional definition of enemy under Article III, Section 3. This element presents the most legally contested question in the case. A court could rule differently. But it is a jury question that reaches the threshold for indictment and does not foreclose the argument as a matter of law.

□ □ □

III.

FINDING OF FACT: THE ADHERENCE AND AID AND COMFORT

The Constitution requires that the defendant adhere to the enemy, giving the enemy aid and comfort.

Finding on Adherence: The cumulative pattern of conduct documented across Parts I through VI of this book establishes the factual predicate for the adherence element.

The consistent alignment of American policy with Russian strategic objectives across two terms is not a series of policy coincidences. The CAATSA sanctions were not implemented despite congressional mandate. The Helsinki Summit endorsement of Russia's election interference denial was delivered despite the unanimous Intelligence Community Assessment. The Ukraine aid freeze was imposed in defiance of congressional appropriation and GAO finding. The NATO withdrawal threat was issued at the precise moment of maximum Russian strategic benefit. The Russia oil sanctions relief was delivered at the precise moment of maximum Russian financial benefit from the Iran war.

Under the Haupt standard, intent transforms an ambiguous act into a treasonous one. The Kawakita standard permits the inference of treasonous intent from the totality of conduct. The totality documented in this book is not ambiguous. Every act in the pattern benefits Russia. Every justification for every act is contradicted by the classified or diplomatic record. Every act is accompanied by a corresponding lie that tracks precisely the element of the treason case the act would establish. The architecture of deception documented in Part V is the strongest available evidence of the adherence element, because it establishes that the underlying conduct was understood to require concealment.

Finding on Aid and Comfort: Multiple overt acts independently satisfy the Cramer requirement of actual aid that actually advances the enemy's mission.

The Russia oil sanctions relief of March 5, 2026, delivered an estimated $150 million per day in additional revenue to the Russian economy at the precise moment that revenue would most effectively sustain Russian military operations and diplomatic ambitions. The Helsinki Summit endorsement of Russia's election interference denial validated the enemy's narrative, undermined the American defensive response to Russian hybrid warfare, and advanced the specific Russian objective of preventing attribution and accountability for its election interference operations. The Ukraine aid freeze of 2019 withheld congressionally authorized military assistance from a nation Russia was actively attacking, creating the specific battlefield window documented in Chapter 8 that extended Russian operational effectiveness. The Lebanon ceasefire denial of April 2026 extended the regional conflict whose primary financial beneficiary was Russia. The NATO withdrawal threat of April 2026 delivered the most credible signal Russia has ever received from an American President that its primary strategic objective was achievable.

Each of these acts, standing alone, satisfies the Cramer actual aid standard. Together, they form the most concentrated cluster of documented aid to a foreign adversary in the American presidential record.

□ □ □

IV.

FINDING OF FACT: THE OVERT ACTS AND THE TWO-WITNESS RULE

Article III requires at least one overt act proved by the testimony of two witnesses to the same overt act.

Finding: This constitutional safeguard, designed to prevent frivolous or politically motivated charges, is satisfied with an evidentiary redundancy unprecedented in the American treason record.

The Lebanon ceasefire denial of April 8, 2026, was witnessed by the Prime Minister of Pakistan, the mediating nation's head of government with direct firsthand knowledge of the negotiated terms, and by the President of France, who confirmed Lebanon's inclusion publicly on the day of the denial. Both are heads of state of sovereign nations with no U.S. domestic political stake in the outcome. Multiple diplomatic sources corroborated their accounts through credible news organization reporting.

The NATO withdrawal threat of April 2026 was made publicly, in all-capitals social media posts and in documented statements by the President and Secretary of State, before an international audience. The NATO Secretary General's refusal to deny the threat at a formal White House press conference is itself evidentiary. The bipartisan Senate response, naming the threat as the fulfillment of Putin's greatest dream, is documented in the congressional record.

The Helsinki Summit of July 2018 was broadcast on international television before the leaders of every major allied nation and a global audience of millions. The specific statement, that the President did not see any reason why it would be Russia, contradicts the unanimous Intelligence Community Assessment and constitutes the most publicly witnessed single act of endorsing a foreign adversary's denial of its own hostile conduct in American presidential history.

The two-witness constitutional requirement does not protect the defendant in this record. The witnesses are not anonymous sources or partisan Americans. They are heads of state, diplomatic officials of independent nations, bipartisan members of Congress, military briefers in classified session, and in several instances, the entire global viewing audience of international television. The constitutional standard has been satisfied with a redundancy that the Framers could not have anticipated.

□ □ □

V.

CONCLUSION OF LAW: THE CONSTITUTIONAL CARVE-OUT FROM IMMUNITY

The Supreme Court's ruling in Trump v. United States (2024) established the most significant procedural obstacle to any treason prosecution arising from this record. The majority created a framework in which absolute immunity applies to core constitutional functions, presumptive immunity applies to official acts, and no immunity applies only to unofficial private acts.

This obstacle is real. It is the current law. This brief does not pretend otherwise.

But the treason clause is the constitutional provision the immunity ruling cannot reach, for reasons grounded in constitutional text, the Framers' recorded intent, and the structural logic of the document itself.

The Textual Argument: Article I, Section 3, Clause 7, the Impeachment Judgment Clause, states that a party convicted in an impeachment trial remains liable and subject to indictment, trial, judgment, and punishment. Treason is the first ground named for impeachment in Article II, Section 4. A ruling that immunizes official acts from criminal prosecution must therefore immunize the first ground for impeachment from the criminal prosecution that the Impeachment Judgment Clause explicitly preserves. That is a textual absurdity. Courts do not reach textual absurdities when a rational reading of the constitutional provisions is available.

The Structural Argument: Treason cannot be an official act because treason is the constitutional definition of the betrayal of the oath that makes official action possible. The immunity doctrine was designed to protect the President's ability to exercise his constitutional responsibilities without fear that every controversial decision will be criminalized. Treason is not a controversial decision. It is the one act the Constitution most explicitly prohibits. Extending immunity to the one act the Constitution most explicitly prohibits would convert the immunity doctrine from a protection of constitutional authority into a protection of the authority's own destruction. The Framers who wrote both the immunity principle through the structure of the Constitution and the treason clause into the same document did not intend one to nullify the other.

The Absurd Result Argument: If the immunity ruling protects official acts, and if a President can commit treason through official acts, then the immunity ruling immunizes the one crime the Constitution names first and most explicitly among the grounds for removal. The Constitution creates an office called the presidency and simultaneously provides that treason is grounds for removal from that office and establishes that a convicted officeholder remains subject to criminal prosecution. Reading the immunity doctrine to nullify all three of these provisions for the crime they most directly address is not constitutional interpretation. It is constitutional destruction. Courts apply the doctrine of constitutional avoidance to prevent exactly this result.

> **The Constitution is not a suicide pact. A reading of the immunity ruling that immunizes treason, the one act the Constitution most explicitly prohibits, would transform the immunity ruling into the mechanism for destroying the constitutional order from within. The rational reading, the historically grounded reading, the reading that gives effect to every provision of the Constitution rather than allowing one provision to nullify the others, is that the treason clause operates as a constitutional carve-out from any immunity doctrine the Court might construct. The Framers who wrote both provisions in the same document did not intend one to nullify the other.**

□ □ □

VI.

FINDING OF FACT: THE SPECIFIC INTENT

Specific intent to betray the nation, rather than accidentally benefit a foreign adversary through misguided policy, is the element whose proof depends most heavily on inference rather than direct evidence.

This brief does not assert that a single document, a signed agreement, or an explicit confession establishes the intent element. None exists in the public record, and this brief will not overstate what the evidence shows.

What the evidence shows is the following. Every act in the documented pattern benefited Russia. Every public justification for every act was contradicted by the classified or diplomatic record. Every act was covered by a corresponding lie that tracks precisely the element of the treason case the act would establish. The architecture of institutional destruction documented in Part VII targeted precisely the mechanisms most capable of exposing and stopping the overt acts.

Under the Kawakita standard, the totality of conduct across two terms, including the overt acts, the lies, and the institutional destruction, permits the inference of treasonous intent. A person who accidentally aligns with a foreign adversary admits the mistake when confronted. A person who intentionally aligns with a foreign adversary constructs an architecture of denial and then dismantles the institutions capable of exposing it. The architecture and the dismantlement are documented in this record.

Finding on Intent: The specific intent element, the most contested and the most dependent on inference, is established by the totality of the conduct pattern, the architecture of lies that tracks that pattern with precision, and the systematic institutional destruction that followed. The jury instruction on consciousness of guilt would apply to the entire documented record.

□ □ □

VII.

THE JUDGMENT: PROBABLE CAUSE ESTABLISHED

The standard for indictment, probable cause to believe that each element of the offense has been established by the totality of the documented evidence, has been satisfied on each element of the constitutional offense of treason under Article III, Section 3.

The allegiance element is established without contest. The functional enemy element is established under the Gadahn standard and the operational doctrine of the identified adversary. The adherence and aid and comfort elements are established by multiple independent overt acts, each of which independently satisfies the Cramer actual aid standard. The overt act and two-witness elements are established with an evidentiary redundancy unprecedented in the American treason record. The specific intent element is established by the Kawakita cumulative pattern inference applied to a totality of documented conduct whose consistent direction is the advancement of the identified enemy's primary strategic objectives. The immunity defense is addressed by the structural constitutional argument that the treason clause operates as a carve-out from any immunity doctrine the Court might construct.

A federal grand jury, presented with the full cumulative record documented in this book's twenty-seven chapters, could return an indictment. The legal argument, that Donald J. Trump committed treason under Article III, Section 3, is not frivolous, not merely rhetorical, and not legally foreclosed. It is a legally cognizable claim that would survive a motion to dismiss and present the constitutional questions it raises to a jury.

Whether a trial jury would convict is a harder question, dependent on the enemy definition's ultimate judicial resolution, the intent element's proof at trial, and the immunity doctrine's future scope. This brief does not assert the verdict. It asserts the probable cause.

The probable cause standard has been met. The indictment is legally justified. The constitutional argument is legally viable. The only remaining question is whether the Republic possesses the institutional will to enforce its own highest law. That question is addressed to the citizens of the United States. It is addressed to the officials who hold their positions in trust for those citizens. And it is addressed to the institutions whose function is to ensure that no person, including the person who holds the most powerful office in the constitutional system, stands above the law that the constitutional system was built to enforce.

□ □ □

"It is the most serious unanswered constitutional question in American history since the Civil War." **This Citizen's Brief**

END OF BRIEF

□ □ □

Chapter Thirty

CONCLUSION

If you have read this book to this point, you are feeling something. Anger, perhaps. Grief. Fear. A sense of helplessness in the face of documented betrayal on a scale that the legal analysis has established is historically unprecedented.

Those feelings are appropriate responses to the evidence. This book would not want you to suppress them. But this final chapter asks you to redirect them. Because anger without direction produces exactly the outcome that the Gerasimov Doctrine describes as Russia's strategic objective: a divided, distracted, and demoralized American public that has lost faith in its own institutions and its own capacity to act.

That is the one outcome this book cannot accept.

The Framers did not build a self-defending republic. They built a republic that depends on the vigilance, the engagement, and the informed participation of the people who live inside it. The accountability mechanisms documented in this book have been weakened by the same pattern of conduct the book analyzes. The inspectors general were fired. The independent oversight was attacked. The congressional accountability function was hollowed out by a political environment that treats constitutional responsibility as partisan. The Supreme Court issued a ruling that created significant procedural obstacles to prosecution.

And yet.

The Republic has survived worse than this. Not automatically. Not because the constitutional architecture is self-executing. But because citizens refused to let it fail. The abolitionists wrote briefs before Lincoln signed the Proclamation. The civil rights lawyers documented the law before the Supreme Court decided Brown. The investigative journalists published what they found before the congressional hearings began. The whistleblowers took notes before the oversight committees subpoenaed them.

The keeping of the Republic has always been the citizen's job. It has never been more urgently that job than it is right now.

This chapter tells you what that job looks like in practice.

□ □ □

First, the Honest Answer to the Question You Are Asking

Before the seven specific actions, the most important thing this chapter can do is answer the question you are probably asking right now.

Why hasn't anyone done anything?

The honest answer is that some people have. The January 6 Select Committee spent two years documenting the evidence and making criminal referrals. Federal and state prosecutors brought charges in multiple jurisdictions. Career officials resigned and testified under oath. Inspectors general forwarded complaints until they were fired for doing so. Sixty federal and state courts reviewed the election fraud claims and rejected them unanimously. The Senate Intelligence Committee published five bipartisan volumes documenting the Russia relationship. The Government Accountability Office twice found that congressionally authorized military assistance was illegally withheld.

The accountability mechanisms functioned. They produced findings. They made referrals. They created the evidentiary record that this book is built on.

What has not happened is the full legal reckoning that the evidence supports. That has not happened for reasons that are themselves part of the story this book tells: the immunity ruling, the weakening of oversight institutions, the political environment that treats constitutional accountability as partisan warfare rather than constitutional obligation.

A citizen who understands this clearly is more effective than a citizen who believes either that the system has completely failed or that the system will automatically correct itself. The system has produced the evidence. The system has not yet produced the full accountability. The citizen's job is to close that gap.

□ □ □

The Seven Things a Citizen Can Do

One: Read the Primary Sources

Not this book. The primary sources this book cites. They are public. They are free. They are available to every American citizen who wants to read them. And they are more powerful than any secondary analysis, including this one, because they are the actual record.

The Intelligence Community Assessment of January 2017 is available through the Office of the Director of National Intelligence. The Mueller Report is available through the Department of Justice. The Senate Intelligence Committee's five-volume report is available through the Senate's website. The January 6 Select Committee Final Report is available through the House of Representatives. The Government Accountability Office's findings on the Ukraine aid freeze are available through GAO.gov.

A citizen who has read these documents cannot be told they do not exist, cannot be told the findings are partisan, and cannot be told that no one has looked at the evidence. The documents are the evidence. Reading them is a form of civic action.

Start with the Intelligence Community Assessment. It is 25 pages. It is clearly written. It is the document that started the documented record of what this book analyzes. Read it. Then read the others.

□ □ □

Two: Talk About It Accurately

Not with outrage and not with conspiracy language. With the precision this book has tried to model.

The word treason has a specific constitutional meaning that most Americans do not know. It is defined in Article III, Section 3. It requires allegiance, an enemy, an overt act witnessed by two people, and specific intent. When citizens use that word accurately, in the legal framework the Framers established, it is more powerful than when it is used as a political epithet that can be dismissed as hyperbole.

Here is the plain-language version of the core argument that this book makes, in the form you can explain to a neighbor or a family member who has not read the book. The Constitution defines treason as betraying the country to its enemies by levying war against it or giving aid and comfort to its enemies. The documented public record, confirmed by bipartisan government findings, shows that a pattern of conduct spanning two terms consistently benefited a foreign government that American intelligence unanimously identified as hostile to the United States, was concealed through a sustained architecture of denial, and culminated in an armed attack on the certification of a presidential election. The legal question this book asks is whether that pattern, evaluated against the constitutional standard, meets the definition of treason. The book argues that it does.

You can say that to someone. It is accurate. It is sourced. And it is a conversation, not a lecture.

□ □ □

Three: Support the Institutions Still Doing the Work

The evidentiary record this book is built on was produced by specific institutions that are still operating and still need support.

Investigative journalism organizations, ProPublica, The Intercept, the investigative units of major newspapers and broadcast networks, produced much of the documented record. Their financial sustainability depends on reader support. Subscriptions, donations, and the active sharing of their work with your networks keeps them viable.

Legal accountability organizations, the Brennan Center for Justice, Citizens for Responsibility and Ethics in Washington, the American Civil Liberties Union, the Lawyers' Committee for Civil Rights Under Law, do the legal groundwork that precedes prosecutorial action. They file the briefs, develop the legal theories, and create the institutional knowledge that shapes how the law is applied. Financial support and public engagement with their work keeps them in the fight.

Whistleblower protection organizations protect the people who take the personal and professional risk of documenting misconduct from the inside. The Government Accountability Project and the Project On Government Oversight support the individuals whose firsthand testimony has been essential to every accountability proceeding this book cites.

These institutions are not self-funding. They depend on citizens who understand their importance.

□ □ □

Four: Know Your Representatives and Make Them Know You

Not a form letter. A specific, sourced, documented communication that demonstrates you have done the work.

The Senate committees with jurisdiction over intelligence, judiciary, and foreign affairs have subpoena power, investigative authority, and confirmation power over the officials who implement the law. The House committees have equivalent power over appropriations, oversight, and the impeachment process. The specific senators and representatives who serve on these committees are the citizens' primary lever on federal accountability.

Find your senators and your representative. Find out which committees they serve on. Write to them, not with a form letter but with a specific question or request grounded in the documented public record. Reference the GAO finding on the Ukraine aid freeze by its specific designation, B-331564. Ask whether they have reviewed the Intelligence Community Assessment and whether they believe its findings should inform sanctions policy. Ask what oversight the committee has conducted of the conduct documented in the Senate Intelligence Committee's five volumes.

Elected officials respond differently to constituents who clearly know what they are talking about. A constituent who demonstrates specific knowledge of the documented record, and who asks specific questions grounded in that record, is a different kind of pressure than a constituent who expresses general outrage. Be the first kind.

□ □ □

Five: Vote Like the Constitutional Order Depends on It

Because it does.

The 2026 midterm elections determine the composition of the congressional committees with subpoena power. They determine whether whistleblowers have protected channels through which to report conduct that executive branch officials would prefer to suppress. They determine whether the statutory framework around sanctions, appropriations, intelligence oversight, and inspector general independence is strengthened or weakened. They determine whether the accountability mechanisms that produced the evidentiary record this book relies on continue to function or are further hollowed out.

This is not a partisan argument. The Senate Intelligence Committee that produced five volumes of bipartisan findings on the Russia relationship was controlled by Republicans for most of its investigation. The Government Accountability Office that found the Ukraine aid freeze violated federal law is a nonpartisan institution. The career officials who testified under oath about the corruption pretext served in both Republican and

Democratic administrations. The constitutional question this book raises is not a partisan question. It is a constitutional question.

The ballot is the most direct democratic instrument available to a citizen. Every election in which the constitutional order is at stake, which is every election, deserves a citizen's full engagement: registration, turnout, and the active support of candidates who take their constitutional obligations seriously regardless of party.

□ □ □

Six: Support State-Level Accountability

The federal accountability architecture is not the only accountability architecture available. State attorneys general and state prosecutors have jurisdiction over conduct that occurs within their states, and that jurisdiction cannot be preempted by a federal immunity ruling that applies only to federal prosecution.

The Raffensperger call, in which the President asked Georgia's Secretary of State to find 11,780 votes that did not exist, was a Georgia crime investigated by a Georgia grand jury. The fake elector scheme involved specific individuals in specific states taking specific actions that are subject to state law. The conduct documented in this book has state-level dimensions that state-level accountability mechanisms can reach.

Citizens can support state-level accountability by staying informed about ongoing state proceedings, supporting state attorneys general who take their accountability obligations seriously, and recognizing that the legal question this book raises can be approached from multiple jurisdictions simultaneously. The federal immunity ruling does not immunize every dimension of the conduct documented in this book.

□ □ □

Seven: Document Everything

The evidentiary record that this book is built on exists because people documented things. Journalists who filed FOIA requests and preserved records. Career officials who took contemporaneous notes. Congressional staff who archived communications before they could be deleted. Whistleblowers who forwarded complaints through legal channels. Diplomats who reported to their own governments what they witnessed at meetings. The documentation is the foundation of every accountability proceeding the record has produced.

If you witness conduct in your workplace, your community, your local government, or your state government that implicates the arguments of this book, develop the habit of documentation. Date, time, location, specific words, specific witnesses. Not for the purpose of vigilante action but for the purpose of creating the kind of contemporaneous record that James Comey's memos provided, that Gordon Sondland's testimony provided, that the Woodward recordings provided: a documented, dated, first-person account of what actually happened.

The habit of documentation is a civic skill and a constitutional one. It is how citizens become witnesses rather than bystanders.

□ □ □

What Citizens Cannot Do and Should Not Try

This chapter would be incomplete without an honest statement about what it is not asking you to do.

Citizens cannot file treason charges. That authority belongs exclusively to the Department of Justice. Citizens cannot override the immunity ruling. That is the Supreme Court's domain, subject to future reconsideration by a future Court on a future case. Citizens cannot compel a prosecution that the executive branch has chosen not to bring.

And citizens must not attempt to take extralegal action in response to even the most serious documented misconduct.

This point is not a legal disclaimer. It is the core argument of this entire book. The treason clause exists because the Framers understood that the greatest danger to a republic is not the enemy at the gates but the person inside the gates who opens them. Responding to a documented violation of the constitutional order by abandoning the constitutional order, by taking matters into your own hands, by treating the documented illegitimacy of an election or a presidency as justification for illegal action, is not defending the Republic. It is completing the work of its destruction.

The only legitimate response to the documented betrayal of constitutional allegiance is to exercise constitutional allegiance more vigorously. Vote. Document. Testify. Organize. Litigate. Legislate. These are the tools of constitutional citizenship. They are the tools that have worked before. They are the tools that will work again.

□ □ □

The Oath Returns

This book began with thirty-five words spoken on a cold January morning.

> *"I do solemnly swear that I will faithfully execute the Office of President of the United States, and will to the best of my Ability, preserve, protect and defend the Constitution of the United States."* — **Presidential Oath of Office, Article II, Section 1**

Those thirty-five words are the legal foundation of this book's entire argument. They are the contract whose breach this book has spent seventeen chapters documenting. They are the statement of allegiance whose violation is the constitutional definition of the highest crime the Republic recognizes.

But the oath is not only the President's.

Every member of Congress swears to support and defend the Constitution. Every federal judge swears to administer justice faithfully. Every military officer swears to support and defend the Constitution against all enemies, foreign and domestic. Every naturalized citizen swears to support and defend the Constitution of the United States against all enemies.

And every citizen who was born to the rights and protections this Constitution provides carries, if not a sworn obligation, then a civic one. The Republic that the Framers built is not merely a set of institutions. It is a practice. It requires active, ongoing commitment from the people who live inside it and especially from the officials who are temporarily entrusted with its power.

The officials documented in this book failed that practice. In some cases catastrophically. In some cases in ways that this book has argued meet the constitutional definition of the highest crime.

But the officials are not the Republic. The Republic is the people. It always has been.

John Adams wrote in 1761 that the very ground of our liberties is the freedom of elections. He understood, seventy years before the Republic had been tested by the conduct this book documents, that the constitutional order is not self-sustaining. It is sustained by the choices of the people who participate in it. By the voters who show up. By the journalists who document. By the lawyers who litigate. By the teachers who explain. By the writers who publish.

By the citizens who read a 400-page legal brief about treason and then ask: what can I do?

You have already done the first thing. You read it. You engaged with the evidence. You took it seriously enough to ask what comes next.

What comes next is the Republic's oldest and most demanding requirement.

Keep it.

> **This brief has made the legal case. The constitutional case is yours to make. It is made every time a citizen reads the primary sources, speaks accurately about what they found, supports the institutions still doing the work, engages with their elected representatives, votes with the constitutional order in mind, supports state-level accountability, and documents what they witness. The Framers gave us a Republic. The keeping of it has always been ours.**

□ □ □

End of A Citizen's Brief

Index

The Legal Case for Treason Against Donald J. Trump

A

B

F

G

H

S

T

Z

Bibliography

SELECTED PRIMARY SOURCES, GOVERNMENT Documents, Legal Authorities, and Reference Works

The Legal Case for Treason Against Donald J. Trump

Publisher's Note: All primary source documents listed below are publicly available through the issuing government agency or congressional body. URLs were verified as of April 2026. Readers are encouraged to access and read these documents directly. Citation format follows The Bluebook: A Uniform System of Citation (21st ed.).

I. Constitutional Provisions

U.S. Const. art. I, § 3, cl. 7 (Impeachment Judgment Clause).

U.S. Const. art. I, § 9, cl. 8 (Foreign Emoluments Clause).

U.S. Const. art. II, § 1, cl. 7 (Domestic Emoluments Clause).

U.S. Const. art. II, § 1, cl. 8 (Presidential Oath of Office).

U.S. Const. art. II, § 4 (Impeachment Grounds: Treason, Bribery, High Crimes and Misdemeanors).

U.S. Const. art. III, § 3 (Treason Clause — the only crime the Constitution defines).

U.S. Const. pmbl. (Preamble — the contractual foundation of the presidential obligation).

II. Federal Statutes

Antideficiency Act, 31 U.S.C. § 1341 (prohibition on obligation of funds in excess of appropriations).

Espionage Act of 1917, 18 U.S.C. §§ 793–799 (unauthorized transmission of national defense information).

Foreign Agents Registration Act (FARA), 22 U.S.C. § 611 et seq.

Impoundment Control Act of 1974, 2 U.S.C. § 682 et seq.

Trading with the Enemy Act, 50 U.S.C. § 4301 et seq.

Treason, 18 U.S.C. § 2381.

Misprision of Treason, 18 U.S.C. § 2382.

Seditious Conspiracy, 18 U.S.C. § 2384.

Theft of Public Money, 18 U.S.C. § 641.

Acts Affecting Personal Financial Interest, 18 U.S.C. § 208.

International Terrorism Definition, 18 U.S.C. § 2331.

North Atlantic Treaty, Apr. 4, 1949, 63 Stat. 2241 (Article 5 mutual defense commitment).

III. Supreme Court Cases

Brandenburg v. Ohio, 395 U.S. 444 (1969) (First Amendment limits on incitement).

Chandler v. United States, 171 F.2d 921 (1st Cir. 1948), cert. denied, 336 U.S. 918 (1949) (objective standard for treasonous intent; conviction of American who broadcast Nazi propaganda).

Cramer v. United States, 325 U.S. 1 (1945) (overt act requirement for treason; Justice Jackson's definition of enemy as 'any party united in hostile purpose against the United States').

Ex parte Bollman, 8 U.S. (4 Cranch) 75 (1807) (Chief Justice Marshall's controlling definition of levying war; assemblage of persons required for treasonable purpose).

Trump v. United States, 603 U.S. ___ (2024) (presidential immunity; absolute immunity for core constitutional functions; presumptive immunity for official acts; no immunity for private acts).

Zivotofsky v. Kerry, 576 U.S. 1 (2015) (President's exclusive recognition power in foreign affairs).

IV. Lower Court Cases

Best v. United States, 184 F.2d 131 (1st Cir. 1950) (Nazi propaganda broadcaster; intent standard for treason).

United States v. Abu Ali, 395 F. Supp. 2d 338 (E.D. Va. 2005) (post-9/11 functional enemy doctrine).

United States v. Hammoud, 381 F.3d 316 (4th Cir. 2004) (material support; hostile purpose standard).

United States v. Trump, No. 23-cr-257 (D.D.C.) (Espionage Act indictment; dismissed on procedural grounds, 2024).

V. Government Reports and Official Documents

A. Intelligence Community

Office of the Director of National Intelligence. Assessing Russian Activities and Intentions in Recent US Elections: Intelligence Community Assessment. ICA 2017-01D. January 6, 2017. Available at: https://www.dni.gov/files/documents/ICA_2017_01.pdf.

Senate Select Committee on Intelligence. Report of the Select Committee on Intelligence, United States Senate, on Russian Active Measures Campaigns and Interference in the 2016 U.S. Election. 5 vols. 116th Cong. (2019–2020). Available at: https://www.intelligence.senate.gov/publications/report-select-committee-intelligence-united-states-senate-russian-active-measures.

B. Department of Justice

Mueller, Robert S., III. Report on the Investigation into Russian Interference in the 2016 Presidential Election. 2 vols. U.S. Department of Justice. March 2019. Available at: https://www.justice.gov/storage/report.pdf.

C. Government Accountability Office

U.S. Government Accountability Office. Anti-deficiency Act: Office of Management and Budget's Apportionment of Ukraine Security Assistance Funds. GAO-20-330R. January 16, 2020. Available at: https://www.gao.gov/products/gao-20-330r.

D. Congress — January 6 Investigation

Select Committee to Investigate the January 6th Attack on the United States Capitol. Final Report. H. Rept. 117-663. 117th Cong., 2d sess. December 22, 2022. Washington, D.C.: U.S. Government Publishing Office. Available at: https://www.govinfo.gov/content/pkg/GPO-J6-REPORT/pdf/GPO-J6-REPORT.pdf.

E. Congressional Budget Office

Congressional Budget Office. The Budget and Economic Outlook: 2025 to 2035. January 2025. Available at: https://www.cbo.gov/publication/60870.

Congressional Budget Office. Federal Budget Deficit Data. Various years. Available at: https://www.cbo.gov/topics/budget.

F. Federal Economic Agencies

Bureau of Labor Statistics. Labor Force Statistics from the Current Population Survey. U.S. Department of Labor. Available at: https://www.bls.gov/cps/.

Bureau of Economic Analysis. Personal Income and Outlays. U.S. Department of Commerce. Available at: https://www.bea.gov/data/income-saving/personal-income.

Department of Housing and Urban Development. Annual Homeless Assessment Report (AHAR) to Congress. Various years. Available at: https://www.huduser.gov/portal/datasets/ahar.html.

G. Nuclear and International Monitoring

International Atomic Energy Agency. Verification and Monitoring in the Islamic Republic of Iran in Light of United Nations Security Council Resolution 2231. Various reports, 2015–2026. Available at: https://www.iaea.org/topics/iran-and-iaea.

NATO. Summit Communiqués. 2017–2024. Available at: https://www.nato.int/cps/en/natohq/official_texts.htm.

VI. Constitutional Convention Records

Farrand, Max, ed. The Records of the Federal Convention of 1787. 4 vols. New Haven: Yale University Press, 1911. (Including James Wilson's statements on presidential treason and the impeachment clause).

Madison, James. Notes of Debates in the Federal Convention of 1787. Reprint. New York: W.W. Norton, 1987.

VII. Secondary Legal Authorities and Scholarship

Hurst, James Willard. The Law of Treason in the United States: Collected Essays. Westport, CT: Greenwood Press, 1971. (Foundational scholarly treatment of the treason clause).

Stern, Michael. 'Impeachment for Conduct Prior to Taking Office.' Congressional Research Service. (Analysis of Framers' intent on the Impeachment Judgment Clause).

The Bluebook: A Uniform System of Citation. 21st ed. Cambridge: Harvard Law Review Association, 2020.

Tribe, Laurence H. American Constitutional Law. 3rd ed. New York: Foundation Press, 2000. (Constitutional framework for executive power and allegiance).

VIII. Investigative Journalism Organizations

The following organizations produced investigative reporting that contributed to the evidentiary record this book analyzes. Their work is cited throughout. Supporting these organizations is one of the seven civic actions recommended in the Conclusion.

ProPublica. https://www.propublica.org. (Independent investigative journalism; financial entanglements, emoluments reporting).

The Intercept. https://theintercept.com. (National security, civil liberties, foreign policy reporting).

The Washington Post. https://www.washingtonpost.com. (Ukraine aid freeze reporting; January 6 documentation).

The New York Times. https://www.nytimes.com. (Russia alignment reporting; financial disclosure investigations).

Reuters. https://www.reuters.com. (International affairs; NATO and Iran reporting).

The Guardian. https://www.theguardian.com. (Foreign policy; alliance deconstruction coverage).

IX. Legal Accountability Organizations

American Civil Liberties Union. https://www.aclu.org.

Brennan Center for Justice at NYU School of Law. https://www.brennancenter.org.

Citizens for Responsibility and Ethics in Washington (CREW). https://www.citizensforethics.org.

Government Accountability Project. https://whistleblower.org.

Lawyers' Committee for Civil Rights Under Law. https://lawyerscommittee.org.

Project on Government Oversight (POGO). https://www.pogo.org.

X. Research Tools Disclosure

In accordance with the AI Disclosure on the copyright page of this book: research for this work was conducted in part using AI-assisted tools including Claude (Anthropic), ChatGPT (OpenAI), and NotebookLM (Google). All research, analysis, legal arguments, editorial judgment, and final content decisions were made by the human authors. The authors retain full responsibility for the accuracy, conclusions, and legal arguments presented in this work.

About The Author

The DocWriteReview Collective is a group of writers, researchers, and legal minds who believe that words matter, evidence matters, and accountability matters. They build documents and apps for a living. This time, they built a case. Their goal is to remind everyone that the American Citizen still has a voice.

* * *

About DocWriteReview LLC

DocWriteReview LLC is a technology and publishing company dedicated to building web-based solutions for nonprofits, law firms, and small businesses. Founded on the principle that access to information and legal tools should not depend on the size of one's bank account, DocWriteReview develops custom, client-owned platforms that serve underrepresented communities.

In addition to its technology work, DocWriteReview LLC., its publishing imprint, which produces civic, legal, and educational titles designed to inform and empower citizens. The Legal Case for Treason Against Donald J. Trump is a DocWriteReview publication.

Connect with DocWriteReview

Website: www.docwritereview.com

Email: info@docwritereview.com

Phone: 202-800-1899

* * *

"The Framers gave us a Republic. The keeping of it has always been ours."

Stay Connected!

Unlock a wealth of knowledge and exclusive deals! Sign up now to receive free updates and special discounts on services and products related to grant writing, commercial lending, and much more. Don't miss out, join our community today!

Website: www.DocWriteReview.com

Email: Info@DocWriteReview.com

DocWriteReview
Consulting, Courses and Content